Ariadne P. Beck

GROUP AND FAMILY THERAPY 1983

Edited by
LEWIS R. WOLBERG, M.D.
Chairman, Board of Trustees,
Postgraduate Center for Mental Health
New York, N.Y.

and

MARVIN L. ARONSON, Ph.D.
Director, Group Therapy Department;
Training Analyst; Senior Supervisor,
Postgraduate Center for Mental Health
New York, N.Y.

BRUNNER/MAZEL, *Publishers* ● New York

Library of Congress Catalog Card No. 72-10881
ISBN: 0-87630-345-9
ISSN: 0276-5594

MANUFACTURED IN THE UNITED STATES OF AMERICA

PREFACE

Group and Family Therapy 1983 is the eleventh volume in an annual series of invited articles by authors from the United States and abroad. From 1973 through 1979, our series was entitled *Group Therapy—An Overview*; its focus was primarily on group therapy. Beginning in 1980, in recognition of the major developments which had been taking place in family therapy, the series was retitled *Group and Family Therapy*.

Each volume is dedicated to a major figure who has made seminal contributions to either group or family therapy (or, in some cases, to both). Previous volumes have been dedicated, respectively, to Asya L. Kadis (group), Nathan W. Ackerman (family and group), Emanuel K. Schwartz (group), Jacob L. Moreno (group), Donald D. Jackson (family), S.H. Foulkes (group), Paul F. Schilder (group), H. Peter Laqueur (group and family), Wilfred R. Bion (group), and Eric Berne (group and family).

Group and Family Therapy 1983 is dedicated to S.R. Slavson, by common consent the "father of group psychotherapy" in the United States, who died in New York on August 5, 1981 at the age of 91.

We have classified the 28 articles contained in this year's collection into the following categories: 1) The Contributions of S.R. Slavson; 2) Theoretical and Technical Issues in Group Therapy; 3) Stages of Development in Therapy Groups; 4) Group Therapy with Special Patient Populations; 5) Group Methods in the Training of Mental Health Professionals; 6) The Family Paradigm in Group Therapy; 7) Theoretical Issues in Family Therapy; and 8) Technical Interventions in Family Therapy.

We wish to thank Dr. David M. Aronson, Ruth R. Aronson, and Eleanor R. Kern for their most valuable help in readying each manuscript for publication. We also wish to thank Lee R. Mackler, Director of Library Services at the Postgraduate Center for Mental Health, for her excellent bibliographic assistance.

THE CONTRIBUTIONS OF S.R. SLAVSON

Our first chapter, by Leslie Rosenthal, reviews Slavson's achievements in facilitating the organizational growth of group therapy in this country. It also explicates Slavson's theoretical contributions and shows how they accelerated the recognition of group therapy as a valued therapeutic modality. In the second chapter, Mortimer Schiffer, who worked closely with Slavson for many years and is the editor of *Dynamics of Analytical Group Psychotherapy*, published by

Jason Aronson in 1979, which deals with Slavson's contributions, describes Slavson's efforts to establish the American Group Psychotherapy Association as well as his ceaseless attempts to preserve the integrity of group therapy practice over a period of four decades.

THEORETICAL AND TECHNICAL ISSUES IN GROUP THERAPY

Anne Alonso and J. Scott Rutan discuss a variety of techniques for dealing interpretively with transferential phenomena in group therapy. They also delineate various abuses of transference interpretations in groups and suggest how these can be avoided. Herman S. Alpert shows how analytic group therapy can be used to elicit conscious and unconscious guilt reactions and to facilitate the discharge of underlying hostility in socially acceptable forms. Michael P. Andronico describes how the group therapist can synthesize symbolic and actual realities by the employment of a variety of special techniques. Of special interest is his use of "minithons"—six-hour group experiences in which family members or other significant figures are temporarily included in the treatment process. Lowell Cooper and James Gustafson present their theoretical views on the dynamics which underlie all brief groups with special emphasis on how unconscious planning is manifest in groups. Normund Wong studies the impact of failures, casualties, and hazards in group therapy on both therapist and patient. He examines the causes of these untoward reactions and offers various preventive strategies which may be profitably employed by the therapist.

STAGES OF DEVELOPMENT IN THERAPY GROUPS

Ariadne Beck delineates the clinical phenomena which typically reveal themselves during the first three phases of therapy groups. These phases, according to Beck, are characterized respectively by issues of 1) contract formation, 2) competition, and 3) differentiation. K. Roy MacKenzie and W. John Livesley, of Canada, writing from the perspective of general systems theory and small group theory, conceptualize developmental stages of therapy groups in terms of a series of interactional tasks. These authors use the concepts of role to express the interrelationships of behavior required by the entire group, as well as by the members' individual characterological structures.

GROUP THERAPY WITH SPECIAL PATIENT POPULATIONS

Fernando D. Astigueta describes various techniques which he employs to provide clinical services to severely disturbed patients in a day hospital setting. Ava L. Siegler describes her use of groups to treat single mothers of oedipal children. The idiosyncratic transference and countertransference issues in these groups are discussed in detail and clinical case examples are offered. Edward S. Soo deals with the management of scapegoating in children's group therapy. He discusses the dynamics of this destructive phenomenon and offers a variety of techniques for circumventing it. Janice de Mocker and David G. Zimpfer describe how psychosocial interventions in groups can serve as valuable adjuncts to various forms of medical treatment.

GROUP METHODS IN THE TRAINING OF MENTAL HEALTH PROFESSIONALS

Valerie T. Angel, Carole Katz, Arlene Litwack, Mary Maffia, Robert A. Mednick, Richard Mingoia, and Rene Rocha discuss their personal experiences in supervision groups in which they participated during their training as analytically-oriented psychotherapists. Michael H. Lawler presents a case to illustrate the interrelationships which obtain between certain aspects of psychoanalytic and general systems theory in the supervision of group workers. Walter N. Stone, Bonnie L. Green, and Mary Grace compare the efficacy of teaching group dynamics by means of leaderless groups rather than by more traditional formats.

THE FAMILY PARADIGM IN GROUP THERAPY

Phyllis Bronstein Burrows describes two research studies which deal with the relationships between patients' experiences in their families of origin and their transferential reactions to therapists in group therapy. Jerome Steiner, by contrast, takes the position that the family is, in fact, an outmoded paradigm for the psychotherapy group. He offers instead a ''master-disciple'' paradigm. Seymour Tozman, Helen Minkowitz, and Gale Mittleman elaborate on an outpatient socialization program which they conceptualize as providing a surrogate family for patients who grew up in dysfunctional families.

THEORETICAL ISSUES IN FAMILY THERAPY

Dennis Bagarozzi and C. Winter Giddings discuss the specific impacts of intrapersonal, interpersonal, and systems processes in family therapy and point out how cognitive processes can aid in integrating these processes. In addition, they recommend a number of intervention strategies for altering cognitive processes in family therapy. John Clarkin, Allen J. Frances, and Samuel Perry explore the implications of the DSM-III classificatory system for family therapy. They suggest ways in which DSM-III can be adapted to family therapy. Neil S. Jacobson and Kathy N. Melman present research data which indicate that behavioral marital therapy can be helpful to couples with sexual concerns when these concerns are explicitly dealt with but that such concerns do not automatically disappear even though other marital issues have been successfully dealt with. Monica McGoldrick and Froma Walsh discuss the systemic implications of loss to illustrate how families respond to crucial events and how the therapist's recognition of a family's behavioral patterns can facilitate systemic change.

TECHNICAL INTERVENTIONS IN FAMILY THERAPY

Joel S. Bergman describes how he employs odd-even day rituals to change both symptoms and systems in his strategic approach to brief individual, couples, and family therapy. Douglas A. Breunlin and Rocco A. Cimmarusti identify seven aspects of therapy which they believe are crucial in achieving rapid changes in the context of their structural-strategic approach to family therapy. Robert Garfield and Linda Schwoeri present a methodology for consulting with families in therapy. They also outline the guidelines which they employ to prepare the family, to conduct the interview proper and carry out follow-up procedures. Stephen E. Levick discusses what he refers to as the "always-never" form of paradox and shows how therapeutic awareness of this concept can help in the formulation of effective family therapy interventions. David Wellisch proposes a model of family treatment that is geared to dealing with the family problems of cancer patients. This model suggests fundamental changes in relation to who is included, when and where the family is seen, and for how long.

In closing, we wish to express the wish that these articles will prove of value to group and family therapists and will enhance the effectiveness of their work with a wide variety of patients.

Lewis R. Wolberg
Chairman, Board of Trustees
Postgraduate Center for Mental Health
New York, N.Y.

Marvin L. Aronson
Director, Group Therapy Department
Training Analyst; Senior Supervisor
Postgraduate Center for Mental Health
New York, N.Y.

CONTENTS

GROUP THERAPY WITH SPECIAL PATIENT POPULATIONS

GROUP METHODS IN THE TRAINING OF MENTAL HEALTH PROFESSIONALS

THE FAMILY PARADIGM IN GROUP THERAPY

CONTRIBUTORS

Alonso, Anne, Ph.D., Director, Treatment Center, Boston Institute for Psychotherapies, Inc.; Director, Post-graduate Fellowship on Psychotherapy, Massachusetts General Hospital, Department of Psychiatry; Clinical Instructor in Psychology, Harvard Medical School, Department of Psychiatry, Boston, Massachusetts.

Alpert, Herman S., M.D., P.C., Assistant Clinical Professor of Psychiatry, Mount Sinai School of Medicine, CUNY; Associate Attending Psychiatrist, Department of Psychiatry, Mount Sinai Hospital, New York City; Attending Psychiatrist, Gracie Square Hospital, New York City.

Andronico, Michael, P., Ph.D., Adjunct Professor of Psychiatry, College of Medicine and Dentistry, Rutgers Medical School; Field Supervisor, Graduate School of Applied and Professional Psychology, Rutgers University, New Jersey; private practice, Somerset, New Jersey.

Angel, Valerie T., M.S.W., C.S.W., Faculty and Supervisor, Community Services and Education Division, Postgraduate Center for Mental Health; Supervisor, Westchester Institute for Training in Psychotherapy and Counseling, Mt. Kisco, New York; private practice, New York City.

Aronson, Marvin L., Ph.D., Director, Group Therapy Department, Senior Supervisor, Training Analyst, Postgraduate Center for Mental Health; private practice, New York City.

Astigueta, Fernando D., M.D., Director, General Psychiatry Unit, Postgraduate Center for Mental Health; private practice, New York City.

Bagarozzi, Dennis A., Ph.D., Associate Professor, Coordinator of Clinical Training, Division of Social Work, East Carolina University, Greenville, North Carolina.

Beck, Ariadne P., M.A., Private practice, Chicago and Indian Head Park, Illinois.

Bergman, Joel S., Ph.D., Senior Faculty, Ackerman Institute for Family Therapy; Visiting Associate Professor of Psychology, Ferkauf Graduate School, Yeshiva University; private practice, New York City.

Breunlin, Douglas C., M.S.S.A., Acting Director, Family Systems Program, Institute for Juvenile Research, Chicago, Illinois; Adjunct Faculty, Department of Pediatrics, University of Illinois, Abraham Lincoln School of Medicine.

Bronstein-Burrows, Phyllis, Ph.D., Assistant Professor, Clinical Psychology Program, University of Vermont.

Cimmarusti, Rocco A., A.C.S.W., Assistant Team Administrator and Family Therapy Trainer, Youth Guidance, Chicago, Illinois.

Clarkin, John F., Ph.D., Associate Professor, Clinical Psychology, New York Hospital-Cornell Medical Center, New York City; Director of Psychology, New York Hospital-Westchester Division, White Plains, New York.

Cooper, Lowell, Ph.D., Faculty Member, California School of Professional Psychology (Berkeley) and Lecturer in Psychology, University of California (Berkeley).

DeMocker, Janice Delahooke, Ed.D., Assistant Professor, School of Nursing, University of Rochester, New York.

Frances, Allen J., M.D., Associate Professor of Psychiatry, Cornell University Medical College; Director, Payne Whitney Outpatient Department, New York Hospital, New York City.

Garfield, Robert, M.D., Assistant Professor and Director of Masters of Family Therapy Program, Hahnemann Medical College and Hospital Philadelphia, Pennsylvania.

Giddings, C. Winter, M.S.W., Assistant Professor, School of Social Work and Department of Psychology, University of Georgia, Athens, Georgia.

Grace, Mary, M.S., Research Coordinator, Central Psychiatric Clinic and Research Assistant II, Department of Psychiatry, College of Medicine, University of Cincinnati, Ohio.

Green, Bonnie L., Ph.D., Assistant Professor of Psychiatry, University of Cincinnati College of Medicine; Director of Research, Central Psychiatric Clinic, Cincinnati, Ohio.

Gustafson, James P., M.D., Professor of Psychiatry, University of Wisconsin.

Jacobson, Neil S., Ph.D., Associate Professor of Psychology, Department of Psychology, University of Washington, Seattle, Washington.

Katz, Carole, M.S.W., C.S.W., Director, Community Education, Faculty Member and Training Supervisor, Institute for Mental Health Education, Englewood, New Jersey; Supervisor, Dumont Mental Health Center, Dumont, New Jersey; private practice, New York City.

Lawler, Michael H., Ed.D., Faculty Member, School of Social Work, Boston College; Lecturer in Clinical Psychology, Harvard Medical School; private practice, Newtonville, Massachusetts.

Levick, Stephen E., M.D., Department of Psychiatry, New York University Medical Center, New York City.

Litwack, Arlene, M.S.W., C.S.W., Director, Child Therapy, Long Island Consultation Center; Faculty Member and Supervisor, Long Island Institute for Mental Health, Queens, New York; private practice, New York City.

Livesley, W. John, M.B., Ph.D., Associate Professor of Psychiatry, Faculty of Medicine, University of Calgary, Canada; Coordinator, Residency Psychotherapy Training and Director, Psychotherapy Services, Calgary General Hospital, Calgary, Canada.

MacKenzie, K. Roy, M.D., F.R.C.P., Professor of Psychiatry, Faculty of Medicine, University of Calgary; Director of Residency Training and Director of Group Psychotherapy, Foothills Hospital, Calgary, Canada.

Maffia, Mary, Ph.D., Faculty Member, Training Supervisor, Institute for Mental Health Education, Englewood, New Jersey; Consultant, VA Medical Center, East Orange, New Jersey; private practice, Englewood, New Jersey.

McGoldrick, Monica, M.S.W., Director, Family Training UMDNJ-Rutgers Medical School and Community Mental Health Center, New Jersey; Faculty, Family Institute of Westchester, New York.

Mednick, Robert A., Ph.D., Staff Psychologist, Long Island Jewish-Hillside Queens Hospital Center, Queens, New York; Training Department Staff, Postgraduate Center for Mental Health; private practice, New York City.

Melman, Kathy Newport, Ph.D., UCLA Neuropsychiatric Institute, Los Angeles, California.

Mingoia, Richard, M.S.W., C.S.W., Administrator, Holley Child Care and Development Center, Hackensack, New Jersey; Adjunct Associate Professor, New York University School of Social Work; private practice, New York City.

Minkowitz, Helen, M.S.W., Supervising Social Worker, Coney Island Hospital, Brooklyn, N.Y.

Mittleman, Gale, M.S.W., Staff Social Worker, Coney Island Hospital, Brooklyn, New York.

Perry, Samuel, M.D., Associate Professor, Clinical Psychiatry; Associate Director of Consultation Liaison Psychiatry, New York Hospital, New York City.

Rocha, Rene, Ph.D., Staff Member, Postgraduate Center for Mental Health; private practice, New York City and Englewood, New Jersey.

Rosenthal, Leslie, Ph.D., Group Therapy Consultant, Center for Modern Psychoanalytic Studies, New York City; Group Therapy Consultant, Nassau County Department of Mental Health; formerly, Group Therapy Consultant, Jewish Board of Guardians, 1956-1975.

Rutan, J. Scott, Ph.D., President, Boston Insitute for Psychotherapies, Inc.; Coordinator, Group Therapy Training, Massachusetts General Hospital, Department of Psychiatry; Past-President, Northeastern Society for Group Psychotherapy.

Schwoeri, Linda, M.A., M.F.T., Therapist, PATH Inc. Community Mental Health Clinic, Philadelphia, Pennsylvania.

Schiffer, Mortimer, M.S., Consultant, Bank Street College, New York City.

Siegler, Ava L., Ph.D., Director, Children, Adolescents and Family Clinic, Postgraduate Center for Mental Health; Director, Prescott Early Intervention Project, Prescott Day Care Center; Associate Clinical Professor, Clinical Psychology, Doctoral Program, New York University, New York City.

Soo, Edward S., M.S., Senior Clinical Supervisor, Jewish Board of Family and Children's Services, New York City.

Steiner, Jerome, M.D., Assistant Clinical Professor of Psychiatry, Columbia College of Physicians and Surgeons, New York City; Attending Psychiatrist, St. Luke's-Roosevelt Hospital Center, New York City; Member of Committee on Religion and Psychiatry, American Psychiatric Association, Washington, D.C.

Stone, Walter N., M.D., Vice Chairman and Professor of Psychiatry, University of Cincinnati College of Medicine, Ohio.

Tozman, Seymour, M.D., Chief, Substance Abuse Services, Department of Psychiatry, Veterans Administration Medical Center, Brooklyn, New York; formerly Chief of Adult Outpatient Services, Coney Island Hospital, Brooklyn, New York; (pending) Clinical Associate Professor, SUNY Downstate, New York.

Walsh, Froma, Ph.D., Associate Professor, University of Chicago; Faculty Member, Chicago Family Institute, Chicago, Illinois.

Wellisch, David K., Ph.D., Associate Professor of Medical Psychology, Department of Psychiatry, U.C.L.A. School of Medicine; Neuropsychiatric Center for the Health Sciences, Los Angeles, California.

Wolberg, Lewis R., M.D., Chairman, Board of Trustees, Postgraduate Center for Mental Health; Clinical Professor of Psychiatry, New York University Medical School, New York City.

Wong, Normund, M.D., Director, Department of Education and Menninger School of Psychiatry; Clinical Professor of Psychiatry, University of Kansas School of Medicine, Topeka, Kansas.

Zimpfer, David G., Ed.D., Professor and Chairman, Counseling and Personnel Services Education Deparment, Kent State University, Kent, Ohio.

The Contributions of S.R. Slavson

Chapter I

S.R. SLAVSON—AN APPRECIATION

Leslie Rosenthal, Ph.D.

On the wall in S.R. Slavson's office at the Jewish Board of Guardians was the framed quotation, "Nothing in this world is as powerful as an idea whose time has come." The idea was group therapy and Slavson was to be its father, mother, midwife, and pediatrician. *The Introduction to Group Therapy*, his first book on group therapy, opened with the statement:

> Among the most important developments in psychiatry and psychology in recent times is the recognition that man is essentially a group animal. The destiny of man, sane or civilized, is irrevocably tied up with the group. His growth and development are conditioned by the group's values and attitudes. In the healthy personalities, group associations expand to include even wider areas and larger numbers of persons. (1, p. 1)

In the mid-thirties he began his monumental work with children's groups at the Jewish Board of Guardians (J.B.G.) where he developed that remarkably potent therapeutic modality, Activity Group Therapy, for latency-age youngsters. Subsequently, a variety of group approaches for adolescents, mothers, and fathers was also developed.

In 1947 Slavson united a handful of colleagues to join him in founding the American Group Psychotherapy Association. In 1951 he launched the *International Journal of Group Psychotherapy*. As its Editor in the first decade, Slavson contributed heavily to the professionalization of the fledgling field and the development of a body of theory and practice based on Freudian principles of psychoanalytic psychology. At the J.B.G. and in his seminars and consulting work to a wide variety of agencies dealing with children, Slavson trained a generation of group therapists including Saul Scheidlinger, Emanuel Hallowitz, Mortimer Schiffer, and this writer. These, in turn, trained many others. In his many appearances at international conferences, in his books, which were translated into fourteen languages, and in his voluminous personal correspondence with group therapists from all over the world, he influenced the practice of group therapy, raised its standards, and catalyzed its growth.

From its beginning at only a few pioneering outposts like J.B.G., group therapy's burgeoning growth has made it an integral part of the clinical services offered in social agencies, child guidance settings, psychiatric clinics, hospitals, and educational and correctional institutions all over the world. Group treatment is so much a part of the contemporary therapeutic arsenal that major psychiatric residency training programs require and offer training experience in group leadership. Also, some of the outstanding schools of social work require the host agencies where their students receive their clinical training to provide a group experience for them.

There are several basic concepts in Slavson's metapsychology of group psychotherapy which were consistently emphasized in his teaching and writing.

1) *Group therapy is a lineal descendant of individual psychoanalytic psychotherapy.* The same dynamic processes of transference, resistance, insight, catharsis, reality-testing, and identification are operative though modified by the group setting. This firm belief in the individual psychoanalytic parentage of group treatment held significant clinical consequences for the approach to the individual member and to the group.

There was an emphasis on a comprehensive and dynamic understanding of each member, preferably achieved prior to entry into the group. In one of my early supervisory conferences with Slavson he surprised me by asking at the very outset, "What are the nuclear problems of each member of your group?" It was Slavson's conviction that through his understanding of the unique dynamics and maturational needs of each member, the group therapist would then devise a therapeutic strategy uniquely addressed to each member. If a young group member who had lost his father at an early age was struggling to saw a piece of wood, Slavson would have the therapist spontaneously go over to help by holding the wood steady. If another child with a different relationship to his father, i.e., an aggressive boy in rivalry with a weak father, were experiencing the same difficulty, the therapist would not intervene unless asked.

Another consequence of the close link to individual psychoanalytic therapy was an overall individually-oriented approach to group therapy. Slavson maintained that group therapy was the therapy of individuals and that approaches geared to the dynamics of the whole group vitiated the potential for therapeutic gain in each member. In the first issue of the *International Journal of Group Psychotherapy* in 1951, Slavson warned that "the placing of primary focus on treatment of the group as an unitary entity, rather than on individual patients, is a development which may prove to be a major crisis." These views, he noted, are reflected in such terms as "group emotion," "group resistance," and "group formation," and the question of whether personality problems "can be rectified by the treatment of groups as groups rather than correcting the imbalance of psychic forces in the individual is a question we shall have to face'' (3, p. 12). In the following years Slavson campaigned vigorously for the autonomy of the individual patient in the group. In a 1957 paper he forcefully disputed the idea of common forces in the group.

> Each patient seeks to achieve his own aim as an individual for his own individual ends and not for the benefit of the group as a unit or for the sake of a common group aim. (4, p. 137)

Slavson conceived of the group as a setting which catalyzed the dynamics of the *individual*, accelerated regression, weakened defences, loosened resistances and provided a matrix for reality testing. In 1964, Slavson wrote:

> Group psychotherapy can never stand alone as a therapeutic tool. By its very nature, it must always base its methods, techniques and understanding on individual psychotherapy. Group psychotherapy is only a modification of individual psychotherapy and not a completely different method. Fundamentally, the focus of treatment in a group is still the individual patient and the dynamics of the individual personality. (5, p. 122)

Yet in the same publication Slavson could offer a statement which encompassed both individual and group orientations:

> Analytic group psychotherapy, with adolescent and adult patients, relies on interpretation of individual and group resistance, interpretation of the individual, multiple and collective (group) transferences, and the attainment of insight by *each* of the participant group members as *individuals*.

Slavson's individually-oriented position was by no means monolithic. In his supervision he was alert to group-as-a-whole manifestations of transference and resistance. He frequently observed that unanimity in a group was an expression of group-wide resistance and often warned therapists against major errors in group management which could plunge a whole group into a state of negative transference. He was also alert to scapegoating as an indirect expression of the group's aggression against the therapist. It is my own observation that within the individual-group parameter, Slavson adopted a more rigid stance in his writing than he did in his supervision and teaching.

2) *The development and expression of hostility are an inevitable component of the therapeutic process, and its prolonged absence from the group arena constitutes a major resistance and may represent a serious problem in countertransference on the part of a therapist who can only tolerate love from group members.* It is an index to Slavson's therapeutic acumen that, in the mid-thirties, when the treatment of children in child guidance clinics was almost invariably

based on seducing them into a positive relation to the therapist, he devised a treatment which elicited and accepted intense expressions of hostility and negative feeling. It may be noted that in the activity groups, when a child or group thanked a therapist for bringing a requested craft material or game, the therapist was instructed to respond that "the office got it." The intervention was specifically intended to avoid placing obstacles in the path of the development and expression of negative feeling. In Slavson's words,

> In psychotherapy, individual equilibrium has to be achieved through prolonged intra- and interpersonal struggle. The therapist must not assume the role of a repressive parent who demands control of hostile impulses or a placid group façade. Hostility is an essential part of therapy. A regimen that supresses it is countertherapeutic. Uninhibited expression of hostility toward the therapist and fellow patients is the major grist in the therapeutic mill; where there is no hostility there is no therapy. (1, p. 164)

3) *The therapeutic import of identification is "the outstanding single force in the genesis of personality and the humanizing of man"* (1, p. 83). Slavson saw identification as a crucially significant aspect of group psychotherapy where the multiple transferences provide multiple models and objects of identification. Since identification also operates in the direction of the therapist, Slavson constantly stressed the need for the group therapist to present himself as a strong but loving model to group members. His recommendations of patients for group treatment were frequently based upon the corrective impact of the group in rechanneling or strengthening distorted or tenuous identifications. In considering referrals to groups, Slavson sought to establish the individual's basic identification as established within his family and frequently envisioned the group as possessing an inherent capacity to redirect a pathological identification through exposure to more constructive models in the group.

4) *Dilution of the transference is a singular modification of transference phenomena in the group setting.* As opposed to individual therapy where the therapist is the sole transference object, groups offer a number of objects and "target multiplicity" occurs. These multiple transference options, in Slavson's view, diminish the intensity of the transference on any one person, though the total quantum of affect may be multiplied many times. This diminution of the intensity of the transference led Slavson to the conclusion that a transference neurosis could not develop in the group setting and that it was therefore not suitable for the treatment of deep individual problems. While well aware of the tendency of group members to unconsciously perceive the group as a preoedipal mother, Slavson apparently did not deem this to be of sufficient therapeutic force to enable the group to effectively deal with major libidinal problems. His strong conviction that patients with serious neurotic conflicts need to attain insight into

their unconscious within a transference relationship of sufficient depth made Slavson a proponent of combined group and individual treatment in these cases. While focusing on the reduction in the intensity and emotional charge of the transference in groups, Slavson also presented some of the singular advantages it provided for those who are unable to assimilate the intensity of the undiluted transference:

> It is particularly helpful to those who feel disloyal toward parents or mates where they develop strong attachments as in individual treatment. Group therapy for such patients is, therefore less threatening and guilt evoking. Dilutions of the libidinal transference is essential for patients, who, because of homosexual trends, are afraid to become involved with a therapist of the same sex. It is also advantageous for individuals who have been so hurt in their earliest emotional relationships that they are fearful of emotional attachments. (5, p. 20)

Slavson did not view group psychotherapy as a modality which could be universally applied. The group with its built-in frustrations of sharing time and therapist, its greater potential for intense emotional stimulation and resultant contagion of feeling, and the ever present possibility for exposure to hostility demand a greater degree of ego strength, resiliency, and flexibility than is required of the dyadic setting with its significantly fewer variables. Slavson held that the first crucial group of two with the mother determined the individual's capacity for subsequent multiple relations. If the individual did not receive the requisite amount of nurturing and gratification, his immature ego could be overwhelmed by the demands and exigencies of the group. It was this deep awareness of the stresses and ego demands of group membership which impelled Slavson's warnings about the encounter group movement which indiscriminately and swiftly exposed members to intense amounts of emotional stimulation without a prior careful appraisal of their capacities to assimilate such dosages.

Slavson also postulated a basic need for group relatedness—a "social hunger" for compresence with and acceptance by one's peers. It is this need for the group and its approval which gives the group the power to modify the individual's character egocentric and maladaptive patterns.

Underlying all of Slavson's work was a deep love of children. His interest in children had led him from initial training in engineering into education at the Walden School where he experimented with creative methods of eliciting and utilizing the innate curiosity of children. He frequently said, "Children cannot be taught; they can only be helped to learn." At the Integration Conferences held periodically at J.B.G. on children in groups, Slavson conveyed that the child being discussed was infinitely precious to him and that the young ego was a treasure to be guarded and protected from harm. It was at these conferences, attended by group therapists, caseworkers treating other family members, supervisors, and psychiatrists, that Slavson's uncanny gift for stepping into the unconscious of a child was often displayed. His ability to accurately predict the ways in which a new child would interact with his fellow group members, or how a specific therapeutic intervention would affect a whole group, was so frequently demonstrated as to become commonplace. He was sharply attentive to the subgroup alliances which developed in groups and carefully noted members' choices of "supportive egos" in other members. He utilized changing subgroup choices as a significant barometer of a child's progress in the group. The sequential selection of a more mature ally or allies after a coalition with a less mature or a submissive ally was a prime index of maturation. Slavson wrote that

> the dynamic of supportive ego is a phenomenon of major importance in group psychotherapy. In children's groups, those who develop such relationships make better recoveries than those who remain isolated or only enter into superficial, floating relationships. (2, p. 211)

Slavson dedicated himself to forming and shaping and articulating an internally consistent, rational, teachable, and effective system of group treatment wedded to Freudian theory. He possessed an ever-flowing fount of energy and creative tension. His mind bubbled furiously with ideas in a ferment which even old age could not still. On the occasion of Slavson's eightieth birthday, Hyman Spotnitz offered a tribute, the final sentence of which seems an appropriate conclusion to this dedicatory statement:

> He has made an indelible imprint on the constructive evolution of mankind through the principles he has developed, the organizations he has sponsored, and the human beings he has rescued and elevated via the group process. (6, p. 402)

REFERENCES

1. Slavson, S.R. *An Introduction to Group Therapy*. New York: The Commonwealth Fund, 1943.
2. Slavson, S.R. *Analytic Group Psychotherapy*. New York: Columbia University Press, 1950.
3. Slavson, S.R. Current trends in group psychotherapy. *Int. J. Group Psychother.*, 1: 7-15, 1951.
4. Slavson, S.R. Are there group dynamics in therapy groups? *Int. J. Group Psychother.*, 7: 131-154, 1957.
5. Slavson, S.R. *A Textbook in Analytic Group Psychotherapy*. New York: International Universities Press, 1964.
6. Spotnitz, H. In tribute to S.R. Slavson. *Int. J. Group Psychother.*, 21: 402-405, 1971.

Chapter II

S. R. SLAVSON

Mortimer Schiffer, M.S.

Group psychotherapy has lost one of its eminent pioneers and major advocates with the recent death of S. R. Slavson at the advanced age of 91. Thus ends the long career of a man whose creative endeavors were associated mainly with groups, starting at the turn of the century when he sponsored cultural enhancement activities with children and adolescents, followed by social group work in community centers, then in progressive education in this country and abroad and, finally, in group psychotherapy.

For four-and-a-half decades Slavson's energies were devoted almost exclusively to group psychotherapy. He was responsible for many original contributions to the theory, principles, and practices of group treatment. Perhaps of equal importance was the leading role he took in launching the American Group Psychotherapy Association, the preeminent professional organization in its field. He stimulated interest in group psychotherapy in this country and abroad, and with the assistance of other interested members of the AGPA, notably W. C. Hulse and Samuel Hadden, and foreign representatives, he brought into being the International Association of Group Psychotherapy. The *International Journal of Group Psychotherapy* was published under his aegis, and he was the first editor of this prestigious publication for many years. Slavson was an active proselytizer for group psychotherapy, and his truly Herculean efforts were responsible for the accredited position it now holds as one of the two fundamental modalities of psychotherapy.

Historical study of the physical, chemical, and biological sciences, including sub-specialties within these fields, reveals linkages between current theories and their applications with antecedent discoveries. A similar related progression cannot be discerned in the beginnings and later evolution of group psychotherapy. One would find it difficult to demonstrate significant relatedness in the psychological premises and methods of the following: J. H. Pratt's fascinating—and successful—utilization of inspirational lectures to groups of tubercular patients, as part of his overall medical treatment; L. C. Marsh's combination of psychiatry and his classes in art and dance; J. L. Moreno's use of "psychodrama"; T. L.

Burrow's imaginative use of psychoanalysis (changed by him later to "phyloanalysis") in residential treatment of groups of patients; P. Schilder's more precise application of classical psychoanalysis with groups; and methods used by S. R. Slavson, L. Wender, W. R. Bion, A. Wolf, and others. Overlooked in the historical roots of group psychotherapy is some of the work of Alfred Adler, during the first two decades of this century, when he employed groups with adolescents to encourage discussions about feelings, conflicts, aspirations, and other matters of universal interest to adolescents during this difficult stage of development. Adler did not look upon this group approach, which is commonly used today for counseling, as psychotherapy, although it undoubtedly had ameliorative effects for some troubled adolescents.

During the early years, some therapists who had been trained in Freudian psychoanalytic theory and methodology held disparate views about how a group could be used as a therapeutic instrument. The methods with which they experimented make one wonder how markedly different procedures could stem from the same body of psychological knowledge. Burrow, for instance, was interested in social (group) phenomena, and he was responsible for many probing articles on this subject (eventually earning for himself the disapproval of the American Psychoanalytic Society, which saw fit to drop this creative thinker from its ranks). Using a group of about 20 patients, students, and psychiatrists living together, Burrow was primarily interested in social parameters affecting treatment of emotional disorders. Wender, and several others, employed didactic lectures to acquaint hospitalized patients with the nature of their emotional pathology. Schilder, at Bellevue Hospital, came closest, perhaps, to analytical group practices currently in use in the manner in which he applied the tenets of Freudian psychoanalysis.

The first comprehensive study and compilation of group psychotherapy was done by G. W. Thomas (8). From this otherwise excellent work the reader gains an impression of a linear, historical development of theory and methodology of group psychotherapy by early practitioners in this country during a period of several decades, starting with Pratt's work in 1907. Yet, such a progression is far from what actually occurred. In no way, however, does this diminish the significant contributions made by the early practitioners, different as they may have been in their theories and the methods they employed.

There *is* one common factor which links the past and the present: a recognition on the part of all the pioneers of the considerable merit inherent in a group for treating emotional disorders. This is a unitary concept, and it served as a unifying force in the subsequent development of this valuable clinical resource.

In a field of interest which has had so many prestigious "pioneers," one wonders why Slavson was awarded a signal honor—that of being the "father of group psychotherapy" (2).

After graduation as a civil engineer from Cooper Union, Slavson was employed in that occupation for a number of years. At the same time he involved himself in cultural activitities with groups of youngsters in the neighborhood where he resided, on a voluntary basis. His first published works dealt with group recreation, the essence of democratic institutions and social problems, and a science curriculum in progressive education. None of these made any references to group psychotherapy. It was not until 1934 that Slavson became interested in groups for helping emotionally troubled children, as Director of Group Therapy at the Madelaine Borg Child Guidance Institute of the Jewish Board of Guardians in New York City. This agency, under the leadership of its imaginative Executive Director, John Slawson, created the first program in group psychotherapy associated with a community service agency. It was here that group psychotherapy became a major part of clinical services for children and their families.

Activity group therapy was the first method Slavson devised in 1934, and it was to be a turning point for him—a beginning of what was to be a long career devoted almost exclusively to group psychotherapy. In a few years, group practice began to assume a professional identity. Many persons who had become interested in this approach joined in regular weekly seminars, including guest visitors from other agencies and in private practice. A common forum came into being. This was formalized when Slavson, assisted by a number of equally dedicated persons, organized the American Group Therapy Association (later changed to the American Group Psychotherapy Association). Annual conferences started shortly thereafter which brought attention to the movement, and the membership roles increased rapidly. Group psychotherapy had become formally launched. These events took place during a relatively short period of time, from 1934 to 1945.

Publications in the *International Journal of Group Psychotherapy* and the annual conferences were the main avenues for disseminating information on group treatment. Slavson wrote prodigiously; he was undoubtedly the most prolific contributor. He was responsible, eventually, for 192 separate publications: 16 books, chapters in books, and articles in professional journals. His writings have been translated into seven languages.

Slavson devised activity and analytical groups for children; para-analytical group psychotherapy for adolescents; analytical and counseling groups for parents of children in treatment; and a special milieu treatment for hospitalized, psychotic patients (3). His first "love" was for children, as typified by his early involvements with them in recreational and cultural groups, and in education, and finally as the first age group he became involved with in group treatment. Slavson's psychological formulations about group psychotherapy came from the children's groups, and they gave direction to group treatment by defining and delineating its primary elements. It was this early work with children's groups which established a fundamental frame of reference for what constituted a therapy group: a psychologically designed small group with a maximum of eight patients, selectively chosen, whose personalities and problems were of a nature to evoke psychologically meaningful interpersonal interactions. This definition holds true, in the main, for all therapy groups with patients of all ages.

Slavson took pains to delineate the nature of the therapist's role in group psychotherapy, comparing its similarities and differences with individual therapy. Because of the complexity of the multiple transference phenomena in groups, he pointed out that the therapist was not as central an object for libidinal and aggressive cathexes as is the case in dyadic treatment. He described the necessary permissive, therapeutic climate of a therapy group, which was in stark contrast to the didactic, directed, leader-dominated group practices of many of the early practitioners.

Some persons tend to associate Slavson with children's groups exclusively, unaware of the breadth of his contributions in other areas of group treatment. As director of group therapy in a large community agency, he was in a strategic position to experiment with innovative groups. He discovered that activity group therapy was insufficient as an exclusive treatment for children with neurotic problems. It was thus that he proceeded into analytical groups. He also employed analytical groups with parents and, when he concluded that some parents did not require such a penetrating therapy, he experimented successfully with counseling groups for parents with children in treatment. It is likely that the antecedents of "family therapy" may be found in the context of these counseling groups and other group experiments at the Jewish Board of Guardians. Nathan Ackerman, who was associated with that agency during the late 1930s and early 1940s, became interested in the group approach through Slavson's work with children and parents. Ackerman, who was interested in families with delinquent children, and the social interactions in such families, organized and conducted several groups of parents.

Slavson never accepted the concept of "family therapy," considering it, instead, a special form of family counseling. He believed that what transpired in discussions between family members and with a therapist did not adhere to the requisites of psychotherapy. At that time, Ackerman did not consider his work with parents' groups as psychotherapy.

Slavson was a seminal thinker and critical evaluator of his own work and that of others. He had little patience for abstruse theories and formulations which lacked substantiation in actual practice. His own ideas on psychotherapy—individual and group—were traditional, explicitly defined in terms of Freudian psychology. He did not consider such "tradition" as pejorative, as some therapists are wont to do. Slavson could not accredit his own premises until he was able to demonstrate their clinical validity in practice. His views were expressed in conversations with the writer in words to this effect:

> I cannot begin to think outside the context of topological elements (id, ego, superego) and the dynamic interrelationships of these psychic structures. I don't see how any therapist can truly comprehend the nature of his work without considering these factors and how they bear on personality, character structure, and symptom formation. Not only diagnosis, but the choice and implementation of therapy are predicated on discerning the nuclear elements of problems.

According to Slavson, psychotherapy has the following elements: transference, catharsis, insight formation, reality-testing, and sublimation. The effects of treatment can be reasonably construed only in the context of these elements, which are germane in all forms of psychotherapy—individual and group, ego level therapy, and deeper, analytical methods. Objective determination of the results of therapy can be made from the feelings of patients after a sufficient time in treatment. When it is successful there is a redistribution of libido, relaxation, and regulation of the superego, ego strengthening, and an improved self-image.

The purpose of psychotherapy is to effect changes in the structural elements of personality. It is a process of altering the pathological features of the psychic trinity—ego, superego, and id. Despite Slavson's definitive constructs as to the nature of psychotherapy and how it could be evaluated, he did not believe that basic change was feasible in personality and character of adult and adolescent patients. According to him, successful therapy helped these patients to understand themselves better, to cope with problems which were unmanageable before therapy, and to ameliorate symptoms. On the other hand, children's personalities could actually be subject to change because they had not yet become crystallized or rigidified.

Precise distinctions were made by him between counseling, advisement, and psychotherapy. The first processes were concerned mainly with situations and specific management problems affecting individuals which were not integrally related to personality and character structure. They were faults in adaptation, but not determined by intrapsychic factors to any appreciable degree. Whereas psychotherapy was intended to bring about modifications in symptoms and inappropriate behavior, counseling and guidance were designed to help clients learn more appropriate ways of managing their problems. Psychotherapy was concerned with making a patient aware of unconscious motivators of inappropriate behavior, symptoms, and feelings, and aimed at relieving the psycho-noxious effects. Counseling and guidance do not attempt to uncover unconscious factors.

In Slavson's own words:

> . . . Psychotherapy is the process through which the structure of the psyche is corrected and/or reconstructed so that an individual can function more efficiently, within the limits of his native capacities, conditioned by his native equipment and as defined by the mores of the culture in which he lives. . . . (3, p. 377)

These formulations on psychotherapy, and group psychotherapy in particular, appeared in an impressive dissertation in the *International Journal of Group Psychotherapy* in 1954, one of a series of ten highly instructive papers which he later incorporated as the first textbook on the subject (6).

In the textbook, Slavson, among many topics, described significant aspects of analytical group psychotherapy with a clarity and succinctness which characterizes all his writings. He delineated the differential effects of treatment of neurotics, character disorders, schizophrenics, and psychotics, describing the indications and counterindications for both individual and group psychotherapy in treating these disorders. He stressed the necessary modifications in standard analytical procedures in ego-level treatment of character disorders, for whom the potential corrective effects of treatment were limited to ego reconditioning. Beyond this they were not accessible to significant modifications.

Slavson's definitive views as to the nature of personality and character structure and the aims and effects of group psychotherapy, emphasize and the centrality of the individual in treatment. The therapy group, and its inherent processes, were construed by him as the *technical instrument* of therapy. This focus on the patient and his or her interpersonal interactions with other group members placed Slavson's orientation in contrast to that of a different concept which was evolving. Some therapists, the British group in particular, considered "group dynamics" and the group-as-a-whole as primary considerations in group psychotherapy.

Yet, from the same classical Freudian orientation from which his conceptualizations about human behavior and group psychotherapy flowed, Slavson could be highly critical of some psychoanalytical practices. He decried the futility of attempting to treat character disorders in psychoanalysis. He considered this a misapplication of psychoanalytic psychology. He possessed a global perception of psychotherapy, in addition to his main interest in group treatment. He considered a group modality as one basic method; he never lost sight of the need for psychoanalysis, or psychotherapy based on psychoanalytical principles for patients with psychoneuroses. Slavson professed no allegiance to one methodology, only to that which proper diagnosis indicated as the best treatment approach. He insisted, repetitively, that only diagnosis and the elucidation of nuclear elements of presenting problems could determine the choice of treatment, which could be group, individual, or both concurrently.

During his later years, Slavson confided his concern with the current state of analytical group practice and the direction it was taking. He believed that some practices had gotten "out of hand"; that some therapists had elevated group pychotherapy to a singular position, and that they were employing it indiscriminately with all kinds of problems, unaware of or insensitive to diagnostic considerations. In the same way in which he found fault with what he considered illegitimate uses of psychoanalysis, he also held accountable group therapists who, in his words, "seemed to have forgotten" the nature of a psychoneurosis and its etiology and the need for dyadic treatment at times.

Well versed as he was in psychoanalytical theriory, Slavson recognized its necessary variances when it was translated into analytical group practice. He differed with some who considered that such mechanisms as transference, catharsis, and insight formation were explicable in group therapy in the same qualitative contexts they held in individual treatment. For example, some therapists referred to "free association" as occurring in groups. Slavson denied this, pointing out that what did take place was more accurately titled "associated thinking," which is quite different. Free association could occur only in dyadic treatment after a patient learns how not to govern his or her thoughts but to let them flow uninterrupted and uninhibited as much as possible. In this way associated content would stem *solely* from the patient's conscious and unconscious memory traces, replete with idiosyncratic symbolic references. Such a process could only be individualistic. He did not deny the value of "associated thinking" in fostering communication in a group. He considered this beneficial in that communications of other group members, including the therapist, would foster interactions between members. This process would evoke from others reactions and interpretations of their own dreams and fantasies, besides responding to the offerings of group members.

Slavson deplored inaccurate, imprecise applications of dynamic psychological principles in group practice, which would inevitably lead to misinterpretations and inefficiency, to the detriment of patients.

Slavson's views on individual and group psychotherapy were far from simplistic, nor were they uncompromising. He could accept the use of group treatment for a patient for whom the more penetrating psychoanalytical therapy was indicated, but who, for reasons of intractable resistance or other factors, was not amenable to dyadic treatment. An experience in a group might render the patient more accessible later. Contrariwise, Slavson sometimes recommended a course in group psychotherapy for patients following successful treatment in psychoanalysis or psychotherapy.

Slavson applied strict criteria in evaluating the methods and results of group psychotherapy. Whereas some therapists were prone to judge patients' florid, acting-out behavior as "free" expression, with therapeutic merit, Slavson pointed out that it was often a resistance. According to him, freedom and permissiveness were necessary attributes of the therapeutic climate of treatment groups designed to relax patients so that they could openly describe feelings about themselves and others. However, the tendency on the part of some therapists to encourage diffuse ventilation and personal "revelations" from patients in fact created anxiety which, in turn, could be expressed in acting-out or, in some patients, withdrawal and silence. There was no substitute in psychotherapy for patients having to work "at" their problems and work them through.

With respect to children, Slavson made a distinction: acting-out behavior by children was a form of communication, an action "language" which revealed feelings and conflicts—for children a natural, expressive pathway.

As the practice of group psychotherapy expanded, innovative methods were being used increasingly, e.g., confrontation, marathons, and other pressure-charged techniques. Slavson interpreted much of the results of such methods as "transference cures," apparent changes brought about through highly evocative techniques and "solicited" expressions of emotivity by a therapist. Emotivity by itself, despite some manifest changes in patients, did not constitute psychotherapy. It could not replace the more necessary, painstaking tasks of psychotherapy and the time required to accomplish them. Anything less constituted temporary remissions. Freud noted this phenomenon:

> . . . When a powerful impetus has been given to group formation, neuroses [or facets of character disorder behavior, according to Slavson] may diminish. . . and temporarily disappear. (1)

Other formulations of Slavson were in pointed difference with current ideas and practices. Prominent was his disbelief in the existence of "group dynamics." This view has almost startling import since it was he who first introduced the term "group dynamics" in a volume which was devoted to a subject other than psychotherapy (4). At the time he was interested in humanistic, social group activities in a democratic society. In their original formulations, group dynamics were identified in the context of normal groups. The dynamics he described have today become basic in the lexicon of terms employed in group psychotherapy, namely, cohesion, neutralization, polarization, mutual induction, identification, interstimulation, intensification, and others. Were he writing today about such concepts in light of his later experiences in psychotherapy chances are he might have modified his original term to "dynamics *in* groups."

Slavson identifies as interpersonal interactions what others term group dynamics. According to him, most observations and interpretations offered by therapists should have the individual at its focus, directly or by inference, depending on a patient's tolerance for and readiness to deal with the material. Analytical group psychotherapy constitutes treatment of an individual *in* a group. This is in contradistinction with the view of others, which holds that the unitary group and its moods, tensions, and behavior are primary. This he considered therapy *by* the group. According to Slavson, group dynamics are present in groups whose members share a *common* goal—normal groups. This is unlike therapy groups where patients have the *same* goal, namely, to be "cured," but they do not have problems in common; rather, they are usually different.

Slavson was well aware that at times a group acted in unison, which had the semblance of a group dynamic. He believed that such unitary behavior usually emanated as a form of negative transference against the therapist, a not uncommon group response. This could be due to a therapist's failure to recognize a crisis situation affecting one member, or the entire group, and thus fail to help the group work it through; or it could be the result of an egregious error by a therapist. The consequence of this could be heightened tension, perhaps protracted periods of silence, or an extraordinary degree of acting-out, with the therapist unable to deal with it.

As early as 1948, Slavson commented on the question of centrality of the individual in group psychotherapy:

> Therapy groups should not be relegated to the realm of mysticism and . . . transcendental concepts should be eliminated from discussions of them. . . . I have taken the opportunity to indicate the semantic discrepancy as well as the epistemological unsuitability of such terms as "group symptom" and "group emotion". . . "Group culture," for example, implies staticism; while psychotherapy is dynamic in its inherent process and in terms of intrapsychic activity. . . . The foundations of group psychotherapy lie in clinical, not sociological or philosophical concepts. Clinical and diagnostic understandings must be dominant here as in any other branch of psychiatry; especially important is diagnosis. . . . (5)

Normal groups would be torn asunder, unable to resolve problems and achieve common goals, without cohesion as a cementing force. In such groups, cohesion is a constant influence during the group's existence, except for occasional, temporary interruptions when differences arise. But, since the coping abilities of the members are essentially normal, the process of neutralization resolves these differences, and the group returns to a state of equanimity. In therapy groups, however, if cohesion is maintained as a pervasive and lasting influence, it blocks the discharge of negative transference and prevents catharsis, which are essential in psychotherapy. Persistent cohesion may represent a combined resistance, or it may result from a therapist's purposive implementation of *status denial* or an example of *aim attachment.*

Slavson questioned the concept of "status denial," namely a therapist's intentional fostering of feelings of equality in members of a therapy group, including the therapist—an existential concept. Status denial purportedly enhances a patient's ability to deal with the here and now rather than to explore the historical contexts of early development in the family. In effect, status denial is intended to foster cohesion in a group and empathic interactions. It was pointed out by Slavson that this blocked catharsis and inhibited the therapeutic process.

In a paper dealing with countertransference, Slavson identified "aim attachment" of a therapist as countertransference. This is a condition wherein a therapist is unduly motivated by a personal need to be successful, to be liked by his patients, to achieve the therapeutic outcomes which he deemed to be most important (7). Such an attitude and the methods used stem from the therapist's insecurity; unwittingly he reveals this from a compelling need to deny the possibility of failure. Such motivation (countertransference) probably accounts for status denial also, a "humanistic," empathic conceptualization of psychotherapy. In keeping with his clearly stated ideas as to the nature of psychotherapy, Slavson held that patients cannot be spared the necessity to work through problems over time, which is not enhanced when therapists actually encourage positive transference relationships through aim attachment and status denial.

During his last years, when Slavson could no longer apply himself to writing to further express his philosophy anent psychotherapy, he communicated his thoughts in personal conversations. He questioned the validity of so-called "cognitive therapy," which stresses the merit of purely intellectual, conative capacities to affect psychic processes. He could see the need for intellectual reflection in counseling and guidance—individual or group—but not in psychotherapy as the sole procedure for ameliorating problems caused by intrapsychic conflict, the basis of most emotional disorders. Among other questions, he wondered how intellectualization in and of itself could affect a patient's early, preconceptual experiences which are responsible in large measure for character problems.

Systems theory, as applied to interpersonal dynamics in groups, was rejected unequivocally by Slavson. He knew the penetrating effects on personality and character development of interactions between family members, but he could discern no "systems" in families, nor in their displaced projections by patients in analytical group psychotherapy. The human psyche is too complex, too idiosyncratic, to be comprehended in a mechanistic context of "systems." He did accept the existence of systems in other social phenomena—the sciences, industrial processes, and some political and socioeconomic phenomena.

In a limited exposition, one risks the possibility of doing disservice to the scope of Slavson's seminal thinking, as well as to the views of others with whom he disagreed. That he held firmly to his beliefs and the practices derived from them does not mean that he resisted innovation. He wrote—and spoke—of circumstances in which a therapist may depart from standard procedures of treatment, in both groups and individual therapy. This allows for didactic, mild confrontation, paradigmatic techniques, encouraging assertiveness in patients, and other procedures, when they are employed episodically in therapy, at psychologically propitious times. But, he could not accept such "strategies," as he called them, as total forms of psychotherapy. A sophisticated therapist knew when—and how—to "break the rules."

The fact that Slavson earnestly defended what he considered responsible practices in group psychotherapy did not stem from iconoclasm. Those who knew him personally recognized his motivation as objective, scientific, and concerned primarily with the integrity of psychological premises and practices derived from them. He was always mindful of the patients' interests. When, in professional conferences, he served as a chairman, a presenter, or as a respondent to presentations of others, his manner was direct, unequivocal, often challenging, but always responsive to the *subject* under consideration. Nevertheless, his acute analyses were bound to elicit personal responses from persons whose concepts and practices he questioned. Slavson was relatively unconcerned at such times about personal factors, and more concerned with establishing the validity of ideas. He was particularly zealous in defending children against the effects of ill-conceived group treatment methods.

It is fitting that we give proper acknowledgment to a man who made many contributions: who was substantially involved in the origins and development of group psychotherapy; who had an important role in monitoring the directions it took over the years; and who labored to insure that the AGPA would remain a preeminent professional organization. Many times Slavson vigorously defended the standards of qualifications for membership in AGPA; he also worked to bind the local affiliate societies of AGPA to the parent organization, insuring that they not become advocates of views and practices antithetical to AGPA.

Slavson planted the "seeds" of group psychotherapy, cultivated them assiduously, and formed the organization which truly gave clinical identity to a relatively new modality of psychological treatment. His complete dedication in pursuit of these goals and his unswerving convictions about what was correct and helpful in ameliorating human ills have provided a heritage few can match. He merits the honors and titles bestowed upon him. For this he is rightfully AGPA's "President Emeritus."

In conclusion, here is a short statement from an unpublished note by Slavson:

It has always seemed to me that the greatest value of therapy groups lay in their permissiveness to discharge hostility, something that no other group or individual relation can permit. For to achieve mental health, one must face his own aggressive feelings and either suppress or sublimate them, or allow himself a moderate amount of hostility without ensuing guilt. Aggression should be spread about thinly, instead of concentrating it on one object. In this very important step toward mental health and inner peace, the ability to reconcile oneself to the inevitability of irrational aggression urges and hostility in oneself and in others is essential. For unless we develop this tolerance, a harmonious social life is impossible to envisage. There is no solution to the problems of mankind or of individuals unless man begins to understand himself and accepts his nature and his unconscious. A step in this direction is to know the function of emotions in life and survival and their indestructability. Then will individuals and nations be more accepting of each other and give themselves a chance.

REFERENCES

1. Freud, S. (1921) Group psychology and the analysis of the ego. *Standard Edition*, 18: 65-145. London: Hogarth Press, 1955.
2. Robinson, D. One hundred most important leaders in the world of health. *Family Health*, 4 (3): 211-223, 1972.
3. Schiffer, M. (Ed.) *Dynamics of Analytical Group Psychotherapy (Chapters 23, 25, 31, 34, 38, 43, 46)*. New York: Jason Aronson, 1979.
4. Slavson, S.R. The dynamics of the group process (Chapter IV). *In: Character Education in a Democracy*. New York: Association Press, 1939.
5. Slavson, S.R. Advances in group and individual therapy: Discussion. *In Proceedings of the International Conference on Medical Psychotherapy, Vol. 3*. London: H.K. Lewis, 1948.
6. Slavson, S.R. A systemic theory. *In: A Textbook of Analytical Group Psychotherapy*. New York: International Universities Press, 1964.
7. Slavson, S.R. Sources of countertransference and group induced anxiety. *In:* M. Schiffer (Ed.), *Dynamics of Analytical Group Psychotherapy*. New York: Jason Aronson, 1979, pp. 341-358.
8. Thomas, G.W. Group psychotherapy: A review of the recent literature. *Psychosomatic Medicine*, 5: 166-180, 1943.

Theoretical and Technical Issues
in Group Therapy

Chapter III

THE USE AND ABUSE OF TRANSFERENCE
INTERPRETATION IN GROUP THERAPY

Anne Alonso, Ph.D., and
J. Scott Rutan, Ph.D.

Editors' Summary. The authors begin by reviewing some general considerations of transference interpretations. Groups are seen as presenting both enabling and inhibiting factors
for the use of transference interpretations and these are described in the context of kinds of
transference and the timing and accuracy of interpretations. The authors conclude with a
discussion of abuses of transference interpretations in group therapy and present an outline
for some of the contributing factors that lead to these abuses.

INTRODUCTION

Since Freud first mentioned the concept of transference in his *Studies on
Hysteria* in 1895 (8), transference has remained a fundamental premise of psy-
choanalytically oriented psychotherapy. It has not been a non-controversial concept, however. Leites (20) provided a very helpful overview of the arguments
surrounding the centrality of transference interpretation as a major analytic technique. He maintained that all the arguments about transference center around
one basic set of assumptions, known as Strachey's law (24), which states that
the reliving of infantile reactions in the transference is a necessary condition and
that *only* transference interpretations regarding those reactions produce therapeutic effect.

While psychoanalysts debated whether change could occur from sources
other than transference interpretations, another debate began concerning the
prospect of generating any usable transference in a group at all. Some analysts
maintained that the presence of other people, the visible stimulus of the therapist,
and the upright position of the patients all served to dilute transference, rendering
it unusable as the primary therapeutic agent. Likewise, the question of whether
free association is truly possible in a group setting is controversial. Blau (2) has
taken the position that free association is not possible in groups.

The authors take the position that the resolution of neurosis occurs in group
in much the same way as in any other analytic modality, given the same level

of intensity and the same investment of time. The degree of freedom of associations is affected by the context, but this is also true in traditional dyadic psychoanalysis. Freud (12) stated,

> We must . . . bear in mind that free associations are not really free. The patient remains under the influence of the analytic situation even though he is not directing his mental activites on a particular subject.

The interpretation of transference maintains its primacy as a change agent in groups. Group therapy provides a setting for the emergence of multiple transference phenomena, all occurring simultaneously. An individual in a group may develop aspects of a transference neurosis toward the leader, any one of or several of his/her fellow patients, and/or the group as a whole. This paper proposes some theoretical and technical considerations for applying the classical method of transference interpretation to working with transference in group therapy. In addition, we will delineate some of the appropriate uses of transference interpretations in group therapy, outline some specific abuses of the technique, and indicate the sources of such abuses. Our goal is to provide guidelines to facilitate the training of psychodynamic group therapists, as well as to provide added clarity about these concepts for more experienced group analysts.

GENERAL CONSIDERATIONS

The management of transference in groups is a complicated and intricate process requiring theoretical clarity and technical accuracy. For example, Anna Freud's (7) distinctions between the three kinds of transference phenomena have major implications for group therapy since all three occur simultaneously in groups and may need to be interpreted differently. She distinguished types of transference phenomena according to degree of complexity. Sandler et al. (23) list these as

> 1) transference of libidinal impulses, in which . . . wishes attached to infantile objects break out toward . . . the analyst, 2) transference of defense, in which former defenses are repeated, and 3) acting out in the transference, in which the transference spills out into the patients' life.

This, in effect, is a displaced transference.

The earliest and most predominant transference phenomenon that occurs in groups had to do with *displacement transferences*, in which members seem to move away from the powerful feelings for a group member or the leader to a displaced memory of their families of origin. For example, a group member who may displace affect about a new group member back to older feelings about the birth of a deformed sibling. While it is certainly true that on other occasions group members can focus on in-group, here-and-now affects in order to avoid more potent and important historical feelings, in this case and many others the group member was reverting back to a far more remote issue in order to avoid the intensity of feeling that was present in the here and now. Ekstein (5) reports a patient whose "association about an aunt could be considered a displacement from the analyst." The anxiety generated by the group situation produces a milieu in which it is often initially safer to place one's family of origin between oneself and the analytic situation. Thus, one frequently hears in a group something like, "You remind me of my sister!", which serves primarily as a defense against the full experiencing and sharing of the feelings between the members of the group.

A second transference phenomenon that occurs regularly in groups is the *transference of defense*, in which the individual unconsciously repeats patterns of affective response and behavior in the group. Group members are ready to address these patterned and repetitious responses since they often generate dystonic responses in some of the members, while inviting an indentification in other members familiar with this defensive maneuver from their own psychic economy.

Finally, and frequently the most difficult to elaborate in a group setting, is the individual's *transference of libidinal impulses toward the leader*. Group-wide transference toward the leader is more common; thus a group may share a view of the leader as cold, warm, intrusive, or distant. Only in very mature groups, when the protective alliance had been firmly established, is it possible for individual members to routinely risk sharing their individual transference images of the leader apart from the group transference. Not infrequently the sharing of the individual transference is the harbinger of the patient's nearing the final stages of group therapy, a very different meaning than the appearance of such material in individual analytic therapy. To share such private material is to risk attack by the other members, which has the effect of raising anxiety and allowing for the working through of the transferred affect. Gray (17) pointed out that "it needs catastrophe to break the reign of transference; happiness apparently will not do." It may well be that the catastrophe of the differentiation from the group is just such a breakpoint for the patient.

While the method of individual analysis is "talking out," the method of group analysis is "acting-out" of the transference in the group. By this, Ackerman (1) did not refer to "acting-out" as an impeding factor, but rather he pointed out that members of groups have the opportunity to act out, or demonstrate their transference reactions by their relations with the various other group members, which will portray their inner conflicts clearly. The preconscious inner conflicts are first available to interpretation, but then the unconscious conflicts, by inference, may be interpreted in the medium of the group.

In individual therapy or analysis, the patient is mandated to speak his feelings rather than act them out. Every effort is made to set up a therapeutic situation which reduces the environmental temptations to do rather than to talk, to fantasize, to dream, and to allow the associations to flow as freely as possible. Acting-out is seen as an interruption of the free associative process and thus is to be eschewed. In groups, the analytic situation promotes a limited, analyzable forum for the acting-out, or more appropriately put, the acting-in of patients' conflicts. One of the major advantages of groups is that patients immediately enter a group and start *having* their problems rather than just talking about them. The group patient is encouraged to relate to the other members and, by definition, to then "act out" his style of object relatedness in the context of the group. Instead of defining acting-out as a resistance to the analytic work, this limited type of acting-out (or -in) is seen as the medium for analysis, on a par with dreams, associations, parapraxes, etc.

A Kleinian understanding of acting-out, having to do with projective identifications, is a more accurate model for applying to groups. Each member is exposed to a variety of objects whom he or she must split, at least initially, in order to maintain equilibrium. This is consistent with Klein's developmental schema in which the baby, unable yet to contain ambivalence, splits the mother into good breast and bad breast fantasies and responds to the mother-environment in alternations of this perception of self and other. The new member in a therapy group is also apt to split, seeing good members and bad members, safe members and dangerous members. Furthermore, the group member is likely to act out the split in the forced relatedness to these people in the group environment. This process forms an adaptive context for acting out the ambivalence within the safety of the group boundaries. This makes the split available to early and persistent interpretation when it emerges in the transference distortions. The container of the group must be shored up, often with a clear group contract which reinforces the parameters of "allowable" acting-out, distinguishing it from destructive forms of acting-out, which are then interpreted as violations of the group contract.

Just as there are factors in groups that facilitate the emergence of transference, so too there are aspects of groups which lend themselves to a distortion of the transference and impede its proper interpretation.

There are three major areas of confusion and concern surrounding the interpretation of transference: 1) the timing of transference interpretation; 2) the accuracy of transference interpretation; and 3) a clear understanding of the source and aims of transference distortion.

Freud's (9) early position was that the analyst should refrain from interpreting the transfernce too early, lest he interfere with the analysis. Freud felt that while the patient's associations flowed, the analyst should say nothing. Recently, this point has come to be questioned on the basis that Freud erroneously assumed the transference neurosis did not exist prior to the analytic situation (cf., Gill and Muslin [13], Loewenstein [21]). In the present era, especially with the increased application of psychoanalytic theory to psychodynamic psychotherapy, early interpretations of the transference are often valued, at least as they are manifest in the here and now between patient and therapist.

As Gill and Muslin (13) state:

> We believe that an extensive examination of analytic case material would show that covert references to the transferences, like resistance in fact, as transference resistance, are present every step of the way and, subject to the usual issues of judgement about when an interpretation should be made, should be interpreted when they appear, even if that be early in the analysis. (pp. 792-793)

Issues of timing have long been considered important, along with concerns about the level of the patient's pathology and the level of the analyst's experience. How much interpretation, how soon, and to what avail are all very important questions.

If we consider ongoing, open-ended analytic groups, the setting must be taken into consideration when determining the timing of interpretations. The process of the group is a continuous stream with a life of its own, and into which the patient steps at a given point in time. Interpretations made in groups are heard by members who are at differing stages of development within the group: One member may be preparing to terminate while another may be in the earliest stages of joining the group and beginning the therapeutic journey. To the extent that the group therapist makes an interpretation of group-as-a-whole transference, he or she may be speaking prematurely for some, belatedly for others (and thus perhaps regressively). Similarly, the interpretation of any single member's transference distortion toward the leader or another member is also heard by other members who may or may not be ready to hear or understand it. No one speaks to just one person in a group. That which is "overheard" can catalyze or inhibit, and the effect of the interpretation must be carefully examined in this light.

THE ACCURACY OF THE INTERPRETATION

Just as no one speaks to only one person in a group, no one ever hears the same message, no matter what words are actually spoken. Each member necessarily filters the heard communication through his or her context. Concerns about the effect and meaning of inexact or incomplete interpretations (cf., Glover [16]), have been the focus of much scholarly inquiry. The application of this kind of intellectual rigor is of major importance to group therapists since interpretations in groups are heard by, and affect, more than one person.

In groups, for example, what constitutes an accurate interpretation for one patient may constitute an inexact interpretation for another. Inexact interpretations, as Glover pointed out, tend to reduce anxiety and shore up the defense of the patient, thereby slowing down the process of analysis. For example, a leader might make an interpretation that a group is resisting sharing affect because of the advent of a new member. The new member might experience a reduction in anxiety, and therefore, in Glover's (16) terms, an increase in repression. For this member the leader's comment might represent an inexact interpretation of his repression, since he is probably dealing with early group concerns such as stranger anxiety and issues of basic trust. The less fearsome interpretation of sibling rivalry may serve to separate him from the group resistance. Another member of the group may hear the interpretation in the context of some working through he has been engaged in around the birth of a deformed sibling, as in the earlier example, and may thus feel enabled to experience his sense of displacement in the heart of the leader-qua-parent. Yet another member may produce an association which fuses her with newborn group "baby." Glover (16), in discussing the therapeutic effect of an inexact interpretation, points out that early analytic improvement is in part related to transference factors and in part related to an increase in the effectiveness of repression, which allows for the building of a therapeutic alliance.

Glover's work suggests that a group therapist's interpretations had best be aimed as accurately as possible toward the in-depth work of the most engaged group member. The interpretation of the deepest level of unconscious conflict will loosen the repression of the members capable of dealing with it, while at the same time increasing the repression of those members who hear it as (or for whom it is) an inexact interpretation. The former population is thus open to deeper levels of work, while the latter population is protected by the reduction of anxiety and increase in repression. Analysis, to be effective, must resolve the affective, transferential bond, both positive and negative. This is done by pushing interpretation to the existing maximum of objective understanding in order to loosen the bonds of repression.

THE ABUSE OF TRANSFERENCE INTERPRETATION

Since the interpretation of transference constitutes such a major part of analytic work, it is important to pay close attention to the abuse of this powerful and fundamental technique. For the purpose of this paper, we make no distinction between abuse and misuse, but rather we assume that this occurs without any awareness or conscious intent on the part of the clinician. It is nonetheless abusive of the therapeutic process to the extent that it distorts or inhibits the aim of analysis, i.e., the resolution of the patient's neurosis as expeditiously as possible.

Glover (16) separates the sources of difficulty in analytic practice due to 1) the case, 2) the technique, and 3) the analyst's personal defenses. We will utilize this outline to investigate the abuse of transference interpretations in groups.

Due to the Case

Many levels of transference are operating simultaneously in a therapy group; thus, it is crucial to attend to the composition of an analytic group so as to ensure a joint capacity among the members for dealing with the group therapist's interpretations. For optimal functioning, an analytic group should consist of members with a similar level of ego development. They may be widely divergent on other axes, but in order to best utilize a treatment which focuses on transference they need to operate from a shared set of developmental assumptions. For a group to contain too wide a range of ego levels usually means that individual responses to transference interpretations are so widely divergent as to inhibit group-wide exploration. This becomes particularly troublesome when the leader is directing his or her interpretations at the deepest level of conflict. The leader needs to know that the overheard interpretation will not be injuriously regressive on the one hand, or superficial and inhibiting on the other hand, for the other members.

Due to the Technique

The multiplicity of transferences in a therapy group present the leader with a confusing array of entry points for transference interpretation. Should the interpretation of the group-as-a-whole process take precedence over the interpretation of the individual within the group? Are peer transferences more or less important than patient-therapist or patient-group transferences? These questions exist alongside the confusion about the meaning of transference delineated by Anna Freud (7) and alluded to above. The literature is riddled with contradiction and confusion and provides little in the way of clear guidelines, especially for the handling of transferences in group settings.

The cognitive confusion about technique can leave the clinician uncertain and anxious, and this vulnerability may then be projected onto the group. This can ultimately result in a well-meaning clinician avoiding transference interpretations altogether, or aiming them at the more comfortable level of transference distortion. The authors have found that considerable experience, both as members of groups and as therapists leading groups, is needed to allow for the development of faith and confidence in the capacity of groups to titrate the anxiety to a tolerable level for different members and the group-as-a-whole. For example, the overly chatty member is usually given the job of interfering with anxiety-producing interventions by the therapist, and the danger is more on the side of the group being overprotected than being underprotected from undue stress.

Due to the Analyst's Personal Defenses

The contagious pull in groups is one of the more powerful disinhibiting factors that leads to a loosening of the patient's defenses. However, the clinician is also pulled into the group contagion and may experience a struggle to maintain clinical neutrality and the integrity of his or her own defenses.

It is difficult to avoid enjoying the idealization of a group, and it is difficult to avoid fearing a group's denigration and scorn. The group therapist who interprets an anxiety-binding defense or transferential distortion always runs the risk of becoming the focus of powerful instinctual assault, both positive and negative, by a whole group of individuals.

The clinician may succumb to his or her narcissistic vulnerabilities and end up using interpretations as a defense, or as Freud (10) said, "Hurling interpretations in the patient's face." This often serves to gain a sense of superiority to the group, to impress them with wit or cleverness, in the service of protecting the leader from narcissistic harm. Similarly, unneutralized sadistic impulses in clinicians may lead to overly incisive, unempathic interpretations.

SUMMARY

The multiplicity of relationships in group therapy requires special and careful attention to the interpretation of transference. While groups provide an intricate array of opportunities for the emergence of transference phenomena, they also present the clinician with certain constraints. The authors maintain that transference does exist in groups at levels of intensity suitable for in-depth interpretation. This paper has outlined some of the special considerations regarding interpretation of transference in groups. By careful attention to exact application of the technique, the analytic method adds rich dimension to treatment in groups.

REFERENCES

1. Ackerman, N. Psychoanalysis and group therapy. *In:* J.C. Moreno (Ed.), *Group Therapy VIII*, Nos. 2-3. Boston: Beacon House, 1949, pp. 204-215.
2. Blau, D. Presentation at a Symposium entitled, "Group Psychotherapy and the Dynamics of Change: Three Theoretical Perspectives," under the auspices of the Northeastern Group Psychotherapy Society, Copley Plaza Hotel, Boston, June 12, 1982.
3. Brenner, C. Some comments on technical percepts in psycho-analysis. *J. Am. Psychoanal. Asso.*, 17: 333-352, 1969.

4. Caligor, J. The analytic therapist in group: Continuities and discontinuities with Sigmund Freud. *Group*, 4: 32-39, 1980.
5. Ekstein, R. An historical survey on the teaching of psychoanalytic technique. *J. Am. Psychoanal. Asso.*, 8: 500-516, 1960.
6. Fenichel, O. *Problems of Psychoanalytic Technique*. New York: Psychoanalytic Quarterly, Inc., 1941.
7. Freud, A. (1969) Difficulties in the path of psychoanalysis. *In:* A. Freud, *Problems of Psychoanalytic Technique and Theory*. London: Hogarth Press, 1972.
8. Freud, S. (1895) *Studies on Hysteria* (translation). *Standard Edition*, 2. London: Hogarth Press, 1956.
9. Freud, S. (1913) On beginning the treatment. *Standard Edition*, 12: 123. London: Hogarth Press, 1958.
10. Freud, S. (1910) Wild psychoanalysis. *Standard Edition*, 12: 140-142. London: Hogarth Press, 1958.
11. Freud, S. (1912) The dynamics of transference. *Standard Edition*, 12: 99-108. London: Hogarth Press, 1958.
12. Freud, S. (1925) An autobiographical study. *Standard Edition*, 20: 40-41. London: Hogarth Press, 1959.
13. Gill, M. and Muslin, H. Early interpretation of transference. *J. Am. Psychoanal. Asso.*, 24: 779-794, 1976.
14. Giovacchini, P. Transference, therapy and synthesis. *Int. J. Psychoanal.*, 46: 287-296, 1965.
15. Gittelson, M. Analytic aphorisms. *Psychoanal. Q.*, 36: 260-270, 1967.
16. Glover, E. *The Technique of Psychoanalysis*. New York: International Universities Press, 1955.
17. Gray, W. Psychoanalytic technique and the ego's capacity for viewing intrapsychic activity. *J. Am. Psychanal. Asso*, 21: 486, 1977.
18. Greenacre, P. The psychoanalytic process: Transference and acting out. *Int. J. Psychoanal.*, 49: 211-218, 1968.
19. Greenson, P. and Wexler, M. The Non-transference relationship in the psychoanalytic situation. *Int. J. Psychoanal.*, 51: 143-150, 1969.
20. Leites, N. Transference interpretations only? *Int. J. Psychoanal.*, 58: 275, 1977.
21. Loewenstein, R. The problem of interpretation. *Psychoanal. Q.*, 20: 1-14, 1951.
22. Ornstein, A. and Ornstein, P. On the interpretive process in psychoanalysis. *Int. J. Psychoanal. Psychother.*, 4: 219-271, 1976.
23. Sandler, *et al.*, p. 638.
24. Strachey, J. (1934) The Nature of the therapeutic action of psychoanalysis. Reprinted in *Int. J. Psychoanal.*, 50: 275-292, 1969.

Chapter IV

A QUANTITATIVE THEORY OF GUILT AND ITS RESOLUTION IN GROUP THERAPY

Herman S. Alpert, M.D.

Editors' Summary. A quantitative theory of guilt is proposed to assist the psychotherapist in detecting ontogenetic sources of conscious and unconscious guilt from the quality of child-rearing, the interpersonal relationship between both parents and their relationship to their children during the formative years. In analytic group psychotherapy, unconscious guilt is made conscious so that the patient becomes aware of its genesis and takes steps to correct what was heretofore unknown. This is accomplished by the interactions between the group members and between themselves and the therapist. Accumulated hostility is released harmlessly in socially acceptable quantities and guilt energies are discharged until a positive balance of affection and well-being is achieved.

In this chapter the author's aim is to clarify the concept of guilt so that it can be practically and appropriately utilized in psychoanalytic individual and group psychotherapy. No attempt will be made to enter into current theoretical disputes regarding the various unsettled and undecided areas in metapsychology, nor will shame be delineated from guilt.

Guilt may be conceptualized as a negative energy unpleasantly experienced by the "self" when conscious, but totally unknown to exist (by the "self") when unconscious. In the human psyche, guilt is the result of a conflict between the superego, or conscience, and the amoral, demanding discharge of the instinctual drive energies of the id. It can be both conscious and unconscious. When one is aware of feelings of guilt, e.g., conscious guilt, actions of contrition and repentence can result to minimize and attempt to eliminate the unpleasant tension generated by this battle in the self between the id and the superego:

> Guilt reactions are readily discharged by some activity which makes amends, or balances the scales of obligation. They are more easily discharged if one is able to rectify the trouble one has caused. States of shame and/or guilt which cannot be discharged or righted lead into "primary process" transformations or psychic symptoms. . . .
> The ego is the term for the ongoing activities of the individual without the individual's awareness of all of them (Chein, 1944). The *self* is the term for the experiencer of these activities. (4, pp. 27-28)

The ego is the "arbitrator," so to speak, to force these opposing psychic energies into a compromise, temporarily acceptable to both. Since neither the energies of the id nor those of the superego are allowed complete discharge because of this "compromise," residuals are stored in the psyche and are repressed or "forgotten." Because the psyche contains a "collector" of these residual guilt energies in variable increments from infancy into adulthod, the quantity of unconscious guilt can accumulate over the years to a grand total far in excess of any conscious guilt, which seeks immediate discharge due to the discomfort it causes.

Factors influencing the input of guilt will vary with the constitution of the infant, the quality of parenting, the beneficial or adverse effects of parent surrogates or important others as role models (e.g., teachers, relatives, close friends), and the nature of the relationship between the parents, and between themselves and their children. Add to these the socioeconomic conditions, accidental injuries to oneself or to others, events of chance, family size, and one's interpersonal relationships with siblings, and the complexity of attempting to evaluate the sources and effects of unconscious guilt becomes apparent.

The earliest guilt begins in infancy when the hungry infant cries to be fed or changed. If the mother replies immediately and doesn't allow a short waiting period before responding, the infant will expect this immediate gratification as a pattern. As a consequence, the personality trait of patience and the optimistic expectation of fulfillment despite the short wait will be impeded, and impatience or fretfulness take root.

By contrast, the mother who refuses to respond in a reasonable period and allows her infant to escalate its cries to the point of anger, manifested by flushed face, copious tears and thrashing about, builds the earliest accumulation of anger against a loved person in the infant psyche, despite the mother's rationalization that she did not want to "spoil" her infant.

Only later when the infant begins to learn the concepts of "good" and "bad," "no" and "yes," does it begin to employ its will and enjoy the power of these antithetical words taught by the parents. At this stage, conflict begins and guilt starts to accumulate. As long as the infant is obedient and complies with the parental wishes and admonitions, it feels "good" with the love and approval given by its parents. If, however, the infant's wishes are thwarted by parental "no's" often quite essential to protect it against injury, anger may be activated against the parent whose love and care it needs, and the guilt growing from being told it's "bad" adds its portion to the initial amount in the "collector" of these energies in its psyche. It is helpful to conceptualize this early conflict between the infant's ego and its conscience (superego) as the prototype of primitive guilt formation on which increments of guilt are added as the infant progresses toward adulthood.

The presence of this unconscious, accumulated guilt can be deduced from the self-punitive reactions and behavior it produces, because it cannot be measured. It can only be approximated as minimal, moderate, or maximal by the degree of suffering it causes the possessor, who may complain of symptoms, inhibitions in attaining goals, or unexplainable periods of anxiety.

Those persons with minimal unconscious guilt can usually tolerate it without discomfort or any external signs of its presence. Actually, no one is totally without some guilt since the training period of a growing child must produce resentment or anger against even the best-adjusted and enlightened parents who must teach the child right from wrong, correct manners, proper treatment of others, and a realization that all its wishes cannot be granted.

Even the most permissive parent cannot allow the complete discharge of the consciously expereinced anger, as a matter of discipline. The child must suppress this anger toward the parent he loves. It finally undergoes repression and remains quiescent but has added itself to the total in the unconscious guilt "collector."

When one undergoes individual or group analytic psychotherapy, the gradual developing insights into the causes of one's difficulties by this unconscious guilt become clear. The individual may even complain of feeling worse than before starting psychotherapy, because the transference onto the therapist of unfulfilled needs of one's parents stimulates the release of some unconscious guilt energy to punish the therapist as a frustrating parent substitute. The therapy group offers multiple opportunities to work through the recall of the many incidents generating guilt with parents, because members recalling conflict situations will stimulate similar memories in groupmates.

Identification with the speaker elicits "me, too!" abreactions with emotional release through ventilation, when other groupmates are stimulated to interact and corrective emotional experiences occur. Insights into why and how the unconscious guilt interferes with their lives are also gained. The sentence imposed as a punishment by their superegos for this guilt is the thwarting of attaining their intended goals, and more severely, the development of a variety of functional symptoms. All is part of the process of absolution for this guilt.

Evidence of the lessening of the amount of guilt by group psychotherapy is the progress a member makes in attaining goals and the successful accomplishment of heretofore blocked endeavors, as well as the diminution or elimination of unpleasant symptoms. The psychotherapy group accomplishes this by being a "laboratory of human interpersonal reactions and emotions." When the group members experience these reactions, they know that they are pledged to describe exactly what they feel without censoring. This is in direct opposition to what occurs in a social group where one is careful to avoid saying what might be hurtful or negatively critical.

As the group becomes the laboratory for the uncensored expression of interpersonal reactions between the groupmates and the leader, as well as between the groupmates themselves, hostile and competitive energies accumulated during one's growth to adulthood against loved parents, siblings, and important others are activated and released. Since hostility cannot coexist with love in the psyche, conflict results and guilt ensues. However, when hostility is expressed to the leader and no retaliation occurs, and when angry interchanges happen between groupmates with no alienation resulting, it is very reassuring to the participants. In this way, appropriate, tolerable quantities of hostility are drawn off, and the positive (love) feelings predominate as the ambivalence diminishes. As a result, a closeness and friendliness develop between the group members.

Since guilt resides within the self, it interferes with one's feelings of well-being and pleasure by blocking the flow of erotic currents and the whole range of positive feelings towards others. Positive balance is restored by psychoanalytic group and/or individual psychotherapy by the discharge of these negative (hostile) feelings which are transferred onto the therapist and/or the members of the group representing family members who lend themselves as targets. The therapist leads the group into recognizing the sources, exploring and interpreting the meaning of these transferences. As the group member expresses his or her frustrations and anger with the therapist and the group members, and yet does not experience the usual rejection or other punishments he/she received at home, he or she improves, because the fantasied destruction due to the years of accumulated hostility does not come to pass. Finally, the realization that the group member would not destroy or be destroyed is convincing and comforting.

The unconscious guilt energy seeks discharge outlets. If conditions outside the self are too dangerous or forbidding, it will attack the inner self (ego) as its target. Actions inviting humiliation, embarrassment, or shame can result to atone for this guilt. An established and prolific writer develops a block, a student fails exams to prevent promotion, an employee inappropriately defies his employer and is fired, and a marriage ends in divorce—these are a few examples of the potential results of expiating this unconscious guilt.

In practice it is important for the psychotherapist to utilize the concept of incremental accumulation of guilt through the formative years from infancy through the training period of early childhood and later, as the personality traits making up character evolve and crystallize.

From the quantitative theory it is useful to consider the therapist and the group members as transference objects, session after session, drawing off fractional amounts of unconscious guilt from the total in the psyche. Thus, the individual is made aware of its presence through interpretation of the noxious effects it produces to prevent the happy and effective functioning in all of life's personal and interpersonal areas.

To elaborate on the process of resolution, group psychotherapy facilitates the "drawing off" of portions of unconscious guilt by supplying multiple transference objects to dilute the intensity of its being made conscious. A "safer" environment is created to express, as well as offer, here-and-now interpretations touching on several levels of the ontogenetic evolution of the individual's psyche.

The effect of the "me, too!" identification by other groupmates acknowledging heretofore "forbidden" and "dangerous" feelings is very reassuring to the groupmate revealing, for the first time, behavior, feelings, or ideas he or she considered weird, shameful, or crazy. There is safety in numbers; when groupmates unite in articulating complaints, anger, sexual fantasies, or other "forbidden" feelings to the therapist-leader, which few would be courageous enough to do in individual therapy, they effect the resolution of the unconscious guilt in a continual manner.

When the scales are tipped finally in the direction of the positive (love) feelings, the improvement in the individual's function and interpersonal relationships is quite apparent to oneself, as it is to family members and close friends. This change is the evidence that a sufficient quantity of guilt reduction has taken place, and in this resolution of guilt a more consistent happiness has been maintained. It follows that the demands of the conscience have been greatly diminished or even transiently eliminated.

Under certain circumstances, unconscious guilt can produce punishment through personal suffering as absolution and compensatory benevolence in adulthood. For example, a middle-aged man suffering from angina pectoris was married to a woman who was quite directive and controlling of his life, in direct contrast to his mother whom he terrorized as a boy with his willful behavior. As a child he was cruel to his younger sister; he had a noninvolved, chronically ill father. He became a most considerate and indulgent son and brother after he married, had children of his own, and moved to another city. He insisted on his sister visiting him on her vacations after their mother died, and he and his wife were most hospitable and gracious to her, much to her pleasant surprise. His sister, who had been satisified with occasional telephone conversations with her sister-in-law and her brother up to this time, marveled at the change in him when she finally consented to visit them. He had learned in group psychotherapy that his angina pectoris was the price his conscience made him pay for being such a brat as a youngster, which he was convinced he must undo by being kind and considerate to his sister, his only surviving family member.

Another group member whose life was affected adversely by guilt collected during his growing-up years finally sought help because of his depression, alienation from friends, and lack of functioning in his business. He and his parents had never gotten along. They constantly criticized his lack of ambition and his refusal to study hard, and pessimistically predicted that he would "never amount to anything." To add insult to injury they constantly compared him to his first cousin of the same age who graduated with honors from college, and was increasingly successful in his work. He envied and hated this cousin, and was furious when his parents would ask, "Why can't you be like Mel?!" His father, who was an alumnus of the college he attended, took pride in the fact that his influence had guaranteed his son's admission, and frequently reminded him that he expected his son to uphold his father's reputation and family name. But this only added to his son's rage. As a result, he neglected his studies, was put on probation, and finally left college. The father was chagrined and felt disgraced by his son's behavior.

In the interim the son had found work so he would not have to be dependent on his father and would only talk to his parents when they sought him out. A few months later both parents were killed in an airplane crash, and he inherited more than $250,000. He proceeded to spend his inheritance wildly and made poor business investments. The group interpreted his need to hurt himslf financially as a result of the great amount of guilt he harbored for wishing "to get his parents off his back" so many times, their tragic death becoming the fulfillment of his wish. During more than five years in group psychotherapy he worked through his anger for his parents' lack of confidence in him, and wept openly when he relived the many times he had wished for their love. His group encouraged him and became the loving parents he had hoped for. Proof of the resolution of his guilt was in his progress in all areas of his life, i.e., greater success financially, and finally marriage to a young woman who made him very happy.

Unconscious guilt is produced by civilization. Everyone accumulates unconscious guilt as a result of the frustration of instinctual drives by the civilizing process. The restrictions imposed by society on these drives which compel their inhibition or modification leave residual quantities of this guilt to accumulate in the unconscious part of the psyche where the "collector" operates.

The grand total in adulthood will depend on how much had accumulated in the "collector" during one's growth and development from infancy onward. The extremes of the spectrum range from becoming the most well-adjusted person with minimal unconscious guilt to the hardened criminal psychopath with never any conscious guilt but a huge amount of unconscious guilt.

"History repeats itself" is a generally accepted aphorism which can also be applied to patterns of behavior passed on from generation to generation. Parents are the models for their children, who initiate the "bad" as well as the "good" examples to which they have been habitually exposed. When the children grow up, they compulsively repeat these "bad" as well as "good" patterns. The "bad" patterns are not always obvious and can be detected only by a trained professional.

For example, the unconscious guilt generated in the growing child because of the anxiety, resentment, and silent criticism of the parents for demonstrating an incompatible interpersonal relationship between themselves finds opportunity for discharge against the "self" in adulthood by the unconsious choice of a spouse capable of repeating the same interpersonal conflicts. When the individual undergoes group psychotherapy, this repetition is readily perceived by group-mates as punishment. Not infrequently the pattern appears as an "opposite." For example, a hostile demanding mother can produce a passive, timid, maso-chistic daughter who tolerates her husband's abuse in silent suffering to keep their marriage together, rather than finally end it in divorce as her parents did.

These elements of interpersonal difficulties become alive again in group psychotherapy and are vividly replayed with groupmates who share experiences, offer interpretations, and give insights that help in the resolution of this accu-mulated guilt and the alleviation of conflict situations in the future.

REFERENCES

1. Bergler, E. *The Battle of the Conscience* Washington, DC: Washington Institute of Medicine, 1948.
2. Chein, I. The awareness of the self and the structure of the ego. *Psychol. Rev.,* 51: 304-314.
3. Knight, J. A. *Conscience and Guilt.* New York: Appleton-Century Crofts, 1969.
4. Lewis, H.B. *Shame and Guilt and Neurosis.* New York: International Universities Press, 1971.
5. Menninger, K.A. *Whatever Became of Sin?* New York: Hawthorne Books, 1973.
6. Piers, G. and Singer, M.B. *Shame and Guilt.* New York: W.W. Norton, 1971.
7. Reik, T. *The Compulsion to Confess.* New York: Farrar, Straus and Cudahy, 1957.
8. Reik, T. *Myth and Guilt.* New York: G. Braziller, 1957.
9. Rogge, O.J. *Why Men Confess.* New York: Nelson, 1959.
10. Stein, E.V. *Guilt; Theory and Therapy.* Philadelphia: Westminster 1968.

Chapter V

THE UTILIZATION OF SYMBOLIC AND ACTUAL REALITIES IN GROUP PSYCHOTHERAPY

Michael P. Andronico, Ph.D.

Editors' Summary. This paper describes an approach to group therapy which synthesizes a variety of theoretical orientations and methods. Methods utilized are: 1) eliciting and working through transference reactions with symbolic relationships; 2) interpretations; and 3) experiential techniques such as role-playing and the use of fantasies. Also discussed are a "minithon" (a six-hour group experience with significant others added) and the temporary incorporation of a family member in crisis situations.

Group therapy offers people an opportunity to resolve the problems they have with themselves and others by providing a microcosm of life in a warm, accepting atmosphere. This safe atmosphere allows for a setting in which people can try out new behaviors as they work through old issues. The presence of other people allows an individual to react in a variety of symbolic and real ways. The symbolic reactions are, of course, transference reactions.

TRANSFERENCE REACTIONS

By allowing the group to spontaneously interact, the therapist promotes these transference reactions among group members. Fried (2) says:

Transferences occur in groups when feelings and defenses (largely unconscious) and other behavior patterns (character traits) or isolated acts (acting out behavior), formerly directed at and associated with primary figures of childhood, are repeated toward the therapist and group members without being related to ongoing stimuli.

The present author agrees with this definition but would add that certain transferential responses of the group members are related to stimuli in the group. These responses can be considered transferential because they can be the result of distorted perceptions of ongoing behavior of the group or a particular group member. People begin to react to others in their usual styles soon after joining a group, if not immediately. Their transferential reactions are usually so obvious that other group members can, and do, point them out. In other instances, an interpretation by the therapist is needed. In either case, the therapist can focus upon these responses by asking, "Does he (or she) remind you of anyone else in your life?" Most people will usually readily identify the other group member as being like someone in their present life, or a significant person in their childhood. When the person does not easily identify someone transferentially, the therapist may go further by describing the present interaction which stimulated the group member's reactions. For example,

> Steve, you got angry when Amelia smiled at Tommy, and I noticed that you also got angry earlier today when Amelia smiled at Tommy. Was there another female in your life that you got angry at when she smiled at another male?

This kind of feedback helps the client to remember and begin to work towards the resolution of his/her issues. As can be seen from this example, the interaction of the group facilitates the discovery of transferential feelings more quickly than individual therapy.

EXPERIENTIAL METHODS

At this point, the therapist has the option of pursuing the transferential feelings in a variety of ways. He or she may encourage the group member to discuss these feelings directly or encourage others in the group to discuss their feelings around what was said as well. An additional possibility is to utilize experiential methods such a asking the client if he would be willing to place the transferential figure, such as his mother, into an empty chair and conduct a dialogue with her. This Gestalt technique (3) facilitates the exploration of the group member's feelings in several ways. By conducting both sides of the dialogue, the group member is better able to become more understanding of the other person's feelings (in this case, perhaps his mother), and indeed, in some instances, actually discover that the other person has or had feelings at all! It also gives the group members an opportunity to discover, or better realize, how difficult they themselves may be to deal with. For example, when role playing his mother, Steve himself may feel that Steve is too demanding of her attention. Another advantage of this role-playing is that when other group members have an opportunity to observe it, they often see things that may be missed by the person doing the role-playing. In this instance, if Steve didn't see how demanding he was towards his mother, someone in the group might say, "Steve, in the past you've spoken about how inattentive your mother was, and maybe she was, but now I see clearly how demanding you are of her."

This, of course, often stimulates others in the group to question their own interactions with significant people in their lives since the precedent for more flexible thinking has been set. Here again, if the group therapist feels that the moment is ripe, he himself may ask, "Has this led anyone else to possibly see his or her own interactions with others in a different way?"

Another experiential approach is the utilization of fantasies. In the above illustration, Steve was able to recognize his mother as crucial in his reactions to Amelia. If he did not, the group therapist might have suggested that John have a fantasy about himself, another male and a female. Steve may then spontaneously have a direct fantasy about himself and his mother and father, or a fantasy that is symbolic of this triangle. Regrdless of whether the fantasy is that direct or more symbolic, the therapist may at this point introduce the role-playing technique and have the group member have dialogues between the various components in his fantasy, similar to Gestalting a dream (4). In this way the group member gets an opportunity to work either directly or symbolically on an unresolved issue.

If the issue is too threatening for the group member, he may work on it symbolically several times to reduce the intensity of the unresolved feeling. For example, if the group member has a fantasy about himself, his male employer, and a female peer or supervisor, this may be symbolic of the triangle represented by himself, his father, and his mother. To the degree that role playing the other two people in the triangle expands his awareness of those other two people and achieves better understanding of their feelings, the group member is also setting the stage for a better understanding and acceptance of his parents' feelings. In other words, this symbolic role-playing allows for a generalization effect and contributes to a more flexible outlook towards others and a reduction in the group members' usually stereotyped perception of interpersonal relationships.

The therapy groups can be utilized in pursuing these more flexible, realistic, and appropriate reactions to others. The group members initially react to others as transferential figures, as mentioned above, but then move onward and practice relating to each other as themselves. In the example discussed above, after Steve has explored his feelings about himself and his mother and father, he may ask Amelia directly for more attention, therefore becoming more adept at getting his needs met directly and effectively. Or, he may say, "I don't care what my mother did, Amelia, what you just did is a deliberate provocation," which indicates a newfound ability to differentiate between past and present events. Or, he may say, "Amelia, I started to get angry at you, but now I realize that if you want to flirt with Tommy, go right ahead," this then showing increased cognitive control over his emotional reactions.

As the emotional basis for certain behaviors begins to be resolved, the group members can offer each other an opportunity to develop and practice certain interpersonal skills. Steve might, for instance, be given an opportunity to ask

Amelia and all other women in the group how he might gain their attention if that is what he wants. Then he may ask them periodically if he is indeed successfully doing what they suggested to get their attention.

WORKING WITH THE PRESENT

In addition to having the opportunity to role play and fantasize past memories and feelings about parents and significant others from the past, group members may also update their feelings in fantasied present involvement with these people. Many, if not most, adults tend to interact with these childhood figures in the same manner they did as children. One way of helping people in the group to better cope with these significant others in the present is to suggest that a group member have a fantasy of bringing someone, such as father or mother, into the group. How the individual introduces this person to the group and role plays the person is very revealing, both to him/herself and to the other members of the group; how the fantasied figure interacts with others in the group is also revealing. For example, a timid, retiring woman role played her mother and was hostile and aggressive, questioning everyone in the group and insisting that her daughter need not be in this group but only needed to listen to her if she wanted to feel better about herself. The group member benefited by the support which she got from the group members, one of whom said, "No wonder you were always shy. With a person like that, nobody can get a word in edgewise!" She also benefited substantially from observing the response of two other group members who were able to relate to her "mother" in polite but assertive ways, thus role modeling for her an alternative way of relating to her mother that she had not thought previously possible.

Others in the group can also benefit from this exercise by directly or vicariously doing it themselves or responding to the way others enact their own situation. For example, someone might say,

> John, I was surprised when you introduced your father and looked down on him. You must be taller than he is, and then it dawned on me that I've been taller than my father since I was 17 years old and I always think of him as taller than me!

THE MINITHON

A more direct method of helping people to experience their conflicts with significant people in their lives is to supplement the regular weekly group therapy sessions with more intense sessions of longer duration, or a "minithon." These minithons (1) could be held annually, and are usually six to eight hours long.

Each group member has the option of bringing in one significant person, usually a spouse or a partner. The prolonged time of the session allows for the invited group members to have ample time to deal with their issues. It is helpful for the group therapist to see those added people sometime before the minithon if they have not previously seen the therapist. This helps to alert the therapist to potential problems, gain rapport, and orient the people to the minithon.

The minithon offers the group members an opportunity to view other members in direct interaction with their significant other, as well as having the chance to have themselves observed by others in their own direct interaction with their significant other. Both group members and the significant others can benefit from this observation during and after the minithon. Some people say,

> I didn't like my wife coming here every week and then telling me that I had all these flaws. Hell, I now see that she's as critical of you people as she is of me! Besides, maybe I could use a little improvement in my approach to others.

Someone else might say at a future group meeting,

> Meyer, you've been complaining about how undercutting Kay is in the group, and how she reminds you of your wife in public. When your wife was here, she really struck me as being pretty supportive most of the time. Maybe you just want a woman to support you 100% of the time and can't take a woman disagreeing with you.

The minithon also allows a rare opportunity for group members to see that they may relate to their significant other in a very different manner than they relate to anyone else. For example, "battleaxe Betty" was frequently criticized for her severe and critical attitude towards all male members of the group, including the leader. She and others in the group were surprised to discover that her behavior towards her husband in the minithon was not critical but blatantly deferential. This provided important material for many future group meetings.

SPONTANEOUS APPROACHES

In addition to the minithon, in which others are brought into the group for a rare but significant session, the therapist may spontaneously include a significant other during a regularly scheduled group session. For example, a woman who recently joined a group had been in severe crisis and was insisting that she be hospitalized. The therapist suggested that she discuss this with with her group and she was accompanied to the session by her husband. Jennifer opened the session by discussing her distress and her anger at her husband. The group members responded by pointing out her interaction with her husband in the waiting room and his reactions to her. The therapist, after gaining the group's permission, invited Pete to join the group and for the next hour they helped Jennifer and Pete to see how they were interacting in a way that could be modified, and indeed was modified right there in the group. Pete was begrudgingly grateful for the suggestion that he stop playing superman and Jennifer decided that she really didn't need to be hospitalized. Then Pete returned to the waiting room while the rest of the group session continued. Of course, situations such as the above are unusual, but the therapy group does offer a setting that can be conducive to such occasional "emergency" situations.

As can be seen from the above, the focus here is upon the exploration, experiencing, and modification of various emotional reactions which occur during group interaction. Each time a group interaction stimulates member reaction, focus is brought onto an individual and then back to the group. If one were to focus entirely on an individual in the group, much of the vital interactive effects of the group process would be lost. The method of moving back and forth between group process and individual work requires more flexibility on the part of both the therapist and the group. There is no simple, rigid regulation as to how one best achieves the "correct" balance between these two modalities, other than each therapist gradually developing his/her own clinical judgment as to when to move from one to the other. One helpful hint may be that when the group appears to be at an impasse, or asks the therapist what to do too often, this may be a good time to discuss group resistance and not to make suggestions to the individual who may be asking at that time.

SUMMARY

Group therapy, as described in this paper, enables people to experiment with new behaviors as they work through old issues. This is achieved by dealing with transference reactions and other, more current responses which are less related to childhood feelings and behaviors. The vehicles for this are group interactions, interpretations and experiential techniques such as role-playing and use of fantasies. Additional methods incorporated into the usual ongoing group therapy sessions are the minithon, a group session of extended time duration with additional members, and the spontaneous incorporation of an additional member in an ongoing session, when appropriate.

REFERENCES

1. Andronico, M.P. Marathon techniques in an outpatient clinic: The minithon. *In:* L. Blank, G.B. Gottsegen, and M.G. Gottsegen (Eds.), *Confrontation.* New York: Macmillan, 1971, pp. 135-146.

2. Fried, E. Basic concepts in group psychotherapy. *In:* H.I. Kaplan and B.J. Sadock (Eds.), *Comprehensive Group Psychotherapy.* Baltimore: Williams and Wilkins Co., 1971, pp. 47-71.
3. Perls, F.S. *Gestalt Therapy Verbatim.* Lafayette, CA: Real People Press, 1969.
4. Simkin, J.S. The use of dreams in Gestalt therapy. *In:* C.J. Sager and H.S. Kaplan (Eds.), *Progress in Group and Family Therapy.* New York: Brunner/Mazel, 1972, pp. 95-104.

The author wishes to express his gratitude to Barbara Dazzo and Meyer Rothberg for their editorial assistance.

Chapter VI

THE DIVERGENT PROBLEMS OF BRIEF GROUPS

James P. Gustafson, M.D., and Lowell Cooper, Ph.D.

Editors' Summary. Some of the problems posed and discussed by the authors in the light of their theory of unconscious planning in small groups are: Where do such groups break down? What must be supplied to negotiate these impasses? What is the content of the clashing interests? What learning is possible from working through these breakdowns of group co-operation? To what extent does the learning apply to the central "focal problems" of the group members? How widely applicable is the transfer of learning? What background struc-tures are necessary to this free play of deeper concerns? What kinds of persons need to be excluded? What is the difference between the more public forms of these brief groups and the more private forms of brief group psychotherapy?

Belief in psychotherapy has, until recently, flowed in certain familiar di-rections. If an individual needed psychotherapy, it would be believed that his or her chances were better in individual therapy than in a group. A longer time in treatment gave a better chance than a short time. If help had to be brief, structured treatment was better than unstructured.[1] If brief help had to be given in a group, people with common problems seemed more likely to get somewhere together than a diverse group (3).

Countercurrents are now evident along all of these dimensions, which make the subject much more interesting, clarity of thinking more important, and in-telligent research necessary.[2] Our studies of brief psychotherapy in groups are very much of the countercurrent, as we propose a method of psychotherapy which utilizes the group, is brief, is relatively unstructured, and takes on a diverse membership.[3]

---

[1]The belief that an unstructured group gives a mild, positive, but relatively invariant effect is reflected in the commonness of the "placebo group" as a comparison with the treatment that the investigator wants to study.

[2] For example, Malan's (20) studies of individual brief psychotherapy refute the inevitability of long-term therapy for dynamic change, while those of Lieberman, Yalom, and Miles (19) on encounter groups contradict long-standing beliefs of several schools of group therapy.

[3] Furthermore, contrary to the prevalent idea that technique should be addressed to common, unifying themes (2), we believe that differences between members are the central technical problem.

We offer here a clinical account of a practical method of treatment, but we are equally interested in the phenomena we describe for theoretical reasons, inasmuch as these practical results, which contradict convention, can be explained by a new theory of group interaction, which we call the theory of unconscious group planning. We limit ourselves in this brief paper to an exposition of this logic in its clinical context. Our forthcoming book (7a) will explicate the theory at many different levels of organization and in relation to many special cases and applications.

UNSTRUCTURED SITUATIONS

Let us begin by returning to the fact that an "unstructured *group*" is felt to be superficial, but an unstructured situation of *individual* psychotherapy is recognized to have potential. Winnicott (26), among many others we could cite, suggests that when you give an individual an unstructured situation in a pleasant, mirroring environment, the individual will begin to play in depth. If the individual is capable of what Winnicott calls "object usage," that individual will begin to play out a central issue in his/her development that has been giving trouble. The individual may begin by relating outside situations in which the trouble is evident, but sooner or later will enact it directly in relationship to the therapist.

THE FAULT WITH GROUPS

Why, we may wonder, do individuals *not* play out their central problems in groups? Let us suppose individuals A and B to be relatively healthy persons who are capable of some work and some friendship. However, A tends to be neurotic about the various limits he has to live with. He is forever trying to *force* others to make an exception for him, as he becomes very anxious, frantic and demanding when his term papers are due, his girlfriend wants to date someone else, and his parents are going to reduce his allowance. Individual B tends to be neurotic about what others ask of her, continually becoming *over-responsible* and often depressed. She accepts every hint of her professors to take on extra reading, she has sex with her boyfriend when she doesn't want to herself, and she rushes home on weekends to be of assistance when her parents have had a fight.

If A and B are in a group together, A is going to begin playing with the possibilities of forcing the other group members to go out of their way for him. He will have no trouble starting this, as he takes more time to explain his life, interrupts others to let them know how he is feeling, and makes sure to talk to the leader after the first meeting. Unfortunately, B in the group is not herself a psychotherapist like Winnicott, so she is going to get herself in difficulty with A very fast. B, we recall, has a recurrent problem of taking on too much responsibility. She is going to listen to A long past her own felt tolerance for him, she is going to allow him to interrupt her own requests for listening, and she is going to get depressed when she sees him talking to the leader afterwards, because she feels no right to ask for extra assistance herself.

It is not long before B notices that her special efforts to be of use are not being noticed, let alone appreciated, by the self-centered A. She is hurt and depressed, and stops playing. It will then not be long before A dimly gathers that his long speeches and interruptions no longer catch the eye of B, who seems to become flat and withdrawn whenever he starts in on something. This takes the fun out of it for A, who begins to worry that he is no longer liked by her. He stops playing also. A and B have canceled each other out, simply by being themselves. It is fair to say that unstructured groups turn out this way for A and B, the most typical of group members, if nothing else is supplied.

WHAT MUST BE SUPPLIED

Hence it is necessary to introduce therapist C, if there is to be a favorable outcome. A can experiment upon C with his tendency to force others, because C will not take too much of it, will interrupt when necessary, and will not prolong the group meeting for him. Thus A can relax, knowing that he will not be able to drive C away when he is most being himself. He will become quite involved with C, playing out his worst tendency in depth.[4]

C is also needed by B, who can experiment safely with taking so much responsibility if C will recognize what B is doing to herself, and wonder what makes it necessary and what would happen if she unloaded the burden. Knowing that C will grasp all of this, B can work herself up into a wretched state of over-tolerance and guilt. She, too, plays out her worst, safely (25).

C not only must take up the right relationship with A and B as individuals, but must also *steer* the group's course evenly between what the two of them

---

[4] We analyze the needs of individual patients in terms of what will be traumatic and what will be protective, with the perspective afforded by the "control-mastery" theory of Sampson (22) and Weiss et al. They hold that individuals have "unconscious plans" to solve their own recurrent problems, which are based upon personal "unconscious theories" of what is apt to be dangerous. The inividual unconsciously tests others to see if this unconscious theory is confirmed by tempting others to repeat what is traumatic. If others do not respond with such harmful behavior, the unconscious theory is disconfirmed, allowing the individual to try out new behavior with some confidence that it will be safe enough. Weiss et al. and Sampson's research has been restricted to individual psychoanalysis. Our own studies have extended these hypotheses to the realm of groups (5-7, 14-17).

require, so that both get the conditions they need. This steering ability, given the predominance of A and B, will be to allow A to play out his excessive forcing of others, yet also allow equal room for B to play out her drama of how helpful she is being to others. Without steering back and forth between these two poles, either A or B is likely to go under and bring on the dead halt we have discussed previously (16, 17).

So far we have been talking only about individuals A and B, mediated by a third individual, our therapist C, who supplies the vital missing capabilities for the group to develop its play. Actually, A is often not just a single individual with the tendency to force his way on others, but rather represents a subgroup A of "forcers." B is often not just a single individual with the tendency to take too much upon herself, but rather represents a subgroup B of "over-responsibles." The whole group, then, will play out this particular drama, of subgroup A tending to force its way upon a guilty subgroup B.

In reality, there are many other versions of A and B that we and other writers on groups have described. There are the divisions between the dependents and the independents (1); the "early winners" and the "early losers" (21); the aggressive men and the receptive women, those who prefer individuation and those who prefer fusion with the group (24); those who want a very rapid tempo of self-revelation and those who want to resist it in good conscience (16, 17); those who want the group tightly reined in to its specific task, and those who want a loose construction (9). *The battle may be joined over any dimension that is an important, emotional working condition for individuals in their social lives.* Ordinarily in a group that lasts eight to twelve meetings, there is only time for one major battle, with a build-up, middle, and end. The principal job for C, the group therapist, will be to steer between the two subgroups that form themselves.

THE DENOUEMENT

If all goes well, as we have described thus far, A and B will push their experiments to the limit, where C apparently cannot protect them. As Winnicott (26) has written, "development is inherently an aggressive act," which seems to take itself beyond the limits of safety. The group therapist, inevitably, seems to be invited to sacrifice one subgroup to save the other subgroup. A number of examples may convey the high energy and the urgency of these group crises. In a very recent group, a pair of very emotional and dramatic women appeared to be bleeding out their hearts, while coldly and rationaly cross-examined by a pair of men. In another altogether different group, several action members led by a rather hyperactive individual nicknamed the "Pizza Man" insisted that the group had to have a pizza party, while the competing subgroup insisted that the purpose was to talk soberly about the members' problems. In a third example, a subgoup claimed the right to go to breakfast and have an independent discussion, while the opposite subgroup left behind was arguing the necessity of everyone accepting responsibility to attend. Finally, in a fourth group, a very speedy and flashy subgroup arranged to pass around a brochure describing a new business of one of their subgroup to be admired, while the opposite subgroup sat silently gnashing their teeth in frustration.[5]

These are what we call "steering contradictions" (16, 17). The group therapist can no longer balance the two subgroups. One of the subgroups forces the situation, so that the group therapist appears to have only two bad choices: to allow subgroup A to carry on with its dramatic domination, sacrificing B; or

---

[5] The theory of small groups we are summarizing in this article contends that an individual seeks to influence social situations to provide conditions favorable for that individual's development. However, different individuals require opposite conditions. Hence there is a necessary struggle between them. This hypothesis allows us to clarify contradictions in the "conventional wisdom" about managing groups. For example, one school of group therapy insists that the group leaders never see individual members for extra individual sessions, but always tell them to bring their concerns back to the group meeting. Another school believes that extra individual sessions are often helpful or essential. In some group therapy groups, you can find group members who are exponents of each school of thought! For example, in the group just referred to in the text, the cool and rational male subgroup believed in forbidding outside contacts, while the emotional and support-seeking female subgroup believed in their importance. In the actual conduct of the meetings, the group therapists tended to allow the male cross-examiners to have their way. They were then called upon by the females in distress for extra time and support. Given that the group was about to have several weeks' break without any meeting, and given the predominance allowed to the males in the meetings, some leaning toward the women was called for and they were given extra time. This balanced the steering of the group, setting up both subgroups with adequate support, which allowed the whole group in the subsequent meeting to pull itself together. In other groups, allowing an extra individual meeting might have an altogether different significance, e.g., that certain members who were dominating got even more attention! In that instance, it might be essential to refuse the request. In any case, the theory presented gives a way to think through the contradiction between opposing camps of conventional wisdom, to make decisions which strengthen rather than weaken the capacity of the group.

A similar point of view, which originates from work in economics, is that of Schumacher (23), who also sees these problems of divergent interests and principles as endemic in current social life: "The true problems of living—in politics, economics, education, marriage, etc.—are always problems of overcoming or reconciling opposities. They are *divergent problems* (our italics) and have no solution in the ordinary sense of the word. They demand of man not merely the employment of his reasoning powers but the commitment of his whole personality. Naturally, spurious solutions, by way of a clever formula, are always being put forward; but they never work for long, because they invariably neglect one of the two opposites and thus lose the very quality of human life. In economics, the solution offered may provide for freedom but not for planning, or vice versa. In industrial organization, it may provide for discipline but not for workers' participation in management, or vice versa. In politics, it might provide for leadership without democracy or, again, for democracy without leadership.'' Schumacher goes on to contrast divergent problems with *convergent* problems, like detective stories or crossword puzzles, which have a built in convergence or solution. Most group theories are convergent theories which make work in groups seem a lot simpler than it is, at the cost of losing the reality of group life and losing the capacity to predict useful interventions (15).

to interrupt the goings-on to protect B from being run over, cutting off A. Either response from the group therapist will collapse the sacrificed subgroup, which then takes the hope out of it for the others. The whole thing will fail right here.[6]

Fortunately, there is a very clear line of solution to these "steering contradictions" which we discovered several years ago (7, 16, 17). We regard these situations as very high-powered tests, conducted by the opposed subgroups in concert, to test whether the group leader has fully appreciated what both sides need. In our fourth example, (16, 17) the group leader had passed earlier tests that he understood how the "pushy" subgroup needed to run things toward fast and intense involvement, actually to take over without his retaliation; on the other hand, he had passed tests of the opposite subgroup of "resisters," who needed to resist going along with anything too fast, until they were ready in good

---

[6] We have been developing our argument here with the assumption that the group therapist is a single individual. An interesting variation, which shows another relevant application of the theory, is that of having group co-therapists. Like all other people, each co-therapist, we assume, is going to push for working conditions that favor his or her own individual development. Very often, the conditions for co-therapist A will contradict those for co-therapist B. For example, A may want to conduct the group to confront its difficulties—perhaps even to force the members to examine what is going on, despite "resistance"— while B may prefer that the leaders take a great deal of responsibility to make things comfortable. A may want to have an atmosphere of maximum openness and confession, while B prefers a group that is more careful and reflective. Like the group members, the co-therapists may divide over any important condition of work. This significant difference is likely to become apparent in the planning meetings and supervision sessions prior to the first group meeting. Then, as the group itself develops its own battle over working conditions, one of two things is likely to occur. Either the subgrouping among the group members will be shaped by the division between the co-therapists, *or* the division between the co-therapists will be assimilated into the subgrouping of the group. (Of course, mutual influence is also possible but the two extremes are often evident. This process parallels the alignment of the various group members into two camps.) In any case, the co-therapists are likely to be either divided into the two subgroups, or both of them may be captured by one of the subgroups. Either of these alternatives can bring on the collapse of the group. If the co-therapists are pulled into opposite subgroups, they may engage in a desperate struggle for control, which they present to the supervisor. At the height of the difficulty in the group (the "steering contradiction" phase), the supervisor will be very tempted to sacrifice one of the therapists to the other, as one appears to have the more "therapeutic" stance. This is a potential disaster, as the sacrificed co-therapist and his or her corresponding subgroup collapse for being treated as "antitherapeutic." This is bad enough for the group, but equally bad or worse for the career of the student therapist, who tends to accept the negative verdict on his or her capacity or promise as a therapist. If the two co-therapsts simply side with one of the patient subgroups, both together, then the other subgroup collapses, as described in the instance of the single group therapist. (For a partial recognition of these phenomena, see Cooper [4] and Winter [27].) Further complexity of theory is called for, when we recognize that each co-therapist, A and B, has his or her own "shadow group," insofar as he or she is part of other influential groups (than the therapy group) which call upon him or her to retain certain beliefs or ways of working. These "shadow groups" can be the family of origin, the family constituted by marriage, a religious group or congregation, a political commitment, a tradition or school of psychotherapy in which the therapist is presently working. When the co-therapists come from shadow groups with widely divergent views on how to work, their working relationship is going to have to find some view to integrate the divergence, without sacrificing one to the other. (We are indebted to Imogene Higbie, Ph.D., for this suggestion.)

conscience. Now the group leader is subjected to the most extreme test: If he turns down the brochure slyly handed to him by one of the "pushers" after it has been passed all around the group circle and examined by each of the members, he quashes and enrages them. If he accepts in the appreciating way he is invited to take, he is in collusion and the "resisters" have been allowed to be run over.

What he did do was to explain his two alternatives, how each would let down half of the group, which he was unwilling to do. Although tempted to fail both of the subgroups, he would not, reassuring both of his understanding of their particular needs. Given this backing for all of them, they were able to work out their own compromise—in this group, between speeding into group activities and holding back until objections were cleared. Both sides could retain their high energy play. This handling of the "steering contradiction" could not be more important: It makes all the difference, we have found, between collapse and triumph.

TREATMENT OUTCOME

What has been learned through this unstructed free play of adults? Given our original example of subgroups A and B, the "forcers" have gotten a dramatic clarification of their tendency to go too far, the "over-responsibles" of accepting too much. Both subgroups have played their tendency to the hilt, making it less likely they will forget it, and now they have arrived at a suitable compromise with others that controls the danger.

This lesson is likely to be a fundamental one, because they are central recurrent patterns of error in the members' lives. What would be the criteria of maximum improvement for a dynamic change (20)? For the "forcers," a maximum change would be the ability to tolerate new limits, without using the maladaptive strategy of forcing others to give in, instead finding some other constructive solution. For the "over-responsibles," a maximum change would be the ability to withstand demands and needs of others, without using the maladaptive strategy of becoming overly responsible for these others, instead finding some other constructive solution. With regard to both of these types, the maximum change requires that the recurrent stress is managed successfully in both work life and private or interpersonal relations. Withdrawal in any or these spheres discounts dynamic change, since the individual has only managed thereby to avoid facing and coping with his major difficulty.

No one has yet carried out such studies of outcome on brief psychotherapy in groups. We, ourselves, expect the following. Although the lessons learned concern the recurrent central problem, we imagine that most group members carry forward their new solutions only within certain realms of their life, e.g., how they may manage themselves in other social groups they are in, or perhaps how they behave in class. It would be asking a very great deal of eight to 12 sessions of group that the individual would connect up the difficulties in every sector of his life, or even that he would get such a good start on this connecting that five-year follow-up would show him in full control. Of this we are skeptical. We ourselves would be satisfied to demonstrate that individuals had had an intense, clear experience of their recurrent problem, which had led to control and mastery of this problem in several areas.[7]

BACKGROUND STRUCTURE

But has this kind of unstructured play for adults been so unstructured after all? Actually, the structure has been there all along, but kept in the background. First, there have been firm boundaries set up, within which play will occur, boundaries of when the group will start and end (boundaries of time), of where it will occur comfortably (boundaries of space), of who will be committed to being there despite the pull of other interests (boundaries of commitment) (10).

Second, there has been the figure of the group therapist, the vital element C between A and B, who is necessary so that A and B do not nullify each other. This group therapist has stayed in the background, letting A and B play in their own way, trusting that they will be themselves, without intrusion. The group therapist has been there all along, mirroring faithfully the different needs of the different subgroups. However, when needed, this group therapist has had to come forward, to be available for use by both parties, to steer the group between their contradictory demands, and finally to avoid the temptation to sacrifice one for the other.

Third, this group therapist has made a series of critical boundary decisions

---

[7] A straightforward way to state the limitation upon learning in groups is to say that most people are very reluctant to revise their central working hypotheses about social life (18). They may admit a revision in one sector of experience, while holding onto the old notion in another. On the other hand, Malan's studies (20) suggest that superordinate structures (central working hypotheses) do get changed in individual brief psychotherapy in many instances, even by persons with rigid characters. In other words, a given vivid group experience may lead to a revision of an relatively subordinate structure (strategy) in one individual, while bringing about a revision of a major, superordinate structure (strategy) in another. Also, a new solution to a long-standing focal problem, which is experienced in a group, may remain subordinate and restricted in its employment by that individual until latter events confirm its central importance. We do not yet understand these critical differences in outcome.

about whom to include in the group, whom to exclude.[8] Persons severely depressed or with psychotic potential have been excluded for being too vulnerable. Psychopathic individuals have to be excluded for being too rapacious. If we are going to set in motion a struggle for development, essentially an aggressive act for all concerned, we must not have persons who either cannot take aggression or who give it out without any limitations of conscience. Finally, the group therapist has had to exclude those who are unable to engage and use others, but who rather hide forever behind a conventional false self.[9] Such persons lack a capacity for "object usage," which is to be able to throw oneself against others for the sake of one's own development, and trust that they will survive it (26).

Thus, there has been a considerable structure of limiting boundaries, of the nonintrusive but available therapist, and of selection, but it has been mostly in the background, something that is also true of good parents.

CONCLUSION

Finally, we would note that this kind of meaningful adult play in groups could take two forms. One is more public, the other more private. In the public

---

[8] It is commonly asked whether persons who are in individual therapy can also be in a group? Of course, those who are *making advances* in their individual therapy, getting control over their recurrent mistakes, are going to want to experiment with newfound capabilities, in many different kinds of social situations. They are going to do this anyway. A group therapy group is particularly useful for such experiments, insofar as the individual has a chance not only to act, but also to reflect upon that action and its consequences upon others. On the other hand, patients who are *doing poorly* in individual therapy, especially *paranoid* patients, can get even worse when group is added to individual therapy. In other words, if it is known from the individual therapy what conditions the patient needs to advance, it is conceivable that the group therapist can be mindful of these conditions in the group and help the patient battle for them. If it is not known what will help the patient from considerable individual therapy, where the individual therapist has had ample opportunity to study the life of the patient, then it may be difficult for the group therapist to grasp the needed conditions in the fray of the group. Can a patient who is in individual therapy with the group therapist also be in his or her group? Yes, but the therapist is apt to be pulled into partiality for this patient, steering the group towards the known needed conditions of this patient, sacrificing the others. Of course, being mindful of this danger, one may be able to resist the temptation, even when the other patients also encourage or suspect it. This is not an easy job for beginners.

[9] How does the group therapist recognize the conventional "false self," which obscures an inability to engage with others? It can be done, admittedly with difficulty, both by history and by the interaction with the interviewer. A useful place to start in the history, when one is concerned about this diagnosis, is with the question, "Who have been the most important people in your life?" One can then look into these relationships, to see what contact and what ability had been managed. A person who has never been able to use anyone earlier in his life is not going to risk trying in a group that lasts eight to 12 sessions (or if he or she does, it is apt to be dangerously out of control). In addition to history, one has the direct opportunity to see if the patient makes emotional contact in the pregroup interviews around a focus of difficulty that makes sense. If there is no "motivation" or "focus" (20) in these interviews, it is unduly optimistic that they will appear in a brief group out of nowhere!

form, members will play out their roles while restricting their discussion to what is publically observable in the group. This may be a group to study its own process, a "study group" (12-15), or a group to discuss work problems or cases, such as a supervision group (8) or a Balint group for doctors to discuss the doctor-patient relationship (11, 12). The other form is more private, in that individuals have agreed to link up their behavior in the group with the events of their personal past and present outside lives. This latter form is group therapy. In either case, it is possible to take a brief voyage of surprising penetration and relevance.

REFERENCES

1. Bennis, W.G., and Shephard, H.A. A theory of group development. *Human Relations*, 9: 415-437, 1956.
2. Budman, S.H., Bennett, M.J., and Wisneski, M.J. An adult developmental model of short-term group psychotherapy. *In:* S. Budman (Ed.), *Forms of Brief Therapy*. New York: Guilford Press, 1981.
3. Budman, S.H., Demby, A., and Randal, M. Short-term group psychotherapy: Who succeeds and who fails? *Group*, 4: 3-16, 1980.
4. Cooper, L. Cotherapy relationships in groups. *Small Group Behavior*, 7: 473-498, 1976.
5. Cooper, L., and Gustafson, J.P. Planning and mastery in group therapy. *Human Relations*, 32: 689-703, 1979.
6. Cooper, L., and Gustafson, J.P. Towards a general theory of group therapy. *Human Relations*, 32: 967-981, 1979.
7. Cooper, L., and Gustafson, J.P. Conflict in group therapy: Management of individual differences. *In:* L. Wolberg and M. Aronson (Eds.), *Group and Family Therapy, 1982*. New York: Brunner/Mazel, 1982.
7a. Cooper, L., and Gustafson, J.P. *Unconscious Planning: Understanding and Working with Small Groups*. New York: Guilford Press, in press.
8. Cooper, L., and Gustafson, J.P. Group supervision and group dynamics: Problems in teaching clinical skills. Unpublished.
9. Gosling, R. Another source of conservatism in groups. *In:* W.G. Lawrence (Ed.), *Exploring Individual and Organizational Boundaries*. New York: Wiley, 1979.
10. Gustafson, J.P. Group therapy supervision: Critical problems of therapy and technique. *In:* L. Wolberg and M. Aronson (Eds.), *Group and Family Therapy 1980*. New York: Brunner/Mazel, 1980.
11. Gustafson, J.P. The control and mastery of aggression by doctors: A new focal problem for the Balint group method. *In:* L. Wolberg and M. Aronson (Eds.), *Group and Family therapy 1981*. New York: Burnner/Mazel, 1981.
12. Gustafson, J.P., and Cooper, L. Collaboration in small groups: Theory and technique for the study of small group processes. *Human Relations*, 31: 155-171, 1978.
13. Gustafson, J.P., and Cooper, L. Towards the study of society in microcosm: Critical problems of group relations conferences. *Human Relations*, 31: 843-862, 1978.
14. Gustafson, J.P., and Cooper, L. Unconscious planning in small groups. *Human Relations*, 32: 689-703, 1979.
15. Gustafson, J.P., and Cooper, L. Unconscious planning by patients for group therapy. *In:* M. Pines and L. Rafaelson (Eds.), *Proceedings of the 7th International Congress of Group Psychotherapy*. New York: Plenum Press, 1981.
16. Gustafson, J.P., Cooper, L., Lathrop, N., Ringler, K., Seldin, F., and Wright, M. K. Co-operative and clashing interests in small groups, part I: Theory. *Human Relations*, 343: 315-339, 1981.

17. Gustafson, J.P., Cooper, L., Lathrop, M., Ringler, K., Seldin, F., and Wright, M.K. Cooperative and clashing interests in small groups, part II: Group narratives. *Human Relations*, 34: 367-378, 1981.
18. Kelly, G.A. *The Psychology of Personal Constructs*. New York: Norton, 1955.
19. Lieberman, M.A., Yalom, I.D., and Miles, M.D. *Encounter Groups: First Facts*. New York: Basic Books, 1973.
20. Malan, D. H. *The Frontier of Brief Psychotherapy*. New York: Plenum, 1976.
21. Mann, R.D. Winners, losers, and the search for equality in groups. *In:* C. Cooper (Ed.), *Theories of Group Processes*. London: Wiley, 1975.
22. Sampson, H. A critique of certain traditional concepts in the psychoanalytic theory of therapy. *Bulletin of the Menninger Clinic*, 40: 255-262, 1976.
23. Schumacher, E.R. *Small Is Beautiful, Economics As If People Mattered*. New York: Harper and Row, 1973.
24. Slater, P.E. *Microcosm: Structural, Psychological and Religious Evolution in Groups*. New York: Wiley, 1966.
25. Weiss, J., Sampson, N., Gassner, S., and Caston, J. Bulletin #4, 1980. Psychotherapy Research Group, Department of Psychiatry, Mount Zion Hospital and Medical Center, San Francisco. Available on request from Ms. Janet Bergman, San Francisco Psychoanalytic Institute, 2420 Sutter Street, San Francisco, California 04113.
26. Winnicott, D.W. *Playing and Reality*. New York: Basic Books, 1971.
27. Winter, S. Developmental stages in the rules and concerns of group co-leaders. *Small Group Behavior*, 7: 349-362, 1976.

Chapter VII

FAILURES, CASUALTIES, AND HAZARDS IN GROUP PSYCHOTHERAPY

Normund Wong, M.D.

Editors' Summary. Hazards in group psychotherapy include possible psychotic episodes, worsening of social functioning and job performance, disruptive behavior, self-injury, or violence to others. Therapists, like patients in a group, may also suffer these ill effects in the group therapy setting. The therapist must help establish constructive group norms, assume responsibility for the welfare of the group members and the group itself, and provide adequate means of helping individuals should psychological damage occur.

Dr. Jones, a renowned medical researcher, decided to become a psychiatrist in his late forties in order to further his work in the field of neuroleptic drugs. He had never married and was content spending much of his day alone in the laboratory. During his first year of residency he performed adequately, diagnosing and treating a large number of patients who stayed an average of two-and-a-half weeks on his ward. In his second year of training he worked in the psychiatric outpatient department, seeing many of his former patients whom he maintained on drugs. As part of his required experience he also began doing group psychotherapy. He and a vivacious, outgoing, young social worker, Miss Smith, were told to start an outpatient group. Both were supervised by Dr. Brown, a bright, eager psychologist, who encouraged them to aggressively recruit patients for the group. Within three months they evaluated 15 patients and placed them all in a group. After six months only two patients remained.

Like Dr. Jones and Miss Smith, the patients shared little in common throughout the life of the group. Some patients had just been discharged from the hospital while others had never needed inpatient care. In the group, there were late adolescents and senior citizens, single and married people, diagnosed as character disorders, schizophrenics, and borderline and narcissistic personality disorders. Some patients stayed only for one visit while two remained for six months. Several patients were rehospitalized during their group experience and there were two suicide attempts.

Dr. Jones sat silent and bewildered during most of the group sessions. As the psychiatrist and senior therapist, he supposedly was the guiding force for the group. Miss Smith was impatient and critical of her colleague and coercive with the patients. To Dr. Jones, group supervision was a form of the Inquisition where the therapists revealed their ignorance and inadequacies before a demanding task-master. Dr. Jones felt that while Dr. Brown was supportive and complementary to Miss Smith and thought he was hypercritical and disrespectful of him. On several occasions Dr. Jones forgot to show up for the group and came late for sessions. He began to develop chronic anxiety and insomnia before and after the group meetings and dreaded the supervisory sessions. He felt Miss Smith was saying derogatory things about him to his colleagues and the faculty. Before the end of the year Dr. Jones informed the training director that he had gained sufficient experience to enable him to carry on his research and he would not need to complete his psychiatric residency. Feeling relieved, he returned to the laboratory and Miss Smith soon announced her engagement to Dr. Brown.

The above vignette is a composite of events which actually took place in a medical school department of psychiatry. This paper was conceived as a consequence of such episodes, and deals with failures, casualties, and hazards of group psychotherapy. The aforementioned incident illustrates these three issues which, in the literature are rarely discussed. When they are, however, the individual patients in the group are generally referred to, not the group therapist or the group as a whole. A clear understanding as to what constitutes a failure, a casualty, and a hazard is lacking. In the foregoing example, were individual patients, the group, Dr. Jones, Dr. Brown or Miss Smith the failures or casualties? Was the group experience hazardous? Covered in this paper are the definitions of these phenomena, their causes, and suggested strategies for their prevention.

DEFINITIONS

In general, a group failure refers to a patient who unilaterally drops out of group psychotherapy or does not improve at the end of the prescribed treatment. There may be premature failures or individuals who terminate group psycho-therapy early and derive little, if any, benefit from their experience, and late failures, or persons who drop out late in the life of the group. The late failures usually derive some benefit from psychotherapy but not to the extent anticipated by the therapist. The term *failure* also may indicate the disbanding of the group following a thorough exploration of the futility of continuing treatment and group failure to attain its expressed goals. The request to terminate may come from the group members, the therapist, or be arrived at by both parties. The term failure also applies to the group therapist. In this instance, despite adequate didactic teaching and clinical supervision and an average expectable group com-position, the therapist fails to bring about improvement in the patients.

The definition of a casualty has ranged from an individual who has "negative feelings about the experience,'' to someone who suffers ''lasting psychotic re-actions'' (4). Estimates of casualties have ranged as high as 50% in a group to as low as 1% (7). In their comprehensive study of 17 encounter groups, Lie-berman, Yalom, and Miles (9) provide us with some reliable and frequently quoted data. They define a group casualty as

> . . . a member whose group experience was destructive. During and following the group he was more uncomfortable and/or utilized more maladaptive defenses and this negative change was relatively enduring. Finally, in our opinion, the encounter group could be impugned as the responsible agent (p. 174).

Casualties may result from the failure of a group. However, a member may become a casualty even if the group is considered a success. Although it occurs infrequently, the casualty or injured party may remain a member throughout the life of the group but, in essence, the individual becomes worse as a consequence of being in the group. A patient, the group, or the therapist may become a casualty as a result of the group experience. It is difficult to assess the amount or degree of distress sustained and to identify casualties stemming directly from a group experience because researchers vary in their definitions as to what constitutes a group casualty. However, that there are readily identifiable and familiar clinical situations where patients become worse as a consequence of being in a group.

What happens to the unsuccessful group therapist or co-therapist? Many would-be therapists become group casualties because of a traumatic group ex-perience. All psychiatric residencies expose the trainees to group psychotherapy and it is the quality of this experience that has a profound and lasting effect on the students. For example, many analytic colleagues are aware that even highly motivated candidates who have had difficult or poorly selected control cases tend to disparage the practice of psychoanalysis and engage in activities other than analysis upon graduation. Similarly, those resident psychotherapists who have had a difficult group experience because of unsuitable patients or disa-greeable supervisory arrangements may shy away from practicing group psy-chotherapy or suffer adverse effects from their experience. The issue is a complex one as the end result is multidetermined. Some individuals have no intention of becoming group psychotherapists when they enter the residency program and have their minds set on becoming analysts, academic teachers, researchers, and practitioners of other therapies, despite their exposure to the group modality. Others feel that they would very much like to practice group psychotherapy although they are unfamiliar with its theory and techniques. Then there are those individuals who are loners by history and never feel comfortable in any group and dread having to conduct a group. There are many mental health professionals who simply do not feel comfortable in group settings.

There is no doubt that group psychotherapy can be hazardous. For instance, the patient may have a psychotic episode, a worsening of social relationships and job performance, or become an alcoholic. There may be the appearance of antisocial behavior, self-destructive acts, perverse sexual activities, a divorce which is impulsive and detrimental to the individual, or drug abuse. A patient may hurt himself or herself or someone else, take advantage of a group member, or harm the entire group. But it is difficult to define a casualty if we treat someone in the group and we do not know his or her previous emotional state prior to entering the group. Do a patient's adverse reactions in the group represent a reenactment of a long-existing pattern of behavior little influenced by the group process, or are they an immediate consequence of antitherapeutic group forces?

Some therapists argue that a worsening in the patient's condition during treatment does not necessarily portend a bad outcome for the individual. Changes in psychotherapy are usually equated with changes for the better, i.e., improvement. Yet it follows that if a treatment produces beneficial results it may also be hazardous and have the capability of producing harmful effects as well. Hadley and Strupp (6) prefer the term "negative effects" in preference to deterioration or casualty because it seems to describe more accurately the problem of the patient's getting worse as a function of the therapeutic influence, in opposition to other factors which may be outside of the psychotherapeutic situation. Psychotherapists know that during the course of treatment patients may fail to improve, or actually get worse before getting better, and that during the termination phase of a psychotherapy we often see a recrudescence of the original symptomatology. Depending, therefore, on when we evaluate the patient in group psychotherapy, we may be talking about a genuine casualty or merely looking at a normal vicissitude in treatment that may result in a successful outcome for the patient. If we employ the term negative effect, defined as a function of the therapeutic influence, we may be more accurate in assessing the impact of group psychotherapy upon the patient, therapist, and the group, and can weed out the extraneous factors that cannot be so easily correlated and understood. There will, therefore, be less confusion regarding what we are measuring and talking about.

In their survey of 150 experts, Hadley and Strupp (6) classify negative effects into two categories. The first is the exacerbation of presenting symptoms and the second is the appearance of new symptoms. Some comments from the experts bear repeating. Lieberman, one of the people surveyed, feels that a negative effect from psychotherapy is not the same as the temporary deterioration that is inevitable in some forms of psychotherapy. Marks notes that we must differentiate between normal and expected regressions from psychotherapy that are temporary and real, and those that have lasting negative effects. Ford reminds us that we must determine whether an observed negative effect is indeed a product of therapeutic intervention or merely an event independent of therapeutic intervention that coincides in time. Marks' definition of a negative effect as a "lasting deterioration in a patient directly attributable to therapy" is concise and comprehensive.

CAUSES OF FAILURES, CASUALTIES, AND HAZARDS

One of the most recognized causes for failures in group therapy is improper patient selection. The group literature states that patients in certain diagnostic categories are poor risk candidates for group therapy. These are individuals who are brain damaged (8, 10), paranoid (5), extremely narcissistic (14), deeply depressed (14), hypochondriacal (13), suicidal (6, 13), addicted to drugs or alcohol (8, 10), acutely psychotic (3, 11, 13), or sociopathic (1, 2). Such patients may require a specialized form of group therapy with a more homogeneous population and well-defined boundaries. They usually do not fare well in conventional outpatient groups. In their haste to get a group under way, inexperienced supervisors and eager trainees frequently ignore or are negligent in performing a careful diagnostic evaluation and may shorten or totally skip the preparatory phase of individual therapy before the patient is brought into a group. Thus, the group embarks on a hazardous and often unknown course where chances for failure are enhanced.

In their study, Galinsky and Schopler (4) divide the causes of casualties into the categories of personal and interpersonal sources. Casualties may be caused by the individual or personal characteristics of group members and leaders. Members are also likely to become casualties if they have a history of psychological instability or disturbance and an inability to comply with group rules. Whether or not they, indeed, do turn into casualties depends on the degree of pathology tolerated in a group. Other predisposing personal characteristics are the presence of inadequate or inflexible defenses, ego weaknesses, disruptive behavior, a lack of attention to the group, and inability to perceive expectations accurately.

Casualties may also stem from interpersonal sources or from the way relationships and rules are structured in the group. There may be a lack of structure in a group, insufficient clarity of norms, and low task orientation. On the other hand, norms that are coercive and force participation before members are ready, require member acceptance of all feedback, and encourage attack on individual defenses are also likely to lead to individual distress or damage. Excessive confrontations and expressions of anger among participants as well as attack or rejection by members or leaders are felt to be harmful. Group members and leaders must understand clearly what their roles and responsibilities are and adopt procedures and rules which are reasonable and moderate. Group leaders with high casualty rates have been described as being highly charismatic, lacking in ability to diagnose problems, insufficiently trained, overstimulating, impersonal, and inactive (9).

Groups with high casualty rates may themselves become casualties. Groups which have as their norms hostile, confrontational behavior, sustained levels of anger, coercion, and too much feedback rarely achieve the stage of cohesion. Members drop out and the group never reaches its therapeutic goals. Sadoff (12) described a group failure and attempted to identify its causes. He concluded that the patients varied so much in their symptoms that they shared little common difficulty except in their social isolation and lack of verbalization. There was no core group or a patient leader who could maintain the group process from week to week. Cohesion did not develop and the patients related basically to the therapist and not to the group. Sadoff noted the lack of post-session contacts between the members and felt that the instability of the membership during the life of the group was a major factor contributing to the failure of the group.

Countertransference problems in the leader may also contribute to the ultimate demise of a group. Sadoff felt that he had attempted unsuccessfully to treat each of the patients individually before they began in the group experience. He realized that he harbored more negative feelings toward the group that failed than he did toward another, more successful group. He resented having to constantly serve as the source of verbal activity and felt that his attempt to put these individuals in a group rather than transferring them to another therapist for individual psychotherapy was significant in the subsequent failure of his group. Sadoff concluded that the therapist's attitude toward the patients as individuals and toward them as a group is extremely important to the success or failure of the group. Likewise, group members should not have similar difficulties in communicating with others. He felt that at least one or two spontaneously verbal individuals are necessary to maintain the group process and drew the interesting conclusion that the therapist's technique may have to vary depending on the overall personality or type of group. Residents and other trainees who feel "forced" into conducting a group may harbor adverse countertransference feelings to authority figures in the group. Ultimately, unless these feelings are brought to light and resolved, the group, its members, and the therapists may become casualties or failures.

A common hazard to the therapist and to the group may come about when the therapist undergoes a life crisis. A review of the literature fails to show any systematic studies supporting the premise that life crises of the therapist have more of an effect on group therapy than do the individual therapies. However, it seems reasonable that a group therapist who is experiencing a personal crisis is less able to engage in therapy without the group patients becoming aware of his or her concerns. By virtue of the greater number of the individuals present, group therapy is more complex and affords far more opportunities than in dyadic treatment for mirroring or involving one or more facets of the therapist's personal life. If the therapist is vulnerable and especially needy, he or she may seek therapy from the group either consciously or unconsciously. While many experienced therapists candidly admit that they derive a certain amount of personal and professional growth from engaging in group therapy, the therapist in distress can go past that which is reasonable and venture beyond the point of no return. A seductive intimacy and coziness may develop, vitiating any therapeutic gains and impeding further growth and therapy. The therapist may become, in effect, a patient in the group. Boundaries between patient and therapist and patient and friend become blurred. Not infrequently, sexual acting-out occurs and the therapist, patient, and group are compromised.

PREVENTION

In this era of accountability and the increasing need for informed consent for medical and psychological procedures, greater ethical and technical obligations are demanded of the group practitioner to minimize failures, casualties, and hazards in group therapy. It has become accepted practice in many communities that the consumer patient be informed of the potential risks associated with any treatment, which implies that the patient be acquainted over a reasonable period of time with the treatment procedure. It is also assumed that the therapist be sufficiently knowledgeable and skillful to create constructive change and to prevent injury during the treatment process. What remains problematic and highly personalized is how the practitioner deals with the unconscious dynamics and resistances when acquainting the prospective patient with group therapy, the sometimes unpredictable, nontherapeutic atmosphere characteristic for a particular group once it is under way, and the occasional unexpected or uncontrollable external circumstances that may disrupt the group.

A number of general guidelines can now be found in the literature which, if followed, provide the therapist with a beneficial experience and assure the group of a successful treatment outcome. Almost all the guidelines pertain to the leadership functions. Group leaders should be carefully screened for emotional and cognitive inadequacies. They should be well trained and committed, caring persons. The leaders should be sufficiently perceptive and skilled to know what the patient needs and wants from the group experience and if the patient has the requisite qualities necessary for successful participation in the group. The leaders must inform prospective members of the risks involved in participation and help regulate the amount of self-disclosure within the group. They must handle crises that arise. The leaders must do a careful diagnostic assessment on each patient so that individuals may not harm themselves or the members in the group. They must assume responsibility for providing protection of a group member if the group itself is unable to offer sufficient support. They must assist the group in tending to damaged individuals or damage to the group-as-a-whole, and they may have to help change group norms if these are too restrictive. The leaders must be careful to avoid the establishment of the role of scapegoat for members who are unable to fend off such a position. The therapists should have the ultimate responsibility for disbanding a group, if the group's difficulties are insoluble, and for referring members for further help if necessary. Group members should be given sufficient preparation to know what is expected of them and what will happen in the group.

Appropriate group composition is felt to be one of the most important means of avoiding destructive interpersonal developments that may result in failures or casualties. The presence of extreme differences among members may cause difficulties and endless bickering. The expectations of the group must be clearly stated and should be compatible with the wishes of the membership. Group norms or rules which promote mutual support and caring and yet allow for the expression of individual differences among the members help diminish the potential for casualties. The leader should have the ability to nurture relationships that are supportive, help regulate personal disclosures when they create subsequent difficulties for members, and exercise good clinical judgment in regulating the amount of give and take in the group.

In closing, it is appropriate to return to the plight of the group therapist and to discuss strategies for preventing failures and lessening the hazards. I find that when trainees have had a successful group experience they tend to continue with the group beyond their training requirement or to undertake another group, despite an avowed interest in a different aspect of psychiatry. Students who have been patients in a well-handled group also feel this way. Those who wanted to specialize in groups feel angry, disappointed, and sustain a sense of lowered self-esteem when the group fails. Those individuals who are loners are glad to get the experience out of the way and make no attempt at running another group once they complete the group requirement. Individuals who had no pretense or desire to become group psychotherapists and who have failed with a group may find comfort in the rationalization that group therapy is not efficacious. They should not be pushed into conducting another group. Trainees, who earlier may have expressed an interest in group therapy, upon experiencing a failure may pursue other, more gratifying areas or may steadfastly plow into another group although feeling very troubled about their lack of previous success. Some loners or schizoid individuals may be quite distressed by the group experience and become even more reclusive or depressed, or show paranoid features. Some trainees never succeed in getting a group going, being continuously involved in evaluating patients and never retaining a sufficient number of patients to run a group. For them, the group venture is demoralizing and narcissistically mortifying. Usually, the impact on the beginning group therapist is evident and easy to ascertain. The supervisor needs to ferret out the motivation, strengths and weaknesses of the student and to consider these factors in the decision to require the trainee to undertake another group if there has been a previous failure.

Then there is the problem of the more experienced but poorly trained or less talented non-student group therapist who continually encounters little success with groups. Eventually, discouragement and self-devaluation ensue. The therapist may seek a personal group or individual therapy experience or reenter group supervision. He or she may obtain further didactic training. However, not all group therapists are so introspective or insightful. Unfortunately, what happens at times is that the group therapist shuns the neutral, therapeutic stance and may destructively act out his or her hostility and frustrations within the group. Such frustrations and anger may appear in the form of countertransference manifestations such as the therapist not permitting patients to graduate from the group or deciding not to work any longer with the group.

REFERENCES

1. Abrahams, J., and McCorkle, L.W. Group psychotherapy at an Army rehabilitation center. *Dis. Nerv. Sys.,* 8: 50-62, 1947.
2. Bach, G. *Intensive Group Therapy.* New York: Ronald Press, 1954.
3. Corsini, R., and Lundin, W. Group psychotherapy in the mid-west. *Group Psychother.,* 8: 316-320, 1955.
4. Galinsky, M.J., and Schopler, J.H. Warning: Groups may be dangerous. *Social Work,* 22: 89-94, 1977.
5. Graham, I.W. Observations on analytic group therapy. *Int. J. Group Psychother.,* 9: 150-157, 1959.
6. Hadley, S.W., and Strupp, H.H. Contemporary view of negative effects in psychotherapy. *Arch. Gen Psychiat.,* 33: 1291-1302, 1976.
7. Hartley, D., Roback, H.B., and Abramowitz, S.I. Deterioration effects in encounter groups. *Am. Psychol.,* 31: 247-255, 1976.
8. Johnson, J.A. *Group Psychotherapy: A Practical Approach.* New York: McGraw-Hill, 1963.
9. Lieberman, M.A., Yalom, I.D., and Miles, M.B. *Encounter Groups: First Facts.* New York: Basic Books, 1973.
10. Nash, E., Frank, J., Gliedman, L., Imber, S., and Stone, A. Some factors related to patients remaining in group psychotherapy. *Int. J. Group Psychother.,* 7: 264-275, 1957.
11. Rosenbaum, M., and Hartley, E. A summary review of current practices of ninety-two group therapists. *Int. J. Group Psychother.,* 12: 194-198, 1962.
12. Sadoff, R.L. The group that failed. *Psychiat. Q.,* 47: 110-116, 1973.
13. Slavson, S.R. Criteria for selection and rejection of patients for various kinds of group therapy. *Int. J. Group Psychother.,* 5: 3-30, 1955.
14. Slavson. S.R. *A Textbook in Analytic Group Psychotherapy.* New York: International Universities Press, 1964.

Stages of Development
In Therapy Groups

Chapter VIII

GROUP DEVELOPMENT: A CASE EXAMPLE
OF THE FIRST THREE PHASES

Ariadne P. Beck, M.A.

Editors' Summary. This paper presents a clinical example of the first three phases in the development of a time-limited psychotherapy group. The author describes three phases and four emergent leadership roles in the development of group structures. Phase one consists of contract formation, leadership selection, and activities which establish the members' intent to become a working group. In phase two, leadership selection is completed, norms and goals for the group are formulated, and methods for handling negative feelings are established. Phase three is the first work phase addressing the substantive issues which brought the participants to the group.

This chapter will highlight the critical characteristics of the first three phases in the development of a time-limited psychotherapy group, so that the clinician can use them as a guide to facilitate the group's progress through this crucial initial formative process. Beck's theory of group development forms the basis of the viepoint to be elaborated here (1-4).

This theory describes the process by which a collection of persons goes about creating the entity we call a therapy group. A therapy group is a system with a structure. It is composed of a set of other systems called persons. It is itself a subsystem of a larger system: an organization, a practice, a program. The theory describes the developmental characteristics of the system formation and the interpersonal dynamics, especially the emergence of four leaders who contribute to this group level process.

The case example is a group which met for 15 sessions (a limit agreed upon in advance) in an outpatient setting. All the clients had been in individual therapy for at least two years. There were six clients—three men, (Joe, Greg, Brad) three women (Diane, Martha, Pat)—and two therapists—both women. A seventh client (Dan) never actually made it to a session of the group. One therapist was a staff member of the clinic and the other a student in training, co-leading her first group. The clients ranged in age from 23 to 52. The group met for an hour and a half once a week. The meeting time had been set for an early evening hour because one of the clients had to be home early. The others agreed to this time, but some of them knew it would mean rushing from work to make it.

On the first evening all the clients showed up except Dan, the person with the time constraint. He called to say that he could not make it because of a problem on his job. The other members were a little distressed to hear this but seemed to understand. The meeting began with an introductory statement by the primary therapist, Alice, regarding the time limit and the focus for the group, as well as a brief introduction of herself. Each member took an opportunity sometime during the first session to introduce him/herself and to address his/her goal in joining the group. Several members used the occasion of self-introduction to begin working in a more self-reflective way. One in particular, Diane, focused on her issues immediately, and Alice, the therapist, responded in a way which facilitated a period of therapeutic work for Diane. This exchange demonstrated, among other things, the way in which Alice worked with one individual client.

In the second half of this first session, another client, Martha, shared with the group a painful experience she had had. She had awakened in the middle of the night in a state of intense anxiety and realized that there was no one she felt that she could call on in a crisis. The other members responded with empathy to Martha, acknowledging individually that at some time in their lives they had had similar experiences and had felt such loneliness. This was a powerful emotional encounter in this group. As the session ended, the time for the next meeting was reconfirmed.

One week later the group reconvened. Martha was sick and couldn't come. Dan again did not appear and this time did not call to explain. The group was distressed about Dan: They were very aware of the 15-week time limitation, and they were eager to get down to business—yet they felt that they had to wait for Dan. About 20 minutes into the session there was a short discussion about him and the group's readiness to move on. One of the members got up and walked over to the empty chair in the circle and turned it around so that it faced away from the group. The group had decided not to wait for Dan—his membership was in effect canceled.

The segment of group interaction described thus far constituted the first phase in group development for this particular group. In general, phase one gives each participant a chance to size up the situation, him/herself, and the others, including the therapists, and to decide whether or not s/he is prepared to participate in a process with this particular set of people. This finalizing of membership is an important task in this phase. As we saw in our example, the group could not proceed beyond phase one until they resolved the question of Dan's participation.

Since phase one begins with a group of people who are mostly strangers to one another, who do not yet define themselves as a group, its focus is to create an initial contract to become a group with a particular task. This phase must also address initial clarification of both individual and group goals and initial identification of certain limits and expectations, thus beginning a process of creating norms. The group participates experientially in a process that first minimally identifies each member to the others. Then, as the phase nears its close, a strong impulse to share or exchange some emotionally meaningful content seems to emerge. There seems to be a mutually felt need to establish a bond with experiences that are common to everyone there. In our example there was an exchange about feeling anxious and alone in the night—an acknowledgment of sharing a poignant, existential human experience.

Several aspects of the system-forming process are apparent in the first phase of group development. First and foremost, all growth is characterized by processes of differentiation and integration. Both of these processes contribute to the group's capacity for adaptation and to the increase of complexity in the group's organization. This particular group started as a collection of strangers. During phase one each of them participated in a differentiating process by taking some of the group time to present him/herself to the others. Each one could stand out in his or her own way. Also during phase one the group members found a topic about which they could all share deep feelings and in relation to which they could affirm their similarity. This experience served an integrative, cohesive function, bringing the members together with the feeling of being a group. During each phase of group development there is some meaningful way in which each of these processes is experienced, often over several different topics in each phase. Each time the focus is on a different set of group-relevant issues. The level of complexity in the group increases as the members experience together, building on their previous knowledge as their information about each member expands.

Another aspect of the system-forming process has to do with defining boundaries, which in turn defines a group identity and further provides a "safe space" within which creative and generative opening experiences can take place. The fairly assertive group of our example was able to define its own membership boundary and to take the first step toward autonomous functioning in the process. A number of other aspects of the group were also defined during phase one. Both an individual and a group level experience with strong emotion helped to define this as a group where feelings would be shared and responded to meaningfully. This is a very important norm for a therapy group, since it relates directly to the primary goal for the group—namely, to facilitate self-understanding.

To continue with the clinical example: As you recall, phase one ended early in the second session. After a moment of silence Joe offered his ideas on how to locate the resources available in the city if one is in an emotional crisis and in need of immediate help. This was a delayed response on his part to Martha's anguish about waking in the night and realizing her aloneness. (Martha, however, was absent and so could not hear Joe's suggestions.) Various members of the group, especially Greg, reacted to these suggestions as being essentially inadequate. Greg, however, said that he too had had occasion to seek such help.

Pat entered the discussion next, to explore her concern about whether it was possible to express anger within the group. She was annoyed with Joe because she considered his discourse inappropriate, but being ambivalent about her anger concluded instead that Joe should be given special consideration. It seemed obvious to Pat that Joe had not had therapy before and therefore didn't know what to talk about. A discussion ensued on whether individual therapy is important and should be a prerequisite to participatoin in the group. Pat implied that it is, but Greg vehemently disagreed with this notion. The group was clearly exploring the possibility of creating a criterion for membership in the group that would eliminate Joe. Greg's intervention put an end to this criterion and effectively held the group together.

Pat's expression of her ambivalence about expressing anger in the group led to a discussion about the desirability of expressing anger in the moment it is felt. Several members talked about competitive feelings that they were experiencing in the group and expressed concern about the "childishness" of those feelings. Joe talked about maturity and expressed the view that maturity should mean that others can no longer hurt you with their anger and pettiness, i.e., maturity is a kind of shield or shell. In contrast, Greg offered the view that one should never desire not to feel pain—to him, maturity is the ability to be vulnerable, to feel pain, and to cope with it.

Greg and Joe then took turns talking about their own issues. Greg talked more openly about his current personal dilemma in choosing between the continuation of a relationship to a young woman, which was clearly heading for a deeper involvement, and the opportunity to take a well-paying job in Washington, leaving the young woman behind. This stimulated Joe to comment on his relationship with his wife, and their disagreement regarding the idea of moving to Arizona. In the midst of this story Joe expressed a kind of disdain toward his wife, making it quite clear that he often just turns her off in his own mind and doesn't pay any attention to what she says.

Joe and Greg seemed to be parallel-playing or competing for the group's attention. Eventually the two men clashed, and at that point Pat and Diane pounced on Joe, again complaining about the topics he raised and the analogies he drew in his lengthy statements. The primary therapist, Alice, entered on several occasions, trying to help Joe to hear what others were saying about him. Finally, both therapists focused their attention on Pat and Diane, exploring the reasons why they had been stopped by Joe from saying whatever they wanted to say in the group. As the session drew to a close, Greg capped the feelings of the group by telling Joe not to treat the group the way he treats his wife, i.e., by ignoring what is said to him. The group members parted with some issues crystallized, but without any resolution.

When the next session began, everyone had arrived except Joe. Martha and Greg got into a playful sparring session about male/female issues, surfacing another latent conflict in the group. Martha said that men have a feeling that just being men makes them superior; Greg said that women have similar feelings, and that in fact they really dominate but don't admit that. The standoff was left unresolved as Diane focused on Joe's absence and expressed concern about whether he would come back to the group. Since Brad had left midstream in the previous session due to a job commitment, and Martha had been absent from the previous session, Greg filled them in on what happened, explaining that the group had given Joe a hard time during the last part of the last session.

Joe came in during this summary. When Greg finished, Joe shared his thoughts and reactions to the last meeting—in particular, the stress that he had felt as a result of the confrontation. He said that he had been upset enough to try to phone the therapist, without success. Not only had he been unable to tune out the group from his mind, but their comments had forcefully impacted on him. He concluded his typically lengthy remarks with the thought that we are all different personalities, that we are bound to irritate each other, but that we have to be willing to give and take, and—most importantly—still have the courage to be ourselves. Joe seemed to be saying that he was hurt but that he could still live with the group. Both Martha and Brad responded in supportive ways to Joe.

Pat and Joe then exchanged feedback on their experiences in the previous session, which led Joe into a self-reflective exploration about the problems he has in communicating with people generally, and his feeling that he gets used by others in negative ways.

Diane responded to this by trying to get Joe to produce even more material on his issues, but at this point it became apparent that this was a maneuver to avoid her own self-disclosure. Greg and Brad noted the fact that the group knew more about Joe than about anyone else so far. They acknowledged that the group had found it convenient to focus on Joe—to "scapegoat" him—but that it was time to get down to work themselves. With this acknowledgment this group ended phase two.

Each phase of group development is characterized by the necessity of attending to certain group level issues. Most frequently these are addressed as though they were personal issues, but occasionally the group members become conscious of the fact that they are grappling with a more general problem. The second phase in particular has these important issues in it; one set has to do with norms, a number of which are processed during this second phase. For example, this group dealt with the following normative questions:

1) How should one get the time and attention of the group?
2) What are acceptable strategies for doing that?
3) What are the appropriate topics or levels of emotional issues to pursue here?
4) Is it appropriate to express anger?
5) Is it safe to express anger?
6) How will anger be managed interpersonally?

A second group level issue addressed in phase two has to do with group goals. In the example group there was a serious concern with the image of maturity and strength which were the hoped-for outcomes of the therapy process. Was the goal to develop strength to withstand conflict and adversity, or was the goal to achieve openness to emotional pain as well as joy?

A third issue of this phase is the leadership-selecting process. In the example group, Joe and Greg were vying for leadership. The group responded by trying to thwart Joe's efforts and eventually turned on him in a kind of attack. Greg and Joe, in fact, filled two of the four leadership roles identified in Beck's theory as emerging in all small groups: Greg became the Emotional Leader of the group and Joe became the Scapegoat Leader. The primary therapist, Alice, filled the role of Task Leader. Martha filled the role of Defiant Leader (1, 2, 3, 5, 9).

Through phase two the group, in attempting to define goals, norms, leaders, limits, and procedures, has focused primarily on structural issues. These are necessary to the establishment of the therapy group and to the formation of a structure. Within this context a number of the members have also been airing their personal concerns. It is not, however, until the third phase of development that the group has the security and space to address personal concerns in depth. Phase two resolves a competitive process, and that resolution allows the group to move on to a more cooperative, opening, enabling process. The competitive behavior has largely been expressed over the formative issues in developing a group structure. Structural issues come up in every phase, but after phase two they usually take less of the group's time to resolve. (Phase five, however, also presents a comparably difficult time for most groups [6]).

To return to the example: As phase three began, Diane shared some of her concerns that seemed to have their beginnings in her childhood experiences, particularly in relation to her father. Greg, Martha, and Joe also shared some negative experiences that they had had with their parents. The group then turned to resolving issues of tension between several pairings within the group: Joe and Pat; Diane and Joe; Martha and Diane; Greg and Diane. Finally they returned to issues of love and attachment in their relationships to their parents, and session three came to a close.

When session four began, there was some rearranging of furniture, some noticing of art in the room, and some discussion of Brad's absence from the session. Joe then picked up the previous week's discussion about parents and shared some thoughts he had had during the week about the difficulties he had had in separating from his parents. Pat then told the group that she had terminated her individual therapy under duress—a conflictual relationship with her therapist. This aroused some fairly intense anxiety in the group, especially in Martha. The members explored issues regarding the question of what evidence there can be that one is making progress in therapy. They then shifted to Diane, and her anxiety when she had felt closed out by Joe's style of communicating (phase two). They reviewed with Joe and Diane the conflict they had had and how it had developed. They seemed to be redoing the issues in the scapegoating process, but from a more open, exploratory, and reflective stance, using the experience to learn something about themselves (8). After the group addressed Pat and her stress situation again, the session ended.

In session five, the group self-consciously addressed the fact that Brad had not yet disclosed himself, and seemed withdrawn. Brad shared something about himself which he felt was embarrassing. His problems emerged in intimate contexts—he had not felt free up to that point to reveal them to anyone. (It was, in fact, a major step for Brad to tell anyone.) Greg then told the group that he had decided to go to Washington to interview for the job out there. The group discussed his issues with him for an extended period of time. As the session closed, Greg expressed a curiosity about the session of the group that he would have to miss. The group reflected on the themes that they had discussed since "they had gotten down to work," and they realized that they shared several issues primarily having to do with love, dependency, and anger. This brought phase three to a close.

The focus of phase three is on the development of effective work skills in the group and on the recognition of individuals, their differences, their unique problems, and their potential contribution to the group. This phase is in dramatic contrast to phase two: It is characterized by cooperation, interest in others, and considerably greater reflectiveness. The achievement of some group norms regarding participation and the successful handling of competitive processes in phase two seem to lead naturally to the question of how individual differences will be handled in the group.

If the tasks of phase three are successfully accomplished, the group achieves a cohesion based on a mutual recognition of individual differences among the members and different goals for growth. Because personal growth is the "work" of a therapy group, this stage must also deal with the problem of developing a communication style that leads to the accomplishment of the work to be done. The basic conditions which are conducive to personal growth must therefore be created. In our case example this was expressed very clearly in the segment when the tensions between various pairings in the group were explored and worked through.

Phase three is characterized by (a) the exchange of information of a personal kind with everyone having an opportunity to express and disclose him/herself, and (b) an experimentation with various modes of communication and their interpersonal implications, ranging from facilitative listening to confrontation. This work-oriented stage has the special feature of allowing everyone to emerge more openly and fully in his or her uniqueness, in an atmosphere that tends more toward cooperation and caring than the previous two phases. In this process information and experience are generated that then allow the group to develop a more functional set of relationships later on.

It seems to be important to the group that everyone participate in the work on personal growth, and in the self-disclosure process in particular, in some meaningful way (the group of course deciding what is appropriate). There is a sense of establishing a basic equality as "known" individuals at this time.

In this group Brad had held back in a visible way until late in phase three. The group put pressure on him to participate. He did not go into his problem in great depth, but the group does not require that. It does seem to require that the risk of self-disclosure be taken during phase three. Also during this period of work on personal growth, the Emotional Leader is recognized clearly by everyone as experiencing a growth spurt. The Emotional Leader usually makes significant changes in his life outside the group, either in work commitments or in intimate relationships, and to some degree shares these accomplishments with the group, acknowledging the significance of their support to him.

As phase three comes to an end, the group reviews characteristics, views, experiences, and problems which they share. The members reestablish a group emotional bond on a basis that now recognizes individual differences while acknowledging some universal similarities and a feeling of equality as participants in the group. From a structural point of view, phase three begins the community of peers which is the basis ultimately of a group which develops a sense of responsibility for itself.

In summary, this chapter has presented a case example of the first three phases in the structural development of a time-limited psychotherapy group. The first phase has as its primary group level task to form a contract to become a group. Evidence is growing, however, to indicate that leadership selection also begins in phase one (7). The second phase of group development is characterized by high tension, competitive behavior, and the scapegoating of one leader. Norms and goals for the group are hammered out during this phase and leadership selection is finalized. The group works out a method for handling negative feelings and anger. When all of this is achieved (and many groups do not succeed

•

at all), the group is ready to begin a cooperative work process. Phase three is characterized by two primary activities: The clients take turns in self-disclosure and in-depth work on their issues, and the group members as well as therapists explore various methods of response in trying to be helpful to each person as they work on their issues. The basic conditions for getting the work accomplished which brought the group together must be established in phase three. In long-term groups phase three may last a considerable length of time as clients work intensively on historical issues primarily. In this case example, the time limit on the group worked against lengthy exploration. In fact, groups seem to have an internal clock and will try to complete all the phases in the time allotted, if they know in advance what the time limit is. The members of this particular group were able to process all the issues rapidly enough to move smoothly through all nine phases to a successful, natural termination.

REFERENCES

1. Beck, A.P. Phases in the development of structure in therapy and encounter groups. *In:* D. A. Wexler and L.N. Rice (Eds.), *Innovations in Client-Centered Therapy*. New York: John Wiley, 1974.
2. Beck, A.P. Developmental characteristics of the system forming process. *In:* J.E. Durkin (Ed.), *Living Groups: Group Psychotherapy and General System Theory*. New York: Brunner/Mazel, 1981.
3. Beck, A.P. The study of group phase development and emergent leadership. *Group*, 5 (4): 48-54, 1981.
4. Beck, A.P., and Keil, A.V. Observations on the development of client-centered, time-limited therapy groups. *In: Counseling Center Discussion Papers*, 13 (5). Chicago: University of Chicago Library, 1967.
5. Beck, A.P., and Peters, L.N. The research evidence for distributed leadership in therapy groups. *Int. J. Group Psychother*. 31 (1): 43-71, 1981.
6. Dugo, J.M., and Beck, A.P. Issues of intimacy and hostility viewed as group level phenomena. Presented at the American Group Psychotherapy Association, New York, 1982.
7. Eng, A.M., and Beck A.P. Speech behavior measures of group psychotherapy process. *Group*, 6 (3): 37-48 1982.
8. Lewis, C.M. Symbolization of experience in the process of group development. Unpublished manuscript.
9. Peters, L.N., and Beck, A.P. Identifying emergent leaders in psychotherapy groups. *Group*, 6 (1): 35-40, 1982.

Chapter IX

STAGES AND ROLES: THE GROUP
AND THE INDIVIDUAL

K. Roy Mackenzie, M.D., F.R.C.P.
and W. John Livesley, M.D., Ph.D.

Editors' Summary. This paper presents a view of the therapy group based on General Systems Theory and the social psychology of small groups. It stands in contrast, therefore, to traditional psychoanalytic concepts of the group-as-a-whole. Developmental stages are conceptualized in terms of a series of interactional tasks. Group development is linked to specific kinds of social role behavior. The concept of role is used to express the relationship between behavior required by the group and individual characterologic structure. This provides a way of understanding individual behavior which is complementary to that based upon a consideration of intrapsychic processes.

This chapter presents a descriptive model of small group functioning based upon developmental stages and social roles. This perspective encourages the clinician to consider the relationship between the group as a whole and the personality of the individual member. The account of developmental stages deals with the interactional tasks which the group must address in sequential fashion for progress to occur. Social roles form the links by which the behavior of the individual can be considered to have meaning for the social system. In this way it is possible to view the contributions individual members make to the accomplishment of group tasks. Thus the stage/role model provides a comprehensive theory for understanding the behavior seen in clinical groups. A synopsis of developmental stages will be presented initially, followed by a consideration of social role behavior and finally a discussion of the implications of social role functioning for group development.

DEVELOPMENTAL STAGES

In recent years there has been an increased interest in the idea that groups progress through a series of stages. A number of studies have shown consistency in stage description and sequencing (2, 10). This perspective is compatible with a general view of living systems as having an inherent directionality toward the development of greater complexity over time. Each stage possesses an organizational structure which emerges as the group attends to its developmental tasks. Change in structure is followed by a period of consolidation around the new set of issues. For each stage a central developmental task is identified which the group as a social system must achieve. As the group system deals with the particular challenge of each stage, the individual members are forced to confront similar issues. This intertwining of social system development and individual events offers significant opportunities for inducing therapeutic change. Groups progress through an invariant sequence of stages providing the clinician with a valuable organizing framework. Our description of group stages will focus on five stages plus termination.

Stage 1—Engagement

The task of the first stage is to resolve the issue of engagement of members. As members become more committed to the group there is a growing sense of group identity, a sense of "groupness." The achievement of this task ensures that the group has emerged as a social system with its own organizational structure. Two mechanisms play an essential part in this process. By comparing common experience and reactions, the members develop a sense of universality, an appreciation that they have had similar experiences and so can understand each other. This provides a focus around which the group may coalesce and achieve cohesive interaction. The second related mechanism involves comparisons between extra-group and intra-group experiences. This information about differences establishes the group boundary as members come to appreciate the ways in which the group is different from other aspects of their lives.

The task for the individual member is to become part of a social system. This is achieved through relatively superficial self-disclosure often of a factual nature. This may be experienced as intensely arousing and threatening, since it brings with it the possibility of being found unacceptable to the other members. Once accomplished, however, it results in a sense of satisfaction that contributes strongly to the development of group cohesiveness. The group interactional climate is characterized by a steadily increasing sense of engagement with a minimum of conflicting material. Stage 1 approaches resolution when membership criteria have been finalized and there is a demonstrated commitment on the part of the members to participate in group interaction.

Stage 2—Differentiation

The task in this stage is to recognize differences among members. The approach to these issues is accompanied by anger and conflict between the members which may be characterized by a high degree of polarization accompanied by exaggerated and stereotyped statements, the unrealistic nature of which goes unnoticed. This helps to resolve the danger inherent in Stage 1 of the prolongation of an uncritical and comfortable environment that is neither challenging nor change-inducing. The group must develop a mechanism for the cooperative exploration of differences in which the assertion of individual ideas and beliefs can be tolerated. Without this mechanism of conflict resolution, a competitive and unyielding approach may result in group fragmentation. Part of this process will involve decisions regarding the way the group should operate, resulting in the emergence of more clearly identified group norms.

For the individual members the threat and challenge are to deal with differences, conflict, and anger: To what extent should they go along with the collectivity and to what extent should they be their own person? The role and function of the leader are often challenged and tested in this regard. The climate in Stage 2 is characterized by a drop in engagement and a marked rise in conflict. The early portion of this stage demonstrates a clear awareness of avoidance of important issues which remain submerged until a breakthrough later in the stage. This stage reaches resolution when conflictual issues have been successfully aired and all members have participated in the assertion of individual points of view. Recognition that the group can resolve conflict is accompanied by a resurgent sense of cohesion and engagement. It is important that the anger experienced in Stage 2 is understood to reflect differences, since this cognitive dimension is an important part of the work during this stage.

Stage 3 — Individuation

The task of the group in this stage is to pursue a deeper understanding of the internal complexity of each member. The cohesion of Stage 1 together with the cooperative style developed in Stage 2 are now put to productive use. The impression created is that the group is now really "working," although the earlier stages were necessary precursors. While the content in this stage is about the individual, the work is conducted through an interpersonal process. To use the language of the Johari window (6), the area "Known to Self" expands during this stage, and there is increasing recognition of internal conflicts and contradictions. This process of reflective introspection is accompanied by deeper levels of self-revelation in which the individual member risks some loss of self-esteem as parts of self are uncovered which may not be appreciated. Collaboration with other group members in the process provides an important source of support.

The climate in Stage 3 is characterized by high levels of engagement and a marked drop in conflict. As members are now more aware of psychological issues going on among themselves, avoidance of important issues will be recognized. This stage approaches resolution when all members have demonstrated the ability to participate in collaborative exploration and engage in deeper self-revelation—a process resulting in a greater acceptance of self as complex. The transition to Stage 4 is marked by emerging evidence of personal involvement among the members. From this point on in the group's life, however, the transition zone between stages becomes less acute and more overlap and blurring occurs in regard to stage-specific characteristics.

Stage 4—Intimacy

Now that the individual members understand each other in complex ways, it becomes possible for them to interact in a more psychologically meaningful manner. The task of Stage 4 is to manage and explore close interpersonal involvement, and thus to experience intimacy. While this process may have an erotic quality, a more fundamental dimension concerns the recognition that members have the ability to influence each other in a reciprocal fashion, so that the importance of relationships must be acknowledged. This process carries with it the threat of rejection by persons the member has come to know in a complex and personal fashion. The inner material revealed in Stage 3 is now reexplored in terms of its application to interpersonal relationships within the group. In Stage 4 the group climate is characterized by continuing high engagement and minimal overt conflict. The initial portion of this stage is often accompanied by a sense of euphoria and excitement which later gives way to an appreciation of avoidance of significant issues. The stage reaches resolution when the members are able to relate nondefensively and demonstrate tolerance of closeness and intimacy.

Stage 5—Mutuality

The task in this stage is to develop an increasing sense of mutual responsibility amongst the members. This exploration of the meaning of closeness carries with it the need to resolve a control dimension between the members, involving a sense of reciprocity and responsibility for others as opposed to either excessive dependency or exploitation in relationships. It should be emphasized that this is not an issue of intimacy related to a recognition of deeper similarities, but rather a sense of the fundamental uniqueness of each group member. This stage, therefore, addresses the danger in Stage 4 of irresponsible closeness. At the same time it brings a threat to the individual of becoming trapped in a relationship in which unequal status hampers individual development. Demonstration of the acceptance of personal responsibility in relationships indicates a high degree of group maturity. The climate during this stage is characterized by sporadic surges of conflict as members test individual autonomy in resolving issues of dependency and dominance.

Termination

The task here is to allow disengagement of members in such a way that they can function as individuals without feeling a sense of demoralization and hopelessness. A number is not given to this stage because it may occur at any point in the developmental life of the group. As in Stage 1, the focus of psychological attention is again directed to the events and issues external to the group. The history of the group and its individual members is reviewed and external objectives and plans are compared and contrasted with in-group events. Critical incidents will be recalled and worked through once more. These mechanisms assist in the process of incorporation of the group as a personally important and lasting experience. There is a danger that the acknowledgment of loss óf the group will be handled through avoidance and denial, thus preventing full integration of the experience. At the same time the stage is accompanied by an acceptance of responsibility for self.

SOCIAL ROLES

Social roles provide another useful way of describing group structure (4, 8). People behave in a group in ways which will evoke from others responses found satisfying. These behaviors gradually fall into patterns so that each member is expected by the other members to adopt predictable ways of interacting. Such behavioral expectations constitute social roles and become part of group norms. Beck and Peters (3) suggest that certain role behaviors are necessary for the group to master the stage-related developmental tasks mentioned earlier. Members finding it most comfortable to exhibit the behaviors demanded by a particular social position may be said to occupy that social role. Thus the concept of role stands at the boundary between the functional needs of the group system and the personality of the individual member (7). Behavior exhibited in the group can be viewed as arising from the interaction between the personal characteristics of the member and the context created by the functional requirements of the group system.

Four social roles will be described in this paper drawn from the literature on informal roles in small groups; the Sociable Role, the Structural Role, the Cautionary Role, and the Divergent Role. These roles relate closely to the two basic dimensions of personality and interpersonal behavior described in numerous studies; affiliation and dominance (5, 9, 11). The four roles represent clusters of behaviors which are important for the group. While at times one member may dominate a particular social role position, it is more common for several members to contribute to each. When composing groups it is useful to try to incorporate a mix of members which has within it some potential for all four types of interaction.

Sociable Role

This role is derived from the ''socio-emotional leader' described by Bales (1). Members displaying this role are gregarious and trusting, as well as supporting and reassuring of other members. They attempt to include all members in the group and emphasize a positive emotional tone. They attend closely to interpersonal process and tend to minimize the expression of differences, negative feelings, and anger. The function of this role for the group is to promote cohesion and facilitate engagement. From an informational point of view, the result of these activities is to make members aware of similarities in their experiences, problems, and reactions. The supportive aspect of this role is particularly critical during the formative stages of the group although it remains significant throughout the group's life. The nonthreatening nature of these members and their positive regard for others make them popular group members. Excessive display of these sorts of behaviors, however, may limit the group's capacity to deal with conflict, difference, and confrontation. Similarly, individual members who display these behaviors to a marked degree will experience anxiety when such negative issues arise.

Structural Role

This role description has its origins in the ''task leader,'' also described by Bales (1), but has been modified to emphasize the way this role functions in therapy groups, where the task is less evident. Members adopting this role are concerned with establishing goals for the group and procedures for attaining them. In this way they structure and organize group activity in a highly cognitive manner, emphasizing explanations and theories and often neglecting emotional implications. In one sense they may appear to be controlling the group but this is better understood as a concern with adherence to conventional behavior rather than as an attempt to dominate. These behaviors are useful to the developing group by helping to establish and maintain a focus upon goals and norms. Later in the group's life, emphasis upon cognitive understanding helps members to clarify issues, thus providing the understanding necessary for therapeutic change. Those adopting this role display a strong sense of purpose and direction which reduces the anxiety felt both by themselves and other group members in early group stages. Excessive presence of this role behavior, however, has a constricting effect on the group by limiting the exploration of affect, while those showing such behaviors in an extreme manner may be viewed as distant and unapproachable.

Cautionary Role

This role is derived from the "defiant member" role described by Beck (2). Those exhibiting this role find it difficult to trust others and consequently behave in a cautious and defensive way. They are hesitant to engage in self-disclosure and their distrust may show itself in a hostile fashion. They are ambivalent about committing themselves to the group and skeptical about its potential benefits. These members model for the group the importance of the individual and prevent the excessively rapid submission into a group consensus. Particularly in the later stages of the group they emphasize the importance of autonomy and the dangers of excessive reliance on the group. There is a danger that if these role behaviors dominate, the group will be prevented from developing cohesion and positive working norms. Those members displaying these behaviors to a major degree may isolate themselves from others thereby cutting off potential support.

Divergent Role

This social role is closely related to that of the "scapegoat." Members enacting this role show a challenging and questioning attitude which is divergent to that adopted by the rest of the group. In terms of information, they emphasize differences rather than similarities, often in an impulsively blunt manner. Their aggressive approach to group participation may elicit the hostility of other group members who see them as insensitive. For this reason they may become involved in a rejecting process. Although they appear insensitive, they have an intuitive understanding which allows them to rapidly identify the sensitive and vulnerable areas of others. The Divergent Role is valuable for the group since the exploration of differences is critical to the differentiation of individual member identity in Stage 2. The polarizing position taken by these members forces the group to develop mechanisms for conflict resolution and at the same time results in the revelation of important personal material as members defend themselves. The function of this role remains important throughout the group's life, the continual rejection of consensus forcing consideration of alternative viewpoints. These members demonstrate that anger and conflict can be tolerated and useful, although excessive display of these behaviors can result in group disintegration. Members adopting this role are often admired and respected by others for their determination and commitment to change.

SOCIAL ROLES AND GROUP DEVELOPMENT

In Stage 1, Engagement, the primary task is achieved through universality which gives rise to a sense of cohesion. Behaviors necessary for this are those associated with the Sociable and Structural Roles. Those adopting the Sociable Role seek to establish a warm and sharing atmosphere, in which self-disclosure can occur. Structural Role behavior helps the groups to identify and define specific issues. The combination of these role behaviors helps to allay anxiety stemming from the unstructured nature of the new situation. The essential information necessary for group formation is that concerning similarities regarding identity, problems, and concerns. This process draws members' attention to in-group experiences and contrasts them with extra-group events.

As the group moves to Stage 2, Differentiation, the task shifts to that of acknowledging differences among the members, a process accompanied by confrontation and turmoil. Divergent Role behavior challenges the consensus and focuses upon dissimilarities between members, adding considerably to the information available for group work. Cautionary Role members may misinterpret this friction as attack and express a desire to withdraw from the group. The possibility of system disintegration produced by Divergent and Cautionary Role performances stimulates "positive" Sociable and Structural Role behavior to counterbalance the threat. Under these circumstances it is easy to lose sight of the contribution being made by the "negative" Divergent and Cautionary Roles, whose behavior forces self-revelation.

Stage 3, Individuation, is characterized by active self-exploration as members address the task of arriving at a deeper appreciation of the internal complexity of each other. The trust characteristic of Sociable Role members allows them to lead in self-revelation. These members provide empathy and support, encouraging similar self-exploration by others. Structural and Divergent Role behaviors force a critical examination of these self-revelations by providing alternative points of view and preventing premature closure. At the same time Cautionary Role behavior is helpful by ensuring that the process does not proceed too rapidly and by reminding members of the importance of maintaining control.

As the group develops beyond Stage 3, role behaviors become less polarized and members demonstrate greater role flexibility. The task of Stage 4, Intimacy, is to apply the increased knowledge of self and others to group interaction through an exploration of the complexity of close relationships. Sociable Role members lead this process initially, but as they become aware of the demands of intimacy and fearful of its implications their enthusiasm wanes. Members displaying Structural Role behaviors experience difficulty with the affective openness of this stage and attempt to divert the interaction prematurely into cognitive terms. This search for meaning, however, remains important, helping to reinterpret experiences into understanding and thus consolidating the process of change. Those who adopt the Cautionary Role find this stage particularly difficult. The demands for interpersonal commitment heighten their sense of vulnerability leading to thoughts of premature termination. Divergent Role members have consistently shown a desire for openness and therefore respond positively to these opportunities. At the same time, the behavior of those who occupy this role may be interpreted by others as abrasive and distancing and indeed such members frequently have a personal history of unsatisfactory attempts at intimacy. Successful passage through Stage 4 is thus particularly satisfying for them and their involvement is of value to the group because it ensures that group events are seen from multiple perspectives.

The central task of Stage 5 is the development of mutual responsibility. Behaviors associated with all roles play an important part in this process. If members are to achieve interactional maturity, they must be able to show greater behavioral flexibility, adopting different role activities with increasing facility and comfort. Just as later stages merge gradually into each other making transitions less easily identifiable, so roles are less conspicuous because the behavior of each individual reflects a more subtle blending of all role dimensions. Nevertheless these behaviors continue to have functional significance for the system. Those who have found the Sociable Role particularly compatible with their personality come to recognize that interpersonal relationships are complex and inevitably involve ambivalence. Those in the Structural Role learn to experience and appreciate an open emotional dimension to relationships. Cautionary Role members develop a tolerance for closeness and learn that it need not be overwhelming, so that they can be a member of the collectivity without loss of individuality. Divergent Role members learn to modulate their confrontive stance so that it becomes stimulating rather then damaging to relationships.

Sociable Role members generally have the most difficulty at termination because of their high sense of engagement in the system and dependence on it. They help monitor cohesion and thus prevent the group from fragmenting prematurely, forcing members to deal with termination. The high engagement of these members leads them to emphasize the importance of the group, thus ensuring incorporation of the group experience as positive and meaningful. This counterbalances the danger that difficulties with separation will color the entire experience negatively. Structural Role behavior, with its focus on task accomplishment, helps to link intra-group learning with everyday circumstances. Those who occupy this role are able to see beyond the group and are therefore able to help all members gain perspective on the group experience, although they themselves will tend to avoid the affective aspects of termination. Cautionary Role members provide a model for autonomous functioning by challenging the fantasy that "there is no life after group." Divergent Role members most clearly express the anger and sense of betrayal lurking within all members.

SUMMARY

This brief presentation of developmental stages and social roles provides a model for understanding the structure of the therapy group. Against this background structure of interactional process a wide variety of specific content themes will be expressed. Both the stage and role descriptions are to some exent idealized. Stages are ways of dividing what is, in reality, a continuously evolving system so as to make it comprehensible by comparing and contrasting the patterns that predominate at different times. In actual practice, progress may not be unidirectional but move back and forth in response to the stress of working on difficult issues or membership change. Social roles can be understood as behaviors critical to group development as well as expressions of personality traits. Any one member may show a mixture of these role behaviors. From the standpoint of group development, the critical factor is the summative presence of each role behavior within the total membership. The stage/role model provides an overall perspective of group events which has been found useful in training and supervision. An additional benefit is that it provides a description of group events which is open to empirical examination.

REFERENCES

1. Bales, R.F. The equilibrium problem in small groups. *In:* T. Parsons, R.F. Bales, and E.A. Shils (Eds.), *Working Papers in the Theory of Action.* Glencoe, IL: The Free Press, 1953.
2. Beck, A.P. Phases in the development of structure in therapy and encounter groups. *In:* D.A. Wexler and L.N. Rice (Eds.), *Innovations in Client-Centered Therapy.* New York: John Wiley, 1974.
3. Beck, A.P., and Peters, L. The research evidence for distributed leadership in therapy groups. *Internat. J. Group Psychother.,* 31: 43-71, 1981.
4. Biddle, B.J. *Role Theory: Expectations, Identities and Behaviors.* New York: Academic Press, 1979.

5. Hurley, J.R. Two interpersonal dimensions relevant to group and family therapy. *In:* L.R. Wolberg and M.L. Aronson (Eds.), *Group and Family Therapy 1980.* New York: Brunner/Mazel, 1980.
6. Luft, J. *Group Processes: An Introduction to Group Dynamics.* Palo Alto, CA.: National Press, 1970.
7. MacKenzie, K.R. The concept of role as a boundary structure in small groups. *In:* J.E. Durkin (Ed.), *Living Groups: Group Psychotherapy and General System Theory.* New York: Brunner/Mazel, 1981.
8. Newcomb, T.M. Role behaviors in the study of individual personality and of groups. *J. Personality,* 18: 273-289, 1950.
9. Schaeffer, E.S. Converging conceptual models for maternal behavior and for child behavior. *In:* J.C. Glidewell (Ed.), *Parental Attitudes and Child Behavior.* Springfield, IL: Charles C. Thomas, 1961.
10. Tuckman, B.W. Developmental sequence in small groups. *Psychol. Bull.,* 63: 384-399, 1965.
11. Wiggins, J.S. A psychological taxonomy of trait descriptive terms: I. The interpersonal domain. *J. Pers. Soc. Psychol.,* 37: 395-412, 1979.

Group Therapy With
Special Patient Populations

Chapter X

A THERAPEUTIC COMMUNITY SETTING DESIGNED TO PROVIDE TRANSITIONAL CLINICAL SERVICES TO THE SEVERELY MENTALLY DISTURBED

Fernando D. Astigueta, M.D.

Editors' Summary. The author describes a program of modified psychoanalytic group psychotherapy integrated with pharmacotherapy within a therapeutic community milieu for the treatment of severely mentally disturbed individuals. The introduction of the group history, a written record of each session (similar to minutes) read aloud at the beginning of each successive session, mirrors the interactions and disclosures of the group members. Primitive defense mechanisms and social maladjustment as witnessed by the group members are interpreted, clarified, and worked through from session to session. The focus is shifted to events or interactions occurring within the temporal and spatial boundaries of the group or other places where the members meet.

THE THERAPEUTIC COMMUNITY MEDICAL MEETING

The therapeutic community medical meeting consists of a weekly 60-minute group session composed of the entire staff and about 15 to 25 patients. The therapeutic activity consists of a combination of modified contemporary psychoanalytic group psychotherapy, psychopharmacology, and reinforcement techniques. Meetings begin with the reading of the written summary (22) of the previous session to promote continuity. The collected written summaries comprise the group history.

Patients are enabled to relive or relieve their maladaptive functioning through interaction in the therapeutic community setting. Medication is integrated into the technique in distinct ways. First and foremost, it relieves many of the patients' symptoms through manipulation of their chemical environment. This enhances their interaction in the group and their ability to discover and rehearse ways to improve their level of functioning. Second, both prescribed and nonprescribed medications are discussed. The effects on the central nervous system are explained. An attempt is made to thoroughly inform patients about chemical effectiveness, target symptoms, and adverse effects with both short- and long-term therapy. Patients are warned by both the staff and peers of the consequences of failing to take their prescribed medication and of the dangerous outcome of medication abuse and self-medication.

In the therapeutic community medical meetings, patients and therapists enter the therapy room together. The therapists and patients are seated in a circle in order to have a complete view of one another. If one of the members is late or absent, the discussion moves to this topic in order to set up the norm of punctual attendance. The most characteristic way of starting the session is by reading the summary of the prior meeting. This seems to produce a sense of continuity and a feeling of being cared for by the therapists. All staff members call the patients by their first names and invite them to reciprocate. The purpose of this is to lessen the vertical or authority vector while at the same time increasing the horizontal (21) or peer vector. These patients are often latently fearful of, or antagonistic towards authority (9, 14). They behave either submissively or are covertly defiant by missing sessions, by being late, or by misusing or not taking medication. Prescriptions are written out during the middle of the session once the interaction is in progress.

The psychiatrist listens attentively and prescribes medication without interrupting the group process. He needs to make himself almost invisible, metaphorically speaking, to discourage direct questioning. The staff maintains the flow of interaction as much as possible within the framework of the here and now. When moments of silence occur the theme of medication is brought back either didactically or to foster interaction. In this manner staff and clients together (17) are able to impart and receive information on the course of treatment and the effectiveness, inadequacy, or toxicity of medication. At the same time intrapsychic, but primarily interpersonal and group phenomena become discernible.

THE GROUP HISTORY

Every group has a history (2) based on the events that have occurred since its formation. A group also has a prehistory established by members who are no longer in the group. The written summary of the previous session read at the beginning of the therapeutic community medical meeting describes the highlights of the preceding session. The collected summaries chronicle the group history. The process of recording, reading, and saving the summaries provides continuity and structure. Each of the medication groups has its own unique history which is used as a confrontational screen for different behaviors displayed by the members over the course of its meetings. The summaries crystallize the observations made about group interaction. They focus on verbal and nonverbal communication (5), seating arrangements, tones of voices, postures, noises, interruptions, and every point that the recorder has detected. While he or she reads, the group members listen with the utmost attention, at times smiling, grunting, nodding, protesting, or adding comments. All of these reactions are carefully introduced into the narrative as part of the group history.

The group history, as it is presented and has developed, increases the participants' awareness of their own interactions, their repetitive patterns of behavior, their assets, and their vulnerabilities. As usually happens within the confines of cohesive groups, all the characterological manifestations of the members come to the surface repeatedly.

The group history also serves the important purpose of preventing disclosure of painful material from the personal history of each individual member. Members are afraid, and rightfully so, that the intrusion into their personal lives would be disruptive to their emotional stability. They do not want to have their secrets exposed. These are dealt with quite adequately and willingly in their individual or small supportive group sessions. In addition, fears of breached confidentiality permeate the group atmosphere, and basic assumptions mainly of the fight-flight (7) type emerge preventing the group work from continuing. Particular skill is required to effectively reinstill an atmosphere conducive to dispassionate self-observation and constructive feedback. Instead of utilizing personal history as in traditional psychoanalytic group psychotherapy, with exploration and working-through of member-to-leader and peer-to-peer transferences, we turn back to the genetic material of the group-as-a-whole and the individual behavior observed since the beginning of membership. Interpersonal distortions (19) are analyzed in the group context relating mostly to manifest behavior of the individuals in the group. Intimate material is seldom disclosed and discouraged if presented. Patients are referred to previous analogous events which took place in the group setting. This technique allows for full participation of all members who, having witnessed past events, signal what is appropriate in terms of group norms and standards.

Some examples will illustrate the above. L. is a young man in his early thirties who is concurrently attending a methadone clinic, and who is highly popular among his peers for his honesty and knowledge about drugs. One day he attended the meeting staggering and with slurred speech. A., a borderline woman, confronted him with his evident drug abuse. L. became anxious, angry, and started to deny this, but subsequently did admit to buying drugs on the street. He was amazed that he was not to be expelled from the group as had happened previously at other facilities. After six months he is no longer abusing drugs, and ready to enter more structured rehabilitation services or to return to school.

R., age 24 and diagnosed paranoid schizophrenic, was afraid to divulge "personal secrets" to other group members who were "as sick as he was." During the second session of the group he noticed that others had problems similar to his and voiced his feelings of persecution. He is now an active member of the group and has a part-time job. He is also grateful that his past personal problems were not raised within the group and that he can contribute with his observations from sessions in order to help himself and others.

B., age 26 and hospitalized several times, always felt badly treated in groups. She experienced them as a personal intrusion. In this group, where no mention is made of personal affairs, she had begun to identify with others and to benefit from the sessions.

One one occasion, G., a staff therapist, asked the group for help in dealing with one of the members whom he was treating individually. Several clients offered him information which enabled him to improve her treatment. The patient, herself, a manipulative drug abuser, laughed at G.'s ingenuity but became more amenable to therapy.

These examples demonstrate the effectiveness of working with here-and-now material and with group history employed as a collective mirror. As illustrated above, this appears to be an effective way of dealing with vulnerable patients who lack sufficient trust to disclose personal and family history. A sense of cohesiveness prevails in the group where members and staff candidly interact with warmth, empathy, and humor.

The therapeutic community medical meeting has the following purposes:

1) To transmit and receive medication information with patients and staff present.

2) To enhance, accelerate, and moderate communication between patients and staff using the theme of behavioral information as a vehicle for that particular purpose.

3) To establish a therapeutic milieu where the director of the program, the program coordinator, supervisors, students, and patients are all visibly exposed to one another.

4) To promote the emergence of both adaptive and maladaptive behavior in order to praise the former and discourage the latter. At this point the group history becomes a therapeutic confrontational screen when maladaptive behaviors and/or negative interactions are reiterated session after session.

5) To foster the formation of small groups by selecting those members whose functioning in the larger groups makes them likely candidates for a more intensive form of therapy.

6) To reorient relationships from leader-centered to group-centered interaction. This is necessary in order to alleviate the all too frequent occurrence of traumatic separations when a therapist leaves the clinic.

7) To teach and render services simultaneously. This conserves lost therapeutic time incurred by patients' absenteeism and by the inexperience of some caseworkers.

The following summary will illustrate the first 75-minute session and the subsequent half-hour post-group staff discussion.

GROUP SESSION

Seven patients and seven staff members were seated in a circle. One of the staff members opened the meeting by explaining the purpose of the group. The group was set up to provide and exchange information on medication being taken by each of the participants. A chart depicting the different psychotropic drugs was displayed on the floor. The patients were invited to identify their medication. Patients and staff members readily started to interact, mentioning names of drugs, doses, personal symptoms, and side effects. Whenever silence occurred, a staff member intervened by pointing out which patients were taking the same medication to establish a common bond. One patient said that there was a "chemistry some people have in common which makes them alike or sympathize with one another." A., a seductive, rapidly self-disclosing member, made a revelation about her sex life. A moment of tense silence followed which was ended by returning to the framework of discussing medication.

This same member, calling the doctor "cute," asked for sleeping pills. Her medication was not helping so she had to take her mother's Valium. Other members were also asked for their opinion. M., a young man, said that A.'s request was quite valid and that she should be given the medication. Others supported him, saying that they took Thorazine which was helpful for sleeping. Another young man, J., said he was doing an experiment with Thorazine, i.e., taking different doses on different days. A., again testing the doctor's authority in her usual provocative and seductive manner, again called this member "cute," while, at the same time, insisting on obtaining her sleeping pills and permission to have a glass of wine. She was directing herself to the doctor who was writing the prescriptions. The other members were watching the doctor as though awaiting word from him regarding A.'s request. The doctor felt placed in a double bind situation (4). It would be dangerous to let her take sleeping pills and wine, but if he didn't let her, he could be seen as a domineering and controlling authority. Because the session was coming to an end, this matter was put off for further discussion either in individual session or group meetings. At this point one of the staff members asked the group about their reactions to this first session. Most of them expressed satisfaction: It had not been as boring as they thought it would be. J. had a fantasy of the doctor addressing a mass of people through a loudspeaker and giving out medication. Others expressed the desire to form small groups where they would be able to talk about other matters besides medication.

STAFF MEETING AFTER THE GROUP SESSION

Staff members were enthusiastic about the session. They found it lively and therapeutic. Some felt that one or two of the silent members would not return. Others remarked that the session had revealed another dimension of the patients. There were different interactions than in the "one-to-one" interview. One of them described how, that same morning, he had had an individual session where both patient and therapist, sitting face-to-face, remained in silence for an extended period of time. Another also mentioned how medication could be used as a vehicle of communication which both enhanced and facilitated the interaction of members. For instance, A., who has the proclivity to reveal intimate information in an immediate and almost shocking manner, could be guided and reoriented just by bringing her back to the original topic of discussion. It is true that other themes were presented and could have been explored, i.e., relationship between mother and daughter, stealing, the therapist seen as omnipotent and frightening, the infringement on moral and social orders of behavior, and the desire to submit to and to defy authority. However, it was considered prudent not to deal with any of these themes at this point because it was the first session. Furthermore, the author wanted to test this new approach of combining the therapeutic community milieu, the teaching (6) of a difficult therapeutic modality, and the utilization of medication in a manner far beyond its pharmacotherapeutic implications.

The staff also have the opportunity to explore issues of countertransference among themselves and with patients. This makes it possible to work through conscious and unconscious conflicts occurring within the working unit. Through an open attitude sustained in a nonjudgmental atmosphere, the purpose of working through the interpersonal problems of the staff can be resolved. This process, in turn, becomes a model for the patient (3).

THE GROUP PROGRESS

In the third weekly session a significant event changed the format of the group. Several patients were actively engaged in interacting around issues of separation and feelings of abandonment by their therapists. At one point, J., a 22-year-old paranoid schizophrenic, noticed that one of the staff members was taking notes. Appearing alarmed, he suddenly and firmly addressed the staff member taking notes and asked her purpose. He was concerned about the confidentiality of the notes. He expressed his fears of having outsiders know about his personal secrets. Tense silence followed. At this time the entire group turned to gaze at the doctor with expressions of mistrust, helplessness, and collective embarrassment. This indicated a dependency (7) on the psychiatrist and raised the specter of professional guilt felt by staff members because of concern about possible breach of confidentiality.

Some moments of suspense passed and then the doctor invited the recording staff member to read the notes aloud. The group members appeared to concentrate on hearing what had been written about them. Some members showed signs of delight especially when their names were mentioned. For example, "I didn't know I was doing that," "I like to feel that someone remembers me," and "That was not exactly so." At this point, the atmosphere of tension, fearful anticipation, and general malaise began to disappear. It had competely vanished by the time the reading of the notes was terminated. J. for once, felt happy and satisfied because his inquiry was acknowledged through the openness and immediacy of the readings. Also, he felt he had initiated a norm (18) in the group which would most probably prevail.

The following sessions were structured to include the reading of the notes 10 minutes prior to the end of the sessions. Since the reading of the notes became so valuable, written summaries of the previous session were read at the beginning of the next session. This supplanted the previous procedure. This technique seems now to be an important part of the group culture and greatly assists in adding structure to the meetings. Attendance is high and the interaction, the concern for others, and the sincerity of self-disclosure have increased. The spirit of the meeting is based on the here and now approach (9) coupled with references to previous sessions recorded in the written summaries. The collected written summaries constitute the group history which is used as a confrontational screen to signal repetitive maladaptive behavior. Individual histories are discouraged in order to prevent the leakage of ''top secrets'' or the emergence of monopolizers (8).

OPERATIONAL TECHNIQUE

The validity of the group history as a confrontational screen becomes enhanced by the utilization of feedback. This technique represents one of the major therapeutic interventions in this type of group for this population. Feedback, when positive, genuine and adaptive, is reinforced and encouraged by the staff. It also serves the purpose of avoiding or mitigating pernicious confrontations. The success in developing trust and therapeutic alliance through group work is enhanced by three factors: 1) The therapists are randomly intermixed sitting in a large circle with the patients; 2) the interaction is framed in a nonjudgmental atmosphere; and 3) appropriate feedback (11) is wisely guided and preferably comes from the patients themselves. The therapist is already aggrandized by the patients' idealized transference (12) and therefore needs to be aware not to perpetuate this omnipotent and omniscient role (10) at the patients' expense. The fact that peers are listening, observing, and interacting enables those involved to feel they are knowledgeable. Peers can also set limits. A comment such as, "You are doing it again," serves to remind the member that he or she is proceeding, once again, in a counterproductive manner which has already been documented in the group history. This observation allows the member to become aware of a new and fruitful realization which stimulates the observing ego toward future productive work. This situation does clearly indicate, however, that certain patients in this large group setting persist in reenacting, over and over again, the archaic and repetitive role originally acquired in the course of their early psychosocial development (15).

S., who takes non-prescribed and illegal drugs as well as prescribed medication, always tries to engage the psychiatrist in prescribing some new medication for her chronic insomnia and her other symptoms. She constantly interrupts the group process in an attempt to obtain stronger medication. She gives the impression that nothing is ever enough, that her needs are unique in comparison to those of others and should be satisfied immediately. Her personal adaptation consists of disregarding the needs of other members in the group. The individuals who compulsively repeat the same egocentric behavioral pattern in this group setting are those who alienate others in everyday life and who react by feeling victimized by the injustices perpetrated upon them.

They feel strongly that any criticism or rejection is absolutely unfounded. They are unable to see the provocative aspects of their own conduct manifested by characterological, hostile, or uncaring attitudes about other people's rights or feelings. These individuals possess a "blind window" (13) in their view of themselves similar to a psychological scotoma (16). A positive group relationship allows for sufficient trust to permit reflective self-observation and insight. These mechanisms are initially perceived by staff members and then by the patients themselves who provide a series of observing egos to supplement the impaired one of the member in question. This is a difficult process since any criticism of behavior may be viewed as rejection or condemnation by the group. The patient may fight this process via denial, displacement, further projection (20), splitting, angry outbursts, statements about leaving the group, and actual flight from treatment. He projects himself from the anxiety and impending depression which follows the introjection of the "bad self-object" (1) and the consequent lowering of self-esteem. If the positive group relationship provides sufficient security and support, he is capable of working through self-damaging behavior in either the group or individual sessions. The patient will eventually give up the rigid archaic self by developing a greater differentiation of self and object and a more flexible character structure.

This point was illustrated by the previously mentioned situation regarding A., who after 10 sessions, is seen seated calmly in her chair, interacting readily with the other members in the group and no longer compulsively demanding more potent sleeping pills. This process allows differentiation of the external real object from the internalized representations of infantile objects which previously were projected on the group members or the therapist. Thereafter, by virtue of the group work (7), the individual realizes the fundamental basis of his external maladaptive behavior in the "there and then" of the real world. This liberating effort brought about by the staff and group members establishes a strengthening of the immature ego. It provides such accomplishments as individuation, insight, improved reality-testing, increased self-esteem, and an improved capacity to relate to others. The individual in question now sees other members as helpers and realizes that help is coming not only from the omnipotent and omniscient therapist, but also from his peers. The latter view of the therapist is frequently dominant in the dyadic situation or when the group is in the early stages of development and the therapist is central in the interaction.

The entire staff have facilitated and enhanced the feedback process by their role-modeling (6), and through their encouraging members to act honestly, spontaneously, and responsibly. These interventions are received as ego-supportive by members, thereby enhancing ego-functioning and structuralization.

The writer would like to affirm that unit staff have developed an awareness of the value of groups as transitional objects ready to absorb separation traumas due to the rotation of therapists. Patient fears of being abandoned by the therapist are reduced. Members know that the group will remain together analogous to a new family stronger than the family of origin. In this setting the group members learn to confide in each other in a way that was not feasible in the original family. The feelings of being listened to, remembered (through the reading of written summaries) and missed when absent makes patients feel wanted and cared for by both members and staff.

SUMMARY

A new program for the treatment of the severely mentally ill integrating several different therapeutic approaches has been described. This program is considered holistic because, for each patient, staff members concern themselves with the personality, the social milieu, and biochemical considerations.

Individual, group, milieu, and behavioral therapy together with pharmacotherapy are administered in an integrated fashion. This works to produce optimal communication between workers and patients.

The special format of the teaching aspect of this unit, where intern-therapists remain for only nine months, generates frequent issues of separation trauma and loss. In order to alleviate the potentially serious consequences, much emphasis has been put on group modalities which tend to absorb and contain the possibilities of unfortunate outcome, such as psychotic decompensations and rehospitalizations, as well as other therapeutic calamities such as dropping out of therapy. Only a very small number of rehospitalizations have occurred since the beginning of this program one year ago. Rehospitalized patients have remained in contact with their therapist until their return to the unit upon discharge.

The unit also acts as a transitional milieu for further referral and disposition to other facilities capable of providing more insight-oriented therapeutic approaches.

The most significant event for the unit is the therapeutic community medical meeting. This is where all patients and staff gather together twice weekly for an hour and fifteen minutes to discuss issues of medication, behavioral changes, and all matters concerned with their functioning in and out of the therapeutic environment. This meeting focuses primarily on the here and now of the session taking place as well as the here and now of the preceding sessions. The sum total of these meetings contains the group history which is used therapeutically through the reading of written summaries at the beginning of each session. This technique is aimed at pointing out repetitive maladaptive behavior. These behaviors are then subject to change through the medium of constructive feedback provided by both the staff and group members.

The patients learn to understand the medication they receive: how it acts in the central nervous system, the symptoms that are being treated, and the side effects produced. The weekly prescriptions are written out during the session by the psychiatrist in accordance with his assessment of the symptoms or pathology emerging during the interaction. Very personal individual problems are not appropriate for discussion in this meeting. These are discussed in the individual sessions or small group meetings especially designed for more intensive and personal psychotherapy.

It appears from the low rehospitalization rate and the qualitatively improved condition of many of the patients that this approach is effective in stabilizing some cases within a disruptive and often resistant population. Further implications of this innovative treatment method remain to be explored.

REFERENCES

1. Asch, S.E. Effects of group pressure upon modification and distortion of judgements. *In:* G.E. Swanson, T.M. Newcomb and E.L. Harley (Eds.), *Readings in Social Psychology.* 2nd Edition. New York: Holt, 1952, pp. 2-11.

2. Astigueta, F.D. The use of nicknames in delineating character patterns in group psychotherapy. Presentation to the annual meeting of the Golden Gate Group Psychotherapy Society, San Francisco, 1968.

3. Bandura, A. Modelling approaches to the modification of phobic disorders. Presented at the Ciba Foundation Symposium, *The Role of Learning in Psychotherapy*, London, 1968.

4. Bateson, G., Jackson, D.D., Haley, J., and Weakland, J. Toward a theory of schizophrenia. *Behavioral Science*, 1: 251-264, 1956.

5. Berger, M. Non-verbal communications in group psychotherapy. *Int. J. Group Psychother.*, 8: 161, 178, 1958.

6. Bernard, V.W. Education for community psychiatry in University Medical Center. *In:* L. Bellak (Ed.), *Handbook of Community Psychiatry and Community Mental Health*. New York, London: Grune and Stratton, 1964, pp. 82-122.

7. Bion, W. *Experience in Group and Other Papers*. New York: Basic Books, 1959.

8. Durkin, H. Analysis of character traits in group therapy. *Int. J. Group Psychother.*, 1: 133-143, 1951.

9. Ezriel, H. A psychoanalytic approach to group treatment. *Brit. J. Med. Psychol.*, 123: 59-74, 1950.

10. Freud, S. (1938) Splitting of the ego in the process of defence. *Standard Edition*, 23: 273-278. London: Hogarth Press, 1964.

11. Glatzer, H.T. Treatment of oral character neurosis in group psychotherapy. *In:* C. Sager and H. Singer Kaplan (Eds.), *Progress in Group and Family Therapy*. New York: Brunner/Mazel, 1972.

12. Kohut, H. *The Analysis of the Self*. New York: International Universities Press, 1971.

13. Luft, J. *Of Human Interaction*. Palo Alto: National Press Books, 1969.

14. Milgram, S. *Obedience to Authority*. New York: Harper & Row, 1973.

15. Parsons, T. Social structure and the development of personality, Freud's contribution to the integration of psychology and sociology. *In: Social Structure and Personality*. London: The Free Press, 1964, pp. 78-111.

16. Pichon Riviere, E. Personal communication, 1955.

17. Rubenstein, R., and Lasswell, H.D. *The Sharing of Power in a Psychiatric Hospital*. New Haven & London: Yale University Press, 1966.

18. Sherif, M. Group influences upon formation of norms and attitudes. *In:* E.E. Maccoby, T.M. Newcomb, and E.L. Hartley (Eds.), *Readings in Social Psychology*. New York: Holt, Rinehart & Winston, 1958, pp. 219, 232.

19. Sullivan, H.S. *The Interpersonal Theory of Psychiatry*. New York: Norton, 1953.

20. Wolberg, A. Group therapy and the dynamics of projective identification. *In:* L. Wolberg, M. Aronson, and A. Wolberg (Eds.), *Group Therapy 1977: An Overview*. New York: Stratton Intercontinental Medical Book, 1977, pp. 151-180.

21. Wolf, A. The psychoanalysis of group. *In:* H.M. Ruitenbeeck (Ed.), *Group Therapy Today*. Chicago: Aldine-Atherton Press, 1969, pp. 92-93.

22. Yalom, I.D. The Theory and Practice of Group Psychotherapy. New York: Basic Books, 1970, pp. 70-104, 440-441.

Chapter XI

CHANGING ASPECTS OF THE FAMILY: AN ANALYTIC PERSPECTIVE ON GROUP WORK WITH SINGLE MOTHERS OF OEDIPAL CHILDREN

Ava L. Siegler, Ph.D.

Editors' Summary. This paper explores the function of the family, mother-child reciprocities in the absence of the father, and special demands which are placed upon the single mother from the psychoanalytic point of view. Group intervention models are presented to meet the needs of these mothers to replace the "family circle" (so strikingly missing in the lives of such women) with the "group circle." Particular transference and countertransference problems implicit in the formation and operation of these groups for the unique population are examined.

In New York City alone, more than 100,000 single working mothers are raising children under six years of age. They represent the growing trend toward single-parent families noted in the past decade (13). The majority are *not* middle-class women who choose to work, or who return to work after a divorce (bolstered by household help, child support payments, and the father's weekend visits with the children). Most are women who *must* work, because they are the sole support of their families. The fathers are unlikely to be available as emotional, social, or financial partners. The mothers must face the complex responsibilities of parenthood alone. The frenetic rhythms of urban life often intensify feelings of uncertainty, apprehension, and isolation, and these women may feel caught in a web of tangled stresses.

For many of these mothers, the day care system provides an alternative to transient caretakers, unreliable family arrangements, or, in some cases, locking a child in the apartment while the mother goes to work. When a psychological problem arises, these mothers are least likely to take advantage of mental health facilities because of a lack of knowledge, time, or finances. Often, their children do not attract the attention of any specific child advocacy group: They are neither psychotic, nor retarded, nor physically handicapped, nor orphaned. Yet they frequently suffer from a wide range of emotional and cognitive difficulties.

When these mothers and their children came to my attention, the need to study the problems of this special population and to create an intervention program that would provide psychological support for these families became apparent. It light of this, an early intervention pilot project was developed within a day care center in Manhattan. This center serves a multi-ethnic group of working parents, 80% of whom are young mothers raising a single child, alone. Roughly 65 three- to six-year-olds are enrolled in the preschool nursery and kindergarten program. The project offers direct, on-site psychological services to the families at the day care center.

Group intervention models were developed that were based on psychoanalytic developmental ego psychology (5, 9, 23). The aim of these models was to understand the function of the family, the nature of mother-child interactions in the absence of the father, and the special demands placed upon the single mother during the oedipal phase of development.

THE FUNCTION OF THE FAMILY

It is the family that forges the links between character and culture. Through family interactions and patterns the child's personality is fashioned. Though family composition and style vary in accord with class and geographic differences, family function—socialization of its young—remains the same.

According to psychoanalytic theory, the family's cultural task is accomplished through a series of complex object relations and object representations established in early childhood, and crystallized by the outcome of normal oedipal struggles between parents and child (3, 7, 16). It follows, then, that alterations in family structure, whether caused by individual or cultural variables, will resound and reverberate throughout development.

In our culture in this century, the dominant family structure has been the nuclear family (that is, the family containing a father, a mother, and more than one child.) However, the absence of a father in the child's formative years, and the presence of a working mother have become an increasing reality since World War II (2, 11, 13, 18). While many observers are alarmed about the social and economic effects of "fatherlessness," little research exists that either documents the psychic consequences of this altered family structure or examines the psychic resources that mothers and their children rely on in order to cope with such a loss.

MOTHER-CHILD RECIPROCITIES IN THE ABSENCE
OF THE FATHER

The existing analytic literature that discusses the one-parent family has emphasized the potentially destructive effects of the father's absence on the development of the child (11, 14, 16). Most writers focus their concern upon the pre-oedipal and oedipal distortions that are inherent in this altered family structure and maintain that the presence of both parents is essential to a satisfactory oedipal outcome. Over 20 years ago, Neubauer blamed "the lack of oedipal stimulation, normally found in the continuous day-to-day interplay between the child and each parent, and especially as evidenced by the relationship of the parents to each other" for causing what he called "a primary imbalance" (16). It is obvious that the continuous day-to-day interplay between the child and the parent, and between the parents themselves, is a widely varying exchange influenced by many factors, some of which have nothing to do with the actual physical presence of the father.

In our clinical investigations we repeatedly found that the effects of the father's absence on the child's development are determined by the ways in which the *mother experiences and defines this event for the child*. Mothers have countless ways of keeping the image of the father alive, or conversely, destroying his image, if that is their wish. While there is no question that it makes a difference if a child is raised in the absence of a father, the more interesting question focuses on what difference it makes.

The meaning of the loss of the father in both the life of the mother and the life of the child depends on whether the loss was incurred through death, illness, separation, divorce or abandonment.

Many of the families studied in the project experienced a severe rejection concurrent with object loss. Many of the young mothers were abandoned by the biological father of the child before or shortly after the baby's birth. Other fathers left later. In charting the course of mother-child interactions during the father's absence, the following variables were found to be critical:

1) personality and level of maturity of the mother;
2) sex of the child;
3) age and developmental stage of the child when the father left the home;
4) existence of other supports for the family at the time of the loss of father;
5) degree to which the father remained available to the family after the separation;
6) mother's experience of her partnership with the father, and her reaction to his departure;
7) child's experience of the father and reaction to the loss;
8) mother's capacity to explain the father's departure to the child;
9) mother's understanding of the special stresses associated with single parenthood.

A descriptive profile, drawn from experiences with these mothers may be helpful in conveying the impact of raising a child alone.

All of the mothers in the project had considerable difficulty being a single parent. They were deeply concerned about the developmental implications that the lack of a father was likely to have upon their child, and this was especially noted in the mothers of male children. Even those mothers who had made new and steady alliances with another man felt some apprehension about the fact that, "It can't be the same. . . . I mean he's not his *real* father."

Those women who had not made a new alliance often felt torn between their wish to act sensitively, responsibly, and knowledgeably about their children, and their desires to have a life of their own, to seek out a new male partner. They were acutely aware of the intensity of their bond to their child. One mother expressed the ties this way: "Tommy and me are a matched set, you know, you can't break us apart." The mothers would often choose relationships with men that were based upon the man's capacity to display affection and protection toward their child. The connection to such a man was often maintained in the face of clearly expressed dissatisfaction with him on other grounds: "He's not what I want in a man, but I hate to leave him because he's good to the baby."

For most of the women, the early years of infant care had been difficult and demanding. They were usually quite young when the baby was born, and the birth itself had often been an unexpected and/or unwelcome event in their lives, interrupting their late-adolescent search for identity and intimacy. Despite the abrupt onset of parenthood, most of the mothers in the project described a surge in self-esteem when they became parents. They felt that they were necessary to the baby, and indeed, many believed themselves capable of being responsible parents at this point, even in the absence of the father.

THE SPECIAL TASK OF THE MOTHER DURING OEDIPAL DEVELOPMENT

Interestingly enough, many mothers began to experience increased apprehension about raising the child alone during the onset of the oedipal years. This differed from the confidence in their capacity to be a "good-enough" mother that they had felt when the child was younger.

Their increased anxiety seemed to signal their own awareness on some level of the psychic meaning of the oedipal triangle, and their recognition that it was going to be particularly difficult to negotiate this phase of development *alone*. Their concerns clustered remarkably about the issues that are recognized as crucial to oedipal resolutions:

1) *Sexual differentiation and the development of sexual identity:* e.g., "Will my son grow up to be homosexual with no man around?"
2) *Object choice:* e.g., "My daughter goes to any man on the subway and asks him to be her daddy. Isn't that bad for her?"

3) *Superego formation:* e.g., "I really worry that with no man around, he won't learn to listen," and "I try to be really tough on the kids, so they'll have self-control and respect for me, because I'm alone."

4) *The crystallizing of ego ideals:* e.g., "I don't know what to tell him about his father. I mean, when he was little it didn't matter, but now he asks me all the time. Was he good or bad?" and "Her father is a real bastard. He never sees her except to give her an expensive toy so he can feel like a big shot, while I pay the bills. But I'm afraid to tell her the truth, 'cause he is her father."

The parent of an oedipal age child must disengage him- or herself from the child's seductive attempts to include the parent in the fulfillment of erotic desires (1, 6, 7, 12, 19). To accomplish this, appropriate limitations and restraints must be placed upon the child. In the one-parent family the mother must absorb the entire role of "frustrator." This increases the child's ambivalence toward her. Single mothers often try to delay taking on this restrictive role; or they attempt to shift the responsibility onto a male figure in their lives, even a transient partner. In this way they may succeed in creating a makeshift oedipal triangle. These mothers are often attempting, with whatever resources they have at their disposal, to create a more complete oedipal drama. Additionally, the discrepancy between the pre-oedipal mother who permitted the child to sleep with her as a comfort to both of them, and the oedipal mother who abruptly permits a man to displace the child in her bed, insisting that the child sleep alone, produces bewilderment, sadness, and rage in the oedipal age child.

In normal oedipal phase development (roughly three to six years old) the child would ordinarily become aware of his/her parents as a couple. This perception represents a developmental achievement. Children begin to perceive the triangular nature of their position vis-à-vis the parents in a unique way that emphasizes their exclusion from the parental relationship. That is, their sense of themselves as singular is, in some sense, sychronized and dependent upon a perception of the parents as a couple. The oedipal age child from a one-parent family does not have this perception of "coupling" available in a continuous and reliable manner. Child and mother must therefore compensate for the resultant blind spot in their vision of the oedipal dilemma. They do this by fantasizing about what is missing in reality, so that the shadow of the father falls upon the developmental path.

Both parent and child struggle valiantly to create an exchange between them that will accommodate the surge of impulses that accompany the oedipal phase. How they enter this phase has, of course, already been partially influenced by distorted and unresolved pre-oedipal issues. Nonetheless, development proceeds, integrating old, imperfect resolutions with the new challenges (16, 19). Certain "pairings" between mother and child that represented a type of generalized response to the oedipal dilemma were observed in the project.* They are listed below.

The Erotic Pair. In this coupling, the mother of the child permits and encourages the child's oedipal overtures, while retaining pre-oedipal modes of relating. She feeds the child's fantasy that he or she is, in fact, the mother's one and only love. This pairing has quite different implications with a male child than with a female child, and varies from those rare instances (in our population) of actual incestuous sexual exchange to the milder erotic feelings expressed in the phrase, "He's Mommy's little man."

The Hostile Pair. In these instances, the emerging sexual desires of the oedipal age child are warded off by hostility. The mother mirrors these feelings by displacing hostility from the child's father onto the child (he's a "chip off the old block"); or, the mother may see the child as an externalization of all she finds despicable in herself; or she may victimize the child in an attempt to master her own experience of victimization at the hands of the father. In these cases, the exchanges between mother and child are suffused with anger. For the male child the father's absence as an inhibitor of his desires for the mother often leaves the boy with no defense against the seductive potential of the mother except distance and/or anger. The female child, on the other hand, without a father to turn toward in her mastery of the oedipal dilemma, is left with the anger that is appropriate to this phase as well as her rage at the mother for depriving her of the father, for "getting rid" of him. The strife between girls at this age and their mothers, in the absence of the father who might have moderated their dispute and competition, is striking, and the girls often feel doubly deprived by their mothers.

The Fearful Pair. In this type of interaction, the mother is overwhelmed by her own impulses, and the child identifies with the mother's anxiety. The mother's perception of her fate is informed by dread, fear, and hopelessness, and she sees herself and the child set adrift, without direction, helpless and surrounded by danger. This perception of danger from *without*, reflects the mother and the child's fear of danger from *within*, with regard to the pull of internal impulses. Sometimes children who experience the mother's terror will attempt to take over the role of parent to their own parent and assume a pre-cociousness that can interfere with appropriate ego development. More often, the child shares mother's agitation and loss of functioning, and retreats from the age-appropriate challenges.

---

*These pairings should be seen as types of reactions in extreme form. They are meant for descriptive use only, and should not reduce our sense of the complexity of intrapsychic conflict for either parent or child.

CLINICAL INTERVENTION: THE RATIONALE

With these clinical observations in mind, the need for many of our families to participate in a process that would help them to understand the special demands of their role as parents, the unique difficulties of approaching that role without a partner, and appropriate ways of resolving these special conflicts of oedipal development were made evident. The following propositions underlie the rationale for clinical intervention with these mothers.

1) All actual (i.e., real) events in one's life are uniquely colored by the psychic structures of the mind.
2) These structures bear the individual stamp of character and the developmental limits of mind and memory.
3) There is a body of knowledge assembled by psychoanalytic developmental ego psychology which, like any other body of knowledge, can and should be shared.
4) Most individuals are capable of responding to such knowledge in rational ways, and there are techniques relevant to parent guidance which can increase the capacity of the individual to make use of this knowledge.

It was not known which model would best suit the needs of this population of single working mothers. The group structure seemed most satisfying for several reasons, primarily because it creates a sense of community, something that seemed strikingly absent in the lives of these young mothers. The group circle, it was hoped, could substitute for the family circle. Ekstein supports these thoughts in a paper that described his understanding of the meaning of the loss of the father in our society:

> The lack of identity, the lack of family bonds, the aimlessness that we frequently face today, perhaps can be counteracted in work with and through groups. . . . I would suggest that the helping professions . . . are now the powerful counter-weights in a society which is in danger of becoming a society without a father (4, p. 442).

Mothers in a group would have a safe haven for the open exchange of ideas, feelings, fears, and wishes. Their shared concerns would create bonds between them, and the group could provide a forum for considering changes. The group would also create an opportunity for multiple identifications; on the simplest level, the single mother would no longer have the sense that she stood alone but would realize that her plight was shared by others. By forming therapeutic groups for these women, we hoped to create a facilitating environment (to borrow Winnicott's phase) for the growth of both parent and child (21, 22, 23).

Still to be decided was what type of group would be most helpful to the mothers. Searching through recent literature on groups yielded no references for treatment models for single parents. Despite the fact that single mothers had become such a dominant social phenomenon, they were not treated as a special group in need of special therapeutic strategies, with a rationale separate from women's groups in general.

Several parameters of the proposed group intervention treatment situation seemed clear:

1) The group could not be called a psychotherapy group because of the general reluctance of our population to commit themselves to anything that could be construed as "treatment." (They did not want to be seen as either "sick" or "crazy.")
2) Maintaining the boundaries of the traditional group setting in which the group members had no contact with each other outside of the group would be impossible since our mothers already knew each other from the day care center.
3) Strict confidentiality would be difficult to maintain within the day care center, and therefore personal revelations would have to be carefully monitored, regression discouraged, and transferential manifestations dealt with quickly.
4) The group had to fill not only an emotional need in our population, but a cognitive one as well. It had to provide a forum for the exploration of parent-child relations and offers mothers the benefit of professional guidance on these issues. Therefore, the group leader could be neither passive nor anonymous.

Two types of groups were created to meet the special needs of our single working mothers: the parent guidance group (an ongoing monthly discussion group), which was open to all parents at the center, and had an attendance rate between 10 and 30; and the mothers' group, which was composed of six to nine women (a fixed membership) who met weekly. The larger parent guidance group functioned as both a child development seminar and parent guidance session. The mothers' group embraced aspects of a women's consciousness-raising group and analytic group psychotherapy. Women were placed in the smaller groups according to specific variables including personality, level of education, language skills, capacity for self-reflection, and presenting problems. The mothers' group offered them a chance to analyze experiences that might never have come to light in the larger, more public parent guidance group. Some of these shared vignettes capture the struggles of a single parent with peculiar vividness.

One young woman, for instance, related an incident in which she was trying to force her stubborn four-year-old to wear her sweater under her coat on a bitterly cold day. The battle between them took place in the elevator, in the presence of several other tenants. Finally, in a fury at the child's imperviousness to her reasonable pleas, the young mother said to the child, between clenched teeth, "You put that sweater on, or I'll hurt you!" Whereupon one of the men in the elevator turned to her and said, "You keep that up, and you'll destroy her!" The mother replied, "That may be, mister, but she's mine to destroy."

This particular incident characterized the passion, problems, and possessiveness of being a single parent. The intense rage felt at being solely responsible for raising a young child, having no support when irritable, ill or helpless, can be debilitating. This helplessness is often mitigated by the recognition that the mother is all powerful and critical to the child's existence.

Single mothers are aware of the potential destructiveness of the intense bond they have to their child. The most primitive expression of this is child abuse; a more commonplace manifestation is inconsistency, i.e., overindulgence versus autocratic discipline. Some of our mothers come to the bittersweet realization that it is only with their child that they had found a love that was stable and enduring. Although this extreme emotional investment in the child can have dire consequences for the child's emerging identity, the bond between them, particularly in the absence of other loving relations can also be, as Christopher Lasch (13) has put it, "a haven in a heartless world."

THE THERAPEUTIC ROLE OF THE GROUP LEADER

The Leader as Idealized Parent

The role of the group leader was given careful consideration. We understood that the absence of a father in these women's family lives was likely to intensify their experience with the group leader, investing the leader with some of the idealized aspects of the missing partner. Slavson (20), for instance, has stated that all group therapies provide an opportunity for the therapist to symbolically acquire the authority of the father, while the group itself can be seen as functioning as a nurturant, protective, empathic mother. It was speculated that this symbolic situation might be further intensified in a group made up of mothers without husbands. An additional factor was the reality that many of these very women in the project had experienced parental deprivation in their own childhoods—usually the loss of their own fathers.

The Leader as New Object

Since many of the single mothers had received inadequate or interrupted parental care as children, a goal of parent guidance was to increase the mothers' potential to acquire new responses, to help them transcend the compulsion to repeat their own childhood pain. The group leader offered herself as organizer and confirmer of new responses, and lent herself as an object available for imitation and identification.

As the clinical work progressed, some of the mothers who participated in the program were found to be suffering from borderline, narcissistic, or impulse disorders which impaired their capacities to cope with both their own lives and those of their children. The group was able to offer them a "holding environment" by providing the ongoing support necessary to permit them to nurture their child with less strain. The group leader, then, functioned as an auxiliary ego for the borderline parent with inner feelings of panic and fragmentation. The other group members with more structured egos often helped the less stable members.

Group processes also encouraged the development of frustration tolerance among members. Through the leader's interventions, the member evidenced a slow accumulation of knowledge, frustration tolerance, and insight. Mothers were then able to bring this ego growth to bear upon their relations with their children (8, 9, 10).

The Leader as "Expert"

In the larger parent guidance group, advice was given on the assumption that it could be received in a spirit of rational responsiveness, provided that the limitations of such advice-giving were also confronted and discussed.* Refusal to give any advice, on the basis that it would be subverted by the underlying power of unconscious processes, did not seem pertinent to our group. However, in order for advice to be meaningful, it was necessary to take into account the development level and potential of both parent and child. If carefully timed, as any effective intervention must be, it can parallel the topic being discussed. The group leader tried to resonate the parents' concerns and mirror them in such a way that the mothers could understand their implications in their own lives.

The Leader as a Link With the Past

One of the most vital ways that parents can be helped to identify and empathize with their children is by helping them recall their own past. Therapists

---

*In this attitude, we were guided by Anna Freud (6), who emphasizes that mothers do not have to change their personalities in order to change their handling of their child.

do this with individual patients; what makes a group different is that remembering is a shared experience. One reason that being the parent of the oedipal-age child is so difficult is that the memories associated with this period of development are not available to most of us (7, 17). In fact, theoretically, they are the very memories that are most likely to have been repressed. Consequently, parents of oedipal-age children are most likely to *act out* their oedipal age experiences with their children, instead of *recalling* them. When it is impossible to revive these memories, an attempt is made to construct a narrative from what we know about normative development that somehow resonates with the parents' own experiences. Here the skill of the group leader required the ability to shift gracefully from an educative to a therapeutic role, sensitivity to individual variation in personality, the willingness to share aspects of her own experience in an unobtrusive fashion, and a capacity to create a forum for the safe exploration of conflict.*

THE THERAPEUTIC ROLE OF THE GROUP LEADER: COUNTERTRANSFERENTIAL IMPLICATIONS

I have outlined some of the unique ways in which the group leader can take on transferential meanings in a group composed solely of single mothers of oedipal-phase children. Now I would like to suggest that similar countertransferential pressures are exacerbated in the therapist of such a group.

The Rescue Fantasy

One of the fantasies which is central to the oedipal experience and expresses its dynamics, is the rescue fantasy, a familiar component in the analytic dialogue.

Acknowledging the absence of the father in these families may also draw the group leader into identifying with the child's wish to displace and dispose of the father, to "rescue" Mommy from his "unwanted" attentions and to triumph by replacing him in her affections. Initial feelings of protection toward these mothers can easily become overprotection without sufficient self-knowledge on the part of the therapist. The group leader under the sway of his/her own unconscious desire can present the therapeutic role in this manner: "I will be 'rescuing' these single mothers from their plight by displacing the absent father as a family authority, and I will become the 'missing link' in the oedipal triangle—no one else is necessary."

*This author is greatly indebted to Dr. Carol Michaels, a valued staff member on the project, who has led the mothers' group for several years. Her resourcefulness, sensitivity, and clinical talents have made the success of these groups possible.

Attitudes and Feelings Toward Men

The group leader must also have a great deal of awareness about his/her feelings toward men. Many of these women are enraged and embittered by their experiences at the hands of men. These feelings spill over into any topic which is discussed in group and they are often not balanced by the pleasanter realities of male-female relationships, since many of these mothers have not formed subsequent bonds. A therapist with hostility toward men is unable to help these women to work through these feelings and easily overidentifies with the rage, treating it *only* in its manifestly justified respects, without treating the latent meaning of these communications.

Environmental Stress: The Pull of Manifest Content

Since many of these women are in social situations which elicit enormous sympathy as well as empathy, the clarity of the analytic therapeutic stance can be easily blurred, obscuring important clinical issues including narcissistic pathology, sadomasochistic maneuvers, and underlying depressive states.

Cecilia, an intelligent, soft-spoken, attractive woman from an aristocratic politically active South American family, was struggling with her six-year-old boy, Paulo, the only child of a brief liaison with a man of limited intelligence, background, and means, who had beaten her during their relationship. She felt that she had raised Paulo "to be strong—not to give in to the system—to be anti-establishment." She was an articulate and impassioned defender of the workers' rights. Following avowed Marxist principles, she had indeed produced a "little revolutionary." But she had not bargained for the fact that he was also uncontrollable, agitated, and unable to use his superior intelligence to concentrate and learn.

She had accumulated, since her brief marriage, many tales of the brutality of men, but she was unaware of the ways in which she sought out these men or the powerful role that "identification with the aggressor" played in her life.

She was unaware of the fact that she alternated between identifying with Paulo in his role as a child and permitting him to express her underlying rage at her own brutal and domineering father, and identifying with this same father and cruelly humiliating Paulo, undermining any autonomy and/or self-esteem he tried to attain.

Hearing her story, one could be easily sidetracked into sympathetic expressions of social injustice and political manifestos, losing sight of the powerful influence of intrapsychic struggles upon the patterns of her life and the life of her child.

Everything emphasized in the method and rationale converges with the ultimate goal for this entire therapeutic program, that is, to create and maintain a setting in which it is possible for the single working mother under stress, to identify and explore her conflicts, and to internalize stronger, more effective ego structures. This project hopes to expand the possibilities in these mothers' lives, to combat the pain of the past, and to restore their hope for the future.

REFERENCES

1. Anthony, E. J., and Benedek, T. (Eds.) *Parenthood: Its Psychology and Psychopathology.* Boston: Little, Brown, 1970.
2. Aries, P. *Centuries of Childhood: A Social History of Family Life.* New York: Knopf, 1962.
3. Blanck, R., and Blanck, G. *Ego Psychology: Theory and Practice.* New York: Columbia University Press, 1974.
4. Ekstein, R. The search and yearning for and rebellion against the father. *International Journal of Group Psychotherapy,* 28 (4): 435-444, 1978.
5. Foulkes, S.H., and Anthony, E.J. *Group Psychotherapy: The Psychoanalytic Approach.* Baltimore: Penguin Books, 1957.
6. Freud, A. The child guidance clinic as a center of prophylaxis and enlightenment. *In:* J. Weinreb (Ed.), *Recent Developments in Psychoanalytic Child Therapy.* New York: International Universities Press, 1960.
7. Freud, S. Three essays on the theory of sexuality. *Standard Edition,* 8: 207-300. London: Hogarth Press, 1961.
8. Greenson: R.R. The real relationship between the patient and the psychoanalyst. *In:* M. Kanzer (Ed.), *The Unconscious Today.* New York: International Universities Press, 1971, pp. 213-232.
9. Hampton, P.J. Group work with parents. *American Journal of Orthopsychiatry,* 32: 918-26, 1962.
10. Hartmann, H. *Ego Psychology and the Problem of Adaptation.* New York: International Universities Press, 1958.
11. Isaacs, S. *Fatherless Children, Childhood and After.* New York: International Universities Press, 1949.
12. Kestenberg, J.S. *Children and Parents: Psychoanalytic Studies in Development.* New York: Jason Aronson, 1975.
13. Lasch, C. *Haven in a Heartless World: The Family Besieged.* New York: Basic Books, 1977.
14. Loewald, H.W. Ego and reality. *International Journal of Psychoanalysis* 32: 10-18, 1951.
15. Loewald, H.W. On the therapeutic action of psychoanalysis, *International Journal of Psychoanalysis,* 4: 16-33, 1960.
16. Neubauer, P.B. The one-parent child and his oedipal development. *Psychoanalytic Study of the Child,* 15: 286-309, 1960.
17. Robbins, L. Parental recall of child development practices. *Journal of Abnormal and Social Psychology,* 66: 261-70, 1963.
18. Rutter, M. *The Qualities of Mothering: Maternal Deprivation Reassessed.* New York: Jason Aronson, 1974.
19. Shapiro, T. Oedipal distortions in severe character pathologies: Developmental and theoretical considerations. *Psychoanalytic Quarterly,* 46 (4): 559-579, 1977.
20. Slavson, S.R. *Child-Centered Group Guidance of Parents.* New York: International Universities Press, 1958.
21. Winnicott, D.W. *The Child, the Family and the Outside World.* Baltimore: Penguin Books, 1969.
22. Wolk, H.H., and Call, J.D. *A Guide to Preventive Psychiatry: The Art of Parenthood.* New York: McGraw-Hill, 1965.
23. Yalom, I.D. *The Theory and Practice of Group Psychotherapy.* New York: Basic Books, 1970.

Chapter XII

THE MANAGEMENT OF SCAPEGOATING IN CHILDREN'S GROUP PSYCHOTHERAPY

Edward S. Soo, M.S.

Editors' Summary. The author describes how group dynamics can activate scapegoating phenomena in children's group therapy. He points out that scapegoating may be symptomatic of developmental deficits in certain groups, group transference and countertransference resistances in operation. He presents a number of illustrative clinical examples.

For those of us who are involved in children's group psychotherapy, the phenomenon of scapegoating is a common occurrence. Toker reported scapegoating in an adolescent group directed toward both a member and the therapist. He illustrated the dynamics of scapegoating through the use of the mechanisms of projection and displacement (4). However, little has been reported on the management of scapegoating in children's group psychotherapy.

The issue of scapegoating can be one of the more difficult, anxiety-producing, and painful interactions that confronts a therapist. Many groups have suffered the destructive influences of scapegoating and its antitherapeutic impact upon the group members. It has often resulted in the demise of groups or, at best, it has been counterproductive in the effectiveness of the therapeutic enterprise. If scapegoating is examined more systematically in relation to its function and underlying dynamics, it can be viewed symbolically as a special form of group resistance arising out of the members' transferences to the therapist, multitransferences of the members to each other, and the transference of the group to the therapist. The therapist's reaction to and his/her task in managing scapegoating in children's group psychotherapy is the subject of this paper.

The propensities of children's groups to develop patterns of scapegoating are multifaceted in nature. Some forms of scapegoating are a by-product of group process and group formation rather than simply a reflection of individual or group transferences.

Regardless of the maturational levels of group members, each potential member who is faced with a new group experience is subject to common anxieties. He or she is vulnerable to exposure of weaknesses from members. The explorations of areas of inadequacies by means of "ranking and snapping" are common events in children's groups. The establishment of a "pecking order" is part of the initial process of group formation and forces members to establish relationships and form alignments based on power. Group tensions and conflicts arise as a consequence of the struggles among members to realign and equalize their relationships with each other. Until relationships are equalized within the group, scapegoating may occur in children's groups (3).

It is at this phase of group development that a therapist may perceive the group's alignments represented by scapegoating as "splitting off" into "good" and "bad" members. If he is impelled by his anxiety to respond to this process, then the group's development will be impaired and scapegoating perpetuated. Scapegoating is transitory during this phase and unless it is persistent the therapist's intervention is unnecessary. The persistence of scapegoating is evaluated as a sign of resistance and determines the need for intervention.

A therapist reported on his adolescent boys' group that after a "pecking order" was established, the scapegoating continued. The group's "tough" members were "sounding off" on a member for having effeminate gestures and a high-pitched voice, and accused him of being a "fag." The therapist felt that the scapegoat's behavior was circumstantial and he attempted to defend him. It only increased the scapegoating by the members. The persistence of the scapegoating was investigated.

The therapist presented evidence of members developing positive feelings toward him. It was concluded that the positive transference feelings aroused in the "tough" members were unacceptable to them. These unacceptable feelings were displaced and projected onto a lower echelon member as his being a "fag." When the therapist understood that the group had symbolically placed its concerns about homosexuality on a convenient member, he was able to discuss the highly charged material of homosexuality more openly with the group. The therapist was receptive to each member's questioning about sexual identity and anxieties about homosexuality. The working-through of positive feelings toward the therapist as homosexual ones reduced the boys' anxieties and the need for scapegoating subsided.

Regression is a necessary and desirable condition for therapeutic work in psychoanalytic group psychotherapy. It is easily fostered by the anxiety generated from group process and group formation. The regressive climate of children's group therapy contributes to potential scapegoating. Regression allows for relaxation of ego controls which helps each member reach his level of emotional fixation and functioning. Under the influence of regression, disturbed children with various developmental and emotional deficits will bring with them their unmet needs and pathologies. These will be transformed into conflictual interactions and defensive behaviors for the individual members and the group-as-a-whole.

Children who show lack of impulse controls, inadequate and confused problems of gender and identification, poor self-esteem and self-images, unsuccessful peer relationships, conflicts with parents and other authority figures, and difficulties in learning come to group treatment with a spectrum of emotional deprivations and suppressed hostilities. One can anticipate the projections and displacements of their frustrations and raged feelings upon each other and the therapist. The need for the members and the group-as-a-whole to find an emotional outlet through scapegoating is obvious. Until treatment is developed for the members to find a more appropriate way of expressing hostile aggression, scapegoating will be a primary choice of expression for regressive behavior.

Those children who suffer from incomplete development of object relations and cannot tolerate internalization of the negative self will subject themselves to extensive use of object-splitting as a primary defense. Opportunities are available to every member of the group to be either a target or an agent for the expression of aggression and hostility. Members whose life histories have developed an identification with the aggressor will assume the role of provocateurs, agitators, exploiters, and victimizers. The "hated or emotionally damaged self" which is unacceptable in itself will seek a convenient substitute to displace their anger on the "hated or damaged object" represented by the victim.

Developmental disruption in early childhood can predispose a member to become a victim. Such a child is prone to be submissive and passive in a hostile environment. As a "negative object" he may serve many functions of projection and displacement for the scapegoaters. He acts as an object of catharsis, the fulfillment of self-hatred, and the recipient of sadomasochistic relationships. He becomes a ready target for others to press their hatred and aggression upon himself and a susceptible partner in the interchange for scapegoating in the group.

Once object relationships are established and stabilized among the members and with the therapist, the reparative process of corrective emotional experience will proceed and the obstacles to emotional maturation will be alleviated. The object-splitting of self and negative object representations will diminish, leading to the diminution of scapegoating as a reciprocal means of expressing hostile aggression. Along with the concomitant healing of the ego and its control over a member's impulses, the attack upon the self and the object will be lifted. The psychic energy will be redirected toward integration of the self. The need for hostile aggression is expended and decathected from the ego. Energy will be made available for the synthesis of emotional growth.

To achieve a balance and cohesion for a given group, special consideration is needed in the selection of members (2, 6). Careful selection of group members helps to minimize scapegoating but will not eliminate it. Poor selection often contributes to the unmanageability of scapegoating in children's groups. It is clear that a preponderance of impulsive and aggressive children will produce a chaotic rather than a therapeutic climate. The overloading of aggressive children leaves more withdrawn or passive youngsters vulnerable to continuous attack.

A child who is retarded, brain-damaged, or psychotic becomes threatening to other children who are more intact. The obvious differences create anxieties and arouse feelings of damage in some, which make the acceptance of a defective member too threatening and intolerable. These feelings are often defended by attempts to reject and expel the defective member from the group. If maintained in the group, the highly deviant child can be easily scapegoated.

Severe sadistic and masochistic children are a perfect match for pathological coupling: To have either one or both in a group is to invite perpetual rounds of scapegoating, which can decimate the group, creating a perverted rather than a therapeutic atmosphere. If the group is fixated in scapegoating, the therapeutic value of the group is at risk. The therapist and other members become a captive audience to continuous disruption. The group is placed in resistance with a secondary gain embedded in sadomasochism. Reexamination of group composition is necessary in order to prevent the destruction of the group by scapegoating. A balanced group can be restored by a regrouping of members to minimize sadomasochistic interactions. The therapist's awareness of his countertransferences in composing groups will avert his need to recapitulate scapegoating. This will leave resistances manifested out of the group treatment rather than from improper selection.

To view scapegoating systematically, a combination of factors is considered:

1) The therapist needs to recognize it as both a resistance in a member and as a subgroup resistance combined essentially as a group resistance.
2) The comprehension of what each child brings to a group dynamically becomes pertinent in understanding the precursors to scapegoating. It is symbolic of the psychodynamic interplay among the members, which should be understood as a dramatization of a reenactment of conflicts in a simulated family situation; the scapegoating is a manifestation of resistance in the transference.
3) Countertransference feelings stemming from incomplete resolution of the therapist's psychic problems often can induce scapegoating in groups. Each therapist must be aware and in control of his unconscious feelings and his identification with the victim, the tormentor, and the scapegoating situation. He is just as susceptible to the regressive pull of the group as the members are, and his reactions to the group must be noted and analyzed.
4) Countertransference reactions from the therapist are vital elements in the understanding and handling of scapegoating. The therapist will have options available to him through analysis of the induced feelings from the transferences to select appropriate interventions in the management of scapegoating.

The analysis and application of countertransference feelings in children's group psychotherapy can provide the therapist with a valuable facility for monitoring the members' and the group's emotional levels of functioning, transferences, and resistances (3). His ability to be in touch with and to separate his countertransference feelings into objective and subjective ones (5) induced by the transferences will assist him to identify and determine more clearly the dynamics of the transferential interaction in the group.

When the induced feelings are analyzed and the types of resistances represented by the scapegoating in the transferences are assessed with reference to each child's life history, the therapist's understanding of the dynamics will follow. His responses will be selective and calculated to be corrective within the dynamics of the scapegoating displayed in the transference.

The therapist's understanding of the dynamics will guard against his acting on the subjective countertransference feelings and discipline the induced feelings for the management of scapegoating.

EXAMPLES OF SCAPEGOATING FROM SUBJECTIVE COUNTERTRANSFERENCE

In a group where scapegoating was ongoing, the victim cried and ran to the therapist for protection. The therapist attempted to reason with the victimizer without success. He reacted with helplessness and ineffectiveness. It was realized through supervision that he had experienced similar encounters with bullies in his youth. His parents had rescued him from his tormentors as a child. When his subjective countertransference resistance was understood, he was able to develop an intervention which permitted the victim to deal with the bully more effectively. His overidentification with the victim and his responding like his parents only reinforced and perpetuated the scapegoating.

In another group, a replacement activity group therapist reported scapegoating after several sessions. Prior to scapegoating, the members were working on their projects without any apparent interaction among the members. They were quiet and ignored the new therapist. The group appeared to be functioning without overt conflicts or difficulties (3).

The scapegoating was generalized without any specific incidents. The weakest member was targeted by each of the members. He seemed to be the recipient of everyone's anger. The therapist was perplexed and it made him feel uncomfortable. He was angry with the scapegoaters. He attempted to rescue the scapegoat, but the scapegoating continued.

When his angry feelings were investigated in supervision, the therapist felt that he was rejected by the group. Initially he was anxious about his competence as a therapist and was concerned about his performance. Instead of being welcomed by the group, he was met with coolness and distance. He thought he could win them over by overtures of friendliness. The group was not ready to receive his reaching-out, and responded with displaced hostility directed at the weakest member. He felt envious of the group's positive feelings toward the former therapist and was angry at the group's rejection of him. He became uncomfortable at their prolonged mourning. Once the therapist became aware of his countertransference feelings, he became less invested in his performance and his need for the group's acceptance. He ignored the scapegoating and stopped his attempts at reaching out. He recognized that the group was in a state of negative transference. As he permitted the group members to deal with their feelings of loss of the former therapist by rejecting the new therapist, the scapegoating diminished.

When the group was transferred to a new therapist, it was emotionally vulnerable to act in regression. The group was suffering from feelings of object loss, rejection abandonment, and separation anxiety. The new therapist's anxiety and zeal had shifted the members' hostility toward themselves. His intervention had precipitated scapegoating.

A therapist of a girls' group was planning to prepare them for her leaving the agency. As she was contemplating this, the group's scapegoating heightened. She became perplexed and postponed preparing the group until the scapegoating was resolved. She felt it was necessary to resolve the scapegoating before she could work through her separation from the group. As she attempted to deal with the scapegoating, the group resistance hardened. It became evident that the therapist's prolonged focus on the scapegoating was an avoidance to deal with the reactions of her departure. When this became obvious to her, she said, ''I guess it's better that they are angry at each other than at me.'' Her anxiety about the group's reaction to the impending separation and loss was picked up by the group. The anxiety was transformed and expressed through scapegoating by the group.

When improper selection of members and countertransference problems of therapists are minimized, scapegoating can be dealt with psychodynamically. Interventions may be appropriately pursued if the precursors of potential scapegoating can be recognized. The therapist should study the prospective victim and differentiate the levels of operation of the scapegoating situation in the group. When he understands it as a symbolic representation of a specific conflict and as a special form of subgroup transference resistance, an intervention can be developed out of the dynamics of the resistance that it serves for the principal members and the group. As a transference object, the therapist is often included in the drama of recapitulation of conflicts, which will provide him with opportunities for the management of scapegoating within the context of the transferences.

Ackerman, Framo, Jackson, and others in family therapy have provided insights on the role scapegoats in the family. The child or parent in question is identified as "bad," "sick," or "crazy" in the pathogenetic development and interactions in the family. He becomes targeted and is symptomatic of dysfunction in the family. Often one or both parents play similar roles in their primary families and the offspring therefore serve as agents in recapitulation and perpetuation of the family's pathological tradition.

A "devoted" child may offer himself as a sacrifice through diversionary tactics in order to save his parents from separation and divorce and become a buffer or a defense against marital strife and abuse. Children who have been designated to play the role of scapegoat in their families of origin will, as an extension of the family's pathology, reflect and reenact their dynamics in the group treatment.

The group as a symbolic mother (1) and the presence of the therapist-adult are a reconstituted symbolic family. They will provide an arena for the individual and multi-transferences to develop and the scapegoat to reenact his role of the deviant in the setting of the symbolic family group.

When individual and multi-transferences are established, the reenactment and recapitulation of each of the members' pathology will appear. Scapegoating as part of the manifest behavior is viewed as symptomatic and symbolic of a group resistance. The dynamics and resistances displayed in the scapegoating are studied by the therapist in the framework of each member's life history and the ongoing transference. The therapist can develop interventions in the context of the transferences to resolve the scapegoating as resistances operating in the group.

EXAMPLES OF SCAPEGOATING AS
TRANSFERENCE RESISTANCE

A highly provocative 10-year-old family scapegoat, with a history of rejection and expulsion resulting from multi-placements, was upsetting the group. He was successful in establishing a "cat and mouse" game between himself and the other members. He would tease, name call, and go to great lengths to provoke the members in chasing him. The other members wanted to "get rid of him." They were vituperous and ganged up on him. The provocateur did not mind and enjoyed himself with the negative attention he received from the group. The therapist unsucessfully attempted to intervene by pointing out his provocative behavior. He was identified with the other members' feelings of wanting to expel the noxious member. Through supervision, understanding of the resistance that the scapegoating represented symbolically in the sadomasochistic "chase" was clarified with the therapist. For the "chase" to be successful the scapegoat needed the other members and the therapist to join in with the game. The therapist was able to elicit the other members' cooperation to frustrate the provocateur's behavior. Once the members ceased to gratify the scapegoat, his masochistic behavior was undermined. The resistance embodied in the symbolic behavior of scapegoating in the "cat and mouse" game was defeated.

The therapist's recognition of the youngster's game, which had replicated his role in his family and had successfully induced the symbolic family group's cooperation in scapegoating him, enabled the therapist to devise a corrective intervention that obviated the acting-out of rejection and expulsion in the group transference. His intervention curtailed the youngster's reenactment which led to verbalization of his traumatic life history.

Billy, Mark, and Raymond were members of another group. Billy, an only child frequently witnessed his parents' arguments and his father's physical abuse of his mother. The parents divorced, and his mother remarried a similar type of person, which ended with many separations. Billy had a history of fighting with peers and behavior problems in school.

Mark, a younger sibling of a single-parent family, was referred to group therapy because of his being picked on by peers and was known as a "cry baby." He often ran to his mother and was rescued by his "big sister." His mother and sister were critical of his performance in school and his being "obnoxious." He was described by them as being like his unreliable father.

Raymond, a middle sibling, was manipulated by his father to criticize his mother as ineffectual. He constantly fought with his two brothers, leaving the mother feeling helpless. He had no friends and was an underachiever in school. He was described as contrary, argumentative, uncooperative, and found little pleasure in play.

As the group's treatment unfolded, each of the youngsters portrayed his behavior and attitudes that blended into an interacting transference situation. Mark's entry with his overbearing bravado easily alienated Raymond and Billy. Raymond retaliated by attempting to set Billy up against Mark for confrontations. Billy was caught in a triangulation of two belligerent members. Each, with his unique life history, coalesced himself into a scapegoating situation. Each was recapitulating his family problems in the arena of the symbolic family group.

The multi-transferences of Raymond, Mark, Billy, and the countertransference reactions to the therapist were mutually interactive. The therapist understood the feelings induced by their interaction. His subjective and objective countertransference reactions were differentiated and analyzed to avoid playing into the members' transferences. His analyzed feelings were utilized to develop a corrective intervention appropriate to the content of the ongoing transferences (3).

The therapist did not rescue Mark like his mother and sister, nor sided with Raymond against Mark like Raymond's father. Instead of getting entangled in their dispute and along with Billy's triangulation, the therapist pointed out how they did not seem to mind the impending scapegoating, but rather they were pleased with the fact that their situation was getting "out of hand." The subgroup angrily rejected the therapist's observations. Billy, Mark, and Raymond's hostility became more open and they verbalized their hatred of their siblings, teachers, and other significant figures in their lives. Subsequently, the scapegoating was given up.

In this instance it was not a question of one child being bullied, and the therapist ignoring him and waiting for the child to develop sufficient strength to stand up against his tormentors. Their unconscious attempts at including the therapist as a transference parental object in their reenactment made it apparent that their scapegoating represented a repetition of their pathogenetic family drama. The study of each child's life history helped the therapist to anticipate and clarify the psychodynamics that the potential scapegoating was to form out of their interaction.

The study of the role and function of the scapegoat, the scapegoaters, and the scapegoating situation becomes comprehensible psychodynamically with reference to the history of each child and the manner the reenactment unfolds in the transference. Recognizing scapegoating as subgroup resistance in the transference is pertinent to the management of transference resistance in children's group psychoanalytic psychotherapy.

SUMMARY AND DISCUSSION

Scapegoating is multi-determined in children's group psychoanalytic psychotherapy.

1) Inappropriate selection in membership and/or an improperly balanced group can produce scapegoating. A balanced group can minimize scapegoating and it will permit the symptom of scapegoating to evolve from the treatment process.

2) Scapegoating can be seen as an initial by-product of peer interaction and struggle for power in the group. As equalization of relationships and power structure among members are established, scapegoating becomes a transitional process of group development. Intervention is unnecessary during this phase of group process unless its persistence is a sign of group resistance.

3) Scapegoating can be seen as symptomatic of a deficit in developmental

and emotional maturation in the members's object relations, identification, and ego structure. Based on the members' maturational needs, corrective emotional experiences are provided by the therapist and the group's interaction in constructive and reconstructive activities.

4) Countertransference problems by the therapist can induce scapegoating which serves to fixate group movement and treatment. This becomes symptomatic of the therapist's resistance and it is best resolved by the therapist's self-analysis or by supervisory process.

5) Persistence in scapegoating can be symptomatic of members' pathogenetic family issues recapitulated in the multi-transferences of the group's symbolic family. The dynamics of the members' life histories prone toward scapegoating are anticipated. The therapist's countertransferences reactions are utilized to develop an appropriate intervention in the context of the transference. The scapegoating is resolved as part of the transference resistance. The recognition of scapegoating as a group transference resistance is an integral segment of the total treatment process.

Dissolving scapegoating as a resistance releases hostility. The hostility becomes more accessible to verbalization. The resolution of hostile aggression becomes ego-supportive rather than ego-destructive. It is unbound energy which frees the ego to control its impulse. The removal of the effects of scapegoating allows the child to develop and complete a more positive identification rather than internalizing the role of victimizer or victim. It permits group members to proceed to define themselves through the process of equalization of relationships with each other and the therapist. It alleviates the need for the child to be tied to a pathogenetic relationship and separate from it. It enhances the progression of maturational development in object relations and the unification of split-object dichotomies, and it provides an opportunity for each child to restructure his psychic energy.

REFERENCES

1. Scheidlinger, S. On the concept of the "mother-group." *International Journal of Group Psychotherapy,* 24: 4, 417-428, 1974.
2. Slavson, S. Criteria for selection and rejection of patients for various kinds of group psychotherapy. *International Journal of Group Therapy,* 5: 3-30, 1955.
3. Soo, E. S. The impact of transference and countertransference in activity group therapy. *Group,* 4 (4): 27-41, 1980.
4. Toker, E. The scapegoat as an essential group phenomenon. *International Journal of Group Psychotherapy,* 22: 3, 320-332, 1972.
5. Winnicott, D. *Hate in the countertransference. Collected Papers.* New York: Basic Books, 1958.
6. Yalom, I.D. *The Theory and Practice of Group Psychotherapy.* (2nd ed.) New York: Basic Books, 1975.

Chapter XIII

PSYCHOSOCIAL INTERVENTION IN GROUPS AS AN ADJUNCT TO MEDICAL TREATMENT

Janice D. DeMocker, Ed.D., and David G. Zimpfer, Ed.D.

Editors' Summary. This article reviews concepts of healing and cure and proceeds to describe the tasks of healing. Both preparatory and adaptational health-related groups are discussed and the nine therapeutic factors at work in these groups are identified: information, clarification, universality, catharsis, peer support, improved communication, helper therapy, modeling, and confrontation. The literature is reviewed with consideration of who benefits, the nature of the group process, and the results of controlled studies. Suggestions are offered for strengthening investigation of this fruitful application of the group modality.

As health care professionals have developed an increasing awareness of the social and psychological needs of patients who are physically ill, there has been growing interest in the use of groups in the medical setting. Between 1970 and the present, a number of studies have described the use of groups as part of medical treatment by nurses, social workers, physicians, psychologists, and physical therapists. The influence of the group members on one another was noted repeatedly, suggesting that there are unique contributions from group interaction that are not found in individual counseling. By examining these studies and relating the findings to the current philosophy in holistic health care, it is possible to describe guidelines for clinical intervention and to suggest hypotheses for further research in the use of groups as a psychosocial adjunct with the medical patient.

TASKS OF HEALING

If we view illness as a biological, psychological and social event (20), recognizing the potential influences of environmental and interpersonal factors upon its onset and course, then we may identify one of the purposes of group intervention as *healing*. Healing within this framework can be defined as the restoration of internal and external harmony. The goals of healing include physical remediation or cure, but go beyond these to include the acceptance of physical change into the person's self-concept, and reintegration of the patient into the family and community (42). Both cure and healing are needed. Healing results in growth that comes from the successful integration of the person into the life-style that his or her level of health suggests is appropriate.

As we have suggested earlier (17), illness is a universal occurrence, not a unique event. Nearly every person will experience a physical illness requiring medical or surgical intervention. As we learn to treat acute health problems with greater sophistication, the survival rate increases and with it the probability of experiencing chronic illness. The counseling and support that a person receives when confronted with a health problem can determine whether he or she finds the experience to be growth-producing or degenerative. Medical problems represent a predictable adult developmental crisis, and the outcomes can be markedly influenced by the educational and supportive intervention which the patient receives.

When individuals recognize changes in their level of wellness, they face four tasks that are part of the healing process. Each task is partially or entirely dependent upon the person's ability to communicate with potential sources of help and to negotiate in his or her own behalf.

Defining the Problem

Symptoms may develop some time before the person becomes aware of their significance. He or she may postpone dealing with medical problems because other activities are effective distractions or because of fear, denial, or the seeming insignificance of early symptoms. Denial may also prevent an obviously ill or newly handicapped person from realizing the full meaning of his or her physical condition. Denial can be viewed as a valuable and healthy mechanism; it allows the person time to gather the resources needed to face illness or incapacitation. Its value is only short-term, however. Healing begins when one can allow him- or herself to become aware of the possible significance of a physical condition or symptom. This provides the base for a realistic assessment of the need for help or support.

Seeking Care

The person's past experience with physicians and hospitals may determine his or her willingness to seek medical care promptly. Positive or negative attitudes are frequently the result of personal experience, but may also develop from the person's observations of parents' or siblings' illness. In addition, parents display attitudes of skepticism and cynicism, or of confidence and trust, which they say developed as they worked with physicians and nurses during the illness of a child. Negative attitudes may result in postponing contact with a health care professional until one feels backed against a wall, either by the severity of the symptoms or by pressure from concerned relatives or friends. This in itself is reason for using whatever effective means we have for maintaining optimal levels of communication between patient and health professionals, recognizing the person's feelings of fear and need for denial, and encouraging his or her efforts to solicit needed support during an illness experience.

In seeking medical care, one may lose power over some aspects of daily life, and may also yield control over his or her fate. The patient is placing his or her well-being in the hands of the health care provider, and then must rely on that other's competence and continuing interest. Characteristically, seriously ill people hesitate to confront or even question the physician or to respond negatively to medical or surgical decisions made on their behalf, because of their fear of abandonment or rejection (21).

Accepting Intervention

The person seeking medical intervention must assume the sick role, with changed expectations for his or her behavior. Hospitalization entails loss of privacy, lowered status, and altered identity. The ill person is excused from the usual role obligations of family member, worker, community volunteer, or student, but is expected to seek actively to be cured. The sick role is a passive one, and patients consistently describe the behaviors that identify a ''good patient'': One must limit the number of requests made to the staff, do as much as possible for oneself, and not complain or cry (DeMocker, Note 1). Patients are aware that caregivers are performance evaluators and that there are penalties for being a bad or uncooperative patient (8, 36).

An illness or a medical procedure that causes incapacitation necessitates dependency for such basic needs as food, maintenance of body warmth, and elimination of body wastes. Medical care is potentially regressive, and the ill person may associate even brief periods of helplessness with the remembered powerlessness of childhood.

Each person in need of medical intervention will also experience fear. Even when facing an elective procedure, there is concern that an unexpected complication may make the intervention more difficult or will be life-threatening. In addition, there is fear of pain, of the unknown, of unpleasant interventions, of outcomes that fall short of the desired level of wellness or of function. With a serious illness or a poor prognosis, the fear may intensify as the potential for its realization increases.

Reintegration

Studies of the influence of support on physiological functioning in stressful situations present evidence of the theoretical importance of a support network for the medically ill (23). The presence of a family member or friend can meet the need of an ill person for the presence of another. Yet the suddenness with which illness may occur, the uncertainty of outcome, and the added stress inherent in the changed living patterns that result from the disability of one of its members often make it difficult for a family to meet the patient's needs for support. The patient's inability to fulfill his or her usual role in the family may result in feelings of frustration, guilt, and a fear of rejection, placing an increasing strain on the relationship between a patient and those close to him or her. Family or friends may feel overwhelmed and guilty. The patient may feel overprotected or abandoned. No one may be able to share feelings or to solicit the help needed to work through them. By examining patterns of communication and encouraging the expression and acceptance of feelings, the ill person may gain increased trust and confidence in those close to him or her (19). The goal is to return the person to a social environment that is at least as supportive and empathetic as it was before his or her illness.

GROUP WORK AS INTERVENTION

As the medically ill person works through the tasks of accepting medical intervention and returning to the family and community, he or she may gain from the unique contributions of group intervention. It is helpful to divide group work in medicine into two categories, according to goals or purposes. We will designate these as *preparatory* and *adaptive* groups.

Preparatory group meetings are planned to assist the person who is anticipating a health-related event such as surgery or childbirth. The group provides an opportunity to share information about the event or procedure, learn techniques for solving anticipated problems, and acquaint the participant with both the process and the personnel they will meet. The group leader may include discussions of feelings or experiences, but there is not heavy reliance on the group for support or emotional catharsis. As an example of a preparatory group, Schmitt scheduled presurgery meetings with patients during which she explained the operative procedure, encouraged their use of medication for pain relief during the early postoperative period, and explained other ways they could minimize their discomfort immediately after surgery (41).

The adaptive group is planned to help members whose illness may have long-term consequences and who must face their disability and maintain or reestablish supportive relationships with significant others. The adaptive group is less structured, of longer duration, and makes use of group cohesiveness and shared experience to provide emotional support. Examples of adaptive groups are the group for stroke patients and their families (15) and group work with emphysema patients, some of whom were terminally ill (35). The adaptive group members share with those in preparatory groups the need to see themselves as capable of functioning effectively in caring for their health needs. In addition, adaptive groups attempt to help their members incorporate loss, disability, or change into their self-concept, as well as encouraging them to work through their concerns over others' expectations of them. The goals and purposes of the group vary with the diagnosis, the situation confronting the participants, their expressed needs and concerns, and the leader's skills and philosophy. Those variables, in turn, determine the type of group most appropriate for the person and suggest which of the therapeutic factors potentially gained from group interaction may be most successfully brought to bear.

Nine therapeutic factors can be identified by reviewing the observations of researchers and the patient comments cited in the clinical studies of group interventions published over the past 12 years. The term "therapeutic factor" has been used in group therapy to refer to the process that "contributes to the improvement of the patient's condition and is regarded as a function of the actions of the therapist, the other members of the group, and the patient himself" (5). Bloch et al. distinguish therapeutic factors from *conditions* for change, such as members' attendance, or *techniques*, which are the strategies that the therapist may adopt in order to bring the therapeutic factors into operation. Although the therapeutic factors are presented here as discrete dimensions, the distinctions among them are not clear-cut, nor do they operate independently of one another. In this way they are similar to the curative factors described by Yalom (46) with reference to psychotherapy. Some of his curative factors parallel those we have identified from examining groups conducted for the medically ill.

Information

Laboratory studies of responses to noxious stimuli (usually electric shock) indicate that the majority of persons prefer information regarding both the timing and the sensations of an impending threatening experience. In a hospital setting, Johnson, Rice, Fuller, and Endress (28) found that informing cholecystectomy patients of the sensations they would probably experience postoperatively significantly reduced the length of postoperative hospitalization and the length of time the patient remained housebound after hospital discharge. Other studies have also indicated that information about the physical sensations the person would probably experience after surgery, plus techniques that he or she might use to control pain or discomfort, resulted in more rapid hospital discharge and less need for pain medication (18, 41). Information about an anticipated event can diminish the person's fear of it and may be used to maintain a sense of control over the experience. In a preparatory group, information is often provided by the leader's use of a structured program of instruction. Adaptive groups are usually less structured, and members may ask for information as they experience a need for it. Helpful information includes not only facts about disease, medical procedures, and hospital routines, but a description of emotional needs as well. People are often surprised to find that others share the same fears, anger, or guilt that they believed to be theirs alone.

New group members may draw on the knowledge of more experienced members when learning new skills or gaining information. The special contribution of the group in teaching renal dialysis patients and their families was noted by the group leaders, who observed that family members seemed to learn far better from peers than from professionals, and were better able to cope after sharing experiences with one another (26, 44).

Clarification

There are specific problems associated with an illness. As the duration or severity of the health problem increases, the problems may also become more intense. The person attempting to alter living patterns to accommodate functional loss at the same time that he or she is working through grief caused by an awareness of the loss may feel awash with anger, discouragement, and helplessness. The wide array of problems characteristic of chronic or terminal illness can be overwhelming: management of pain, relationships with family and friends, participation in therapeutic surgical or medical intervention, and maintenance of independence (45). By identifying specific problems, establishing priorities, and focusing the person's problem-solving resources, it may be possible to diminish anxiety and their sense of helplessness. A group may be able to encourage its members to be open in sharing their experiences by the closeness in the relationships, reciprocity, and interpersonal attraction (5). As the members are able to self-disclose, they can draw on the group for clarification of problems and for practical solutions that others have found to be helpful.

Universality

Interaction with a group provides the ill or disabled person with an opportunity to compare his or her feelings and perceptions with those of others who face similar problems. Citing "universality" as a therapeutic gain in group psychotherapy, Yalom has observed that the members' awakening awareness that their experiences were not unique was a "powerful source of relief" (46). This contribution of the group was identified by several clinical observers (8, 25, 37, 43). The group offers two valuable perspectives to its members: how others experience the disease or intervention, and how other members perceive oneself. Members of a group established for persons who had recently experienced heart attacks were able to confront one another over excuses they offered for noncompliance with essential routines (39). Members of another group gained courage from observing the progress of those who suffered disabilities similar to their own (7). Solutions for practical problems and the recognition of non-facilitative behavior patterns were frequently shared among members. The group also afforded an opportunity for leaders or members to suggest novel ways of perceiving themselves in relationship to the disease. For example, Campbell and Sinha (9) attempted to change members' perception so that illness was viewed as a challenge, rather than an enemy. They presented illness as a problem-solving task.

Catharsis

There is frequently a strong need, particularly among those persons facing chronic illness or disability, to express feelings of despair, anger, and helplessness. Members appear to gain relief from the expression and sharing of feelings, particularly those feelings that are painful or possibly unacceptable. Clinical researchers have noted that the opportunity to ventilate anger and despair led to more balanced thinking and planning as the group members were encouraged to focus on their remaining potential (4, 15, 30). Some of the groups also afforded their members a safe means of working through the hostility and anger toward the medical establishment that is often generated by chronic illness. The opportunity for expression of negative feelings appeared to facilitate patient-staff communications, and heightened staff awareness of the needs and the strengths of the patients (32, 34).

Peer Support

Feelings of isolation commonly accompany physical illness. Patients express the belief that others who have not felt the pain, fear, and helplessness associated with their malady cannot understand their experience. These persons may benefit from the opportunity to share with others who face a similar health impairment. Cohesiveness often develops rapidly in a group composed of those who have similar problems. The deep concern that patients develop for one another diminishes their isolation and helps them to accept loss and to move on. Disease causes increased strain on family and marital relationships. With the increased dependency on doctors and mechanical equipment, peer support becomes increasingly important.

Groups with open-ended or revolving membership can offer special advantages in peer support. The encouragement and teaching of the more experienced group members may help a newly disabled member to develop and rehearse new skills in a setting that is not threatening. For example, an amputee may practice with one hand those activities that he or she will need to be able to perform routinely after hospital discharge. Others in the group can provide support and suggestions. In another situation, the practice may take the form of learning to articulate needs clearly, to improve listening skills, or to set limits for self or others. Group supportive feedback provides the mechanism by which a person may examine and evaluate new behavior patterns.

Improved Communication

Increased dependency may cause a person to avoid dealing directly with problems that arise in relationships with others when he or she cannot risk alienating them. Group interaction provides training in listening to others without judging them, and in communicating one's own needs clearly. It may also be used as a medium for settling problems between patients and staff or among patients in a long-term hospital setting.

Groups which include family members provide the opportunity to examine patterns of communication between patient and family. The group can provide feedback to correct behaviors or attitudes that are not facilitative, and family members can be encouraged to express feelings and to indicate the ways they believe other members might be helpful. An increasing number of groups have been planned for family members only, to meet their need for information about the illness and related hospital procedures and routines, to facilitate members' sharing concerns and stresses related to the illness, and to give emotional support to the family (2, 14).

Helper Therapy

Group members function not only as receivers, but also as givers of help. Participation in a group encourages the members to focus on needs beyond their individual selves, and each gains an increased sense of personal worth from realizing that he or she has something of value to offer other members. For handicapped persons who have come to view themselves as dependent on family and community, the opportunity to feel needed and useful represents a significant stimulus for changed self-concept. When specific skills are necessary, such as those required of families performing home hemodialysis, members actually teach one another. The more experienced families gain in self-confidence by relating the ways they have solved disturbing or unexpected problems (26).

Modeling

When groups are used to assist persons to adapt to a specific medical illness, cohesiveness often develops quite rapidly as the members recognize shared experiences and problems. In a cohesive group, members are eager to meet the expectations of the group. Other members' successes provide a yardstick against which persons may measure their own performance. The accomplishments of others also offer hope to persons struggling with the same problems or handicaps.

In the open-ended, ongoing group that accepts new members during its course, modeling is facilitated by the periodic influx of new members with varying degrees of experience. In a closed group, a similar variation of skill levels may be attained by composing the group of members with different levels of readiness and competence regarding the task of the group.

Confrontation

The person with a chronic disease or handicap can plan more effectively if his or her assessment of personal strengths and limitations is relatively accurate. Without forcing the person to give up a defense that is still needed, the group may be able to assist its members to view the future more realistically. The group may need guidance from the leader in distinguishing between potentially harmful confrontation that forces a group member to accept reality for which he or she may not be prepared, and helpful confrontation with here-and-now behavior patterns that are not facilitative for oneself. Patterns of dependency or other maladaptive behavior may be challenged through feedback from the leader or the group, resulting in changes that are more satisfying for the person and his or her family.

There is often a wide discrepancy, particularly in persons with a handicap, between their own concepts of self and their ideal self-image. The group helps to narrow that distance, both by enhancing self-concept and by promoting a more appropriate ideal image (33). Information about the course of the disease and an accurate appraisal of the prognosis encourage realistic planning. Although death is a constant possibility in many chronic diseases, people are not helpless victims; they can contribute much to the final outcome (26). With knowledge of the purpose and necessity for medications, diet, exercise, and rest regimens, the patient can plan life-style changes with the support and encouragement of the group.

CLINICAL USE OF GROUPS

The use of groups for medically ill persons raises many of the same questions that are common to group work in other settings. Who will benefit from group intervention? How long should the group continue? What qualities of leadership are the most facilitative? How can desired change be verified and measured? Several of these will be addressed in the following sections.

Who Benefits?

Based on a review of the literature from 1956 to 1974, Cunningham, Strassberg, and Roback (13) describe three types of patients that have been treated in groups: patients with physical symptoms that are partly a result of, or aggravated by, psychological stressors; patients with somatic complaints that do not appear to have a physical basis; and patients with incapacitating or life-threatening illness such as multiple sclerosis, renal failure, or cancer. Our examination of the studies published from 1970 to early 1982 indicates that the majority of the groups described in the literature were aimed at assisting those patients in the last category: patients who were adjusting to marked changes in physical capacity, self-image, and life-style. In addition, there appears to be an increasing use of groups to help the families of both adult and pediatric patients with their own feelings of anxiety and grief, and to draw them into fuller participation in the care and support of their ill member. Several groups were planned to include both patients and families, providing assistance for pregnant adolescents (1), emphysema patients (35), and patients on hemodialysis (26, 44). These groups had, among other goals, the sharing of feelings and an increased ability to find solutions to shared problems. Other groups were planned only for the families: of burn victims (2), children with leukemia (3), and home dialysis patients (14). In nearly every instance, the groups were homogeneous; that is, each group was planned for the persons, or families, confronting a specific disease entity. The symptoms of cancer patients were varied, depending on the body areas involved in metastatic spread of the disease, but there was no evidence that this diversity decreased the cohesiveness of the group or the members' perception of the commonality of their experiences (37, 45).

These groups all may be described as adaptive groups. Their purposes were to provide support, diminish anxiety, and change behavior. They drew upon several or all of the therapeutic factors described earlier; the extent to which each factor was present in the group work appeared to vary with the purposes of the group and the style of the leader.

In addition, a small number of groups were preparatory, serving to help their members through an anticipated event or intervention. One group was designed to assist pregnant women who anticipated delivery by Caesarean section by supplying information, answering questions, and providing for the expression of feelings about members' inability to deliver normally (10). Hypertensive patients were treated by group intervention in order to increase their understanding of the disease, decrease anxiety, and increase compliance with the prescribed medical regimen (11). The therapeutic factors identified in these groups were information and clarification, with some opportunity to express sadness, anger, and guilt (catharsis). The remaining preparatory groups surveyed were planned for presurgery patients, and dealt with their pre- and postoperative routines, information about the surgical procedure, and expression of concerns and feelings. By defining the needs of the group members and setting appropriate goals for meeting their needs, it is then possible to identify the therapeutic factors that will be the most effective in helping the group to reach the goals.

What Is the Group Process?

Approximately half of the adaptive groups described phasic shifts over time. It is possible to examine the stages that were identified and relate these to other variables such as duration, membership, and leadership style.

Time is a factor often associated with progress in a group, yet there was a surprising absence of correlation between group process and duration. One group had achieved a supportive-confrontive atmosphere by the fourth meeting (16), while others did not even after several months (22, 25). Although the actual duration did not appear to affect group process, there may have been a relationship between the *scheduled* duration and change in the group. It seemed that the group moved more slowly to the stage of shared feelings and mutual support when the members anticipated that meetings would continue over several months.

The single most important variable influencing the group process appeared to be the leader. Leaders varied along a number of dimensions: activity, directiveness, experience, and emphasis upon teaching. Several groups appeared to develop particular ability to self-explore and to support their members. The leaders were described as being supportive, nondirective, reflective (24), and clarifying and moderately confrontive (34). Well over half of the groups were co-led; however, the number of leaders, their status, and their experience did not appear to influence the process. The leader qualities that appeared to be significant were the ability to be nondirective, reflective, and concerned, and to trust the group. It also appeared to be helpful if the leader had some information that related to the physical problems confronting the group members.

The characteristics of the members appeared to influence the group process in several specific instances. One of the predictable stages of group interaction is a confrontation or challenge of the leader by the membership. Although in several groups the members began to take over leadership or maintenance functions (35, 40), this was done in most instances without confrontation. There were two exceptions: first, the suspicion and anger of the visually handicapped group members toward the sighted leader (29) was heightened by the fantasies about him that developed because the members could not see him. The second exception occurred in prenatal groups for adolescents where the potential conflict with the leader appeared to be exacerbated by the girls' identification of the leader as the mother from whom they were attempting to gain independence (1, 31).

Group process was also influenced by the extent of loss experienced by the members, and the resulting need for grief work. Grieving was expressed through anger or sorrow (15), and also through reminiscing about "the good old days," reviewing hobbies and activities that were no longer possible, and talking about well-known people who had had similar experiences and had recovered sufficiently to resume their normal living patterns (24, 34, 39).

By examining the group interaction across studies, we identified a three-stage process: 1) *exploration,* with specific, concrete discussion focusing on disease symptoms or problems external to the patient; 2) *support* for the expression of feelings, especially about illness or loss; and 3) *group maintenance* characterized by mutual support and concern, confrontation, and sharing of leadership and maintenance functions. This third stage depends not only upon the responses of members as individuals, but also upon the attainment of a particular quality of interaction within the group.

What are the Outcomes?

The studies measured or described outcomes that included physical change, improved functioning, and subjective evaluations. Within the category of physical responses are the physiological (such as blood pressure and pulse) and those that Schmitt and Wooldridge (41) call interactional and define as variables that are determined by the interaction of patient with care provider (i.e., amount of pain medication or length of hospital stay). These might also be called "negotiable" outcomes. The physiological and negotiable outcomes are both objectively measurable, usually available in the patient's hospital record, and relatively resistant to the patient's conscious attempt to manipulate. Physical responses were used as dependent measures in two studies, using myocardial infarction patients as subjects (27, 38).

Several studies indicated functional changes by describing the group members' ability to relate more successfully with hospital staff, family, or other group members. Hypertensive patients exhibited more realistic expectations and better decision-making skills, and were less withdrawn (11). Unwed mothers appeared to have a more positive attitude toward pregnancy, decreased anxiety in labor and delivery, better relations with the health providers (16), and were better able to meet the demands of the mothering role (31). Mann and his associates (33) observed that some of the spinal cord injured men in their group took more risks and responded more actively in ways that benefited their rehabilitation. Many cardiac patients "reorganized their daily activities and modified their type A behavior" (6) as the result of a group organized to facilitate their reintegration into family and social life after coronary surgery.

Finally, some studies used patient satisfaction as an outcome measure. Meetings were described as "helpful" before Caesarean section (10). Rehabilitation patients volunteered their satisfaction with their group (24), and patients undergoing hemodialysis commented that it was useful to learn from others' experiences (26). Some leaders cited increases in attendance as indicating the demand for the group experience (35, 40). Stroke patients responding to the questionnaire used by Oradei and Waite (34) all agreed that it was helpful to learn that others had concerns and feelings similar to their own.

Conte and Karasu (12) reviewed eight controlled studies that used group therapy as an adjunct to medical treatment for patients with peptic ulcer, ulcerative colitis, asthma, and cardiovascular disease. They evaluated the research design as "adequate" or "good" for six of these and five of the six showed positive results.

CONCLUSIONS

Group work for the medically ill may serve not only to prepare members to understand and utilize medical technology, but also to assist them in accepting change in their health status and in continuing as a functional part of family and community. The holistic health care movement lends impetus to the use of group interventions by providing evidence that the presence of an empathic support system may have beneficial effects on physiological functioning, and that information may aid ill persons to retain a perception of control over their health, thus promoting optimal physical functioning. The studies of group work in medicine over the past 12 years offer a rich variety of patient diagnoses and leader styles in groups that have been perceived as helpful by most of the members. Coupled with documentation of improved physiological outcomes from several experimental studies which described a lower rate of subsequent serious cardiac events following coronary disease, shorter hospital stay, and less pain medication required after surgery, the studies suggest that groups seem to be an effective tool in the care of the physically ill person.

That there is a preponderance of descriptive studies is characteristic of a relatively new field of investigation; it also reflects the clinical orientation of the majority of the investigators. With the descriptive data available in the existing literature, it should now be possible to establish cause and effect relationships through the increased use of experimental designs. Group composition, duration, continuity of membership, and leader style are all manipulatable and potentially fruitful variables. For this reason, establishing causality has benefits for the clinician as well as importance for the researcher.

The correlation in several studies between degree of investment in the group and resulting improvement in self-concept and ability to function raises two research questions: Does the development of a stage three group process, characterized by mutual support, concern, confrontation and shared leadership, cause this improvement? And how may a group be brought to this level of functioning in the shortest time? We would reaffirm the need for additional studies designed to document the therapeutic effect of group work for the medically ill, to identify which therapeutic factors may be exploited most effectively, and to suggest the most efficient ways to develop these factors in group interaction.

REFERENCE NOTE

1. DeMocker, J. D. Components of the helping relationship in health care. Doctoral dissertation, 1983.

REFERENCES

1. Adams, B., Brownstein, C., Rennalls, I., and Schmitt, M. The pregnant adolescent—A group approach. *Adolescence*, 44: 467-485, 1976.
2. Bayley, E., and Moore, D. Group meetings for families of burn victims. *Topics in Clinical Nursing*, 2: 67-75, 1980.

3. Belle-Isle, J., and Conradt, B. Report of a discussion group for parents of children with leukemia. *Maternal-Child Nursing Journal*, 8: 49-58, 1979.

4. Bilodeau, C., and Hackett, T. Issues raised in a group setting by patients recovering from myocardial infarction. *American Journal of Psychiatry*, 128: 73-78, 1971.

5. Bloch, S., Crouch, E., and Reibstein, J. Therapeutic factors in group psychotherapy:A review. *Archives of General Psychiatry*, 38: 519-526, 1981.

6. Boisvert, C. Convalescence following coronary surgery: A group experience. *Canadian Nurse*, 72: 26-27, 1976.

7. Bouchard, V. Hemiplegic exercise and discussion group. *American Journal of Occupational Therapy*, 26: 330-334, 1972.

8. Buchanan, D. Group therapy for kidney transplant patients. *International Journal of Psychiatry in Medicine*, 6: 523-531, 1975.

9. Campbell, D., and Sinha, B. Brief group psychotherapy with chronic hemodialysis patients. *American Journal of Psychiatry*, 137: 1234-1237, 1980.

10. Conklin, M. Discussion groups as preparation for Caesarean section. *Journal of Obstetric, Gynecologic and Neonatal Nursing*, 6: 52-54, 1977.

11. Conte, A., Brandzel, M., and Whitehead, S. Group work with hypertensive patients. *American Journal of Nursing*, 74: 910-912, 1974.

12. Conte, H., and Karasu, T. Psychothearpy for medically ill patients: Review and critique of controlled studies. *Psychosomatics*, 22: 285-315, 1981.

13. Cunningham, J., Strassberg, D., and Roback H. Group therapy for medical patients. *Comprehensive Psychiatry*, 19: 135-140, 1978.

14. D'Afflitti, J., and Swanson, D. Group sessions for wives of home hemodialysis patients. *American Journal of Nursing*, 75: 633-635, 1975.

15. D'Afflitti, J., and Weitz, G. Rehabilitating the stroke patient through patient-family groups. *International Journal of Group Psychotherapy*, 24: 323-332, 1974.

16. Danforth, J., Miller, D., Day, A., and Steiner, G. Group services for unmarried mothers. *Children*, 18: 59-64, 1971.

17. DeMocker, J., and Zimpfer, D. Group approaches to psychosocial intervention in medical care: A synthesis. *International Journal of Group Psychotherapy*, 31: 247-260, 1981.

18. Egbert, L., Battit, G., Welch, C., and Bartlett, M. Reduction of post-operative pain by encouragement and instruction of patients. *New England Journal of Medicine*, 270: 825-827, 1964.

19. Engel, G. Grief and grieving. *American Journal of Nursing*, 64: 93-98, 1964.

20. Engel, G. The biopsychosocial model and the education of health professionals. *Annals of the New York Academy of Sciences*, 310: 169-181, 1978.

21. Franzino, M., Geren, J., and Meiman, G. Group discussion among the terminally ill. *International Journal of Group Psychotherapy*, 26: 43-48, 1976.

22. Graham, E. Young parents' group. *Journal of Nurse-Midwifery*, 20: 15-19, 1975.

23. Heller, K. The effects of social support: Prevention and treatment implications. *In:* A. Goldstein and F. Kanfer (Eds.), *Maximizing Treatment Gains: Transfer Enhancement in Psychotherapy*. New York: Academic Press, 1979.

24. Heller, V. Handicapped Patients Talk Together. *American Journal of Nursing*, 70: 332-335, 1970.

25. Henkle, C. Social group work as a treatment modality for hospitalized people with rheumatoid arthritis. *Rehabilitation Literature*, 36: 334-341, 1975.

26. Hollon, T. Modified group therapy in the treatment of patients on chronic hemodialysis. *American Journal of Psychotherapy*, 26: 501-510, 1972.

27. Ibrahim, M., Feldman, J., Sultz, H., Staiman, M., Young, L., and Dean, D. Management after myocardial infarction: A controlled trial of the effect of group psychotherapy. *International Journal of Psychiatry in Medicine*, 5: 253-268, 1974.

28. Johnson, J., Rice, V., Fuller, S., and Endress, M. Sensory information, instruction in a coping strategy, and recovery from surgery. *Research in Nursing and Health*, 1: 4-17, 1978.

29. Keegan, D. Adaption of visual handicap: Short-term group approach. *Psychosomatics*, 15: 76-78, 1974.

30. Kelly, P., and Ashby, G. Establishing a group. *American Journal of Nursing*, 79: 914-915, 1979.
31. Kolodny, R., and Reilly, W. Group work with today's unmarried mother. *Social Casework*, 53: 613-622, 1972.
32. Lonergan, E. Humanizing the hospital experience: Report of a group program for medical patients. *Health and Social Work*, 5: 53-63, 1980.
33. Mann, W., Godfrey, M., and Dowd, E. The use of group counseling procedures in the rehabilitation of spinal cord injured patients. *American Journal of Occupational Therapy*, 27: 73-77, 1973.
34. Oradei, D., and Waite, N. Group psychotherapy with stroke patients during the immediate recovery phase. *American Journal of Orthopsychiatry*, 44: 386-395, 1974.
35. Parry, J., and Kahn, N. Group work with emphysema patients. *Social Work in Health Care*, 2: 55-64, 1976.
36. Parsons, T., and Fox, R. Illness, therapy, and the modern urban American family. *Journal of Social Issues*, 8: 31-44, 1952.
37. Parsell, S., and Tagliareni, E. Cancer patients help each other. *American Journal of Nursing*, 74: 650-651, 1974.
38. Rahe, R., O'Neil, T., Hagan, A., and Arthur, R. Brief group therapy following myocardial infarction: Eighteen-month follow-up of a controlled trial. *International Journal of Psychiatry in Medicine*, 6: 349-357, 1975.
39. Rahe, R., Tuffli, C., Suchor, R., and Arthur, R. Group therapy in the outpatient management of post-myocardial infarction patients. *International Journal of Psychiatry in Medicine*, 4: 77-78, 1973.
40. Rosin, A. Group discussions: A therapeutic tool in a chronic diseases hospital. *Geriatrics*, 30: 45-48, 1975.
41. Schmitt, F., and Wooldridge, P. Psychological preparation of surgical patients. *Nursing Research*, 22: 108-116, 1973.
42. Sheldon, A. Toward a general theory of disease and medical care. *In:* A. Sheldon, F. Baker, and C. McLaughlin (Eds.), *Systems and Medical Care*. Cambridge: MIT Press, 1970.
43. Singler, J. Group work with hospitalized stroke patients. *Social Casework*, 56: 348-354, 1975.
44. Sorensen, E. Group therapy in a community hospital dialysis unit. *Journal of the American Medical Association*, 221: 899-901, 1972.
45. Spiegel, D., Bloom, J., and Yalom, I. Group support for patients with metastatic cancer: A randomized prospective outcome study. *Archives of General Psychiatry*, 38: 527-533, 1981.
46. Yalom, I. *The Theory and Practice of Group Psychotherapy*. New York: Basic Books, 1975.

Group Methods in the Training
of Mental Health Professionals

Chapter XIV

PRINCIPLES IN THE ANALYTIC GROUP SUPERVISION OF LEADERS WHO SUPERVISE THERAPISTS USING A GROUP PROCESS MODALITY

Valerie T. Angel, M.S.W.,
Carole Katz, M.S.W.,
Arlene Litwack, M.S.W.,
Mary Maffia, Ph.D.,
Robert A. Mednick, Ph.D.,
Richard Mingoia, M.S.W., and
Rene Rocha, Ph.D.

Editors' Summary. The authors describe specific principles which they believe are helpful in facilitating analytic supervision in groups. These are 1) atmosphere; 2) the supervisory leader; 3) focusing; 4) group supervision processes; and 5) resolution experience. The authors focus on the preconditions necessary for the generation of the resolution experience within the supervisory process as well as on its impact on supervisees and their patients.

The purpose of this paper is to conceptualize and make explicit particular principles we have found to be central to the effective* analytic supervision of leaders who supervise therapists using a group process modality.

Our intention is to offer a contribution to the field of analytic group supervision by drawing from the data of our experience in a supervisory group. Therefore, this paper will be limited to extrapolations of our experiential data derived from our personal participation in analytic group supervision. The requirements for our entry into the analytic supervision group were that we each had previously

---

This paper is dedicated to the late Dr. Benjamin Fielding, Dean of Fellowship Training at the Postgraduate Center for Mental Health. It was under Dr. Fielding's tutelage in an experimental program on the processes of analytic group supervision that the principles we describe in this paper were examined over the course of 10 months. Thanks to Dr. Fielding's deep caring, creativity, and therapeutic vision, we were provided with a group supervisory learning and research experience which was filled with the richness of his supervisory vision. It is from Dr. Fielding's ideas and data of our group supervisory experience with him that the principles set forth in this paper derive.

*By "effective" we mean the activation and facilitation of the "Resolution Experience" described in a later section of this paper.

received psychoanalytic training, and were supervisory leaders of our own supervision groups concomitantly with our membership in a supervisory group for leaders.

The structural boundaries of the supervision process which this paper addresses consist of a unit of three central referents, each having impact on the other. The first referent is the relationship and processes operative between the therapist and patient. The second is the supervisory process where the individual therapist receives supervision in a group supervision modality. The third is the group supervisory milieu where the group supervisor of individual therapists receives supervision, that is, where leaders who supervise individual therapists in group supervision themselves enter into a group supervisory process in order to enhance the effectiveness of their respective supervisory groups. The diagram below makes graphic the boundaries of the supervision structure to which this paper attends.

For purposes of exposition, the principles which follow have been set into five categories: atmosphere, supervisory leader, focusing, group supervision process, and resolution experience.

The principles which are described in each of these categories, when activated in the experiential life of the supervisory structure, are mutually interdependent. That is, the experiences which one principle represents require the presence of concomitant or sequential experiences as represented in the other principles. For example, principles specific to the "focusing" category require prerequisite and ongoing experiences specific to the "atmosphere" and "supervisory leader" categories.

ATMOSPHERE

A central principle in the creation of an analytic group supervision process is the establishment and maintenance of a nurturant and, as much as possible, anxiety-free atmosphere. It is within such an affectively toned group context that the processes intrinsic to learning and specific to the goals of group supervision can best be facilitated.

The climate for this is characterized by a pervasive group attitude of caring. Each group member experiences and comes to trust in a noncritical, nonjudgmental, accepting, gentle, and supportive "holding environment" (4). Inherent in this group attitude is an appreciation and valuing of each group member, and an awareness and respect for all to have defenses, resistance, and conflict. When such an atmosphere is created in the life of the supervision group, the issues of personal competence and competition are generally neutralized. In their place occurs a collective concern for mutual helping and learning.

In an atmosphere in which caring and mutual respect and helping are felt, the ulterior personal agendas of individual group members become secondary to the specific objectives and tasks of the supervisory group. Therefore, problems in the maintenance of focus as described in a later section become minimized.

With the maintenance of a felt empathy in the group, members implicitly come to present their specific problems voluntarily. This precludes an authoritarian imposition of scheduling or requiring members to present. It is the tone of the group milieu which activates the willingness of members to present, share, interact, and utilize the richness of the group process.

Rather than a closing over of material specific to the content and supervisory needs being presented, a group atmosphere of genuine appreciation for the pre-

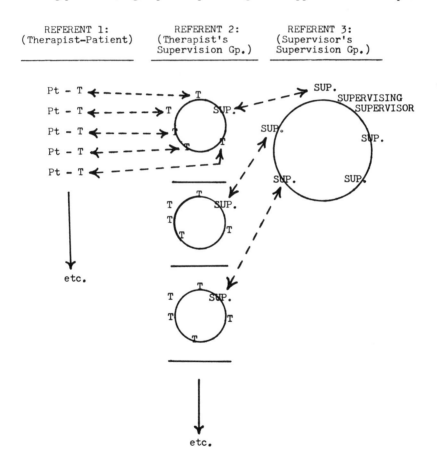

DIAGRAM 1: Graphic representation of the three referent supervisory structure.

senter leads to a searching and collective exploratory process. Therefore, associations and affective experience provoked within each group member are given over to the pursuit of meeting the presenter's specific supervisory needs.

When critical, agitating, or tangential processes emerge, the nurturant group atmosphere allows such group experiences to be utilized in the service of understanding the material presented and furthering the supervisory goals. Moreover, when group members feel the intrinsic caring of the supervision group, they come to expect that any affective or associative experience may have specific meaning to the supervisory need presented. The group member, therefore, assumes responsibility for facilitating the supervisory process in the direction of meeting the emergent supervisory need.

In an analytic supervision group in which the characteristics of a nurturant and caring atmosphere prevail, group members experience an implicit feeling of not being alone. Therefore, those frustrations and unified group struggles which occur become open to the realm of creativity, a place where uncertainty can be invited rather than avoided because of personal insecurity.

We have found that when such a group atmosphere is created and maintained, supervisory transformations which occur in the experience of group members are transmitted down through the entire chain of supervisory contact as shown in Diagram 1. That is, such transformations which occur in the supervisors' supervision group become active in the therapists' supervision group, and finally become reflected in the individual therapists' work with their patients.

SUPERVISORY LEADER

The nature of the supervisory leader's presence and actions in analytic group supervision process is crucial. It profoundly affects the formation of the group atmosphere and impacts on the direction of the group in meeting the goals of supervision.

The group leader enters into and maintains him- or herself in the group supervisory process with an intrinsically genuine attitude. This attitude is composed of several interdependent characteristics. For example, we have found that the supervisory goals and resolution experience are best facilitated when the leader speaks softly, listens softly, and exudes a special caring and sense of dignity for the group members and the group-as-a-whole. This contributes to maintaining a nurturance and sense of security in the supervisory group atmosphere.

By establishing such a leadership role, group members are affected in a particular way. The need for specific kinds of resistance, defenses, or other processes which may impair a group sense of cooperation and trust are diminished.

Another principle we have found to be central in facilitating the group supervisory process has to do with the leader's position in response to the group process and supervisory material presented. When the leader takes his lead from the postulate that creativity has no rigidity, he establishes a specific kind of modeling. In such a mode of experience, the leader suspends personal investments in superimposing theoretical canons. Instead, he remains "open" (3) to a specific listening experience largely free of judgments and predisposed explanations. We have found that often the emergence and processes occurring in the "resolution experience" are blocked or impaired when predisposed theorizing and intellectualizing occur. Such processes often occur at particular vulnerable points as manifestations of anxiety reactions to the emergent transformations in the resolution experience.

By the leader's assuming such a posture of open listening, he or she allows for and facilitates all of the group members to be open to such a mode of listening. When an open listening process is present, the supervisory group is freer to utilize its full repository of life experience. Each presenter then feels surrounded and "held" by emotionally attendant, open-listening, and nonjudgmental fellow members. Within the leader's posture of open listening, interpretation is rare.

The group leader frees the group to use its full repository of life experience by establishing a model of open listening to the presenter and the group. The leader draws from his trust in the rich life experience of each group member, and "takes leads" from the emergent experiences of others in the group. From this position, the leader conveys a sense of appreciation and value for the experiences of the group members. The leader uses the presentations of the group members' experiences and the group processes which these set in motion as important contributions in guiding the group supervisory process.

Another principle we have found to be significant in facilitating an effective group supervisory process is the leader's establishing and maintaining a specific and highly personal *frame* of focus (2). This frame of focus is characterized by a keen attention to the needs of the presenter as well as the processes operating in the group which assist in identifying the presenter's supervisory needs. In this frame of focus, the leader not only models "open listening," he also facilitates a kind of group attention to the presenter in which the group members *feel* what the presenter feels. With the leader's guidance through this modeling, the manifest and latent meanings of the presenter's communications are given a specific group structure in which to be heard, received, processed, and responded to.

The leader's actions and guidance in the supervision group are responsible for establishing the central focusing process so vital to the analytic group supervision experience. This focusing process will be discussed in the next section.

A concluding principle specific to the leader is that he strives not to leave out or ignore anyone in the supervisory group. We have found that often when a group member feels left out, this signals an aspect of the presenter's supervisory need which has been ignored. The leader knows that while the focus must be on the presenter's supervisory needs, ancillary needs relevant to the presenter may be enacted in the group by other members. Well-timed and specifically focused attention to the other group members may ultimately assist in bringing about fuller attention to the needs of the presenter, and facilitate the resolution experience within the emotional life of both the presenter and the group.

FOCUSING

Central to activating an effective analytic group supervision process in which the resolution experience emerges is the group's focusing upon the group member who presents a supervisory problem. Focusing is a multifaceted group process in which the group attends, hears, and reacts in specific ways to the manifest and latent meanings of what and how the presenter communicates.

Principles which we have found to be nuclear to the focusing process rest on the postulate that contained within the presenter's communications are therapeutic conflicts ultimately related to the patient-therapist dyad. Therefore, the presenter is seen as the bearer of those conflicts which require supervisory attention and care. However, while this postulate is assumed, we have found that the focus must be directly on the emergent needs of the presenter. The principle here is that before the supervisory group attends to issues of the patient or therapist, it focuses on identifying the presenter's problems and meeting his or her supervisory needs. We have found that when this focus is maintained in the group through the resolution experience, the nature of the conflict which created the therapeutic impasse between therapist and patient or therapist and supervisor becomes clarified. This clarification occurs through a unique emotional and cognitive experience. We have found that this leads not only to a deeply felt clarification made in this group process but also becomes transmitted down through the chain of supervisory contact to the locus of the problem in the patient-therapist dyad.

The process of focusing proceeds after the foundations of the group supervisory atmosphere and supervisory leader modeling functions have been established. We have found that the sharper the focus about the nature of the supervisory conflict or problem, the closer we come to the inner experience of the presenter.

With opening listening active in the group process, the group attends to the *exact* words of the presenter. Often the leader may ask the presenter, "Let me see if I heard you correctly," followed by the leader or other group members repeating the exact words of the presenter.

Although the presenter may use expressions such as "I'm stuck," "I'm confused,'' or "I don't know where to go with this supervisee (or patient),'' they do little to clarify the nature of the conflict which created the need to present. The knowledge of the presenter's supervisory needs comes from observing and attentively listening to the presenter's exact words, the way the presenter speaks to the group about the supervisee or patient, and the effect that these presentations have upon the group members and group process. This is sometimes reflected in the way group members feel toward the presenter, or their experience in the group. The full meaning of what the presenter's needs may be will only become apparent as the group process unfolds.

Another principle specific to the focusing process refers to the group members' attunement to the urgency or nature of the presenter's need to present. If the group members can reflect back to the presenter an awareness of the meanings of what is being said and convey a genuine appreciation of this material, the presenter experiences an internal validation of the experienced problem. This experience allows for the reduction of anxiety and generally leads to the revelation of more affectively-toned material central to the presented problem, as well as the presenter's relationship to the supervisee, therapist, or patient.

Under such conditions, the focusing process highlights the intensity of feelings and the content which unfolds. When the focusing process is on target and the necessary conditions regarding atmosphere are maintained, the nucleus of the supervisory problem emerges along with a freedom and willingness to learn.

Often, the presenter will inform the group in words or nonverbal expression whether the group is on target in its responsiveness to the presenter's supervisory needs. The full meaning of the presenter's internal request and supervisory need from the group will only be known when the presenter expresses satisfaction either verbally or by some bodily movement. This often occurs as a soft smile. The principle intrinsic here is that only the presenter can be the final and conclusive judge of the accuracy of the group's focusing.

A final principle in relation to the focusing process is a sensitive structuring of what material should appropriately be dealt with in supervision. Here the leader gently guides and holds the boundaries of focus to material representative of the intrapsychic life of the patient, therapist, or group supervisor, as expressed through the emotional life of the presenter. While the focus is maintained within the confines of this material, the intrapsychic lives of each group member are clearly affected and touched.

When the focus strays to tangential issues or into the personal life of the presenter, the refocusing process occurs. The group, guided by the leader, utilizes such misfocusing to facilitate greater responsiveness to the presenter's supervisory needs.

Focusing on the presenter's needs occurs within the context of the ongoing group process. Therefore, the specific characteristics of the analytic group supervisory process deserve particular attention since it is these processes which animate the supervisory experience.

GROUP SUPERVISORY PROCESS

Utilization of a group process modality for the supervision of therapists and supervisors has similar general goals to those of individual supervision. All supervision aims at promoting the growth and learning of the therapist, and facilitating constructive therapeutic action within the therapist-patient dyad. However, we have found the group process modality to have unique advantages in analytic supervision. Because of the multiple person structure of a group and those processes intrinsic to a group milieu, the complex of actions alive in the group process become resources for the supervisory function.

All group members are exposed to a plethora of associations, affective experience, and viewpoints. The unconscious repertoire and process of each group member is placed at the service of the group supervisory function. When utilized effectively, we have found that these resources animate a particular individual and collective experience. This experience provides direction, information, and an emotional context instrumental to the resolution of supervisory or therapeutic conflicts introduced by the presenting member of the group.

Another unique attribute of the group analytic supervisory process is that it intrinsically addresses the question of what to do with the communications of the presenter. The group becomes the instrument through which teaching and learning are established and promoted.

We have found that the group process facilitates a sharpening of the listening process and increases the observational field because of the greater availability of ideas and feelings. The richness of these processes helps move the group members closer to an individual and collective understanding of the supervisee and/or patient. Through the group experience the presenter is availed a unique experience since a number of peers articulate their inner experience of the patient, the presenter, and also the group itself. The congruence of affect between one or several members and the presenter can create a relaxation of tension in the presenter, which is felt by all the group members through their identification with the presenter. This process is experienced even though various individuals in the group may be at different stages of identification and satisfaction. Naturally, the more the members of the group are attuned to the needs and feelings of the presenter, the better the group can focus on the presenter's supervisory needs.

The group leader gently guides the group toward an increasing utilization of the group process in order to sharpen the target of focus. However, if the group supervisor were the only member who attended to the presenter's needs, it would not be possible for an effective group supervisory process to develop. Where the group processes are utilized effectively, each group member actively helps the presenter and other group members to work through each problem whether it be with a supervisee, patient, or within the supervisory group. This process of helping is initially activated in response to the presenter's implicit request for caring and attention to a specific supervisory need.

We have found that an essential element in the group supervisory process is the way in which the group supervisor deals with not having the answers. By the leader or the group members' reflection of this dilemma within the group process, the group can contain feelings of frustration or a sense of impotence. This conveys an acknowledgment and appreciation for the process of the group as a primary mode of learning and problem resolution.

To utilize and highlight the group process the leader might ask at the beginning of a group supervision meeting if there are any reactions to the last group meeting. The leader thus utilizes the group process to recognize the evolving experience of the group members, as well as the presenter.

Another unique advantage of group supervision is that each group member learns from the experience of the presenter in the group. Often, there is a myriad of parallel processes (1) which arise within the group or become observable to group members. These group processes serve to stimulate a collective experience in which the transformations which occur in the presenter simultaneously or ultimately occur, to varying degrees, in the other group members. This permits a greater accessibility of impact from supervisory contact. These impacts reverberate throughout the entire supervisory structure which we have outlined in Diagram 1.

Each member actively participates in the creation and living-through of those prerequisite experiences out of which the resolution experience occurs. It is the group process which strives to generate and bring these conditions and resolution experience to fruition.

RESOLUTION EXPERIENCE

All of the work which goes on in the group contributes to the creation of a resolution experience in the life of the presenter. This might be described as an experiential state in which the presenter feels genuinely helped, cared for, and understood on profound levels.

When the resolution experience is attained, the entire group experiences a parallel state in which feelings of inner freedom and joy occur. This mutual group sharing is essential to the process.

While the focus remains on the presenter, the resolution experience is a shared one. In order to achieve the resolution experience, each group member must enter into his or her own internal processes parallel to and concordant with those of the presenter. In these moments of emotional identification with the presenter, there is generally increased sharing and a deep collective feeling of group unity.

This is a rather delicate process. Each member must join it or, at a minimum, not interfere in order for the resolution experience to take place. A characteristic of the resolution experience is that both the presenter and group members feel a vulnerability due to a reduction in defensive activity and a heightened intimacy.

Even a subtle insensitivity in timing, wording, or body language can be felt as an interruption of the resolution experience. We have found that criticism, competitiveness, or any other form of aggression will potentially dispense or fragment the resolution process for varying lengths of time.

However, while the resolution experience is delicate, it is not fragile. It can be reapproached many times and from many directions when necessary. There is a tenaciousness in the group's efforts toward the resolution experience similar to the developmental drive toward integration. It provides its own rewards.

The actual amount of time devoted to a resolution experience is an important factor. Because of the vulnerability felt in these moments, it can be tempting to move out of it too quickly. It is helpful to allow the experience to be recognized and felt by all group members before shifting away.

The next step is often heralded by the presenter's verbalizations of the feeling of having been helped. Very often the presenter refers back to the original problem with new insights, renewed energy, and new ideas regarding ways to work with the supervisee or patient. A new and open internal position is found. The presenter often subsequently reports being able to enter into a state of emotional concordance with the supervisee or patient and thereby experiences freedom from what had previously been a countertransferential encumbrance. Our experience has shown repeatedly that the efforts of the resolution experience soon resonate throughout the entire supervisory structure.

REFERENCES

1. Ekstein, R. and Wallerstein, R. *The Teaching and Learning of Psychotherapy* (2nd ed.). New York: International Universities Press, 1972, pp. 177-196.
2. Fielding, B. Focusing in dynamic short-term therapy: Three case studies. *Colloquium,* 2: 64-78, June 1979.
3. Fielding, B. Group supervision: The interaction of therapists and a supervisor that facilitates and hinders learning in group. *Colloquium,* 2 & 3: 28-36, December 1979 & June 1980.
4. Winnicott, D. *The Maturational Process and the Facilitating Environment: Studies in the Theory of Emotional Development.* New York: International Universities Press, 1965.

Chapter XV

ISOMORPHISM AND FREE ASSOCIATION: A CASE ILLUSTRATING THE INTEGRATION OF PSYCHOANALYTIC AND GENERAL SYSTEMS THEORY IN THE SUPERVISION OF GROUP WORK

Michael H. Lawler, Ed.D.

Editors' Summary. The author uses case material from group supervision to suggest the complementarity of certain aspects of psychoanalytic theory and general systems theory. Specifically, he discusses the concepts of free association and isomorphy. The use of the former reveals possible sources of resistance, whereas the latter provides an explanation of the dynamics of change which occur in the several human systems involved in this case. Finally, he suggests that Freud and von Bertalanffy share in common a focus on nonobservable causes of observable phenomena.

The purpose of this article is to present a case illustrating the application of specific principles of both psychoanalytic and general systems theory. These two metatheories are rooted deeply in distinctive paradigms of thought, which in turn dominated the thinking in several generations of Western orthodox science. The two paradigms are most often discussed as contrasting, representing very different approaches to investigating the nature of living phenomena. However, this author suggests that specific principles from each of the theories are similar and complementary in nature.

THE CASE

Lifehouse (a pseudonym) is a halfway house for adolescents located in the northeastern United States. It is a residence for up to eight young men and women requiring either temporary or long-term housing. A staff of three to five live in the residence. Historically, the house staff have maintained contact with

---

Portions of this paper were presented at the American Group Psychotherapy Association Annual Meeting, Houston, Texas, February, 1981. The author wishes to thank Dr. Helen Durkin and Dr. Robert Gordon for their criticisms of earlier drafts of this paper.

parents and siblings of residents, depending on resources and the current "house philosophy."

At the time in question, the house was expanding its involvement with parents and families through the establishment of a weekly parents' group, consisting of five to nine parents. I was contacted to provide supervision for the two social workers who were co-therapists of the group.

The parents' group was a supportive, "adaptational" group (11) with limited therapeutic goals. The group provided a regular opportunity for parents to discuss the common experience of an adolescent family member living in LifeHouse, develop cohesion through this identification, explore the circumstances surrounding the event, exchange advice regarding common conflicts, and express their wishes about the future. The group could also provide a means of "cooling out" crises and detoxifying to some extent the intense affect that most often goes hand-in-hand with such developmental derailments.

The group was a pilot project for LifeHouse and as summer approached, the group neared an ending. The date of the final meeting was announced by the co-leaders. In supervision, the co-therapists began to present material which indicated individual and group-as-a-whole response to the impending termination. Some of the contents and dynamics suggested parallel themes of individuation, dependency, and loss which also existed within a family and/or marital pair.

The above observation about the group was presented to the co-therapists, along with the suggestion that they be less active in the next session and allow the material to develop more exclusively from the group. The following week they again presented material, more manifest this time, which indicated responses to ending. The co-therapists, however, presented other concerns. In the supervisory session which followed, the content, dynamics, and observable patterns remained the same. The group material increasingly revealed responses to impending termination. The co-therapists, however, continued to present concerns other than what the group material seemed to indicate. The characteristics of those concerns included interventions with individual members or couples, feeling ignored by the members, and feeling increasingly "frustrated" and "irritable" because "the group has become unresponsive."

The co-therapists seemed increasingly depressed and withdrawn as they continued to request some solution for the "unresponsiveness" of the group. I, in turn, experienced the co-therapists' "unresponsiveness" to my supervisory efforts. I once again suggested that the group and individual dynamics were in response to termination. As the now familiar repetitive pattern unfolded, I decided to turn inward and listen to my own feelings.

It is difficult, retrospectively, to capture precisely that experience and nearly impossible to use ordered, written language to describe the sequence and experience of those associations. Recollection of the sequence is roughly as follows: feeling ignored and helpless, feeling angry and then guilty and saddened. From these associations a phrase emerged: "not taking care of them right." The word "right" felt ominous. Next came a sentence: "There is a right way and only one right way." A picture of me trying to do the "one right thing" for my parents came clearly in my view, the longing to care for them and be cared for by them. Thinking about my family of origin, the word "divorce" emerged.

Shifting to the present, the word "divorce" stood out in relationship to the co-therapists. I became conscious of the fact that for several weeks now the manner of presentation by the co-therapists had altered drastically. While previously much dialogue occurred between the co-therapists and eye contact had shifted evenly among the three of us, I now realized that they had not been looking at or speaking with each other for some weeks. Recalling a comment by a colleague, H. Grunebaum, I thought to myself: "They act as if they are emotionally divorced." The thought occurred to me that I had missed the here-and-now divorce due to its intensity and focused on the background "divorce" of the co-leaders and the group.

I sensed a deep underlying connectedness for all of us amidst my associations. My difficulty verbalizing the connection reaffirmed the trustworthiness of the associations. After one of the co-leaders finished a statement, I spoke: "I feel a sense of divorce. Between you, us, and within the group. I don't understand it, but it feels very real and important. What do you make of it?" One of the co-leaders spoke after a pause: "That is an odd way to put it, but yes, I suppose we are divorcing in a sense." One of the co-therapists had been offered a new job; it was an advancement in career and was in a distant part of the metropolitan area. The news had been communicated to the co-therapist a few weeks earlier. It meant that the attachment formed during the work would end or change dramatically.

Following this announcement, a lively conversation began between the two therapists. They spoke of mixed feelings about the coming event, pleased about the success but saddened at the loss it meant. They spoke warmly of their times talking over coffee after the group and following supervisory hours. Their work together had evolved into a collegial relationship they valued highly. Now, the hope of a continued intimacy was foreclosed by the choice of one to accept the new job. At the close of the hour, there was a tender silence between them; afterwards as they rose to leave, each said: "We had best say goodbye to you also. . . . Supervision with you is ending also." This closing remark revealed another level of the significance of my associations and provided a further clue as to my own idiosyncratic blindspot in the resistive condition.

I decided not to make any explicit connection between what had transpired in supervision and the phenomenon occurring within the group. The co-therapists also made no direct references to this supervisory session and what then transpired in the group.

The final supervisory sessions included lively exchanges between the co-therapists regarding the termination process in the group, their respective responses, the manifest and latent reactions of various group members, and their feeling that this was the central theme of the group. They discussed the parallel between parental dynamics respecting the group's ending and family dynamics and adolescent behavior which preceded an admission to LifeHouse. They compared notes about how they viewed each group member's expression of the affective and historical themes of attachment and loss. They seemed to feel that they and the group were partners in the process of saying goodbye.

They also said goodbye to me and I to them. We exchanged views evaluating the supervision and each expressed some personal feeling about me as a supervisor.

TWO PRINCIPLES: FREE ASSOCIATION AND ISOMORPHISM

The work described above illustrates the soundness and compatibility of two principles which are cornerstones of two metatheories: psychoanalytic theory and general systems theory. Most therapists are familiar with the principle of free association, its origins, and its uses in therapy as developed by Sigmund Freud in the years 1892-1896 (2, 4). In his early work, Freud considered the technique of free association to be a means of enabling the person to rediscover the repressed experience and affect. The "unbearable memories" (13) are returned to awareness; free association was the tool for accomplishing abreaction (undoing the process of repression).

Few clinicians are familiar with general systems theory and the principle of isomorphism. General systems theory is not to be confused with the nonspecific and popular use of the word "system" as a synonym for such words as "interactional," "group," or "interpersonal." Erwin Laszlo provides the following brief definition of the general systems perspective:

> This means thinking in terms of facts and events in the context of wholes, forming integrated sets with their own properties and relationships. Looking at the the world *in terms of such sets of integrated relations constitutes the systems view.* (7, p. 19)

The major, initial author associated with this metatheory is Ludwig von Bertalanffy (14), a biologist who developed his ideas beginning in the late 1920s. He believed that certain "puzzles" in biology were not resolvable so long as the effort to understand them was constrained by reliance upon the prevailing scientific models and methods (6, see chapters 4 and 10). He viewed the prevailing models as reductionistic/mechanistic schemata focusing upon limited variables and linear causality. From the perspective of the scientific historian, the body of principles and theory now referred to collectively as general systems theory may mark a revolution of paradigms in contemporary scientific thought. The principle of isomorphy is one of several major principles developed by von Bertalanffy and others. This principle is concerned with the proposition that all living systems have shared underlying structure and/or functions. In a speech in 1967 before the American Psychiatric Association, von Bertalanffy stated:

> These traits are common to biological, behavioral, psychologic and social phenomena; there are, as it is called, isomorphisms between biological, behavioral, psychologic and social phenomena and sciences. (14, p. 37)

H. Durkin, a therapist who pioneered in the application of this metatheory to clinical work, has remarked about isomorphy:

> All kinds and levels of systems reveal certain fundamental isomorphies of structure and function whose interaction determines their mode of operation. (1, p. 12)

Across the boundaries of living systems, one can discover basic underlying operations of a like manner, patterning of structure, or function which exhibits a commonality between the systems. Edgar Levenson, in speaking of the anthropolological work of Lévi-Strauss, says:

> In Lévi-Strauss' deep structure, the same pattern will emerge whether the person is organizing his village streets, his cooking patterns, his traffic systems or his family kinship relationships. For Lévi-Strauss, this pattern will be innately the same for a Parisian or a Kwakiutl. (8, p. 34)

For example, in our own culture, the red color means stop and the green means go. If we wish an intermediate symbol, we choose yellow; it is halfway between green and red on the spectrum. The ordering of go-caution-stop is the same as green-yellow-red. The color system and the signalling system share this isomorphy; one is a transformation of the other (8, p. 35).

In a recent and excellent article, Peter Steinglass (12) refers to the "systems perspective," meaning a perspective which places great weight on patterning and pattern recognition. This approach contrasts with the scientific method of the nineteenth century and the scientific model underlying the origins of psychoanalysis, namely, the use of deductive reasoning, a focus upon limited variables, and a presumption of linear causality.

Isomorphy can refer to an aspect of the intrapsychic process, the manifestations of individual personality in a group of nonrelated persons, the manifestations of commonality in the family group, or as Lévi-Strauss suggests, to patterning in cultural rituals which reveal a common guiding principle. One can think of it as our deepest inner rules, manifest in a wide variety of environments over time.

DISCUSSION: THOUGHTS ON THE INTEGRATION OF PSYCHOANALYTIC THEORY AND GENERAL SYSTEMS THEORY

In the LifeHouse case, there are several distinct systems: the group-as-a-whole, the group and co-therapist system, the supervisor and co-therapists, the co-therapy pair, and the respective individual intrapsychic systems of each participant. I suggest that there is an isomorphy present. For our discussion, it will be referred to as the isomorphy of "response to attachment and loss." It might be argued that there are two isomorphic structures present. One is that which manifests itself in the resistive phase and the second is that which manifests itself in the supervisory and group sessions following the one recounted in this paper. At this point, I think of this phenomenon as one isomorphy which changes rather than two distinct isomorphies.

The observable manifestations of this isomorphy can be sketched using behavioral and affective material. Affectively, it includes the feeling of frustration, sadness, anger, warmth, and regard expressed by various people involved. Behaviorally, it includes withdrawal and overactivity, bickering and avoidance—all manifest in the parents' group, the co-leader system, and the supervision system.

In terms of interior processes, the supervisor's countertransference difficulties are a piece of the isomorphic structure. My unconscious denial of my value to the co-therapists, their loss of me, and my valuing of them are elements in this countertransference prior to the moment when, to paraphrase Racker, a sufficient part of me became free to associate to the feelings and utilize the result (9). The countertransference is a special part of my own idiosyncratic response to matters of attachment and loss rooted in my early childhood and familial system. Each system, individual and collective, was involved in what Durkin terms a morphostatic repetition (1).

The idea that isomorphies are evidenced by such material is not commonly agreed upon. It has been my own clinical experience that such material provides the initial clues about the existence of such central individual, group, or familial structures/dynamics.

The intervention which followed from my associations revealed the denied affects and theme of attachment and loss within the collegial friendship system of the co-therapists. Fragments of what had been repressed surfaced immediately. The result was a frank exchange of the previously blocked affects. I assumed that this fragment/phenomenon was a part of the whole and isomorphic in the other interpersonal and intrapsychic systems. For example, I assumed that the denial of affect in this relationship was linked to the inability to hear the expression of attachment and loss by members of the group. If it was indeed isomorphic, a change in one system could affect the related systems without explicit verbal instruction.

Some might suggest that the co-leaders are the leading subsystem for the group-as-a-whole. If a change occurs in that leading system, it will have more potency (3, 5). Others would perhaps view the group-as-a-whole as the leading subsystem. The author is suggesting that the isomorphy itself is the leading subsystem from the standpoint of the phenomenon of change and from both the analytic perspective and systems perspective. If the isomorphic structure or element changes, all other systems manifesting that isomorphy will change (3). The transformation of the attachment-loss dynamic in one system (the co-therapists as friends) was transmitted in those other systems where this dynamic was structurally isomorphic (co-therapists as workers, supervisory triad, and the parents' group).

In the LifeHouse case, the psychoanalytic belief in the existence of the unconscious is crucial to discovering the initial aspects of a resistive process.* On the other hand, the positive changes in each of several interconnected systems are explained in part by the principle of isomorphy. This principle from systems theory provides an explanation for the observation of like changes in several systems in the absence of any conscious verbal/cognitive connection (insight) in the supervision.

Free association, one of the earliest notions developed by Freud, can therefore form a conceptual link between psychoanalytic theory and general systems theory. The goal of free association is the uncovering of unconscious material (10). Writers, beginning with Freud, frequently employ the word "connection" in discussing this principle. Free associations can reveal the unconscious underlying connections among seemingly diverse content or between event and affect. The practice of free association gives clues to the unconscious; it unbinds the surface habits of mind to reveal deeper structures.

Isomorphy is a principle by which von Bertalanffy attempted to explain the underlying structures and processes observed in the field of biology. As abstract and diffuse as the principle may be, it is clearly concerned with noting underlying commonalities and organizing principles of life process/activity.

Freud and von Bertalanffy share a common conceptual ground, attempting to solve like conceptual puzzles based on direct observation. Both were focusing upon underlying processes or structures. The case illustrated in this paper suggests

---

*This belief in the unconscious is in sharp contrast to much of the prevailing opinion among systems-oriented family therapists who appear to have thrown the "baby out with the bath water" in their rebellion against the psychoanalytic model and adoption of the systems perspective.

that the two principles are not simply complementary in the abstract, but can work hand-in-hand in the living process of therapeutic intervention.

The free association method of psychoanalysis brings a very specific tool by which the therapist can better understand and intervene respecting resistance to change. The concept of isomorphy from general systems theory brings an understanding of how and/or why change can occur in various interconnected systems (intrapsychic and interpersonal), without specific cognitive, explicit insight.

REFERENCES

1. Durkin, H. The development of systems theory and its implications for the theory and practice of group psychotherapy. *In:* L. Wolberg and M. Aronson (Eds.), *Group Therapy.* New York: Stratton Intercontinental Medical Book Corp., 1975.
2. Greenson, R. *The Technique and Practice of Psychoanalysis.* New York: International Universities Press, 1967.
3. Jackson, D. The individual and the larger contexts. *In:* W.G. Gray, F.J. Duhl, and N.D. Rizzo. (Eds.), *General Systems Theory and Psychiatry.* Boston: Little, Brown, 1966.
4. Jones, E. *The Life and Work of Sigmund Freud, Vol. 1.* New York: Basic Books, 1953.
5. Kernberg, O. Leadership functioning and organizational regression. *International Journal of Group Psychotherapy,* 28: 3-25, 1978.
6. Kuhn, T.S. *The Structure of Scientific Revolutions.* Chicago: University of Chicago Press, 1962.
7. Laszlo, E. *The Systems View of the World: The Natural Philosophy of the New Developments in the Sciences.* New York: George Brazilier, 1972.
8. Levenson, E.A. *The Fallacy of Understanding.* New York: Basic Books, 1972.
9. Racker, H. *Transference and Countertransference: An Inquiry into the Changing Structure of Psychoanalysis.* New York: International Universities Press, 1968.
10. Saul, L. *Psychodynamically Based Psychotherapy.* New York: Science House, 1972.
11. Spotnitz, H. *In:* H.I. Kaplan and B.J. Sadock (Eds.), *Comprehensive Group Psychotherapy.* Baltimore: Williams and Wilkins, 1971.
12. Steinglass, P. The conceptualization of marriage from a systems theory perspective. *In:* T.J. Paolino and B.S. McCrady (Eds.), *Marriage and Marital Therapy.* New York: Brunner/Mazel, 1978.
13. Thompson, C. *Psychoanalysis: Evolution and Development.* New York: Grove Press, 1950.
14. von Bertalanffy, L. General systems theory and psychiatry—An overview. *In:* W.A. Gray, F.J. Duhl, and N.D. Rizzo (Eds.), *General Systems Theory and Psychiatry.* Boston: Little, Brown, 1969.

Chapter XVI

LEARNING GROUP DYNAMICS: COMPARISON OF A LEADERLESS AND TRADITIONAL FORMAT

Walter N. Stone, M.D., Bonnie L. Green, Ph.D., and Mary Grace, M.S.

Editors' Summary. This article examines learning during a group dynamics training program in which a leaderless model was compared with a traditional model. Using a crossover design with two leaders each conducting the training in a leaderless or traditional fashion, no overall differences in learning between the formats were found. It was concluded that the cognitive component overshadowed learning during the experiential phase and accounted for the ho-mogeneous learning which took place. Leadership and Group Attraction Questionnaires completed at two-week intervals during the 16 weeks of training showed that one leader was rated higher than the other, whichever format was used. This difference appeared to influence the group attraction ratings during the early portion of the training but not in the latter portions. This finding supports the notion of a shift from leader to peer-oriented responses in the group development.

INTRODUCTION

The primary goal of group dynamics training in the Department of Psychiatry at the University of Cincinnati is the learning about group-as-a-whole dynamics and processes. Neophyte group therapists who have been exposed to individual (dyadic) work often do not grasp group concepts but see them as discontinuous with their previous experience. The shift in the student's perspective in examining phenomena from an intrapsychic or interactive framework to a group-as-a-whole viewpoint does not come easily.

Yalom (18) has suggested that the primary method of educating students to group dynamics is through a combination of experiential and cognitive elements. Experiential training is conducted across a spectrum of models which may be viewed as a number of dichotomies (1). One dichotomy is that of therapy versus training; a second is interpersonal versus group-as-a-whole; a third is process versus content. No available model includes all ways of conceptualizing groups. Any particular choice emphasizes one or several salient viewpoints, but the student eventually must become aware of these dichotomies.

The cognitive component which is used to raise the experiential learning to a conceptual framework has further broadened the number of possible training formats. For instance, didactic material may be given before or after experiential training (9) or it may be integrated in some portion during the experiential sessions (6, 13).

In our continuing explorations of differing models we began to explore the value of a leaderless group (8). We were unable to locate any mention of such a format in our literature review. There probably was good reason for the absence of a leaderless group as a training device, since it would be difficult to help participants learn leadership functioning from this type of experience. Moreover, there was fear of psychological damage resulting from loss of the leader's containment or control functions and consequent chaos. Nevertheless, there seemed to be potential benefit to the trainees from examining group processes without a designated leader. The shift would be away from authority relations to peer relations, thereby highlighting tasks of sharing, conflict resolution, power, and powerlessness. Learning about authority relations would occur through fantasy with no real object present. Finally, it was hoped that trainees would focus on the learning about the group processes and be less concerned with "how do you actually lead a group?"

The absence of a leader does not necessarily imply lack of structure for the training group. Structure was provided in the course description which included time and space assignments, as well as the outline of the training. Groups were scheduled to meet for 90-minute sessions once weekly for 16 weeks. The first four weeks were traditional didactic sessions with the designated faculty instructor leading discussion of assigned readings. The following 12-week 90-minute sessions were divided into two segments: the first 60 minutes were experiential; the final 30 minutes were processing and integrating data derived from the experiential component. Two variations of the experiential component have been studied. In one variation the leader assumes the traditional role, commenting upon or interpreting group processes as they occur. In the other, the leader is present in the room taking process notes, but remains silent during the experiential component. In the 30-minute segment leaders in both formats assume a traditional educational role, helping facilitate discussion and cognitive integration of the just completed process.

As reported previously (7), participants in these groups evaluated their learning at the completion of the 16 weeks of training by means of a questionnaire adapted from Correa et al. (3). Participants in the leaderless group rated their overall learning lower and felt less prepared to lead a group than those in the traditionally led experiential groups (7). However, the group leaders much preferred the leaderless format and felt this format enabled them to teach group dynamics very effectively (8).

The present study had a twofold purpose: 1) to compare the learning which takes place in the leaderless and the traditional formats utilizing a questionnaire which asked trainees to respond as if they were the group leader; and 2) to study the differential effects of the two formats upon leadership evaluation and group attraction. In both formats the only difference was as described, that is, during the 60-minute experiential segment in meetings #5 through #16.

METHODS

Design

The research plan was to study four separate training groups—two each year for two years. The major experimental design was to alter the leader's role during the initial hour of the experiential sessions (weeks 5 - 16). The two roles were: (a) the traditional leader who would explicate group processes as they occurred; and (b) the leader who would remain a silent observer, in essence establishing a leaderless group. Both leaders took an active teaching role in the discussion component when a cognitive synthesis of the experience was the focus. The person who led in the traditional fashion the first year assumed the leaderless role in the second year and vice versa. This resulted in four groups: Leader A, leaderless; Leader A, traditional; Leader B, leaderless; and Leader B, traditional.

Subjects

Groups were led by faculty psychiatrists who had a firm commitment to psychodynamic group therapy. Leader A was training to be a psychoanalyst and had five years of experience leading groups. His general approach to group leadership and teaching was open-ended. Leader B was a general psychiatrist who had been conducting group training for 12 years. His group leadership technique was similar to that of Leader A. His teaching style, however, was considerably more structured.

The group members were psychiatric residents who had completed 18 months of training (middle of the R-2 year) and graduate social work and psychology trainees. Groups were limited in size to 12 members and an effort was made to form heterogeneous groups with regard to sex and professional discipline.

Measures

The Group Therapy Questionnaire (GTQ-C) described by Wile (17) presents 21 common group incidents. For each incident, the respondent could choose one or more of the alternatives he or she might be likely to make as the leader. Responses derive from a variety of theoretical approaches to group therapy. The choices include interpretation to an individual or the whole group, role-playing, behavioral techniques, questions, expression of feelings, silence, and structuring responses. The GTQ-C was administered twice: the first time prior to the first didactic meeting, and the second time following the last experiential session.

A Leadership Questionnaire assessed feelings about the leader (i.e., competence, admiration, understanding, effectiveness, and desire to be with him in a future group). Each question was rated on a nine-point scale from "not at all" to "very much." Scoring range could therefore be from 6 to 54 with a midpoint of 30.

A Group Attraction Questionnaire assessed the degree to which participants felt attached to and involved in the group (i.e., the group facilitated my goal attainment, I liked the group, I would try to dissuade members who wanted to leave, I felt included in the group, and I imagined the group worked together in comparison with other groups). This Questionnaire included five questions with a range of 5 to 45 and a mid-point of 25.

The Leadership and Group Attraction Questionnaires, initially adapted from Lieberman et al. (11), had previously been used in a study (15) in which correlations within the questionnaires were high. Leadership and Group Attraction Questionnaires were administered biweekly, beginning with the first didactic session (i.e., weeks 1 through 15).

RESULTS

Forty-one trainees participated in the groups over a two-year period (29 residents, eight social work students, four psychology trainees). Most of the residents were men; most of the social workers were women. The four groups were approximately equal in size, having between nine and 11 participants. Proportions by sex and professional discipline were similar for each format/leader combination.

Responses on the GTQ-C were examined by leadership stance (traditional, leaderless) and person of the leader (A, B). There were no differences in initial or final scores by either dimension for the total number of choices, or by specific item. Thus, neither stance nor leader affected the types of responses that students felt they would make if they were leading a group themselves.

On the other hand, there were some changes for the overall group indicating the type of learning which occurred in the training sessions. Table 1 shows the means and standard deviations for the *total* group on the GTQ-C. It can be seen that one of the changes which occurred between the beginning and end of the

Table 1
Initial and Final Mean and Standard Deviations on the GTQ-C for the Overall
Group (N = 42)

	Initial		Final	
Item	x̄	s.d.	x̄	s.d.
1. Silence	2.5	3.2	6.6	5.7
2. Group Directed	6.5	3.8	5.4	4.3
3. Reassurance-Approval	5.0	3.2	1.9	2.2
4. Subtle Guidance	3.0	2.5	1.1	2.1
5. Structure	3.9	2.1	2.8	1.9
6. Attack	.1	.3	.1	.4
7. Member Feeling	14.9	3.7	9.2	5.8
8. Leader Feeling	3.5	4.2	1.1	3.3
9. Leader Experience	.5	.7	.2	.4
10. Clarification-Confrontation	5.3	3.3	3.3	3.3
11. Group Dynamics Questionnaire	12.8	4.2	11.3	5.3
12. Group Atmosphere Interpretation	8.5	4.3	10.0	5.5
13. Group Dynamic Interpretation	8.9	4.4	10.3	4.9
14. Psychodynamic Interpretation	4.4	3.8	4.8	3.2
15. Personal Life	4.0	3.4	1.2	1.9
16. Past & Present	1.3	2.0	.2	.6
17. Behavior Change	1.2	2.2	.1	.4
18. Nonverbal	.5	1.1	.2	.8
19. Role-playing	1.3	2.1	.2	.5
TOTAL # of choices	88.1	21.0	70.0	20.6
TOTAL Psychodynamic items (1, 7, 10-14)	57.3 (65%)		55.5 (79%)	

course was a significant narrowing of choices (t = 4.66, df = 41, p < .001). The average total number of responses chosen at the beginning was 88.1, while the average number at the end was only 70.0. This was accounted for almost completely by the decrease in non-psychodynamic responses as designated by Wile (17). It can be seen that the proportion of psychodynamic choices was relatively high to begin with (65%). The absolute number of those choices stayed about the same, but since the overall number decreased, the proportion increased (to 79%). Thus, by the end, over three-quarters of the student responses were psychodynamic.

Within the psychodynamic responses there was a tendency for group members to decrease individual dynamic choices, and to increase the number of group-oriented responses (group atmosphere interpretation, group dynamics interpretation) and "silence." Unfortunately, the questionnaire is not completely consistent with regard to whether the items labeled the same way in different situations are group-directed, or individual-directed. Thus, it is not really possible, in the present study, to assess this change.

Responses to the Group Questionnaire and the Leadership Questionnaire were examined by a three-factor analysis of variance design. Such an analysis allows the main effects (stance of the leader, and person of the leader) to be examined separately for their effect on questionnaire responses, and to be examined in combination (stance and person). These two factors were "between" groups (i.e., people were in one group only). "Within" all subjects was the third main factor: time (measurement was repeated on eight occasions regardless of group). The total number of subjects who had complete data on these questionnaires over time was 37.

For the Leadership Questionnaire, there were two significant main effects and no interactions. Collapsing across time and stance, the two leaders, A and B,

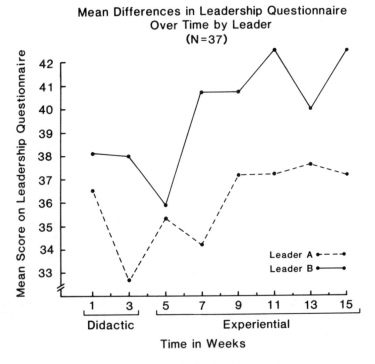

Figure 1.

were rated differently (F = 7.58, df = 1/33, p < .01). Numerically the difference was not large, but Leader B was rated consistently higher ($\bar{x}$ = 40) than was leader A ($\bar{x}$ = 36).

Participants' response to the Leadership Questionnaire also showed a significant difference over time (F = 3.45, df = 7/231, p < .002). This difference is represented in Figure 1. Both leaders had ratings which decreased following the initial sessions, but increased and leveled off once the experiential component had begun. As mentioned, while B's ratings were significantly higher, the slope of the lines did not differ significantly.

The Group Attraction Questionnaire was analyzed in the same fashion. The analysis of that questionnaire showed one significant main effect and two marginally significant interactions. As found on the Leadership Questionnaire, differences over time were significant for Group Attraction as well (F = 3.3, df = 7/231, p < .002). There was a gradual increase in ratings of the groups over time. Figure 2 shows these ratings by leader. The increase was most dramatic for Leader A, whose groups started off relatively low in the earlier sessions but became much more attractive between the weeks 7 and 9. Leader B's groups, on the other hand, showed more variability from rating period to rating period, but no obvious trend up or down over the long run. This interaction nearly reached significance (F = 2.00, df = 7/231, p < .06).

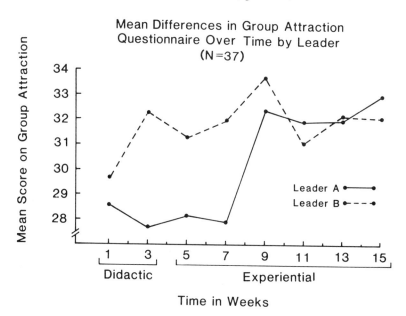

Figure 2.

Table 2
Means by Stance and Leader for the
Group Attraction Questionnaire (N = 37)

	Leader A	Leader B
Traditional Stance	30.0	34.1
Silent Stance	30.5	29.4

The only finding in this report involving stance of the leader was a Leader by Stance interaction on the Group Attraction Questionnaire. Table 2 shows this interaction. While leader A's group was rated as moderately attractive whether he was teaching in the silent or the traditional stance, leader B's groups were differentially rated depending on his role. When he took the silent role, his group was rated at about the same level as that of leader A. When he was teaching in the traditional role, however, his group was rated as highly attractive (F = 3.87, df = 1/33, p < .06).

For purposes of examining the discipline of the participants, social workers and psychologists were combined into a "non-physician" group due to their low numbers. At the initial administration of the GTQ-C, the ony item which differentiated physicians from non-physicians was subtle guidance. Physicians chose this response significantly more often (t = 2.63, df = 40, p < .02). There was also a tendency (t = 1.77, df = 40, p < .09) for non-physicians to choose self-disclosure more frequently. All differences disappeared by follow-up.

DISCUSSION

One of the major purposes of this study was to evaluate differences in learning which took place when the experiential portion of group training was conducted without a leader as contrasted to its being conducted with a traditional leader. Within the overall framework of the training, there were no differences in type of learning between the two formats. Participants in both formats showed similar learning patterns which were characterized by a diminution of non-psychodynamic responses on the GTQ-C from the initial to the final time. There was no change in the number of psychodynamic choices, but the proportion of these choices increased from about two-thirds to more than three-quarters of the total.

Thus using the GTQ-C as a measure of learning, the present study shows an overall change consistent with departmental ideology (14), but no changes related to teaching format.

When the data are examined closely, additional intriguing leads for studying the effects of group training emerge. While the number of psychodynamic responses chosen by the participants changed very little over time, there seemed to be an increase in group-as-a-whole interpretations and a decrease in more individual responses. This would correctly reflect the educational goal of the training. Unfortunately the GTQ-C was constructed so that considerable overlap existed between questions or interpretations categorized as psychodynamic and those categorized as whole-group. Even so, there is some suggestion that trainees had begun to conceptualize whole-group responses.

The absence of difference between the two formats (leaderless and traditional) suggests that much of the integration of learning takes place immediately following the experiential segment in the 30-minute integrative review. It seems that any potential differences in learning in the experiential portion were obviated because the processes were carefully explicated by the leader-teacher. As Lieberman, Yalom and Miles (11) have so clearly demonstrated, a cognitive component is an essential part of learning. Thus pulling together and explaining the group processes in the 30 minutes immediately following the experiential sessions could make more similar the two experiences and generalize the learning for the students (8).

In a previous communication (7), we reported findings from these group participants who rated their learning at the completion of the training. When the leader assumed the traditional role, participants felt they learned more in general, could generalize their knowledge to future group situations, and felt more adequately prepared to conduct a psychotherapy group than participants in the leaderless model. These ratings, reflecting the students' evaluation, are not incompatible with finding no significant differences between models as measured by the GTQ-C. The subjectively more negative ratings of the leaderless groups may be a reflection of the differing methodology, since the GTQ-C measured responses to given situations and not subjective judgments.

Initially, we had suggested that the leaderless format removed structure, which raised anxiety and interfered with learning. However, the responses may also be a measure of the trainees' disappointment at not having a leader who would serve as a model. Such a wish is almost universally present in training groups even when this is not the goal of the training. For example, Redlich and Astrachan (12), using a rigorous Tavistock method, reported that trainees felt knowledgeable about group processes but incompletely prepared to conduct group psychotherapy. One of the underlying reasons for instituting a leaderless group in the first place was because the relatively silent leader in the traditional or Tavistock models was often inappropriately imitated by trainees when they began conducting a psychotherapy group. In order to fulfill trainees' goals of becoming group psychotherapists, other segments of training need to be added to the basic courses and experiences in group dynamics (i.e., observing a group, role-playing, or leading a group with supervisor [4, 5, 10]).

The second major component of this study was the comparison between the two formats on the ratings of two group dynamic phenomena: group attraction and leadership evaluation. The crossover design enabled us to examine separately the contribution of the leaders' personal style as well. The findings on the Leadership Questionnaire showed that leaders clearly were rated differently, regardless of the stance they utilized. In addition, there was change over time. Beginning with the portion of the training which includes the experiential component (week 5) there was a gradual rise over the next six sessions when the ratings leveled off. The relative differences between the leaders remained about the same over time. Since there is no difference in rating patterns across the two formats (leaderless and traditional) and since we would expect no scorable ratings of leadership after the leaderless segment (i.e., if ratings had been collected after the experiential portion), we believe that the ratings which were gathered after the entire 90 minutes evaluate a combination of teaching and leadership, but primarily the teaching style. Thus it seems that as students are more exposed to a teacher and understand the teaching style, ratings will increase. However, as we have shown, some teachers are viewed as more effective than others.

Group attraction ratings also increased over time. However, this trend was probably confounded by the effect of the leader on group attraction. Although only approaching statistical significance ($p < .06$), the trends for the two leaders as shown in Figure 2 indicate that initially leader A had an impact which appeared to interfere with group attraction. The relative disenchantment with leader A's teaching style may be reflected in the didactic portion of the training (week 3) where the spread between the two leaders was the largest of any of the samplings. During the early experiential sessions, attraction to groups led by A were still lower than B, but by midway through the training the ratings converged. These findings interestingly support the traditional notions regarding group formation: Members of groups initially are leader-focused; but as the group develops, members turn to one another (2, 16). Thus if leader A's style was such that group participants were less attracted to him, then overall group attraction would be lower in the early meetings. With the development of the group and with benign leadership, most groups can form strong, attractive, and cohesive bonds among the members.

Lieberman, Yalom and Miles (11) observed that leaders may not be aware of participants' subjective responses during relatively short-term T-group experiences. Both leaders in the present study subjectively preferred the leaderless model because they felt freer to observe and study the group phenomenon without the pressure of having to intervene (8). However, these preferences were not reflected in differences in learning as measured by the GTQ-C, and in fact were contrary to students' perceptions of their learning (7).

The leaders' enthusiasm for the leaderless model probably arises from a natural wish on the leaders' part to experiment and try new methods of teaching. Even though each group process is different, there is a level of repetitiousness in teaching the same course yearly. A change in format, like the famous Hawthorne effect, may be experienced as stimulating and exciting merely because of the change. Thus, leaders were probably less attuned to the members' subtle attitudinal differences between the two formats, particularly in the light of no readily observable differences in learning. Such a finding suggests the need to monitor the inevitable changes which are introduced into teaching formats, since some changes may turn out to be counterproductive for the students, even though the teachers express enthusiasm for the change.

In reviewing this study, several shortcomings of our outcome measures emerged. What comes into focus is the difference between the process of conceptualizing group phenomena and the tactical considerations of intervention. A student may learn a good deal about the whole group functioning and be unable to translate that understanding into effective interventions. The GTQ-C asks students to respond to the various situations depicted as if the students were the group leaders. At this stage in training the more important task would be to ask how the situation could be understood. The questions might be framed to include both individual and group-as-a-whole perspectives. Then, as a second step, the student could be asked to formulate an intervention. Much more data would ordinarily be necessary for this latter task. Such a format might more sensitively reflect educational goals and effectively evaluate learning.

REFERENCES

1. Bascue, L.O. A conceptual model for training group therapists. *Int. J. Group Psychother.*, 28: 445-452, 1978.
2. Bennis, W.G., and Shepard, H.H. A theory of group development. *Human Relat.*, 9: 415-437, 1956.
3. Correa, M.E., Klein, E.B., Stone, W.N., and Howe, S.R. A bridge between training and practice: Mental health professionals learning in group relations conferences. *Social Psychiatry*, 16: 137-142, 1981.
4. Dies, R.R. Attitudes toward the training of group psychotherapists: Some interprofessional and experience associated differences. *Small Group Behav.*, 5: 65-79, 1974.
5. Dies, R.R. Current practice in the training of group psychotherapists. *Int. J. Group Psychother.*, 30: 169-186, 1980.
6. Goldberg, C. *Encounter: Group Sensitivity Training Experience.* New York: Science House, 1970.

7. Green, B.L., Stone, W.N., and Grace, M. Learning group dynamics training: The effects of silent versus traditional training formats. *Psychiatry*, 46: 130-138, 1983.
8. Hall, J.M., Stone, W.N., and Kunkel, R.L. The development and exploration of group experiential training models. *Group 5* (3): 3-12, 1981.
9. Horwitz, L. Training groups for psychiatric residents. *Int. J. Group Psychother.*, 17: 421-435, 1967.
10. Lakin, M., Lieberman, M.A., and Whitaker, D.S. Issues in the training of group psychotherapists. *Int. J. Group Psychother.*, 19: 307-325, 1969.
11. Lieberman, M.A., Yalom, I.D., Miles, M.R. *Encounter Groups: First Facts*. New York: Basic Books, 1973.
12. Redlich, F.C., and Astrachan, B.M. Group dynamics training. *Am. J. Psychiat.*, 125: 1501-1507, 1969.
13. Roman, M., and Porter, K. Combining experiential and didactic aspects in a new group therapy training approach. *Int. J. Group Psychother.*, 28: 371-387, 1978.
14. Stone, W.N., Stein, L.S., and Green, B.L. Faculty and resident commitment to varieties of psychiatric treatment. *Arch. Gen. Psychiat.*, 24: 468-473, 1971.
15. Stone, W.N., and Green, B.L. Learning during group therapy leadership training. *Small Group Behav.*, 9: 373-386, 1978.
16. Tuckman, B.W. Developmental sequences in small groups. *Psychol. Bull.*, 63: 384-399, 1965.
17. Wile, D.B. What do trainees learn from a group therapy workshop? *Int. J. Group Psychother.*, 23: 185-203, 1973.
18. Yalom, I.D. *The Theory and Practice of Group Psychotherapy*. New York: Basic Books, 1975.

The Family Paradigm
in Group Therapy

Chapter XVII

THE DYNAMICS OF MEMBER-LEADER TRANSFERENCE IN GROUPS: A FAMILY REPLAY

Phyllis Bronstein-Burrows, Ph.D.

Editors' Summary. This article focuses specifically on transferences to the leader as reenactments of members' childhood relationships with their parents. Two studies are described which use 1) systematic observations of member-leader interactions, 2) judges' ratings of members' early memories, and 3) scales measuring early parent-child relationships to measure transferences to the group leaders. Significant correlations found in both studies support the hypotheses that transference to a leader does occur in certain kinds of group situations and that it tends to be negative or positive according to the member's early relationship with the parent of the same sex as the leader.

I first became interested in unconscious group processes before I had ever led or even been in a therapy or training group. I was teaching introductory undergraduate courses and became aware, after the same thing had occurred semester after semester, that some students from the first day of class seemed to like me and want to please me, whereas others seemed uninterested or even hostile. This polarization tended to diminish over the course of the semester as the students got to know me better, but with very few exceptions the initially friendly students remained friendlier than the initially distant ones. I began to suspect that their responses had little to do with me—that they were bringing something with them to the class from that very first day that affected their perceptions and expectations of the teacher in front of them.

To explore this idea, I developed a rough scale which asked students about their attitudes toward and expectations of female verses male teachers (sample item: Who would be likely to give you a higher grade? Whom would you be more likely to argue with?) I chose sex as the key variable because it is one of the few pieces of information students always have about a teacher from the beginning, in addition to the fact that she or he is the authority in charge of the class. Within the scale I buried a subscale of several items that attempted to discover which of their parents they had had a more close, positive relationship with. Scores on these two scales correlated highly ($r = .64$, $p < .05$) in a same-sex direction—that is, students who were more positive toward female teachers tended to report that they had had closer relationships with their mothers than with their fathers, and students who were more positive toward male teachers tended to report the opposite. Though the finding did not of course demonstrate a causal relationship, it raised the possibility that people were, in effect, bringing a piece of their families with them into the classroom, and that their initial (and often lasting) perceptions and expectations of the authority figure in front of them were in some way affected by the childhood relationship they had had with the parent of that same sex. Whether they might also have been bringing in other remnants of early family dynamics I was not at that point able to speculate, but it did seem likely that a kind of parent/teacher transference was occurring in a predictable way. I began to wonder whether this process was not merely a classroom phenomenon, but one that occurs in all groups in which someone is designated as leader or authority figure.

Transference, however, as I discovered when I began to explore the group literature, is a problematic concept. Some theorists have posited an early "regressive" phase, in which members simultaneously become like dependent children, perceiving the group leader as an omnipotent father, often with the group-as-a-whole perceived as a maternal entity. Others have suggested that the group leader is perceived as a mother, while Scheidlinger (7), on the other hand, has challenged the whole notion of a uniform "group regression," claiming that shared fantasies are far from being the same in each individual. It seems, then, that transference in groups has been the subject of little agreement among practitioners and theorists, and of minimal systematic research.

Certain basic questions need to be much more rigorously and systematically explored—namely, whether transference actually does occur, and if it does, then in what form and under what circumstances? More specifically, is a group leader always perceived as a parent figure, and if so, is it as an archetypical, omnipotent image that everyone shares, or do members individually visualize their own parent—or do both those phenomena occur, but at different phases of the group (7)? If the leader is seen as a parent figure, what determines whether it is as a "mother" or a "father"—sex, appearance, manner (e.g., tall or short, nurturant or authoritarian)—or the need of a member to have a particular parent image in the group at that time? Does an aloof leader tend to evoke a negative transference, and a warm, active leader a positive one, or are they merely evoking appropriate here-and-now responses to unfriendly or friendly behavior?

To seek initial answers to these questions, I conducted two separate studies on different groups.* There were two main hypotheses:

1) Transference to an authority figure does occur, and it occurs most markedly in the initial stages of a group.

---

*For more complete reports of the research, see Burrows (4, 5).

2) The form the transference takes is individually determined, depending on the sex of the leader and a member's childhood relationship with that parent of that same sex.

It seems likely that the transference process is most pronounced in the early phases of a group because, as Slater (8) and Yalom (9) have pointed out, the unfamiliarity of the situation and the uncertainty about rules and structure are likely to arouse anxiety, and thereby heighten dependency feelings toward the person in charge, so that members unconsciously come to perceive the leader as a parent figure. And since the group leader's personality is at this point unknown, it seems plausible that members will perceive him or her in terms of their own individual early experiences—in effect, as one of their own parents. Yet the leader is not a complete blank screen upon which either parent may equally well be projected. She or he is visibly male or female, and I suggest that it is this one most salient cue that generally determines whether a father or a mother transference occurs.

STUDY 1

Method

Subjects were the 15 members of a self-analytic group that met for one-and-a-half hours, four days a week, as a seven-week group dynamics course at the Harvard Summer School. The group members, nine females and six males, ranged from 18 to 25 years of age, and were all college students or recent graduates. A male graduate student and I (also a graduate student at the time) served as co-leaders. All sessions were tape-recorded.

At the end of the first week of meetings, I rated members' feelings toward the two leaders, based primarily on scoring from the tapes of member-to-leader behavior within the group. There were 13 categories of positive acts and 13 categories of negative acts, ranging from such direct behaviors as agreeing, complying, ignoring, and challenging, to such indirect ones as criticizing the course structure, or agreeing or disagreeing with someone who had just challenged the leader or criticized the course structure.

However, the final ratings used in the analysis were my own global estimates, which took into account not only specific within-group acts, but also general nonverbal behavior (e.g., smiling, nodding, seeking, or avoiding eye contact), and any out-of-class contact initiated by members to the leaders during that first week, including the act of handing in the first assigned paper. After one week of meetings there was not a sufficient sample of relevant acts from all members to make for meaningful comparative frequency measures. Thus it made more sense to provide evaluations of the overall quality of each member's behavior, which took the quantitative data fully into account. These evaluations (labeled Member-Leader Affect Ratings) estimated members' positive or negative affective orientation toward each of the two leaders separately, and then algebraically summed the two estimates, to indicate which of the two a member was more positively oriented toward.

At the end of the first week, members handed in their first paper, for which they had been asked to describe in detail two or three of their earliest childhood memories, and to relate them to general feelings about themselves and to their feelings about entering the group. The memories (but not the papers) were then given to three independent judges, each with expertise in either group or family interaction; they were asked to evaluate the relationships with authority figures that members portrayed in their memories. A rating system similar to the one used for the Member-Leader Affect Ratings was used. Each judge, then, provided an Authority Figure Orientation Rating for each of the 15 members. The ratings of the three judges were averaged for each member, and these average Authority Figure Orientation Ratings were correlated with the Member-Leader Affect Ratings assigned earlier.

Results

There were a total of 36 memories reported by the 15 members. Twenty-seven memories focused on parents (21 on mother and/or father, and six on "parents" as a unit), seven focused on non-parent authority figures (teachers, babysitters, grandparents), and five did not overtly focus on authority figures at all. However, all members referred to parents in at least one of their memories. The judges' inter-rater reliability coefficient was .9. The Product Moment Correlation between the Member-Leader Affect Ratings and the Authority Figure Orientation Ratings was .69 ($p < .005$, one-tailed), giving substantial support to the two hypotheses. It appears, then, that in this kind of unstructured group situation, members' initial interactions with a male and female leader will tend to reflect feelings they had toward much earlier male and female authority figures, most usually their parents.

Illustrations

At this point, a few selections from the transcripts may provide useful illustration. For example, Member A (female) responded to an interpretation made by the male leader (R) during the third session with:

Well, I was really glad [R] said something. . . . And I thought it was really good because, I y'know, didn't realize those things. I thought it was helpful.

She also sought him out during the first week to ask for guidance and reassurance about the paper assignment, and then made sure to hand her paper in to him. On the other hand, she had responded to my initial describing of my nondirective role with, "I think it's really good that [P] defined her position, because we can't rely on her for anything," and subsequently avoided proximity and all verbal and nonverbal contact with me. Her memories were as follows:*

> My most vivid early recollection is very clear in my mind. My parents and I were visiting some friends in the vast mountainous area of Northern California. We were out in their backyard, an open terrace which dropped steeply to a field below. I was swinging on a sofa hammock which overlooked the dropoff, and somehow managed to fall down the slope. My father desperately ran down the stairs and rescued me. I seem to remember that the adults were much more concerned over the whole affair than I was, because I knew that I'd be saved.
>   Another distinct recollection was the time the girl-next-door didn't invite me to her birthday party. Her name was Irene and I had thought we were good friends. All my other friends were invited. I stayed home and cried all night. My mother felt badly for me and told me that Irene was not a nice person, but that didn't help. She was a year older then me. . . .

Here the father is viewed as all-powerful and all-protective ("I knew that I'd be saved"), whereas the mother is totally ineffectual ("that didn't help"). Also, we are told that the rejecting, not-to-be-counted-on female friend is older than Member A. The feelings toward male and female authority figures (and perhaps females older than herself) correspond to Member A's interactions with the two leaders during the first week of the group, in which the male leader was seen as gratifying, and sought out for guidance and reassurance, whereas the female leader was viewed as not to be relied on. In addition, although there were no direct negative interactions with me at this time, I scored her behavior toward me in the negative nonverbal category. On the final exam, in analyzing what might have inhibited learning for her in the group, Member A directly revealed some of her feelings:

> I felt inhibited at first by [P]. Maybe I was jealous of her (she was [R's] partner); maybe I feared her disapproval too much. At any rate, I tried to hide from it by pretending that she didn't exist. I only related to [R] (i.e., giving him my papers). My shining day was the day [P] didn't come to class.

Member O (male), on the other hand sought me out before class to hand his

---

*Names and some details have been changed to protect the anonymity of the members.

paper in, asked to speak to me after class and then did so, smiled often at me, always sat near me, and sought frequent eye contact. He also avoided all contact with the male leader, not only during the first week, but through most of the summer. His memories were as follows:

> I was playing with my toy soldiers. I was around at my grandmother's house. I recall my grandmother working in the kitchen. My grandfather had returned home from work. He looked at me and commented: "You're always playing with those silly sticks and soldiers!" My grandmother stood up in defense and said: "I bet you can't build a bridge like he can!" I continued on with my intense play with vivid imagination put into action of the toy soldiers and accompanied by constructed bridges made out of ice cream sticks. During the course of playing I recall how I used to set up strategic set-ups where the two opposing sides would encounter each other and capture the enemy but done in a manner of least possible act of violence.
>
> My father caught a mouse in a trap that was set in the bedroom. The mouse was still alive and so he gave it to our cat. I was sitting on the table in fear and squirmed at the sight of the cat devouring the little mouse.

In both of these memories, the male authority figures are threatening. The child, however, avoids direct confrontation; in the second instance, he can only take refuge on the table, whereas in the first, protected by a strong female authority, he is able to act out a fantasy conflict where he is in control of both sides. His orientation toward male and female figures here clearly corresponds to his interaction (and lack of interaction) with the male and female authority figures of the group.

STUDY 2

Method

Subjects were the 19 members of a self-analytic group that met for one hour, three times a week, as a semester-long course at Harvard. They were mostly male (n = 17), and mostly undergraduate (n = 16), with a male senior faculty member serving as leader. All sessions were tape-recorded and all were observed from behind a one-way glass by members of a graduate seminar, who used SYMLOG (1) to score the group interaction and met with the group leader afterwards to discuss their observations. Over the course of the semester, I scored all member-to-leader acts using the same 26-category instrument described in the previous section, and confirming my observations afterwards with the tapes of the sessions. Each member's percentages of positive and negative acts to the leader were then computed to adjust for differences in frequency of participation; these percentages were then algebraically summed (percentage of positive acts minus percentage of negative acts), to arrive at a positive or negative total Interaction Score.

The main analysis included 15 consecutive sessions, beginning two weeks into the semester (to allow the membership to stabilize), and ending around the middle. The cut-off point was determined by an announced style change on the part of the leader, after which his participation level increased substantially, and which may have had an effect on members' interaction with him (5).

At the end of the semester, group members filled out a Parent Orientation questionnaire, which was intended to measure the affective quality and intensity of members' early childhood relationship with each of their parents. The first half was a nine-item Mother Scale, and the second half an identical nine-item Father Scale. Sample items were: "My mother (father) praised me when she (he) thought I did something well," "I talked over my problems with my mother (father)," and "My mother (father) found fault with my appearance," with a four-point response choice ranging from "Often" to "Seldom, If Ever." The reliability of the scales has been previously established. A Parent Orientation Scale Score, obtained by subtracting the Mother Scale score from the Father Scale Score indicated which parent a member recalled having had a closer, more positive relationship with. These Parent Orientation Scale Scores were then correlated with the member-to-leader Interaction Scores with the prediction of a relationship between the two—i.e., that Father-oriented members would tend to have more positive Interaction Scores, whereas Mother-oriented members would tend to have Interaction Scores that were either substantially less positive, or else negative.

Results

Since no differences were found in the responses of the two female group members, they were not considered separately in the data analysis. Two members who did not fill out a Parent Orientation questionnaire were excluded from the analysis. The Product Moment Correlation between the two sets of scores was .6, which is significant at the .005 level (one-tailed). Thus, support was again provided for both hypotheses—that transference to an authority figure does occur, and that the form it takes is individually determined, depending on the sex of the leader and a member's early relationship with the parent of that same sex.

Illustrations

The following examples from the transcripts illustrate how Father-oriented and Mother-oriented members differed in their interactions with the leader. The differences were noticeable from the very beginning of the first session. When the leader explained the inactive role he would be playing, in which he would now "recede from leadership position, and just let the group go ahead," two members began immediately to question him on whether the group could do nonverbal exercises. The following dialogue ensued:

> Dr. B.: Well, I feel at the moment that I'm being put under pressure to sort of keep on in the leader role. . . . In the syllabus you've got indications that a great deal is up to you. So without either saying yes or no or maybe or anything, I'll just turn it back . . .
>
> Jeff: Well, I think in this matter at least you *do* have a role here, as a professor and as a resource person. There are certain things that we need to know about. . . . So you do have a role there, perhaps, whether you wish to take that role or not.
>
> Stanley: An important part of the course, though, is to see what we can do by ourselves. . . . I'd be sort of curious about people's expectations, coming into the course (he states his own expectations). . . . It seems that the room is a little cluttered to do nonverbal stuff.
>
> Sean: . . . I'm not saying I want everybody to stand up right now and do something nonverbal, y'know. I mean, just, I think we should be *free* to let it develop. . . . I don't think there should be an arbitrary thing that says we *can't* develop in that direction. . . .

Here we can see that Jeff and Sean were challenging both what they perceived to be the course structure (exclusively verbal interaction) and the leader's non-directive role. Stanley, on the other hand, spoke on behalf of the course structure, tried to comply with the leader's wishes by getting the group going on its own, and opposed the other two members' counter-structure pressure to use nonverbal techniques. By mid-semester, Jeff's and Sean's member-to-leader Interaction Scores were the most negative in the group, whereas Stanley's Interaction Score was highly positive. The Parent Orientation Scale given at the end of the semester showed Jeff and Sean to be Mother-oriented (with Sean extremely so) and Stanley to be Father-oriented.

As the group passed through various developmental stages (e.g., [2], [3], [6], [8]), transferences to the leader continued to be evident. The preceding example was characteristic of the early dependency phase, which manifested itself throughout the first five sessions. As the group moved toward a "revolt," the transferences became more obvious. At the start of the sixth session, the group got into an extended discussion of parents, with many members sharing information about their relationships with their own parents. When the leader attempted to link the conversation to feelings that might currently be running in the group, the following ensued:

> Dr. B. . . . I suspect that some of the things that have been raised here are

pertinent to this situation too—that is, how are you going to get along with the authority figure in this group, do you feel in harmony with him or not . . . ?

Sean: You say "the authority figure." I think it's . . . it would be interesting to find out who is the authority figure for everyone in the group. When you said it, you implied it was you, but it doesn't necessarily have to be . . .

Seth: [to Dr. B.] You can really overinterpret things pretty easily.

Ed: In terms of an authority figure, I don't really think there is one. Because it's different from a parent, where that authority is pre-established. . . . I mean, who's it gonna be here? Who's got a hold over anybody in here, really? Nobody.

Bob: [to Stanley] . . . Do you have something to say, or are you bored?

Stanley: . . . I'm listening, and I'm not bored at all. Especially when the professor here draws his analogies to some dynamic of the group.

Betsy: . . . I tend to forget Professor B. is there until he says something [laughs]. And I'll either accept it or I won't.

Here, Sean, Seth, Ed, and Betsy were all openly discounting the authority of the leader, while Bob attacked Stanley, the member most consistently identified with the leader (both by his own admission, and in the group's perception). Stanley, on the other hand, expressed his admiring interest in the leader's interpretations. Ed, Betsy, and Bob, like Sean, all turned out later to be highly Mother-oriented (Seth did not fill out the Parent Orientation Scale). Further, in the session immediately following, before the leader arrived, Sean, Ed, and another member, Sheldon, gleefully took over the end of the table where the leader normally sat, with Sheldon sitting in his chair. Sheldon, next to Sean, had the most highly Mother-oriented score in the group.

QUESTIONS TO CONSIDER

It is important at this point to consider alternative explanations for the findings. First, there is the possibility that the leaders, rather than being the passive receptors of members' transferences, were in some way directly evoking members' affective responses to them. For example, a leader might have behaved more positively toward some members and more negatively toward others, each of whom might plausibly be expected to have reciprocated in kind, with an appropriate here-and-now response to friendly or unfriendly behavior.

An examination of the behavior of the leaders, however, suggests that this was not the case. In the first study, during the observed initial four meetings, the leaders played a studiedly inactive and impartial role, directing their occasional questions or interpretations to the group as a whole rather than to individual members. In the second study, the observers' SYMLOG ratings of the leader's interpersonal behavior over the entire course of the group showed him to be generally friendly and task-oriented, with no differences toward individual members on the friendly/unfriendly dimension.

Second, there is the possibility that the leaders, rather than simply being inactive objects of transference, were in fact behaving in such ways as to evoke particular kinds of transference responses from the members. One fairly common interpretation is that a leader's aloof manner will tend to evoke negative transferences, whereas a warm positive manner will tend to cause the repression of negative feelings, so that negative transferences are not in evidence. Another possible explanation for the findings is that the leaders' behaviors stimulated the recall of particular *kinds* of parental memories, which perhaps had little to do with the *overall* early relationships members had with their parents.

I would argue that the behavior of the leaders did evoke particular responses and did, in Study 1, stimulate the recall of particular kinds of memories, but that these are in fact essential parts of the transference process. It appears that the leaders' initial aloof manner contributed to the heightening of members' anxiety and dependency needs, while providing a "blank screen" for transference projections. Yet clearly members did not all experience a negative transference; the responses toward each of the leaders (as well as the memories reported in Study 1) were by no means affectively homogeneous across the group. Some members saw safety and affection in a leader's silent demeanor, whereas others saw threat or abandonment. Some of the memories involved being rescued, protected, or rewarded by an authority figure, whereas others involved being intimidated, reprimanded, or let down. It would seem, then, that the transference process is an interactive one; a leader's passive manner helps trigger it, reviving past feelings and events in each member individually, which in turn shape each member's present-day expectations of and responses to that leader.

Furthermore, there is evidence from Study 1 that the authority relationships revealed in the memories do reflect the overall emotional tenor of members' early parental relationships. In other available data sources (papers, exams, sociometric questionnaires, and verbal statements), eight of the 15 members revealed information about their relationships with their parents, and in seven of these instances, the relationships described corresponded closely with those portrayed in the memories.

The results of the two studies presented here are provocative. The findings give strong support to the hypotheses that member-to-leader transferences do occur and that they are individually determined, depending largely on the sex of the leader and a member's early relationship with the parent of that same sex. However, these hypotheses and related questions that were dealt with only briefly here and/or in previous articles (4, 5) (such as the relationship between early family interaction and overall within-group functioning, the relationship of early non-parent authority figures to present transferences, and the way transferences may develop and change as the group moves through its developmental phases) certainly warrant much more extensive investigation. Sibling transference is another area that invites study, which could perhaps be explored using early sibling memories, group sociometric data, and member-to-member interaction scores. I hope that the questions and methods introduced here will provide the bases for additional study.

REFERENCES

1. Bales, R.F., Cohen, S.P., and Williamson, S.A. *SYMLOG: A System for the Multiple Level Observation of Groups.* New York: Free Press, 1979.
2. Bennis, W.G., and Shepard, H.A. A theory of group development. *Human Relations,* 9 (4): 415-457, 1956.
3. Bion, W.R. *Experiences in Groups.* New York: Basic Books, 1959.
4. Burrows, P.B. The family-group connection: Early memories as a measure of transference in a group. *Int. J. Group Psychother.,* 31 (1): 3-23, January 1981.
5. Burrows, P.B. Parent orientation and member-leader behavior: A measure of transference in groups. *Int. J. Group Psychother.,* 31 (2): 175-191, April 1981.
6. Mann, R.D. *Interpersonal Styles and Group Development.* New York: John Wiley, 1967.
7. Scheidlinger, S. The concept of regression in group therapy. *Int. J. Group Psychother.,* 18: 3-20, 1968.
8. Slater, P.E. *Microcosm.* New York: John Wiley, 1966.
9. Yalom, I. *The Theory and Practice of Group Psychotherapy.* New York: Basic Books, 1970.

Chapter XVIII

THE FAMILY—AN OUTMODED PARADIGM
FOR THE PSYCHOTHERAPY GROUP

Jerome Steiner, M.D.

Editors' Summary. According to the author, it is only in ideal situations that a son achieves parity with his father even after he establishes his own household. In most kinship systems throughout the world, the father continues to retain a position of preeminance and power. If the therapist establishes a psychotherapy group in order to fulfill the requirements of this "ideal" family, he assumes a task which is impracticable for most patients. The author suggests, instead, the model of master and disciple, wherein the disciple becomes a master and the pupil becomes the teacher. In the familial model, the author maintains, relationships remain hierarchical and vertical, whereas in the master-disciple model relationships become horizontal.

Both the family and the psychotherapy group are small, face-to-face social systems (9), their members always attempting to establish an equilibrium between the demands of the social roles and individual needs and emotions that define them (6). Generally, the family and the group are similar because they exist within the same cultural framework. At first, love, support, attention, and care are revealed in nurturing behaviors. Later they are expressed in preparing a member for departure from the group. In group therapy, these particular family behaviors are encouraged and examined. Relationships in the group are assumed to be transferences from the family situation, and interactions are interpreted as partially reenacted members' personal histories; changes in the as-if family are stressed.

However, the institution of the family in our cultural climate is far from ideal, and the model assumed as the biological unit has little basis in fact. The premise that when the member matures and is able to exercise authority comfortably he leaves the group and establishes himself in a social or family group is questionable. Families are *extended* in most of the world. Authority resides in an elder person outside of each of the subfamily units; members do not leave unless they are misfits. The structure of the group using the hierarchical family paradigm can only succeed in preventing parity between patient and therapist and, hence, prevent the fullest flowering of the patient's creativity and growth toward mutuality with others.

Specific roles define the family, and some are not present in any other group (14), except by analogy. The survival needs of children must be met within the framework of the needs and expectations of parents, who have individual and marital as well as parental roles. Within the family, communication itself is taught and used as part of the process of transmitting cultural information concerning adaptation. Individuals are seen as possessing drives, and the fulfillment of particular drives which need other people requires that the other (the object) be receptive. Relationships in homeostatic systems are reciprocal, and finding receptive objects results in a sense of hopeful relationships in which there is trust of gaining fulfillment of needs. The family member learns that the "other" person is essential to him or her and is the counterpart of his/her own selfhood regardless of any particular interaction (17). The growing child also learns to be the object of others, of the strivings and assertiveness of others (3). It is felt that the internalized experience of attachment to others provides the security necessary for movement out of this group at maturity. Ideally, persons moving through this process attain mastery of the environment and, by the process of abstraction, aim for psychic mastery in all problem areas. As the family members learn to identify their unique qualities in coping with childhood problems within that social unit, so they later learn to delineate themselves in the world-at-large.

The family, in actuality, is not the same as this theoretical model. It is subject to conflicts brought about by cultural change, the speed of that change, and the psychological states of its members. Conversely, members of faulty family units have damaged self-esteem; they cannot trust or be intimate, nor do they have a sense of equality with others. They see everyone as a potential authority and not as a friend (1). Togetherness is needed to produce the strength that makes autonomy possible when the mature offspring departs. Distorted togetherness leads to distorted separations. Perhaps the "sick" family is one of the causes of a culture in which there is so much maladaptation.

> There is a trend toward a sense of lostness, aloneness, confusion of personal identity, and a driven search for acceptance through conformity. One effect of this trend toward this orientation is to throw each person back upon his family group for the restoration of a sense of security, belongingness, dignity, and worth. The family is called upon to make up its individual members in affection and closeness for the anxiety and distress which is the result of the failure to find a safe place in the wider world. Individuals pitch themselves back on their families for reassurance as to their lovableness and worth. This pressure to compensate individual members with special security and affection imposes upon the family an extra psychiatric load . . . the family tries, but it achieves at best a precarious success; often it fails (2, p. 57).

Despite the shortcomings of the family institution, its members have an unconscious loyalty to their particular family system. Their symptoms, the observed behaviors which get them in trouble, represent victimization for their loyalties and for their unconsciously shared agreement not to hurt any member of the family by change in any one person (4). A person is conflicted between a desire to undergo change for his own happiness and his desire to be loyal to the family group. Movement in one direction produces guilt feelings and movement in the other social isolation.

According to Margaret Mead, only the patterns of protecting and nurturing are always there, even during periods of rapid social change, migration, epidemics, and wars, whether in primates or in humans. Other functions—those of the satisfaction in interactions, the teaching of adaptational skills, and the parental behavior as an audience for the child's increasing independence, autonomy, and achievement—are not always present (11).

Those who do group and/or family therapy feel that the appropriate treatment of the individual is in a social setting. In early work with groups, the specific dynamics involved in the interaction of their members and the group leader were not explored. These patients did better than those who did not have such a group experience. Group treatment was seen as a lecture class (Pratt), a method of persuasion (Déjérine), or reeducation (Lazell). Freud, however, hypothesized that the therapist was the symbolic parent and the group members were symbolic siblings—all interacting in such fashion because of the transference (15). Group relationships began to be examined as analogous to the family in terms of multiple transferences. Furthermore, the faulty learning and emotional travail which give rise to maladaptive resolution of conflicts, both between persons and between the intrapsychic demands of biological needs and the dictates of reality, occur within the context of growth within the family system. Since man is a social animal, group therapists have felt that these problems would best be resolved within the context of the small group.

> The therapy group may serve as "transitional family" for the patient who feels he cannot survive within his own family. Faulty patterns of familial adaptation, recapitulated in the group situation, may be examined and changed; this is possible with a minimum of anxiety, there is "the reward" of the other family (group) dependency gratification. Within the quasi-familial group, anger can be expressed more safely because of the dilution of the transference to authority. The threat of intimacy, on the other hand, may be handled by the patient's moving away temporarily without experiencing the fear of being abandoned (21).

Regardless of the number of patients seen together, the therapist must win the allegiance of the healthier and more reasoning parts of their personalities in order to modify the sick and detrimental parts. The patients must discover that the therapist understands and accepts them as humans and not as "things," while he rejects their destructiveness and distorted value attitudes (2). It is the role of the therapist to create a setting in which people can risk looking clearly and objectively at themselves and their actions. The therapist, unlike the patient, does not fear the unknown; he dares to ask questions when the patient is ready. He is also able to admit lack of knowledge to the patient, and when he makes assumptions he is clear that these are assumptions and that he must check them out over time. He is not suspicious and has the attitude that the patient is doing the best he can.

Pain is reduced through the careful handling of loaded material and feelings are related to facts. The patient is reeducated toward accountability rather than feelings of blame and is able to see the influence of past models on his own expectations and behaviors and the delineation of his role and functions. As time goes on the patient is able to give up some of his defenses as they are less necessary. His protective armor is disturbed as he faces himself and is required to make decisions and to investigate and accept himself. The therapist must see himself as little different from the members in terms of facing life's paradoxes; the treatment situation not only resembles life but is a portion of life itself and the therapist must act as a guide and model until members are ready to accept him as an equal.

In group psychotherapy, the group is the agent of change and the therapist is the group's manager; each group member must find his own purpose (12). The therapist's significance to the patient decreases as the patient is ready to leave, but the patient's perception of the therapist must become more congruent with who the therapist actually is. The patient must realize that his charisma, the perceived omniscience and omnipotence, are things of the past and are neurotic formulations.

The patient comes to treatment suffering and requesting care. He is in a dependent position, and this position is used to establish the authority of the therapist, in order that he might manipulate and catalyze. In the doctor-patient model, authority of one person over another is necessarily implied, if not directly invoked. An individual who is "sick" and feels himself to be in need expects that he will receive some kind of help, be that succor or some kind of expertise. A parental agency is one which protects infants in their helpless state. The image of the physician, likewise, is exalted. The father always lays down rules and regulations and sanctions and punishments, so these are projected both to God and to the physician/therapist from whom nurturing, protection, and the like are required. The good father not only does this but is available in the service of the growth and development of the potential of the children. It is easy to see why Freud identified the psychoanalyst in terms of the prototype of father (8).

Nurturing and protection require a hierarchical relationship between parent and child; teaching which is necessary for growth also requires a hierarchical relationship. Authority is a quality of assurance, superior judgment, the ability to impose discipline, and the capacity to inspire fear. It may be difficult to define the idea of power and the strength attached to it which are involved in this concept. When one defines authority one is attempting to interpret the conditions of power, give the conditions of control, and define strength. Authority is not a thing—It is an interpretive process which seeks for itself the solidity of a thing (19). Time never permits completion of such a process and insofar as it is frustrated, there is freedom.

Freud was concerned with the irrational forces conditioning the power which determines how a person will perceive the environment. Whatever happened in childhood leaves persistent images into adulthood. During periods of anxiety, there is a regression; a person feels infantilized and revives those images of strength which are "over" him. One might question whether the multiple transference of group members to the group therapist as father is a "natural" phenomenon, a result of intrapsychic forces derived from family upbringing, or the result of social conditioning, wherein the loving and nurturing qualities of a parent are ascribed to social roles in addition to the specific tasks involved. The physician is seen as fatherly as well as expert in treating illness (22).

In the ideal family, parents have roles which involve "giving up" authority and permitting the child to assume increasing responsibility for himself and for the family interactions themselves. Of course, the authority of the parent is maintained because it is granted through *noblesse oblige*. If family members are able to give up their loyalties to old roles and old patterns of achieving homeostasis, the achievement of authority is possible. However, if family members object and maintain old loyalties and old styles of maintaining family balance, there occurs conflict between family members, role substitutions wherein one person acts in an age- or sex-inappropriate fashion, or permanent immaturity. In the idealized family described before, the child is able to assume authority as he/she is granted it and moves out and establishes his or her own family, becoming its authority. The child, having assumed the role of "head of the house," behaves in a fashion which respects the experience of elders; he does not obey them. This is true in only a very small part of the world. Most of the time, the family is an extended system, and the range of hierarchical authority includes greater numbers of persons as children are born. It changes only by the death of those in authority.

It is not necessary to appeal to concepts of transference to understand the individual's relationship to the therapist. Man needs an authoritative system because he cannot bear the thought of death which comes with an appreciation of the facts of the world, from self-consciousness and an identification with himself as a biological creature.

> Psychology is the last and youngest offspring of religion, more specifically of the age-old belief in the soul. Yet just as a political and economic ideology of equality

and liberty could not fulfill their early promises neither could it replace religion. . . . To appear rational . . . it had to deny . . . the belief in the soul and to rationalize man's desire for immortality in terms of a psychological equality or likeness, which in turn perpetuates the willful assertion of different . . . from which we are suffering now. (13, p. 61)

In order to feel comfortable, man must have a concept of authority to which he can appeal and a concept of sharing something which will give him immortality; this can be a culture, a political system, and so forth. Immortality of the physical self is replaced by creative perpetuation of a social self. If society is moribund, the individual must be liberated by rebelling against the system and taking over from existing authority rather than fitting within its strictures (13). I agree with Rank that it was unfortunate that Freud saw growth as a modified recapitulation of family relationships in the analytic situation. The model is mechanical. Through a series of interactions in childhood, the character is determined. By establishing equivalencies in the therapeutic situation, other determinants produce changes in the individual. There is no freedom of will or of choice. For some, "science" demands that everything be understood, and this is possible only if behavior is determined by known antecedents. All behaviors are not solely determined by forces impinging on the person.

When the patient is able to do more than attempt to satisfy the unfulfilled needs with which he came to treatment to the transference relationship, he attempts to form a "real" relationship with the therapist. At the end of the therapeutic process, both the therapist and the patient emotionally accept termination of the relationship and must have the capacity to live separately. Residual needs must be satisfied in other ways. The most "difficult problem of contemporary psychiatry is the resolution of the transference neurosis" (23). The individual is now able to move away from the father as he would have been able had the family interactions permitted in the ideal circumstances. However, his behaviors are determined by the resolution of conflicts arising within the original family. Autonomy is seen as the relinquishing of old patterns. One might hope that with maturation the individual has greater access to natural processes within himself and society, releasing a certain amount of "creative" energy (24). Attention must be paid to the actualization of the person because of factors inherent in the interaction between two equal human beings. The relationship of therapist and patient is a new experience in the present wherein a person achieves personal autonomy.

Rosenbaum appreciates the problem of setting up the group as a "special" organization with a father at its head.

In most cases psychotherapy becomes a religious quest, and in fact, it is a psychological religion, which it should not be (16).

Group therapy is not simply an exploration of self in a situation removed from life. It is an expressed part of one's life experienced now. The group has security in the father figure, and could, therefore, solve its existential dilemmas of man's place in creation with mutual reinforcement from member to member. Frequently, the group therapist becomes a secular priest and when he accepts this role he does so because he has not faced his own fears of life. He falsely encourages the patient to believe that the inquiry into the unconscious will solve life's tragedies. However, it must be understood that we are all involved in the struggle. Initially, the patient has "faith" and a need to believe in the therapist. Unfortunately, he cannot believe himself. Power is granted to the therapist. Hopefully, the therapist will not exploit it. The therapist helps the patient find an answer meaningful to him. The patient's search is for a belief and order which will comfort him and bring him out of chaos. Often, patients move from therapist to therapist, collecting gods. Anxiety is part of the human condition. The task is to confront and accept life's absurdities and paradoxes (16). How does the therapist avoid the dilemma of being seen as a perpetual authority, if he views his group and teaches them to view it as a kind of family with himself as the parent? If group therapy is to bring a patient closer to the ideal of freedom, it must deal with the problems of authority inherent in the doctor-patient relationship. Of course, not all therapists would agree that this is the goal of treatment. They may believe that the purpose is more than relief of symptoms or the teaching of better mechanisms of adaptation or resolution of conflict.

It is my belief that the function of psychotherapy, as in all other endeavors which "teach," is the ultimate change of the individual in order that he transcend the person he was and approach the world with a sense of freedom and an ability to create relationships with others, with the world-at-large, and with himself, which did not exist before. This process can never end.

A free individual is one in relationships with others. The strategy of these relationships is not wherein another is an object to be manipulated. A feeling of satisfaction is a feeling that is mutual with another, or it is nothing. Relationships may take place in terms of external goals, money, power, or pride of possession; they may take place in terms of the selfish indulgence of the needs of one party to the transaction or with self-absorption by either person. However, only a relationship which deepens and extends is mutual (25).

> The purpose of life is not achieved through self-actualization or self-realization alone, but rather through self-transcendence and an orientation around causes greater than oneself and persons other than oneself. (5, p. 107)

Mullan (12) believes that group therapy, practiced existentially, corrects the therapist's concept of power and "infinite" knowledge. He sees himself as little different from all the members in terms of facing life's paradoxes. The magnified self-image is reduced; he is no longer the clever analyst, intellectual and isolated. The concepts of therapeutic alliance and transference are not applicable to the existential method. The group meeting does not *resemble* life outside; it *is* life. Learning takes place as it would at any other stage of life. The therapist is a "special" kind of leader—not caught up in the semantic structures involved in group as family and therapist as parent. His task is to help reorient others toward the meaning of life and reduce the self-centeredness which comes from suffering which cannot be explained, and which the individual has no ability to control. The therapist must assist the patient in the discovery of personal relevance in which we transcend ourselves, creating ourselves anew and achieving the management of the anxiety which is the result of being alive (17).

A group psychotherapy situation which is based on the model of the family will perpetuate the problem of maintaining an unrealistic appreciation for authority and the non-achievement of equality with the therapist. I see no way out of this dilemma other than every patient in group therapy "learning to become" a participant of stature equal to the therapist himself, as in the group of master and disciples other than the cult.

A cult is, indeed, a substitute family. The aim of the cult is not the freedom and parity of all members but a continued dependency on the leader who *represents* transcendent power. Members rise above their ordinary stations by participation with him in this particular group; they do not become masters themselves. The aim of the cult is not freedom, but obedience to certain sets of norms, rules, and regulations which assure participation in unending power and thus guarantee a kind of immortality. It reduces the existential threat of death and dealing with the necessary suffering which is part of life on this planet. In the relationship of master and disciple, however, the master attempts to *reveal* transcendental aspects of the "upper" worlds and "universal light" (10). With this revelation and understanding on the part of the disciple, the disciple is trained to become a master. Once he shares in this he becomes the equal of the person who has taught him.

The religious existentialist and mystic know that the fundamental problems of a person are his separation, estrangement, and alienation. This estrangement is an internal problem of psychological disturbance. The social problem is a tendency toward separation and isolation as a person "evaluates" and judges his environment (7). Conflicts, anxiety, doubt, and suffering are part of life on this earth. Death is inevitable and affirms life as a process. In the quest for relinquishing despair and accepting the state of being on earth, a person must seek for himself in the midst of a loving and mutually supporting community. Mutuality and empathy are the solutions to despair. Loving is not analyzed away but also accepted as part of the human condition.

Factors such as loving, acceptance, and interest are of primary importance to successful psychotherapy. Theoretically, these should be available. The mystical encounter is never possible without them; they are always present in the model of the master and his disciple. Both the therapist and the master must distinguish between neurotic suffering and everyday suffering. In the initial stages of psychotherapy, one party has a need and the other has a reputation or ability to help with that particular need. These are nontranscendent in nature. In order to be helpful, however, the therapist must be seen and accepted as a person. Both patient and therapist exist in the same community in relationship to the same world. Only then can the therapist be helpful at a later stage in the treatment (18). After the therapist helps free the person from maladaptive patterns, he must stay with the patient and guide him as a partner in the confrontation of the suffering which comes from living itself.

Hence, it is best to give up the family paradigm which has inherent in the model so many difficulties vis-à-vis parity, and, perhaps, adopt the paradigm of the master and disciples. The master is a member of the elect. He has knowledge and the method of achieving knowledge. His function is to teach those methods to the disciples in order that they participate in that same knowledge. Having learned, the disciples join the master as a member of the elect and the hierarchical distinction between them vanishes.

REFERENCES

1. Ackerman, N. *The Psychodynamics of Family Life: The Diagnosis and Treatment of Family Relationship*. New York: Basic Books, 1958, p. 75.
2. Ackerman, N. Behavioral trends and disturbances of the contemporary family. *In:* I. Galdston (Ed.), *The Family in Contemporary Society*. New York: International Universities Press, 1958.
3. Boszormenyi-Nagy, I. A theory of relationships: Experience and transaction. *In:* I. Boszormenyi-Nagy and J. Framo (Eds.), *Intensive Family Therapy: Theoretical and Practical Aspects*. New York: Hoeber, pp. 49-561.
4. Boszormenyi-Nagi, I. Loyalty implications of the transference model in psychotherapy. *Arch. Gen. Psychiat.*, 27 (3): 374-380, 1972.
5. Bulka, R.P. Hasidism and logotherapy: Encounter through analogy. *In:* R.P. Bulka (Ed.), *Mystics and Medics: A Comparison of Mystical and Psychotherapeutic Encounters*. New York: Human Sciences Press, 1979, p. 107.
6. Committee on the Family, Group for the Advancement of Psychiatry. *Treatment of Families in Conflict: The Clinical Study of Family Process*. New York: Science House, 1970, pp. 253-254.
7. Frankl, V.E. *Man's Search for Meaning: An Introduction to Logotherapy*. New York: Simon and Schuster, 1973, p. 27.
8. Freud, S. New introductory lectures in psychoanalysis. *In:* J. Strachey (Ed.), *Standard Edition*, 22: 3-182. London: Hogarth Press, 1968.
9. Jackson, D.D. Transference revisited. *In:* D.D. Jackson (Ed.), *Therapy, Communication and Change: Human Communication*. Vol. 2. Palo Alto: Science and Behavior Books, 1973.
10. Lipshitz, M.A. *The Faith of a Hasid*. New York: Jonathan David, 1967, p. 221.

11. Mead, M. The contemporary American family as the anthropologist sees it. *Am. J. Sociol.*, 53: 468-475, 1949.
12. Mullan, H. Existential group psychotherapy. *In:* H. Mullan and M. Rosenbaum (Eds.), *Group Psychotherapy: Theory and Practice.* New York: Macmillan, 1978, pp. 392-393.
13. Rank, O. *Beyond Psychology.* New York: Dover, 1941, p. 61.
14. Reik, T. *Pagan Rites in Judaism.* New York: Farrar-Straus, 1964, p. 163.
15. Rosenbaum, M. Group psychotherapy: Heritage, history and the current scene. *In:* H. Mullan and M. Rosenbaum (Eds.), *Group Psychotherapy: Theory and Practice.* New York: Macmillan, 1978.
16. Rosenbaum, M. Toward an ethic and philosophy of group psychotherapy. *In:* H. Mullan and M. Rosenbaum (Eds.), *Group Psychotherapy: Theory and Practice.* New York: Macmillan, 1978, pp. 31-40.
17. Satir, V. *Conjoint Family Therapy.* Palo Alto: Science and Behavior Books, 1967.
18. Schachter, Z.M. The dynamics of the yehidut transaction. *In:* R.P. Bulka (Ed.), *Mystics and Medics: A Comparison of Mystical and Psychotherapeutic Encounters.* New York: Human Sciences Press, 1979, p. 8.
19. Sennett, R. *Authority.* New York: Vintage Books, 1981, pp. 17-19.
20. Spero, M.H. Discussion: On the nature of the psychiatric encounter between Hasid and master. *In:* R.P. Bulka (Ed.), *Mystics and Medics: A Comparison of Mystical and Psychotherapeutic Encounters.* New York: Human Sciences Press, 1979, pp. 63-65.
21. Steiner, J. Holistic group therapy with schizophrenic patients. *Int. J. Group. Psychother.*, 29 (2): 195-210, 1979.
22. Steiner, J. Ethical issues in the institutionalization of patients. *In:* M. Rosenbaum (Ed.), *Ethics and Values in Psychotherapy.* New York: Free Press, 1982.
23. Whitaker, C.A., and Malone T.P. *The Roots of Psychotherapy.* New York: Blakiston, 1953, pp. 51-113.
24. Wilson, R.N. The courage to be leisured. *Soc. Forces*, 60 (2): 282-303, 1981.
25. Woocher, J.S. The Kabbalah, Hasidism, and the life of unification. *In:* R.P. Bulka (Ed.), *Mystics and Medics: A Comparison of Mystical and Psychotherapeutic Encounters.* New York: Human Sciences Press, 1979, p. 107.

Chapter XIX

THE SOCIALIZATION PROGRAM AS SURROGATE FAMILY: THE MILIEU AS A MODEL FOR OUTPATIENT CARE

Seymour Tozman, M.D., Helen Minkowitz, M.S.W., and Gale Mittleman, M.S.W.

Editors' Summary. The authors elaborate on an outpatient milieu socialization program which they have employed to meet the requirements of chronic mental patients at their institution. Such a program provides a surrogate family for patients with absent or dysfunctional families. As such, the rap group milieu program exhibits the dynamics of "the healthy family" with similar parameters and is in essence a "true" family. The authors feel that such a program provides a desired model for a broader-based outpatient approach, offering much more than a conventional clinic for patients whose needs transcend traditional approaches.

INTRODUCTION

Deinstitutionalization of state mental facilities has impacted greatly on community-based clinics not geared to meet the needs of a severely disturbed population. Previously, community clinics operated on a principle of prevention ". . . under the conviction that early intervention would prevent more serious and prolonged emotional disturbance. . . ."(1) In consequence, less severe diagnoses (i.e., situational problems and the neuroses) predominated. Deinstitutionalization mandated that all mental health services be provided in the least restrictive environment. The acute hospitals geared for short stay now had to reduce the stay further in face of larger numbers. This was now the norm for chronically mentally ill patients who had often been custodially cared for over four to 10 years and were now housed in boarding homes and SROs (20). These clients with more extant and chronic mental disorders were now referred to these same community-based acute clinics for aftercare, thus creating a schism between what was the mandate of the community clinics, and the requirements (aftercare,

---

The authors wish to appreciatively acknowledge the helpful suggestions of Florence Lim, R.N., M.S.N.

maintenance, and habitat) of the patients they were beginning to service in large numbers—a schism which is today far from resolved.

The authors have previously reported on an outpatient rap group socialization program—an innovative large group therapeutic milieu which was devised in response to the needs of a changing clinic population. Such a program has exhibited a modicum of success, as we indicated, and is continuing to produce effective results with a rather small capable staff (22). We feel that an analysis of the dynamics of such a model program would be in the interest of other workers who wish to follow suit with similar types of programming for the chronically mentally ill patient.

In our view, in fact, an elaboration of such a milieu model is the preferred modality of treatment for most types of outpatient care, with traditional clinic care (i.e., weekly individual or small group psychotherapy) being adjunctive rather than primary. One of the authors has run such a milieu program with alcoholics and addicts, as well as the chronically mentally ill. Intrinsic in the successful initiation of such a program are the concepts of a camaraderie, spirit, family, and parenting. Such a milieu program offers to these clients much more than conventional clinic treatment. It offers a therapeutic environment and a sense of belonging to a supportive network, a family.

HISTORY OF THE CONEY ISLAND HOSPITAL RAP GROUP

The chronic patients in our mental hospitals are not only people hospitalized because of severe mental dysfunction, but they are also a poorly educated, poorly trained, inadequately socialized segment of our population. . . . The high percentage of chronic mental patients who have been or who are on welfare, the low level of their vocational and educational attainment, and, in particular, their alienation and isolation are salient characteristics of this group as significant as their mental impairment. (15, p. x)

In September 1977 Coney Island Hospital (CIH) opened a 30-bed inpatient psychiatric unit providing to the Adult Outpatient Clinic a steady flow of patients with history of hospitalization who were generally more seriously impaired than heretofore. These patients were found to be devoid of family ties by loss, attrition, or alienation. The limited resources and relationships they did have were often found to be pathological, destructive, or disconnected. Since the winter holiday season is a time for togetherness, turkey, and family, their lack was palpably exacerbated for our clients and one could sense a profound despair within the clinic as that time approached. The C.I.H. rap group began as a pilot project in the winter holiday season of 1977 "as a 90-minute group of 15 patients with a limited treatment goal—to help the isolated patient get through the Christmas-New Year Holidays. . . ." (22).

The group began as a pilot project since neither the administration nor many of the clinical staff were very enthusiastic, necessitating our establishing the value of this approach before we could expect much support. We had anticipated this response as a normative one, for promulgating outpatient "therapy" via an unwieldy, large group was not in accordance with the tenets of existing clinic policy. Nor was it the model of treatment to which most clinicians had learned to aspire in their schooling and early professional years (19). Maxwell Jones had certainly described such an approach, but not under our conditions, nor on an ambulatory basis (8, 9).

In operationalizing our program, we decried the use of a formal referral system or a fee, at least initially, in order to provide easy access to it. The group was open to all clinic-registered clients who were invited to attend through brightly decorated posters or by word of mouth. The response was very gratifying and by the end of January the group's size had doubled. One could sense a perking up of the clinic doldrums both on the part of patients and involved staff. Even the noninvolved and initially resistant staff perceived a new spirit.

As the program proceeded, it became more cohesive and organized. Expansion to three half days was encouraged and accepted by all. Despite the subsequent imposition of a fee and the need to set up an official referral system, the group remained cohesive. A surprising esprit de corps emerged, felt by both patients and staff. The staff came to know all the patients in the clinic who in turn knew all the staff, and there was a new sense of trust and oneness. Although we did not elucidate this even to ourselves, we were providing for many of the needs and characteristics which would be normally met by intact and healthy families (3, 10). In effect, we replaced missing family and became a surrogate family.

FAMILY DYNAMICS AND THE RAP GROUP

The parameters of what constitutes a healthy family have been described by Beavers (3) and Kaslow (10) and our surrogate family interestingly displayed many of these characteristics.

As the rap group evolved, it became a unit, an organism. It became alive and began displaying dynamic characteristics as a family entity. Patients felt special as a part of this unit and thus more positive toward the clinic itself. There was a strong identification with the socialization program. Members joked, laughed and cried together, expressed their anger, and were accepted. Such unity and oneness reflect a systems orientation manifest in the healthy family. All rap group members perceived themselves as having special relationships with each other. There was a realization that the whole was more than the sum of its parts (10).

Relationships developed and intensified. There was a sense of brotherhood and camaraderie within the group. Patients joined one another in social activities outside the rap group setting. Members began to hold parties, visit one another when sick, and even nursed very ill fellow members back to health. The rap group became financially self-supporting, collecting voluntary dues on a weekly basis to pay for refreshments, parties, and special activities. The group members decided to hold monthly parties to celebrate every member's birthday. A loan fund was set up for members in financial need, with a patient committee deciding how the funds were to be used. The rap group members painted and redecorated the dilapidated room used for their meetings. A lending library was established and people exhanged poetry, recipes, and articles of group interest.

Boundaries were established between the group and the world at large. The rap group had a clear, definite structure that was also flexible. There developed a sense of identification—"them" and "us" in a positive way as indicators of the family unity. The facilitation of interpersonal relations was a major factor and at one point we felt we were conducting "relationship therapy."

A sense of individuality and uniqueness developed in which patients did not have to agree to be liked. There was a sense of wholeness and yet also one of differentiation. From the staff standpoint, complementarity of roles evolved. Initially the male therapist greeted the patients and oriented them to the group, while the female leader facilitated the intragroup interactions. Later these differentiated roles blended and became more diffuse and flexible. The initial male therapist had a knack for making sense from the apparently loose associations of many patients, enhancing their sense of individuality and status within the group.

The group displayed democratic characteristics as described by Kaslow (10) and others as power issues. In some sense staff functioned as good parents using maternal and paternal role models, though predominantly there was a sense of maternal nurturing. The concept of a program being "mother" has been described by us previously (21) and has been well defined by others (14, 17, 18).

In a healthy family the parents have egalitarian roles. There is a division of function; however, there is flexibility within this and function can be switched when necessary. The parents share executive functions and do not compete for control. It is not necessary to be right all the time or even to agree. The therapists role modeled this by often sharing with the patients their points of difference and resolution.

Most importantly the therapists encouraged the emergence of increasing self-government on the part of the patients. Thus the members took on the executive functions of the "family unit." Initially, there were informal group role assignments. However, these evolved to the point where a chairperson, vice-chairperson, secretary, and treasurer were elected for a three-month period. Rotating committees were formed for setting up clean-up and shopping, as well as a sunshine fund through which committee members sent cards, made phone calls, and even visited members who were ill or had not shown up in the group for a while. Lastly, a committee drew up a handbook in which to orient new members, explain the traditions, structure, and rules of the group.

The rap group conceptualized as a family unit was geared for evolution and change. Thus, as children grow up and become independent they leave the family unit. This was a natural and desired outcome of the group process.

This dynamic was observed in the group home when some members moved from a silent, somewhat isolated, nonparticipating role to a more involved role and then onto a leadership role where they exhibited a clear sense of identity. Finally at this time, with a good deal of support from the rap group, they would test out this role by gradually moving to the outside world, e.g., college or a job. They would return to the group frequently to discuss their progress and encourage other members to go forth in a similar manner. There were wave-like series of group members who moved from the position of child, to adolescent, to parent in the rap group and then to the outside of the therapeutic community. However, during a crisis some members would come back to the group (for succor and encouragment) before returning to the outside world.

Patients verbalized feeling a new sense of mastery which they exercised by writing to the hospital administration when the program was reduced at one point. They complained also about their fees and asked for more money for the program. The therapists experienced discomfort here, as a parent might, when a maturing offspring asserts his or her independence. Critical to the bonding process in any group is the ability to express emotions and emotionally charged issues in a sympathetic environment (23). In this context, in the rap group a wide variety of emotional experiences had been shared including areas not easily broached, such as rape, child abuse, self-inflicted injury, and suicidal ideations. The inadvertent death of a member was a highly charged issue and mutual mourning was cathartic and bonding—for staff as well as patients.

Joyful experiences were also related and shared, including success at work and love. The members shared the joys together of a gallery acceptance by an artist patient, a law school acceptance by another, and a nursing scholarship by yet another of their compatriots.

Another characteristic which evolved during the group process was a spirit of compromise which Beavers (3) refers to as the ability to negotiate. Again, not everyone need agree; disagreements are acceptable and normal; however, a mutually beneficial resolution needs to surface. Thus, in our group when a problem with regard to new members developed, threatening the status of older more established members, the established group first tended to obstruct new membership, but realizing the need for flexibility and outreach, the members then became "greeters" of new patients and trustees of the program. They also subsequently developed an orientation manual for the novice members. Thus, an area of friction became an area of productivity and harmony.

An elemental aspect of our program which bears some scrutiny was the spirit, or "life-force" of the program. We would aver that without this aspect such a program would not be able to carry out its function. In the family model, transcendental and moral values are alluded to involving some sense of a harmony in the universe or sense of purpose. The program dealt with these transcendental spiritual philosophical issues in a significant manner which will be discussed later.

Issues in the Surrogate Family Approach

The sense of parenting is a crucial factor in the successful implementation of such a program or unit. This, of course, is consistent with a familial approach in which there are, symbolically at least, parents, extended family, sibs, and the outside world. Certain aspects of psychiatry seem pediatric in nature, and there has to be a structure and a firmness, with concurrent affection and trust. This does not mean there cannot be some sharp differences. We speak also of growth and change, and in this sense, the children grow up, for which this program gears. It is important to understand this in terms of family, not in terms of infantilization or paternalization which are antitheses of our goal. In growing, there is disengagement or graduation from the program. There are also issues of separation and loss as in the family when members leave for good or ill.

In our "family" there are paternal and maternal figures. The maternal approach predominates in its nurturing and caring, but there is also clear paternal strength and authority in an affectionate manner with a blending of these functions. Scheidlinger (17) alludes to sexual acting-out when a maternal group becomes paternal in orientation. At times we noted sexual behaviors which undoubtedly were not too therapeutic and may have been based on this dynamic. Therapeutic tensions and frictions did occur periodically in so large a group and under pressure of work. Nonetheless, some of the sexual behaviors were positive and represented normal activities in people who heretofore had no sexual relations whatever. Again, we are talking about a patient population that represented state deinstitutionalization in our facility and that manifested a wide range of very difficult pathologies (12).

The group, then, became an organism—an entity unto itself with living characteristics. There was bonding and cohesion with the ability to express positive and negative emotions. Catalyzing this sense of life was the spiritual force which made the group become alive, an entity. One of our initial workers, himself a highly religious and spiritual person, facilitated this spirituality, inculcating his sense of oneness with the universe, and a higher order of things. This was effected using rather broad spiritual principles and ideas, attempting to avoid fixation on any one leader. We felt such a fixation could be the nucleus for formation of a cult of some kind, which we certainly wished to avoid. The spiritual force should be examined as an element in treatment, for it can be a potent catalyst and even effect dramatic change, as Pattison and Pattison (13) have remarkedly described with homosexuals becoming heterosexual. In working with recidivistic addicts, one of the authors (Tozman) also noted that in many instances eschewing addiction was accompanied by religiosity almost of addictive proportions and in those instances drug recidivism was attenuated. Psychiatry is beginning to take note of these spiritual elements and incorporate them in treatment (5).

We were very aware of these spiritual considerations, though also of the recent Jim Jones suicides, and the cult-like metamorphosis of Synanon, a once highly touted treatment facility for addicts. Alcoholics Anonymous, is a good example of the spiritual being applied to highly salutary ends. We had positive dealings also with the self-help group, Recovery Inc., which we encouraged our patients to attend, noting nonetheless, the tendency to apotheosize its founder Abraham Low (11). The issue of therapy versus cults has been dealt with at some length by Galanter (6, 7), Shaver et al. (16), and Deutsch (4), who allude to the cult as family.

Thus there can be pitfalls to a familial approach. However, within certain clear limits, with good sense and sane leadership, the spiritual aspects are powerful and critical for healthy change.

As we reported (22) we claim modest success and many of our patients have remained free of hospitalization through the entire five-year tenure of the socialization program at this writing. Others decompensated and were supportively helped by their peers in the program as well as by staff. Many were hospitalized and rehospitalized through a revolving door (as all chronic illnesses remit and exacerbate), eventually to improve and graduate from the program. Some did not and a small group whose needs were much higher than we could meet could not be managed in such a program. One young woman eventually was, after numerous inpatient admissions (15 or 16 in three years), placed in a state hospital for long periods and then in a custodial home. Her presence in the rap group was very disruptive and on many occasions she had to be dealt with individually (conventional treatment having failed long before this), sapping staff energies. To this end, a separate treatment room (retreat) for her was set up for a time—essentially an open isolation type area which at least sequestered and quieted her. Even at that, the mood was similar to an Alcoholics Anonymous meeting when a very drunk individual might appear, shaking up those who are trying to get well.

As patients improved and became more socialized, it became necessary to think in terms of graduation and outside agencies. Vocational rehabilitation and jobs were essential to this end, and there was ongoing prevocational involvement. Recovery, Inc. was utilized, A.A. (where appropriate), the local Y, and the numerous senior citizens agencies of the locality where indicated. Weaning from the ''family'' or nest was sometimes difficult and patients who were now really at volunteer level had to be at times firmly encouraged to move into the community. One such patient, an elderly but youthful female and a patient in the clinic for three years, left under such circumstances but did return to the program after a year's productive absence with new though much less severe symptoms. She was gladly welcomed back (a returning child) and her symptoms abated rapidly. Our goal was to return her to the community more speedily this time and we did so successfully after four months.

Separations were at times difficult, though group process ameliorated this. There was communal mourning, as when a key member suddenly died of status epilepticus because she had not taken her anticonvulsive medication. This graphically indicated the value of medication in certain instances even to intransigent patients. Emotionally charged issues were ameliorated and diluted in the group and facilitated the bonding process. Staff leave-taking also was less of a critical separation since there were ready connections with other therapists (like an aunt or uncle taking over for a lost parent).

CONCLUSION

We have attempted to describe some of the dynamics of a successful socialization program which evolved from a rap group to a therapeutic milieu, providing efficient and effective care to chronic mental patients with a wide range of difficult pathologies. Intrinsic in such a milieu is an esprit de corps and a sense of nurturing—in a sense of family.

As has been noted (2) religion and quasi religion have deflected from proper treatment. We as social scientists are applying an aspect of what has been a draw in these sometimes negative movements to what we hope is a more scientific, therapeutic, and salutary end. It is our view that an overall milieu approach can be very successful and should be thought of in terms of a viable outpatient modality in conjunction with conventional therapies. We would like to see the milieu as the primary modality with conventional therapy available and adjunctive.

REFERENCES

1. American Psychiatric Association. Rehabilitating the mentally ill in the community: A study of psychosocial rehabilitation centers. Washington, D.C.: A.P.A. Joint Information Service, 1971.
2. Baer, H.A. Prophets and advisors in black spiritual churches: Therapy, palliative or opiate? *Culture, Medicine and Psychiatry*, 5: 145-170, 1981.
3. Beavers, W.R. A theoretical basis for family evaluation. *In:* J.M. Lewis, W.R. Beavers, J.T. Gossett, and V.A. Phillips (Eds.), *No Single Thread: Psychological Health in Family Systems*. New York: Brunner/Mazel, 1976, pp. 46-80.
4. Deutsch, A. Tenacity of attachment to a cult leader: A psychiatric perspective. *American Journal of Psychiatry*, 137: 1569-1573, 1981.
5. Favazza, A. Modern Christian healing of mental illness. *American Journal of Psychiatry*, 139: 728-735, 1982.
6. Galanter, M. Charismatic/religious experience and large group psychology. *American Journal of Psychiatry*, 137: 1550-1552, 1980.
7. Galanter, M. Psychological induction into the large group. *American Journal of Psychiatry*, 137: 1574-1579, 1980.
8. Jones, M. Therapeutic community practice. *American Journal of Psychiatry*, 122: 1275-1279, 1966.
9. Jones, M. *Beyond the Therapeutic Community*. New Haven: Yale University Press, 1968.
10. Kaslow, F.W. Profile of the healthy family. *Interaction*, 4: 1-15, 1981.
11. Low, A.A. *Mental Health Through Will Training*. North Quincy, MA: Christopher Publishing House, 1950.
12. Pabis, R., Mirza, M.A., and Tozman, S. A case of autocastration. *American Journal of Psychiatry*, 137: 626-627, 1980.
13. Pattison, E.M., and Pattison, M.L. "Ex-gays": Religiously mediated change in homosexuals. *American Journal of Psychiatry*, 137: 1553-1562, 1980.
14. Ruiz, P. On the perception of "mother group" in T-groups. *International Journal of Group Psychotherapy*, 22: 448-491, 1972.
15. Sanders, R., Smith, R., and Weinman, B. *Chronic Psychosis and Recovery*. San Francisco: Jossey-Bass Inc. 1967.
16. Shaver, P., Lenauer, M., and Sudd, S. Religious conversion and subjective well-being: The healthy-minded religions of modern American women. *American Journal of Psychiatry*, 137: 1563-1568, 1980.
17. Scheidlinger, S. On the concept of the mother-group. *International Journal of Group Psychotherapy*, 24: 417-428, 1974.
18. Schlindler, W. The role of mother in group psychotherapy. *International Journal of Group Psychotherapy*, 16: 198-200, 1966.
19. Stern, R., and Minkoff, K. Paradoxes in programming for the chronic patients in a community clinic. *Hospital and Community Psychiatry*, 30 (9): 613-617, 1979.
20. Talbott, J.A. Care of the chronically mentally ill—Still a national disgrace (an editorial). *American Journal of Psychiatry*, 136: 658-689, 1979.
21. Tozman, S., and DeJesus, E. Portrait of a pusher/mother. *Journal of Clinical Psychiatry*, 39: 656-659, 1978.
22. Tozman, S., Hanks, T., and Minkowitz, H. The rap group: A milieu treatment model for the chronically mental ill in an outpatient setting. *International Journal of Group Psychotherapy*, 31: 233-246, 1981.
23. Yalom, I. *The Theory and Practice of Group Psychotherapy*. New York: Basic Books, 1970.

Theoretical Issues in
Family Therapy

Chapter XX

THE ROLE OF COGNITIVE CONSTRUCTS AND ATTRIBUTIONAL PROCESSES IN FAMILY THERAPY: INTEGRATING INTRAPERSONAL, INTERPERSONAL, AND SYSTEMS DYNAMICS

Dennis A. Bagarozzi, Ph.D., and C. Winter Giddings, M.S.W.

Editors' Summary. In this article the authors discuss the development of cognitive constructs and their effect upon interpersonal and family processes. Relationships among intrapersonal, interpersonal, and systems processes are discussed, and cognitive processes are shown to play a central role in the integration of these three realms of experience. The role of cognitive processes in the generation and maintenance of dysfunctional behavior is explored and intervention strategies for modifying cognitive processes and correcting faulty behavior patterns are discussed.

The ideas and procedures put forth in this paper are a result of our collaborative endeavors, over the past few years, to devise a meaningful integration of intrapersonal, cognitive, behavioral, and systems conceptions of family process and treatment. In our view, each conception and its attendant treatment strategies represent complementary rather than competing or mutually exclusive views of human behavior, family functioning, and behavior change. All are seen as subcomponents of a larger, more inclusive systems approach. In our clinical work with distressed couples and families, we attempt to address the behavioral, cognitive, intrapersonal, interactional, and transactional aspects of intimate human systems.

If one wishes to understand the complex relationship among purely behavioral, interactional, and transactional processes and intrapersonal and systems phenomena, one must attend to (a) the symbolic as well as the literal meaning of behaviors and events, (b) the analogic as well as the digital aspects of human communication, (c) the command as well as the report components of messages exchanged between and among family members, and (d) the connotative as well as the denotive dimensions of verbal expressions, physical gestures, etc.

In order to understand the treatment process described in the body of this paper, the reader should be aware that we make a number of assumptions about the nature of intrafamilial behavior. These are discussed below in the following sections.

THE EFFECTS OF COGNITION, PERCEPTIONS AND ATTRIBUTION ON FAMILY PROCESS

Our clinical work with couples and families is based upon the premise that family members respond to their environment, to situations, to events, and to other family members in accordance with how these events, persons, etc. are subjectively perceived by them. Family members attribute meaning and intentions to the behaviors exhibited by others. They often respond to these hidden meanings and intentions rather than to the actual behaviors themselves. It is difficult for family members to modify their perceptions and attributions of intentions of others, because family members tend to view each other in terms of fixed, often stereotyped, ''ideal'' models which have become internalized.

In the case of husband-wife relationships, the internalized ''ideal'' model of a spouse actually represents a composite image which has been constructed by the person and is based upon his/her perceptions and reconstructions of emotionally charged experiences with significant members of the opposite sex (e.g., parents, grandparents, siblings, relatives, etc.). These internalized representations, structures, images, or schemata are not readily accessible to one's conscious awareness. Neverthless, they color how one perceives and behaves toward members of the opposite sex.

Individuals tend to seek out and attempt to marry persons whom they perceive will behave in accordance with their ''ideal'' internalized cognitive representations. This cognitive matching process takes place at both conscious and unconscious levels of awareness.

We are not using the term ''ideal'' in its literal sense. By ''ideal'' we mean an enduring schema or image which does not necessarily represent perfection. By ''ideal'' we mean one's internal model which becomes the standard against which all prospective mates are judged.

Family sociologists (18) have summarized the wealth of research dealing with mate selection, marital stability, and marital satisfaction. These writers have reviewed a number of empirical findings which suggest that mate selection is an active process wherein both individuals seek out potential mates whom they believe will fit their internal cognitive models of ideal spouses. In the initial stages of relationship formation, physical attraction and similarity on a number of salient dimensions are important (e.g., race, ethnic background, religion, socioeconomic status, intelligence, age, values). As the relationship progresses, more subtle and less tangible factors become crucial in determining whether the relationship will progress or dissolve. These factors include the fulfillment of complementary needs, satisfactory role fit, and a congruence between the role expectations for one's future spouse and the actual role performance of that individual. Lewis and Spanier (18) propose that the greater the congruence between one's ideal spousal concept and the actual behavior of one's spouse, the greater will be the quality of the marriage.

In addition to cognitive matching, another important process takes place during the courtship period and early stages of marriage which we term "mutual shaping toward the ideal."

In this process, spouses tend to reinforce those behaviors, characteristics, traits, roles, etc. of their mates which are congruent with their ideal cognitive image and representation. However, behaviors, characteristics, and so forth which are not consistent with these internal images tend to be ignored, denied, or defended against if they cannot be assimilated into the spouse's "ideal" image. Since these discrepant behaviors are ignored and not reinforced, they tend to become extinguished. Any behaviors and characteristics which deviate drastically from those which are expected, which cannot be extinguished through non-reinforcement and are not assimilated into one's "ideal" model, will be punished by the spouse.

Spouses tend to exhibit those behaviors and characteristics which are continually reinforced and tend to refrain from exhibiting behaviors which have been punished by their mates.

In addition to being the product of one's perceptions and reconstructions of experiences with significant members of the opposite sex, one's "ideal" image also consists of various models to whom one has been exposed. Obviously, the most important models are one's parents. Lewis and Spanier (18) cite some empirical findings which suggest that the greater the person's exposure to adequate role models for marital functioning the higher will be the quality of his/her marriage.

Finally, the "ideal" image also becomes a repository for those denied and unacceptable aspects of the self that have been repressed, as well as for those split-off and conflicted object relationships which have been internalized (7). Suggestive empirical support for this assumption again is drawn from the Lewis and Spanier (18) review. These writers cite numerous studies which lead them to postulate that the more conflicted and unhappy one's experiences were in his/her childhood, the less likely that individual would be to enjoy a satisfying marriage. Similarly, these reviewers identify a number of studies which show a positive correlation between a healthy self-concept and a successful and satisfying marriage.

In sum, the "ideal" spousal image is the structure which strongly influences how one processes information about one's spouse and affects how one behaves toward him/her.

The Use of Punishment in the Mutual Shaping Process

As we have stated above, the mutual unconscious shaping between spouses consists of three related processes: (a) reward for those behaviors which are consistent with the "ideal"; (b) extinction of behaviors which cannot be assimilated into the "ideal"; and (c) punishment of those responses which are resistant to extinction.

The use of punishment, however, creates serious problems in interpersonal relationships; there exists a considerable body of empirical literature which shows that the more spouses resort to punishment to get their mates to conform or to change undesirable behaviors, the more distressed the relationship will tend to become. Similarly, research has shown that the use of coercion and punishment by a spouse often results in the reciprocal use of punishment by his/her mate. Such mutually coercive behavior tends to escalate.*

The integration of the intrapersonal and the behavioral becomes possible if one accepts the premise that spouses frequently attempt to induce their mates to behave in accordance with their internal cognitive "ideals," attribute meanings and intentions to their mates' behavior which are consistent with their internal representations, respond to these projected "ideals" as if they were real, and punish their mates for behavior which deviates too far from the "ideal" to be assimilated into it or extinguished through selective inattention.

Relationship Rules and Family Process

Systems theorists assume that marital behavior is governed by fixed rules of exchange (14, 15). Social exchange theorists have assumed that spouses evaluate the fairness of conjugal exchanges according to the norms of equitable sharing and distributive justice and that prolonged perceptions of inequity between spouses leads to marital dissatisfaction. When punishment and coercion are used to reestablish equity, a reciprocal escalating spiral of mutual punishment and coercion ensues (4, 5).

It is important to note that a dissatisfied spouse responds to what he/she

---

*For a review and discussion of the empirical literature dealing with the use of coercion and punishment between spouses, see Bagarozzi (5).

perceives to be a violation of the fair exchange system. However, the rules for exchange may never have been negotiated explicitly by the spouses. It is possible that spouses hold vastly different views about the type of exchange rules which are to govern their system. Recent empirical investigations suggest that equity is only one form of distributive justice and that other types of exchange rules (e.g., equality and Marxist sharing) also may be used depending upon how one perceives the relationship (2, 16, 17, 23). It is easy to understand how difficulties can arise between spouses who do not share the same exchange rules.

Strayhorn (25) also has focused on the various meanings that a single behavior can communicate to one's spouse. For Strayhorn (25), behaviors carry important messages concerning the sender's feelings about the evaluations of his/her mate which convey more to one's mate than the actual pleasurable or displeasurable value of the behaviors themselves. Problems arise whenever the sender's rules and receiver's rules for the same behavioral message do not correspond.

Intrapersonal and Interpersonal Homeostasis: The Delicate Balance

The active quest for and ultimate selection of a potential mate who closely resembles one's "ideal" is an example of cybernetic goal seeking and mapping. This behavior serves a homeostatic function, because the closer the match between the "ideal" and the object, the less one is forced to modify his/her "ideal" representation.

Similar matching along behavioral and interactional dimensions also occurs. For example, homeostasis is maintained, to a large degree, if one is able to find a mate whose interactional style does not require major changes in one's characteristic way of relating.

However, perfect matching rarely occurs, and power struggles often develop in relationships, because spouses attempt to coerce their mates into behaving in ways which are consistent with their "ideal" representations and strive to achieve a correspondence of rules for exchange and behavior through the use of punishment and negative reinforcement.

Through mutual shaping, interaction patterns become fixed and redundant. These give the system its unique character. We conceptualize these redundant and cyclical behavior patterns as overt manifestations of unconsciously negotiated compromises between spouses concerning the rules which are to govern the exchange process in particular and husband/wife interaction in general. These compromises also support intrapersonal equilibrium because they allow each spouse to maintain, intact, his/her cognitive "ideal" and do not require modifications of any significance in characteristic modes of relating. Since the "ideal" is projected onto one's spouse who has been intermittently reinforced for behaving in character, transference and countertransference reactions frequently occur. In such situations, psychic equilibrium is maintained because acting out transferential behaviors towards one's spouse frequently allows one to continue to behave in an "as if" fashion.

We do not wish to give the impression that "ideal" structures and behavior patterns are rigidly fixed and not subject to modification through informational inputs from the external environment. Cognitive structures do change through the complementary processes of assimilation and accommodation and interaction patterns do change over time. However, such change takes place gradually in accordance with the step function (1), is evolutionary rather than revolutionary, and is first order as opposed to second order.

Functional and Dysfunctional Compromises

The effectiveness of any compromise solution reached by spouses can be judged according to the degree to which the compromise allows for change or serves to curtail the growth, development, interpersonal effectiveness, and problem-solving capacities of all family members as well as the manner in which it affects the viability of the family system as a whole.

The presence of psychiatric symptoms in a family system can be seen as a sign of a severely dysfunctional compromise. Psychiatric symptoms serve as excellent examples of compromise solutions which are attempts to maintain one's intrapersonal equilibrium (8, 9, 10, 13), while also preserving a precarious family balance (11, 12, 19, 20). Symptoms are symbols which communicate universal messages that there is an unresolved conflict within the system, that there has been a systemic compromise, that some part or parts of the system are in morphostasis, and that the system has a reduced coping capacity. However, symptoms also convey messages which are unique to the individual and to the particular system of which the individual is only a subcomponent (9). When symptoms are seen as symbolic communications about both intrapersonal and interpersonal conflicts, and therapeutic task becomes one of devising interventions which address both intrapersonal and systems dynamics. While some behaviorists have questioned the homeostatic interpretations of symptomatic behavior (6, 21, 27), others have come to appreciate that behaviors targeted for modification by clients frequently have symbolic significance for them, and that the presenting problem behavior represents important intrapersonal and interpersonal conflicts of which the client may be unaware (22).

The Role of Children

Just as individuals construct "ideal" spousal models, parents create "ideal" models of children. The young child is extremely vulnerable, because his/her behavior comes under the direct stimulus control of both parents who can shape his/her character. Frequently, parents do not possess similar "ideals" for children. Consequently, both parents may attempt to shape competing and incompatible responses in their children through the use of a variety of learning procedures. For example, a mother verbally punishes her son for fighting with a school chum and praises him when he avoids any social confrontation. His father, on the other hand, rewards him for the same behavior, teaches him how to fight, and exposes him to aggressive models. In addition, the child also becomes the object of projective identification for both parents. Finally, the parental compromise may come to rest in the child. In such cases, the child may become symptomatic, and his/her behavior can be seen as representing a compromise for all three levels simultaneously, i.e., intrapersonal, interpersonal, and systemic.

The symptomatic behavior of a bulimic adolescent girl, treated by the first author, provides a good example of how this balance is accomplished, First, the compulsive bingeing and vomiting, practiced in secret, were seen as symbolizing her intrapersonal and unconscious attempts to free herself from an enmeshed relationship with negative maternal introjects, to defend against deep oral-dependent strivings, to feed herself, and so forth. Second, at the interpersonal level, her behavior caused both parents to become extremely concerned and attentive. Their solicitous behavior also served to reinforce the problem. Finally, the bingeing and vomiting were seen as a metaphor for the covert power struggle between the parents, and the girl's behavior began to fulfill many of the homeostatic roles common to the "identified patient" (e.g., homeostat, protector, scapegoat).

THE TREATMENT PROCESS

Assessment Considerations

When a couple or family comes in for treatment, an initial assessment interview is conducted. Several factors influence the degree to which this interview is structured along purely behavioral lines. These include: (a) the nature of the presenting problem; (b) its severity; (c) its duration and history; (d) the family's ability to use standardized instruments and inventories; (e) the philosophical orientation of the family and the degree to which this orientation is compatible with a behavioral approach; and (f) the family's willingness to make behavioral observations and to collect baseline data.

The assumption we make is that unless contraindicated by certain factors (e.g., a severely dysfunctional member or a history of unsuccessful treatments) a direct behavioral approach is attempted first, before moving to a strategic mode of therapy (24). Couples and families for whom a behavioral format is considered inappropriate can be interviewed in a less formal manner by using procedures similar to those suggested by Haley (11) or Watzlawick, Weakland, and Fisch (26).

Initial assessment should encompass the following areas:

Interactional. This includes communication; problem-solving style; types of behavior change strategies; redundant and repetitive behavioral cycles; the contexts in which they occur; and interpersonal and situational factors which maintain dysfunctional behavior.

Cognitive factors. These include family members' attributions of intention to other family members' behavior; conscious perceptions of others; descriptions of how each family member thinks others "should" behave; descriptions of how all family members are expected to behave in order to resolve the presenting problem; and descriptions of how all family members will behave once the presenting problem has been resolved.

Affects. In addition to exploring the feelings associated with the above domains of experience, the therapist should inquire about each person's feelings about coming to therapy and seeking professional help.

Once this phase of assessment is complete and target behaviors have been identified, specific behavioral homework assignments are prescribed for the couple or for all family members if an entire family is being seen. Response to these first order change attempts provides additional diagnostic information, because repeated failure to complete homework assignments may be a sign of resistance.

In order to determine the reasons for failing to follow through on prescribed tasks, the therapist should devote part of a session to helping the couple or family explore those factors which they believe have prevented them from completing their assignments. This should be done in a non-accusing, supportive, and non-threatening manner which conveys the therapist's genuine concern. It is important for the therapist to determine whether homework assignments were not completed because they threatened to disrupt the intrapersonal, interpersonal, and systemic balance or whether environmental and situational factors made it difficult for family members to follow through. In addition, the therapist must rule out the possibility that performance failure was not due to poorly planned or inappropriately timed assignments, to unclear or nonspecific directives, or to skill deficiencies of family members. If nonperformance is a result of any of these factors, the therapist must make the appropriate corrections and reassign the task before concluding that failure to perform was an indication of resistance. However, if the therapist finds that task failure is not due to any of the above factors, the therapeutic focus then becomes one of overcoming resistance.

Overcoming Resistance

We refrain from overt confrontation of defenses and attempt to deal with resistance in an indirect fashion. We accept all reasons offered by family members for not completing assigned tasks in order to avoid power struggles with family members in which the ''homework'' becomes a triangulated issue between the family and the therapist. Frequently, a spouse or family member is singled out as the ''culprit'' who failed to do his/her part. By accepting everyone's explanation, including the ''culprit's,'' we do not reinforce the scapegoating and mutual blaming which are common in distressed families. We also refrain from prescribing additional assignments until we believe that the family will be able to carry them out successfully.

During this time, we attempt to modify those cognitions which we believe contribute to maintaining the presenting problem. The procedures used to achieve this end are outlined below:

1. Exploring attributions and interpretations of others' behavior. The purpose of this strategy is to correct faulty attributions and interpretations of malintention made by family members. For example, a husband is asked to discuss his understanding of his wife's repeated failure to be on time for appointments. After this is done, the wife is asked to discuss her understanding and motives concerning this same behavior. How the therapist intervenes will depend upon the wife's response. For example, statements of positive or neutral intent are accepted and reinforced by the therapist. However, if malintention is admitted, the therapist should explore the reasons for such a response. Frequently, one finds that negative behavior is a reciprocal response to what was perceived as a malintentioned act exhibited by another family member. For example, the wife is late for appointments because she perceives her husband's coming home late for dinner as a sign of his insensitivity and disrespect for her. When this occurs, the therapist can reframe the spouses' actions as behavior change attempts that were ineffective. Finally, the therapist can positively connote the spouse's intentions. For example, if the wife is late because she spends a lot of time dressing, putting on her makeup, etc., this behavior can be described as her efforts to make herself attractive for her husband. Positive connotation in the last example is used to modify the "ideal" image.

2. *Revealing the thoughts, feelings, and self-statements made about other family members whenever malintentions are perceived.* This strategy is used to get at the internal monologue that often serves as an antecedent cue for coercive and punishing responses. The therapist's role is to help the person become aware of thoughts, feelings, and self-statements whenever he/she perceives the behavior of others to be malintentioned. Next, the therapist teaches family members to acquire noncoercive problem-solving responses as substitutes for inflammatory self-statements, feelings, and internal monologues. For example, the perception of malintent can become a cue for a family member to "check out" the actual intentions of others before responding in a retaliatory fashion. In our work with violent spouses, we teach the violent partner how to recognize internal cues which precede violent behavior. These feelings, thoughts, and self-statements then become cues for temporarily leaving the scene in order to "cool off." During this cooling-off period, the violent spouse is taught to replace the angry chain of self-statements with an internal monologue which leads to more prosocial and constructive problem-solving (3).

3. *Uncovering unfulfilled expectations which are perceived as rule violations of unverbalized contracts.* This procedure follows logically from the two outlined above. Usually, perceptions of malintention are based upon a family member's conviction that an exchange rule or implicitly negotiated contract has been violated. Uncovering the contract and its attendant quid-pro-quo rules then becomes the therapeutic task. Once the therapist brings these rules (which take the form of unfulfilled expectations) to light, explicit contract negotiation can be attempted.

4. *Discovering the symbolic meaning of behaviors exchanged between spouses and among family members.* The following strategy has been used to deal with resistance to negotiating explicit contingency contracts in marital therapy. However, its principles can be applied to most relationships where the parties involved are reasonably insightful and psychologically minded. The procedure is as follows.

Each spouse identifies a behavior that he/she would like his/her mate to exhibit in order to improve the relationship. A quid-pro-quo contract is negotiated wherein each spouse agrees to perform the desired behavior for his/her mate. When a spouse resists fulfilling his/her part of the contract, a discussion of the symbolic significance of the behavior in question is undertaken. The symbolic meaning of the behavior is discussed in terms of its meaning for the individual and its meaning in the relationship. Here again, attributions and expectations surface. Frequently, a spouse is asked to describe the importance of the behavior in terms of earlier life experiences. For example, a husband tells his wife that hs is afraid to tell her he loves her because doing so as a child only resulted in ridicule and rejection from his parents. The wife, on the other hand, may reveal that when her husband tells her he loves her she feels the warmth and caring she experienced as a child in her interactions with her deceased father.

In addition to achieving the therapeutic goals outlined above, these strategies also serve to bring about modifications in the "ideal" images of family members. The final strategy of this treatment phase attempts to gain direct access to the "ideal" images themselves.

5. *Exploring "ideal" images within the context of the family.* Gaining knowledge of the conscious aspects of the "ideal" can be achieved through direct inquiries about each person's wishes and fantasies concerning the "perfect," "ideal," or "model" spouse, children, siblings, and parents. Less conscious and negative aspects of the "ideal" can be found by asking family members to identify those aspects of other family members' problem behaviors which they dislike because they remind them of themselves or significant others in their lives (e.g., parents, siblings, relatives). While this process is straightforward and direct, it does offer some insights into less conscious aspects of the "ideal" image. An example is offered below.

Recently, the first author treated a family whose presenting problem was the 12-year-old daughter's refusal to attend school on a regular basis. She feigned sickness, expressed fears of ridicule from classmates for her obesity, and offered numerous excuses for not attending classes which were accepted by both parents. Behavioral approaches failed because both parents were unable to cooperate in carrying out homework assignments. Exploring each parent's "ideal" image of this child proved to be enlightening. Father had projected many of his denied and repressed aspects of himself onto the child. He repeatedly attacked those traits in her. Mother, on the other hand, was involved in an enmeshed relationship with the daughter, with whom she was closely identified. She treated the daughter as she would have liked to have been treated by her distant and aloof parents. When asked to describe differences between herself and her daughter, the mother paused for a long time. The only difference she could identify was their ages!

This revelation cleared the way for the next treatment phase. Mother was put in charge of the daughter. Her task was to help the child achieve appropriate age and sex role behavior. She was labeled as an expert on female behavior who, because of her unfortunate childhood experiences, could help her daughter avoid the same unfortunate experiences she had had with peers. The father's assignment was to reinforce his wife's attempts to help their daughter grow up.

After several weeks of ambivalence, mother told the daughter she had to attend school regularly. After one week of full school attendance, the mother described this experience as "giving birth" to her daughter again. Treatment then turned to the marital relationship, and the daughter was no longer included in treatment. As the parents began to focus on their relationship, attributions, unverbalized expectations, and contracts, the mother was able to identify several differences between her and her daughter.

Once resistances have been overcome, we focus our attention on restructuring the family system and revert to the strategies outlined above whenever necessary. Sometimes paradoxical injunctions are employed in rigidly homeostatic family systems. For example, a 21-year-old son who was not working and living at home with his parents was arrested for vagrancy. This arrest brought the family in for treatment. During the explorations of each parent's "ideal" image of him, it was discovered that he was identified by his father with the father's older brother who continued to live a vagrant life-style but had managed to live with his parents until their death. However, the father's brother managed to stay out of trouble with the law. A paradoxical injunction prescribing the son's symptomatic behavior was devised and assigned to the entire family. All family members were required to visit the father's brother and the "identified patient" was to ask his uncle to teach him how to be a "successful vagrant." This prescription had the effect of having the son begin an earnest campaign to find a job. Treatment then focused on the marital relationship.

CONCLUSION

In this paper, we have outlined a number of techniques designed to focus on the intrapersonal, interpersonal, and systemic aspects of family process. The interplay among the three is complex and difficult to decipher; the degree to which one chooses to focus on one dimension over the other two probably is a matter of personal style and comfort as well as theoretical persuasion and clinical expertise.

The bulk of this paper has been devoted to describing techniques we have developed to deal with resistances which we believe stem from cognitive structures and rules, which are rigidly fixed and strongly influence our perceptions and behaviors toward significant others. The goal of treatment is the modification of these structures so that they become less rigid and fixed, allow for the assimilation of discrepant information about others, and enable the person to learn and exhibit new behaviors which are more socially effective, personally satisfying, and foster the growth and development of the family system as a whole.

REFERENCES

1. Ashby, W.R. *Design for the Brain*. New York: John Wiley, 1954.
2. Bagarozzi, D.A. The effects of cohesiveness on distributive justice. *J. of Psychol.*, 110: 267-273, 1982.

3. Bargarozzi, D.A., and Giddings, C.W. Conjugal violence: A critical review of current research and clinical practices. *Am. J. Fam. Ther.,* 11 (1): 3-15, 1983.
4. Bagarozzi, D.A., and Wodarski, J.S. A social exchange typology of conjugal relationships and conflict development. *J. Marr. Fam. Coun.,* 39: 53-60, 1977.
5. Bagarozzi, D.A., and Wodarski, J.S. Behavioral treatment of marital discord. *Clin. Soc. Wk. J.,* 6: 135-154, 1978.
6. Eysenck, H.J., and Rachman, S. *The Causes and Cures of Neurosis.* London: Routledge and Kegan Paul, 1965.
7. Fairbairn, W.R. *An Object Relations Theory of Personality.* New York: Basic Books, 1954.
8. Fenichel, O. *The Psychoanalytic Theory of Neurosis.* New York: Norton, 1945.
9. Freud, A. *The Ego and the Mechanisms of Defense.* London: Hogarth, 1937.
10. Freud, S. Neurosis and psychosis. *In:* J. Strachey (Ed.), *Standard Edition of the Complete Psychological Works of Sigmund Freud, Vol VI.* London: Hogarth, 1975.
11. Haley, J. *Problem-Solving Therapy.* San Francisco: Jossey-Bass, 1976.
12. Haley, J. *Strategies of Psychotherapy.* New York: Grune and Stratton, 1963.
13. Hartmann, H. *Ego Psychology and the Problem of Adaptation.* New York: International Universities Press, 1958.
14. Jackson, D.D. Family roles: Marital quid pro quo. *Arch. Gen. Psychiat.,* 12: 589-594, 1965.
15. Lederer, W., and Jackson, D.D. *The Mirages of Marriage.* New York: Norton, 1968.
16. Lerner, M.J. Social psychology of justice in interpersonal attraction. *In:* T. Huston (Ed.), *Foundations of Interpersonal Attraction.* New York: Academic Press, 1974.
17. Lerner, M.J. The justice motive: Equity and parity among children. *J. Per. Soc. Psychol.,* 29: 539-550, 1974.
18. Lewis, R.A., and Spanier, G.B. Theorizing about the quality and stability of marriage. *In:* W.R. Burr, R. Hill, F.I. Nye, and I.L. Reiss, (Eds.), *Contemporary Theories about the Family, Vol. I.* New York: Free Press, 1979.
19. Minuchin, S. *Families and Family Therapy.* Cambridge, MA: Harvard University Press, 1974.
20. Minuchin, S., Rosman, B.L., and Baker, L. *Psychosomatic Families: Anorexia Nervosa in Context.* Cambridge, MA: Harvard University Press, 1978.
21. Nathan, P. Symptomatic diagnosis and behavioral assessment: A synthesis. *In:* D.H. Barlow (Ed.), *Behavioral Assessment and Adult Disorders.* New York: Guilford, 1981.
22. Nelson, R.O., and Barlow, D.H. Behavioral assessment: Basic strategies and initial procedures. *In:* D.H. Barlow (Ed.), *Behavioral Assessment of Adult Disorders.* New York: Guilford, 1981.
23. Shapiro, G. Effects of expectation of future interaction on reward allocation in dyads: Equity and equality. *J. Per. Soc. Psychol.,* 31: 873-881, 1975.
24. Stanton, M.D. An integrated structural/strategic approach to family therapy. *J. Marr. Fam. Coun.,* 7: 427-438, 1981.
25. Strayhorn, J.M. Social exchange theory: Cognitive restructuring in marital therapy. *Fam. Proc.,* 17: 437-448, 1978.
26. Watzlawick, P., Weakland, J., and Fisch, R. *Change: Principles of Problem Formation and Problem Resolution.* New York: Norton, 1974.
27. Wolpe, J. *The Practice of Behavior Therapy.* New York: Pergamon, 1969.

Chapter XXI

FAMILY CLASSIFICATIONS AND DSM-III

John F. Clarkin, Ph.D.,
Allen J. Frances, M.D.,
and Samuel Perry, M.D.

Editors' Summary. This paper explores the implications of DSM-III for family therapy and ways in which future nomenclatures might be modified to make them more useful for family therapists. Because DSM-III is explicitly a classification of individual psychopathology, it provides very little data pertinent to the selection and planning of family treatment. Two possible future innovations in the multiaxial system are suggested: 1) replacing the currently categorical Axis II personality disorder section with a dimensional interpersonal system; and/or 2) developing an Axis VI classification of family pathology.

In July of 1980, the American Psychiatric Association published its greatly revised official nomenclature of psychiatric disorders, the Diagnostic and Statistical Manual, Third Edition (2), which is now universally known by its diminutive, DSM-III. This radically innovative classification system has already had an unprecedented impact on psychiatry and also on related mental health disciplines. Several hundred thousand copies were quickly printed and sold, and journals and scientific meetings have become filled with lively debate about its merits and limitations.

DSM-III differs from its predecessors (the never very popular nor influential DSM-I and DSM-II) in its descriptive orientation, characterized by specific operational criteria defining each diagnostic category, and in providing a multiaxial system that allows the clinician to describe the patient more comprehensively than previously had been possible. Using the multiaxial system, the clinician can indicate the patient's clinical syndrome, underlying personality disorder, physical condition, precipitating stressors, and adaptive functioning during the past year. Despite this multidimensional view of the patient, certain variables that crucially affect the choice of treatment are not included. This limitation is especially apparent in regard to the selection and planning of family therapy. Disagreement, even resentment, has arisen among some clinicians who argue that because the DSM-III is explicitly a classification of individual pathology, it implicitly neglects interpersonal therapeutic approaches—or at the very least fails to provide information that would support their selection.

It is obvious that the much acclaimed "atheoretical" approach of DSM-III is not really atheoretical at all (no system of nomenclature can be) and within DSM-III there are any number of unrecognized, but possibly important, theoretical assumptions. One of these is that family pathology constitutes a precipitant to individual disorder but is not itself to be conceived as a psychiatric disorder or to be classified and rated independently. This decision was probably necessary given the purpose and individual orientation of DSM-III and the current lack of research evidence supporting various methods of classifying family pathology, but it clearly establishes a narrow limit of usefulness of DSM-III for family therapists. Those who study and treat families come to believe that the whole of family pathology adds up to something much more than (or different from) the sum of its individual parts and that a method of classifying the family interaction in which the patient participates can conceivably add an important dimension to classification of individual and syndromal diagnosis.

DSM-III makes only passing reference to disordered functioning occurring within the larger family unit. There is, in fact, only one section in DSM-III in which parent-child or marital problems are mentioned at all and this section is titled, "Conditions Not Attributable to a Mental Disorder that Are a Focus of Attention or Treatment." In all other instances, the manifestations of family pathology can be diagnosed only insofar as they have precipitated in the individual family members enough symptoms to qualify them for one or another DSM-III diagnostic category. For instance, many patients who meet criteria for a diagnosis of "adjustment disorder" (i.e., "a maladaptive reaction to an identifiable psychosocial stressor") are likely to be responding with individual symptoms to a problem in the family system. The DSM-III multiaxial method of diagnosis does provide Axis IV to help describe this. Axis IV is a dimensional 1 to 7 rating of the severity of psychosocial stressors occurring in the patient's life within the year preceding his or her presentation. This axis was included in recognition of research evidence indicating that life stress, including marital and family stress, may importantly influence the individual's vulnerability to psychiatric disorder and that acknowledgment of such stress may assist in treatment planning.

For virtually every diagnosis in DSM-III, family therapy might under particular circumstances be the treatment of choice or at least an important adjunctive treatment. On the other hand, there is no DSM-III diagnosis that by itself rules family treatment in or out. There are, in fact, only a few hints provided in the multiaxial diagnosis that will suggest whether family treatment is likely to be indicated. Axis IV, the rating of psychosocial stressors, is the most helpful. For patients who present with high ratings of family stressors, family evaluation and treatment certainly should be considered. This is especially true if the Axis I diagnosis is Adjustment Disorder. Patients diagnosed as parent-child or marital problem ("no psychiatric disorder") will almost always require family evaluation and generally will be treated within the family context unless there are particular contraindications to this. Beyond these few rules of thumb, DSM-III offers little hint about the utility in the given situation of a family evaluation or treatment.

Family therapists are not alone in voicing objections to the DSM-III. Some psychodynamic psychiatrists, for example, have objected to the relative emphasis on overt behavior to the exclusion of more intrapsychic phenomena; they have suggested adding an axis that would include information more useful for psychodynamic therapists (19). Fortunately, the Task Force of the American Psychiatric Association never presumed that psychiatric nomenclature had reached its final state of development with completion of the DSM-III. Those involved in its design welcomed and responded to suggestions while the DSM-III was being developed and tested; and, in that same spirit, they have stated that the multiaxial system was intended to be an evolving classification responsive to the accumulation of new data and experience. Various subspecialties within the mental health profession now have the responsibility of conceiving and testing their own modifications and additions to make future diagnostic manuals more relevant to their work.

The first section of this paper will compare the DSM-III Axis II categorical diagnosis of personality disorder with a dimensional system of interpersonal diagnosis that may be useful for family therapists. We then explore the advantages and disadvantages of the various available methods of classifying families, at least one of which might become a useful Axis VI addition to DSM-III. It will become obvious that the development of a nomenclature of family pathology has not yet attained the same level of detail, precision, and sophistication as has the DSM-III classification of individual disorders. This is not at all surprising. We have been diagnosing individual psychopatholgy for millenia, but have only just begun to think of families as units for diagnostic labeling. Moreover, family pathology is inherently more complex and multivariate than is individual pathology and therefore more difficult to reduce to categories and operational criteria. As Tolstoy (40) noted in a different context, families that manage to attain happiness do so in similar ways, but those that are unhappy suffer in their own particular, individualized, and hard to classify ways. The final section illustrates some of the conceptual and practical options and difficulties encountered in the attempt to classify families.

INTERPERSONAL MODIFICATION OF AXIS II

The question naturally arises whether there are, or could be, other methods of individual diagnosis that might replace or supplement DSM-III to more usefully guide the decision as to whether and which kind of family treatment is indicated. This is an area that is ripe for valuable future research in family theory and practice. It would be a great advance to have reliable instruments to measure the impact of the family on individual psychopathology and vice versa and to assess the accessibility of the social system to therapeutic intervention.

A dimensional method of interpersonal diagnosis with possible utility as a replacement for the currently categorical Axis II has been offered by McLemore and Benjamin (5, 23). They criticize DSM-III, along lines similar to our previous discussion, for showing "near total neglect of social psychological variables and interpersonal behavior." Instead, they submit that "rigorous and systematic description of social behavior is uniquely critical to effective definition and treatment of the problems that bring most individuals for psychiatric and psychological evaluations." McLemore and Benjamin suggest that almost all diagnoses of functional mental disorder are implicitly made on the basis of interpersonal behavior. They review the history of dimensional interpersonal classifications, most especially Leary's, and highlight their clinical and scientific advantages over traditional psychiatric nomenclature, including DSM-III. The various interpersonal methods differ in their specific characteristics but all consist of measures of the patient's functioning along a variety of interpersonal dimensions. For instance, in Leary's system, these are the masochistic, distrustful, sadistic, narcissistic, autocratic, hypernormal, overconventional, and dependent. The patient's interpersonal diagnosis also immediately constitutes an invaluable prediction of the reciprocal behaviors the patient is most likely to "pull" from others.

It is clear how helpful such a system may be for predicting and measuring interpersonal interactions among individual family members. Benjamin (6) offers a detailed clinical vignette illustrating how her method describes and predicts interpersonal behaviors in a troubled family. The ratings serve many diagnostic, therapeutic, and research functions:

(a) explicit charting of family members' disturbances;
(b) clear specifications of treatment goals;
(c) detailed elaboration of the social contexts of problems;
(d) reconstruction of the developmental history of this context across generations;
(e) ongoing monitoring of change over time;
(f) objective criteria for improvement;
(g) useful therapeutic impact when ratings were fed back to family members to impart insight about their contribution to difficulties in family interaction.

The interpersonal method certainly has some appeal for the family therapist since it highlights how individuals in a family interact with one another. This method could be used to establish an empirical typology of family interactions, to predict necessary interventions, and to measure change. Despite the enormous research and clinical potential of interpersonal systems, certain cautions are nonetheless in order. These systems have had limited use to date and need further validation. Moreover, the claim made by McLemore and Benjamin that interpersonal diagnosis could or should replace all of DSM-III is quite misleading. Many psychiatric disorders are, in fact, only peripherally or secondarily interpersonal and are instead best understood within other frames of reference. Moreover, to the extent that a psychiatric disorder has discernible boundaries and is not disturbed normally, it is generally advantageous to retain a categorical rather than a dimensional approach. Although schizophrenia is indeed a very problematic, categorical concept with unclear boundaries, it remains a worthwhile heuristic entity that might be buried in a list of dimensional scores. The dimensional interpersonal method may find its best role as a future replacement for the now categorical DSM-III Axis II personality disorder section. It will not ever, in our opinion, replace the whole diagnostic system.

AXIS VI FOR FAMILY CLASSIFICATION

It seems inevitable that psychiatric diagnosis will, at least for the foreseeable future, remain multiaxial. This approach has demonstrated many advantages and has already been receiving wide acceptance. It is, however, very unclear which and how many axes are most crucial for inclusion in a diagnostic nomenclature and there is no particular reason to suppose that the current five axes will persevere forever. Subspecialty groups (like family therapists) will do well to design for themselves axes that are specifically pertinent for their own work. Once developed, an "Axis VI" classification of family pathology might be appended informally to DSM-III diagnoses in settings where family therapy is practiced, and tested for possible eventual inclusion in DSM-IV.

Table 1 lists many proposed dimensional and/or categorizational schemes by author and indicates the focus (marital or family unit), the relevant dimensions and categories, and the methodology used to derive the system. We will review here a few representative family and marital systems of classification from Table 1 and discuss their possible utility as an Axis VI for DSM-III (or DSM-IV). For a family system of classification to gain status as an independent axis, it will have to demonstrate:

1) reliability;
2) validity;
3) usefulness in treatment planning; and
4) acceptability to clinicians of varying theoretical orientations.

The four models reviewed in some detail below are all of recent origin and are relatively unsubstantiated. None has gained wide clinical acceptance. Nonetheless, they and some of the other systems in Table 1 show enough potential to encourage a concerted research effort to determine if a family classification can become a useful supplement to individual diagnosis. We have picked for representative review a self-report system involving theoretical dimensions of family structure and interaction (29), a self-report system assessing the family environment (28), a rating system for a specific dimension of family functioning found to be related to individual patient course of illness (7, 8), and finally, a test of family problem-solving style that predicts engagement in treatment (10). Our review of previous attempts to categorize families will provide background for the conclusion section of this article in which we point out the conceptual and practical problems involved in designing and formulating any family typology.

Family Cohesion and Adaptability Matrix

Olson and colleagues (30) developed a promising model of family typology by integrating previous attempts reported by investigators in sociology, psychology, and psychiatry. The typology has two major dimensions: family cohesion and family adaptability. Family cohesion is the emotional bonding between members of the family, and relates to such issues as independence, autonomy, coalition, boundaries, pseudomutuality, undifferentiated ego mass, and other concepts described in the family theory literature. The second dimension is family adaptability, that is, the capacity of the family when confronted with situational or developmental stress to change its rules, power structure, role relationships, and styles of negotiating.

To complement the clinician's assessment of the family, Olson and his colleagues (29) have developed a self-report instrument by which individual family members can measure their perception of the family's cohesion and adaptability. A four-by-four matrix is created with 16 possible cells and the family is assigned to cells accordingly. The instrument, while potentially quite useful in terms of defining a family and planning its treatment, reflects the problems of any self-report and needs further validation. Even if the particular instrument has problems, Olson's conceptual model holds great promise since it taps two dimensions that are highly relevant for family therapists.

This model has already been put to some empirical test with signs of at least moderate success. Russell (34) evaluated families with adolescents and differentiated their functioning into high and low groups. He then assessed the families in terms of cohesion and adaptability. He found that the lower functioning families were on the extreme edges of Olson's conceptual matrix, sug-

Table 1

Dimensional and Categorizational Schemata for Family Function/Dysfunction

Author	Focus	Dimensions	Categories	Methodology*
Reiss & colleagues (10, 31)	Psychiatric inpatients and their families	Family coordination Family configuration	Environment sensitive Consensus sensitive Achievement sensitive Distance sensitive	E

Lewis & colleagues (21, 22)	Normal, dysfunctional, and severely dysfunctional families	Overt power
		Parental coalition
		Closeness
		Family mythology
		Goal-directed negotiation
		Clarity of expression
		Responsibility
		Invasiveness
		Permeability
		Range of feelings
		Mood and tone
		Unresolvable conflict
		Empathy
			Optimal families
			Competent but pained families
			Dysfunctional families
			  a. Dominant-submissive
			  b. Conflicted
			Severely dysfunctional families
			  a. Dominant parent
			  b. Chaotic
				E

Olson & colleagues (29, 30)	Dysfunctional families	Cohesion
		Adaptability
			Family system types:
			  Chaotically disengaged
			  Flexibly disengaged
			  Structurally disengaged
			  Rigidly disengaged
			  Chaotically separated
			  Flexibly separated
			  Structurally separated
			  Rigidly separated
			  Chaotically connected
			  Flexibly connected
			  Structurally connected
			  Rigidly connected
			  Chaotically enmeshed
			  Flexibly enmeshed
			  Structurally enmeshed
			  Rigidly enmeshed
				E

Source	Population	Dimensions	Types	
Ryder (36)	Functional and dysfunctional couples	Husband's potency or effectiveness Husband's degree of impulse control Degree of wife's dependency Wife's attitude toward sex Wife's orientation toward the marriage		E
Brown & colleagues (7, 8, 41)	Schizophrenic identified patients and families	Expressed emotion		E
Moos (27, 28)	Functional and dysfunctional families	Personal growth Relationships Systems maintenance	Expressive-oriented families Structure-oriented families Independence-oriented families Achievement-oriented families Moral-religious-oriented families Conflict-oriented families	E
McMaster Model (11, 12)	Functional and dysfunctional families	Problem-solving Communication Roles Affective responsiveness Affective involvement Behavior control		E
Ackerman (3, 4)	Psychiatric outpatient families		Externally isolated family Externally integrated family Internally unintegrated family Unintended family Immature family Deviant family Disintegrated or regressed family	C_2
Richter (32)	Psychiatric outpatients		Family symptom neurosis Family character neurosis	C_1

Author	Focus	Dimensions	Categories	Methodology*
Gehrke & Kirschenbaum (16)	Psychiatric outpatients		Repressive family Delinquent family Suicidal family	C_1

Serrano et al. (37)	Adolescent identified patient and family		Function the adolescent serves in family:
			  infantile maladjustment reaction in adolescence
			  childish maladjustment reaction in adolescence
			  juvenile maladjustment reaction in adolescence
			  preadolescent maladjustment reaction in adolescence
				C_1

Goldstein et al. (17)	Adolescent identified patient and family	Locus of conflict
		Overt versus covert pathology
			Adolescent inpatient and family:
			  aggressive, antisocial
			  active family conflict
			  passive-negative
			  withdrawn-socially isolated
				C_1

Riskin & Faunce (33)	Normal and pathological families		Multiproblem families Constricted families Acting-out or underachieving child-labeled problems Families with significant undiagnosed problems Normal families	C_1
Minuchin (24)	Normal and abnormal families	Disengaged Enmeshed		C_1

Reference	Population	Dimension	Categories	Method
Mittelman (25, 26)	Dysfunctional couples		Aggressive dominating spouse with passive-submissive partner Emotionally detached spouse with partner craving for support Intense competition between spouses Helpless spouse with extremely considerate mate Alternating assertiveness and helplessness in both spouses	C_i
Gehrke & Moxon (15)	Dysfunctional couples	Content of marital conflict	Conflict over masculine-feminine roles Sadomasochistic conflict Detached, demanding conflict Oral dependent conflict Neurotic illness conflict	C_i
Lederer & Jackson (20)	Functional and dysfunctional couples	Power	Symmetrical marital relationship Complementary marital relationship Parallel marital relationship	C_i
Solomon (38)	Normal and abnormal families		Classification by life cycle phase: marriage birth of first child and child-rearing individuation of family members departure of the child(ren) integration of loss	T
Wertheim (43)	Normal and abnormal families		Morphostasis versus morphogenesis Open versus closed to influence	T

*E-empirical investigation; C_s-systematic clinical investigation; C_i-clinical support; T-theoretical gesting that the proposed model correlates with clinical impressions. In a similar study, Sprenkle and Olson (39) applied the model to clinical couples and found that they had extreme scores when compared to nonclinical couples.

Family Environment Scale

This self-report instrument (28) uses 90 true/false items to assess the family environment. Three major areas are evaluated: personal growth, relationships, and systems maintenance. Each major area is subdivided. The dimension measuring personal growth has five subscales: independence, achievement, moral-religious, intellectual-cultural, and active-recreational. The dimension measuring relationships has three subscales: family cohesion, family expressiveness, and family conflict. The dimension measuring systems maintenance has two subscales: organization and control.

To test the utility of this instrument, Moos and Moos (28) collected self-report from 100 diverse families. The results were cluster-analyzed to yield empirical categories of families. Six distinct clusters emerged:

1) expressive-oriented (emphasis on open expression of feelings, ideas, and problems);
2) structure-oriented (emphasis on organization and cohesion);
3) independence-oriented (emphasis on assertiveness, self-sufficiency and personal decision-making);
4) achievement-oriented (emphasis on competitiveness at work, school, and within the home);
5) moral-religious-oriented (emphasis on ethical values and fairness); and
6) conflict-oriented (emphasis on ambivalent interactions, particularly conflicts between hostility and dependency).

In addition to determining these clusters, Moos and Fuhr (27) have used an environment scale to plan treatment for the case of a 15-year-old female who sought counseling because of deterioration in her academic performance. The test responses revealed specific family difficulties and helped guide the therapeutic interventions.

Family Problem-solving Styles

Reiss (31) developed a classification schema based upon his observation that families have distinctly different styles of problem-solving when given a specific task (card-sorting). He noted, for example, that families with a schizophrenic member tried to maintain a close and uninterrupted agreement at all times and, while striving for a common solution to the assigned problems, ended up doing poorly. In contrast, families with members who were delinquent attended very well to cues from the external environment but did not attend to cues from each other. Reiss was cautious in interpreting these data and indicated that the different problem-solving styles did not necessarily relate causally to the nature of the psychopathology in the individual patient. Nonetheless, he suggested that a method for categorizing the problem-solving styles of families might be helpful in planning treatment.

With this in mind, Costell and Reiss (10) used a problem-solving task to predict how families of psychiatrically hospitalized adolescents would engage in treatment. The families were classified along two dimensions: configuration (the family's productive use of each other's problem-solving skills) and coordination (the degree of harmonious working together among the family members). Of note, families with high configuration and high coordination ("environment-sensitive families") became engaged members of the inpatient treatment community. Families with low configuration and low coordination on the problem-solving task ("distance-sensitive families") were at a high risk for noncompliance and nonengagement with the therapeutic environment. They remained inconspicuous, felt little cohesion with the group, and had poor attendance at scheduled therapeutic events.

Family Emotional Expression

During the past 25 years, Brown and his associates (7, 8, 35) have been interested in how psychiatric inpatients function after discharge and how the emotional involvement with others in the home may influence the recurrence of psychiatric symptoms and the need for rehospitalization. In an exploratory study, Brown and his co-workers (7) found that discharged male patients with intense emotional ties to parents or wives had a poor prognosis. In a more systematic investigation (8) they were able to document that, when patients were discharged and returned home to live with relatives with whom the emotional involvement was intense, those patients were more likely to suffer a relapse of florid symptoms even when the severity of the psychiatric illness at the time of discharge was taken into account.

On the basis of these findings, an instrument was devised to measure the inpatient's relationship with family members (9). The semi-structured interview assessed the amount of "expressed emotion" between the patient and other family members. Data from this instrument indicated that the level of emotion expressed by relatives when measured shortly after a schizophrenic patient was admitted to the hospital strongly correlated with symptomatic relapse following discharge. This potentially predictive observation by the British group was later replicated by Vaughn and Leff (41, 42) and has led to other studies relating the hostile overinvolvement of relatives to the outcome of index schizophrenic patients. This research has, in turn, affected treatment planning. For example, Falloon and others (13) have described how three families with a schizophrenic member and rated high in "expressed emotion" responded to a 15-week family therapy specifically designed to reduce the intense emotional involvement. Future research, such as that being currently conducted by Anderson, Hogarty, and Reiss (1), may indicate that "expressed emotion" is an important family variable not only in the course of schizophrenia, but also in the course of serious depressions and other psychiatric illnesses.

Most relevant for possible inclusion in future Diagnostic and Statistical Manuals will be those dimensional and/or categorical classifications of families that have been empirically derived and/or tested on clinical populations, especially where there are additional contrasting data on normals or nonclinic populations. To summarize, at the time of this review, the work of Reiss et al. (10, 31), Lewis and colleagues (21, 22), Olson and colleagues (29, 30), Brown and colleagues (7, 8), Moos (27, 28), and Epstein and colleagues (11, 12) have some empirical basis on clinical populations but much more obviously needs to be done. The dimensions that seem most promising include communication, negotiation and conflict, affectivity, system and boundary issues, individuation, and behavioral control. Table 2 lists these dimensions as they are evaluated or quantified by methods of patient and family self-report, clinical rating by individual observer, or by scores derived from a common task or problem situation that is presented to the family by an investigator.

CONCEPTUAL AND EMPIRICAL PROBLEMS

1. Pathology Versus Normality

In the DSM-III, Axes I, II and III categorize pathological phenomena whereas Axes IV and V rate stressors and adaptive functioning. If an Axis VI is added to categorize the family system, a decision must be made whether this additional axis should be oriented toward psychopathological or normal functioning. Brown's system (7) of categorizing the family's "expressed emotion" is clearly concerned with pathological hostility and overinvolvement. In contrast, Olson's method (30) of categorizing a family's cohesion and adaptability considers a wide range of behaviors which need not be abnormal. A possible com-

Table 2

Prevalent Dimensions of Family Function/Dysfunction

DIMENSION	VANTAGE POINT		
	Self-Report	Clinical rating	Task
Communication, negotiation and conflict	Negotiation (Olson); decision-making (Olson); conflict (Moos)	Unresolved conflict (Beavers); goal-directed negotiation (Beavers)	Coordination (Reiss); configuration (Reiss)
Affectivity	Emotional bonding (Olson); cohesion (Moos)	Affective responsiveness (Epstein); affective involvement (Epstein); empathy (Beavers); expressiveness (Moos); range of feelings (Beavers); mood and tone (Beavers); closeness (Beavers); affective-instrumental and sexual (Epstein)	
System and boundary issues	Family boundaries (Olson); coalitions (Olson); rules (Olson); organization (Moos)	Systems management and maintenance (Epstein); invasiveness (Beavers); permeability (Beavers); parental coalition (Beavers); power (Beavers)	
Individuation	Independence (Moos; Olson); assertiveness (Olson)	Responsibility (Beavers)	
Behavior control	Discipline (Olson); control (Moos)	Behavior control (Epstein)	

promise would be to select for Axis VI those kinds of familial interactions which may be normal in moderation, but would at least imply family psychopathology when rated at extreme levels.

2. Categorical Versus Dimensional System

Frances (14) has discussed the pros and cons of using either categorical or dimensional systems when diagnosing individuals. He concluded that professionals trained in the medical tradition are inclined toward the categorical system, while mental health professionals from fields other than medicine, such as sociology or experimental psychology, are more inclined to distinguish a family by degree rather than kind. The two methods can also be used simultaneously: One can begin with a multidimensional system and then perform cluster analysis in order to empirically determine categorical types. DSM-III now uses categorical diagnosis for Axis I, II, and III, dimensional ratings for Axis IV and V. A family Axis VI could be dimensional or categorical depending upon which method turns out to be empirically the more useful.

3. Rating the Family as a Unit Versus Rating the Individual's Interaction With the Family

Those clinicians who work frequently with families are more prone to see the family as a distinct entity which can be characterized in terms of how it functions, develops, changes, establishes its boundaries, and interacts with the outside world. Those less familiar with family therapy are more inclined to assess the way an individual responds to separate family members and the family-as-a-whole, as well as how the family responds to the identified patients. To oversimplify, given an individual with schizophrenia, some therapists would categorize the entire family, whereas others would evaluate primarily the interaction between the indexed patient and the other family members. The typologies summarized above illustrate these two different ways of describing a family. Some of the systems, such as those of Reiss (31) and Wertheim (43), rate qualities of the family as a unit whereas Brown's rating of "expressed emotion" presupposes the existence of an identified patient with a specific diagnosis (schizophrenia) and then rates the behavior of other family members.

4. Empirical Problems

Many empirical problems must be resolved before a family typology can be added to the DSM-III and be useful for clinicians of varying persuasions and interests. Of these obstacles, the highest no doubt will be to establish dimensions which not only can be measured reliably, but also can show some validity in categorizing families. The fact is that, at this point, no one knows precisely which characteristics of a family are most relevant in terms of the etiology, course, and treatment of the major psychopathological entities. Until a family classification is shown to be reliable and valid, we cannot expect colleagues less inclined toward a systems approach to accept and use it.

CONCLUSIONS

The DSM-III assumes the family problems may precipitate a psychiatric illness, but that family pathology is not in itself a disorder to be separately and specifically classified. Many have expressed disappointment about DSM-III's failure to guide treatment selection, including that of family therapy. Given the present state of knowledge, this disappointment is unreasonable. DSM-III was never intended to be, and clearly cannot be, a comprehensive statement about every variable that is important to treatment planning for most or all modalities. The manual is meant to provide no more than a scaffold upon which a more complete formulation can be printed, a formulation that will inevitably include data and hypotheses about the individual's family and social system and about which therapeutic approaches will be potentially most beneficial. The DSM-III's failure to specify indications for family or other therapies reflects less on the manual and more on our relative lack of knowledge and agreement about which type of treatment correlates best with which types of patient variables. As the present review demonstrates, there is as yet no widely used and proven system of classifying families that would be suitable for an official nomenclature. However, since family interactions seem most relevant to symptomatic behaviors in individuals (18, 43), further research is to be encouraged on specifying such family interaction for inclusion in future editions of the Diagnostic and Statistical Manual.

REFERENCES

1. Anderson, C.M., Hogarty, G., and Reiss, D.J. The psychoeducational family treatment of schizophrenia. *In*: M. Goldstein, (Ed.), *New Developments in Interviews with Families of Schizophrenics.* San Francisco: Jossey-Bass, 1981.
2. American Psychiatric Association. *Diagnostic and Statistical Manual of Mental Disorders (3rd ed.).* Washington, D.C.: American Psychiatric Association, 1980.
3. Ackerman, N.W. *The Psychodynamics of Family Life.* New York: Basic Books, 1958.
4. Ackerman, N.W., and Behrens, M.L. A study of family diagnosis. *Am. J. Orthopsychiat.,* 26: 68-78, 1956.
5. Benjamin, L.S. Structural analysis of social behavior. *Psychological Review,* 81: 392-425, 1974.

6. Benjamin, L.S. Structural analysis of a family in therapy. *J. Consult. & Clin. Psychol.*, 45: 391-406, 1977.
7. Brown, G.W., Birley, J.L.T., and Wing, J.K. Influence of family life on the course of schizophrenic disorders: A replication. *Brit. J. Psychiat.*, 121: 241-258, 1972.
8. Brown, G.W., Carstairs, G.M., and Topping, G.G. The posthospital adjustment of chronic mental patients. *Lancet*, II: 685, 1958.
9. Brown, G.W., and Rutter, M. The measurement of family activities and relationships. *Human Relations*, 19: 241, 1966.
10. Costell, R., and Reiss, D.: The family meets the hospital: Clinical presentation of a laboratory-based family typology. *Arch. Gen. Psychiat.*, 39: 433-438, 1982.
11. Epstein, N.B., Bishop, D.S., and Levin, S. The McMaster model of family functioning. *J. Marriage and Family Counsel.*, 4: 19-31, 1978.
12. Epstein, N.B., and Bishop, D.S. Problem-centered systems therapy of the family. *In:* A.S. Gurman and D.P. Kniskern (Eds.), *Handbook of Family Therapy*. New York: Brunner/Mazel, 1981.
13. Falloon, I.R.H., Liberman, R.B., Lillie, F.J., et al. Family therapy of schizophrenics with high risk of relapse. *Fam. Process*, 20: 211-221, 1981.
14. Frances, A. Categorical and dimensional systems of personality diagnosis. *Comprehensive Psychiatry*, 23: 516-527, 1982.
15. Gehrke, S., and Moxon, J. Diagnostic classification and treatment techniques in marriage counseling. *Fam. Process*, 1: 253-264, 1962.
16. Gehrke, S., and Kirschenbaum, M. Survival patterns in family conjoint therapy. *Fam. Process*, 6: 67-80, 1967.
17. Goldstein, M.J., Judd, L.L., Rodnick, E.H., et al. A method for studying social influence and coping patterns within families of disturbed adolescents. *J. Nerv. Ment. Dis.*, 147: 233-251, 1968.
18. Holahan, C., and Moos, R.H. Social support and psychological distress: A longitudinal analysis. *J. Abnor. Psychol.*, 90: 365-370, 1981.
19. Karasu, T.B., and Skodol, A.E. VIth axis for DSM-III: Psychodynamic evaluation. *Am. J. Psychiat.*, 137: 607-610, 1980.
20. Lederer, W., and Jackson, D.D.: *The Mirages of Marriage*. New York: W.W. Norton & Co., 1968.
21. Lewis, J.M. The family matrix in health and disease. *In:* C.K., Hofling and J.M., Lewis (Eds.), *The Family: Evaluation and Treatment*. New York: Brunner/Mazel, 1980.
22. Lewis, J.M., Beavers, W.R., Gossett, J.T., and Phillips, V.A. *No Single Thread: Psychological Health in Family Systems*. New York: Brunner/Mazel, 1976.
23. McLemore, C.W., and Benjamin, L.S. Whatever happened to interpersonal diagnosis: A psychosocial alternative to DSM-III. *Amer. Psychol*, 34: 17-34, 1979.
24. Minuchin, S. *Families in Family Therapy*. Cambridge: Harvard University Press, 1974.
25. Mittelman, B. Complimentary neurotic reactions in intimate relationships. *Psychoanal. Quarter.*, 13: 479-491, 1944.
26. Mittelman, B. Analysis of reciprocal neurotic patterns in family relationships. *In:* V.W. Eisenstein (Ed.), *Neurotic Interaction in Marriage*. New York: Basic Books, 1956.
27. Moos, R.H., and Fuhr, R. The clinical use of social-ecological concepts: The case of an adolescent girl. Submitted for publication.
28. Moos, RH., and Moos, B.S. A typology of family social environments. *Fam. Process*, 15: 357-371, 1976.
29. Olson, D.H., Bell, R., and Portner, J. FACES: Family Adaptability and Cohesion Evaluation Scales. Mimeograph, University of Minnesota, 1978.
30. Olson, D.H., Sprenkle, D.H., and Russell, C.S. Circumplex model of marital and family systems: I: Cohesion and adaptability dimensions, family types, and clinical applications. *Fam. Process*, 18: 3-28, 1979.
31. Reiss, D. Varieties of consensual experience: II. Contrast between families of normals, delinquents and schizophrenics. *J. Nerv. Ment. Dis.*, 152: 73-95, 1971.

32. Richter, H.E. *The Family as Patient.* New York: Farrar, Straus & Giroux, 1974.
33. Riskin, J., and Faunce, E.E. Family interaction scales: I. Theoretical framework and method. *Arch. Gen. Psychiat.*, 22: 504-537, 1970.
34. Russell, C. Circumplex model of family systems. III: Empirical evaluation with families. *Fam. Process*, 18: 29-45, 1979.
35. Rutter, M., and Brown, G.W. The reliability and validity of measures of family life and relationships in families containing a psychiatric patient. *Soc. Psychiat.*, I, 38-53, 1966.
36. Ryder, R.G. A typography of early marriage. *Fam. Process*, 9: 385-402, 1970.
37. Serrano, A.C., McDonald, E.C., Goolishian, H.A., et al. Adolescent maladjustment and family dynamics. *Amer. J. Psychiat.*, 118: 897-910, 1962.
38. Solomon, M.A. A developmental, conceptual premise for family therapy. *Fam. Process*, 12: 179-196, 1973.
39. Sprenkle, D., and Olson, D. Circumplex model of marital systems. IV: Empirical study of clinic and nonclinic couples. *J. Marr. Fam. Counsel.*, 4: 59-74, 1978.
40. Tolstoy, L. *Anna Karenina.* New York: Bantam Books, 1960.
41. Vaughn, C.E., and Leff, J.P. The influence of family and social factors on the course of psychiatric illness: A comparison of schizophrenic and depressed neurotic patients. *Brit. J. Psychiat.*, 129: 125-137, 1976.
42. Vaugh, C., and Leff, J. The measurement of expressed emotion in the families of psychiatric patients. *Brit. J. Soc. Clin. Psychol.*, 15: 157-176, 1976.
43. Wertheim, E.S. The science and typology of family systems. II: Further theoretical and practical considerations. *Fam. Process*, 14: 285-309, 1975.

Chapter XXII

INTEGRATING BEHAVIORAL MARITAL THERAPY AND SEX THERAPY

Kathy N. Melman, Ph.D. and Neil S. Jacobson, Ph.D.

*Editors' Summary.*The literature on sex therapy and marital therapy remains separate despite the fact that most couples enter therapy with both sexual and nonsexual relationship problems. Data are presented on a sample of distressed couples seeking behavioral marital therapy. Preliminary evidence suggests that behavioral marital therapy is relatively effective in helping couples with sexual concerns when those concerns are directly dealt with. However, sexual problems do not disappear automatically when other relationship problems are successfully treated. Moreover, behavioral techniques in the absence of explicit sex therapy interventions are not sufficient for eliminating sexual dysfunctions.

For the most part, the two areas of sex therapy and marital therapy have remained separate and isolated from one another. Typically, marital therapy texts devote little attention to sexual problems (cf., 7, 12), and the converse is true among sex therapy books (10, 14). While the experts may isolate the two problems and specialize in either sex or marital therapy, distressed couples fail to respect this dichotomy. The purpose of this chapter is to review what little work has been done on the relationship between sexual and nonsexual marital problems, and then to report some of our own data on the effectiveness of behavioral marital therapy (BMT) on sexual dysfunctions and concerns.

REVIEW OF THE LITERATURE

Based on his extensive clinical experience, Sager (17) estimates that almost 75% of the couples seeking therapy have a mixture of marital discord and sexual problems in varying proportions, regardless of whether their chief complaint is marital distress or a specific sexual dysfunction. Stuart and Hammond (18) note that while sexual problems are very common in couples seeking marital therapy,

Preparation of this manuscript was supported by grant #5 R01 MH33838-03 from the National Institute of Mental Health, awarded to Neil S. Jacobson.

they are often neglected by marital therapists. Similarly, sex therapists often do not attend to marital issues or they refer out couples who present with both marital and sexual difficulties.

Masters and Johnson (14) set the stage for sex therapy, focusing on only sexual concerns with little attention to the marital interactions. Couples with significant marital distress or individual psychopathology were excluded from their select, highly motivated, middle-class sample (20). When brief, structured sex therapy is offered to less select populations, less promising results have been obtained. For example, Lansky and Davenport (9) offered sex therapy, using a Masters and Johnson approach, to an unselected working class group of seven couples. They found that most of these seven couples did not do the assigned exercises or demonstrate improvement in their sexual functioning. Four of the seven couples appeared to have significant marital problems which were actually aggravated during sex therapy. Powell, Blakeney, Croft, and Pulliam (15) also offered a Masters and Johnson approach to couples where one or more partners had a sexual dysfunction. While 14 of the 16 couples would be considered treatment successes in terms of demonstrating a reversal of their presenting sexual dysfunction, six of these 16 couples needed referrals for marital therapy at the end of the sex therapy program.

There is a growing consensus that brief sex therapy, without considering the marital relationship, is incomplete (1). Heiman (6) reported that approximately 80% of the couples she has seen in sex therapy also had significant marital problems. For 30% of these sex therapy couples, the marital distress actually interfered with successful treatment of the presenting sexual dysfunction.

Many are now asserting that competent marital therapists must be well trained in dealing with both nonsexual and sexual concerns (17, 18). Sager (17) argues convincingly that therapy is facilitated when both marital and sex therapy are available to couples, regardless of their presenting complaint. Assuming that the therapist is competent in both areas, the question that arises is how to integrate marital and sex therapy. A major dilemma is when to focus on marital therapy, sex therapy, or both forms of therapy for a particular couple. In deciding upon the initial treatment strategy, Heiman, LoPiccolo, and LoPiccolo (5) recommend assessing the functional role which a sexual dysfunction plays in a relationship. A dysfunction may be a means of avoiding intimacy, expressing resentment, gaining control, or retaliating for other grievances in the relationship.

Sager (17) proposes that the relationship of the discord to the dysfunction is a crucial factor in determining the initial therapeutic focus when treating couples with both significant marital and sexual difficulties. In evaluating the qualitative nature of the discord and the temporal relationship of the dysfunction to the discord, he has found that couples can be divided into three categories, reflecting the extent to which the discord causes or results from the sexual dysfunction. For the first group, in which a sexual dysfunction produces secondary marital discord, he proposes that sex therapy be generally the treatment of choice.

For the second group, in which marital discord in other areas negatively affects sexual functioning, Sager's (17) treatment recommendations are less clear. He notes that while marital therapy may be the treatment of choice, sex therapy may also be indicated as an initial strategy if the couples' positive feelings toward one another are strong. A trial of sex therapy with these couples may result in rapid relief of symptoms and create a favorable and hopeful therapeutic environment for dealing with other marital issues.

For Sager's (17) third group, severe marital discord and hostility preclude the possibility of good sexual functioning. He suggests that for these very distressed couples, immediate sex therapy is contraindicated and marital therapy should be the opening strategy. After or during improvement in the marital relationship, sex therapy techniques could also be initiated. Similarly, Stuart and Hammond (18) assert that serious discord and hostility make sex therapy extremely difficult and potentially destructive to the marital relationship. They add that a couple's capacity for affectionate cooperation is probably the single most valuable predictor of successful outcome in sex therapy.

Roffe and Britt (16), in their effort to develop an empirically based typology of marital interaction which included treatment implications for couples seeking sex therapy, arrived at conclusions very similar to those of Stuart and Hammond (18) and Sager (17). They separated 246 couples into three types of marital relationships based on their responses to the Taylor-Johnson Temperament Analysis questionnaire. A Conflict-Centered relationship, in which at least one spouse scored high on the hostility trait, characterized one group. For these couples, who exhibit an atmosphere of accusation, criticism, anger, and resentment, they recommend initially addressing marital issues and then integrating sex therapy with the later stages of marital therapy. For another group, characterized by a Passive-Constrained relationship, the treatment recommendations are less clearly delineated. Roffe and Britt (16) conclude that the third group, couples with a Congenial-Affectionate relationship, are most likely to benefit from a brief, sex therapy intervention.

Some have also suggested that the *type* of presenting sexual dysfunction may provide additional clues as to its relationship with significant marital problems, and the extent to which the latter must be attended to during sex therapy. Libman, Takefman, and Brender (11) state that sexual problems may be differentially associated with the quality of the marital relationship. Stuart and Hammond (18) have observed that nonsexual relationship conflicts seem to be associated more often with problems of inhibited sexual desire, secondary orgasmic dysfunction, secondary erectile dysfunction, and delayed ejaculation. In contrast, they have noticed that marital factors seem to be less significant in cases of premature ejaculation, primary orgasmic dysfunction, primary erectile dysfunction, and vaginismus. It is interesting to note that those dysfunctions thought to be relatively uncomplicated by underlying marital difficulties are also the ones which have responded best to brief sex therapy (5).

Along similar lines, Kilmann (8), after reviewing the literature on female orgasmic dysfunction, concludes that secondary orgasmic dysfunction seems to be more often associated with marital discord than primary orgasmic dysfunction. He suggests that women with secondary orgasmic dysfunction would show greater gains than women with primary orgasmic dysfunction in treatments emphasizing communication training. Kilmann (8) bases his notions to some extent on two studies by LoPiccolo and his associates (13, 19). One study found that a standard sex therapy program was highly successful in altering the orgasmic responses of women labeled as primary but not secondary orgasmic dysfunction. All six of the preorgasmic women became orgasmic during coitus, whereas the majority of the secondary anorgasmic women did not. In examining possible reasons for the differential treatment response of these two groups, it was found that the secondary couples entered therapy with more disturbed marital relationships than the primary couples. They conclude that for the majority of secondary dysfunctional couples, therapists should closely examine and treat the existing marital problems.

Some investigators have tried to assess the relationship between marital and sexual problems by studying the differences between couples who present with a marital versus sexual concern as their chief complaint. Frank, Anderson, and Kupfer (4) assessed 20 couples seeking marital therapy and 25 seeking sex therapy at two separate clinics within the same university. They found that the two groups were similar in the degree of sexual and marital difficulties and in demographic characteristics. They state that

> . . . Just as the couples seeking marital therapy were beset with numerous sexual difficulties, the couples seeking sex therapy seemed to be experiencing considerable marital discord'' (p. 560).

Libman, Takefman, and Brender (11) also compared the sexual and marital functioning of couples seeking sex therapy (n = 15) with couples seeking marital therapy (n = 10), and included a third group of nondistressed couples (n = 15). They found that the marital distress group was the most debilitated, with both the lowest marital adjustment scores and a degree of sexual deterioration which was comparable to the sexual dysfunction group. Similarly, Berg and Snyder (1) attempted to differentiate couples presenting marital distress as their primary concern (n = 45) and couples with sexual distress as their chief complaint (n = 45), using an inventory developed by Snyder, the Marital Satisfaction Inventory. While it was possible to differentiate couples with generalized marital distress from those with specific sexual dysfunctions, the actual numerical differences between the two groups were small and the profiles appeared to be very similar in their patterns of elevation across scales. One difficulty with all three of these studies (1, 4, 11) is that the range of presenting sexual dysfunction was diverse, including various male and female dysfunctions. Given the differential degree of marital discord observed in couples of varying sexual dysfunctions (8, 18), studying such a heterogeneous sample is problematic.

One final type of empirical investigation has been the comparative treatment outcome study. Crowe, Gillan and Golombok (2) randomly assigned 48 couples with a variety of male and female sexual dysfunctions to one of three groups: 1) a modified Masters and Johnson sex therapy program with male and female therapists; 2) a modified Masters and Johnson sex therapy program with only one therapist; and 3) marital therapy without sex therapy and with only one therapist. All of the conditions included relaxation training, communication work, and developing marital contracts. Only the marital therapy group did not include the structured sex therapy interventions such as sensate focus exercises. The discussion in the marital therapy sessions focused on nonsexual marital issues, emphasizing the view that all sex problems are essentially relationship problems. Crowe et al. (2) reported that the couples in all three groups improved after therapy on variables assessing both sexual and more general relationship satisfaction. In general, there were few significant differences in outcome between couples receiving both sex and marital therapy versus marital therapy alone. However, the authors failed to report on actual changes in sexual dysfunction symptoms (e.g., percentage orgasmic during coitus).

Everaerd and Dekker (3) randomly assigned 42 couples with a presenting complaint of female primary or secondary orgasmic dysfunction to one of two types of therapy, a modified Masters and Johnson sex therapy program or communication therapy which included listening effectively, verbalizing and reflecting feelings, productive conflict management, and assertive behavior. The couples initiated the problems which were discussed; when sexual issues were raised in the communication training group, the therapists refrained from providing specific sex therapy suggestions or activities. Sexual satisfaction increased for the women in both treatments, but sex therapy led to more rapid increases in sexual satisfaction, as well as greater increments in overall relationship satisfaction.

Thus, although marital and sex therapists write as if their subject populations were nonoverlapping, they may in fact be writing about the same population. Yet there has been very little written, and no systematic research about the sequencing and timing of marital and sex therapy interventions in the same

couple. For certain types of couples exhibiting certain types of sexual disturbances, it appears that sex therapy must be preceded by marital therapy. Moreover,
there is some evidence that the great majority of married couples seeking therapy—regardless of presenting complaint—have sexual disturbances.

THE EFFECTS OF BEHAVIORAL MARITAL THERAPY (BMT) ON SEXUAL DYSFUNCTION AND DISTURBANCES

At the University of Washington's Center for the Study of Relationships
(CSR), BMT is provided in a clinical research setting. Since the CSR was set
up to evaluate the effects of "marital therapy" interventions, and since we
acknowledged that Masters and Johnson's (14) sex therapy techniques were the
treatment of choice for sexual dysfunctions, couples were excluded from our
program if the primary presenting complaint was a circumscribed sexual dysfunction. However, if there were primary complaints in addition to a sexual
dysfunction, the couple was accepted for treatment. This decision was based on
three considerations: 1) Since we believed that many sexual problems were
secondary to nonsexual relationship issues, we predicted that the former would
disappear automatically if the latter were successfully dealt with; 2) even if they
did not disappear automatically, we thought that standard marital therapy techniques would be effective in dealing with sexual dysfunctions, to the extent that
the latter are secondary to the former; 3) even if we could not modify the sexual
complaints, we could refer to a sex therapist after the nonsexual areas had been
treated.

Similar to the estimates provided by Sager (17), we have found that the
majority of couples seeking marital therapy also have significant sexual concerns
and/or dysfunctions. More specifically, 32 of the 48 couples, or 67% of those
seeking therapy at the CSR, had a significant sexual concern or dysfunction.
Thirty-five percent had a specific sexual dysfunction, with secondary orgasmic
dysfunction being the most common type of presenting sexual dysfunction in
this sample. Table 1 provides a summary of the number of marital therapy cases
presenting with each type of sexual dysfunction. One couple presented with both
a desire phase disorder and secondary orgasmic dysfunction and another couple
presented with both a desire phase and primary orgasmic dysfunction. Treatment
involved standard behavioral marital therapy (BMT) including both behavior
exchange and communication/problem-solving training procedures (7). Due to
research constraints, none of the treated couples received any of the standard
sex therapy techniques or exercises. Instead, when we decided to treat a couple
despite a presenting sexual complaint, we assumed that the sexual problems were
secondary to nonsexual relationship issues.

Table 1
Incidence of Specific Sexual Dysfunctions
in Couples Seeking Marital Therapy

Dysfunction	Number of Cases (N = 19)	
	Frequency	Percentage
Primary Orgasmic Dysfunction	2	10.5
Secondary Orgasmic Dysfunction	8	42
Female Desire Phase Disorder	4	21
Vaginismus	1	5
Secondary Erectile Dysfunction	2	10.5
Premature Ejaculation	2	10.5

The efficacy of BMT has been well established in previous studies (7). However, on the basis of this current sample of couples, there is no evidence that sexual complaints disappear automatically as other aspects of the relationship improve. Moreover, when the presenting problems include a sexual dysfunction, there is no evidence that BMT is effective in eliminating the dysfunction without the addition of sex therapy techniques. For couples whose presenting problems included sexual concerns (e.g., low frequency) without an explicit dysfunction (n = 7), in three cases these concerns were addressed in the same way that any other relationship problem would be handled. All three of these couples exhibited improvement in their sex lives, based on both therapist and client reports. Of four couples whose sexual problems were not directly addressed, only one exhibited improvement. Thus, it appears that when sexual concerns are dealt with in the same way as other relationship concerns, they can be successfully treated within a structured behavioral approach to marital therapy. However, they do not disappear automatically, even when other problem areas are resolved.

It is interesting to speculate as to why the sexual concerns were not directly addressed in over half of the cases in which these concerns were voiced. In two of these four cases, the clients decided that they did not want to work on their sexual problems in therapy. In the other two cases, therapist "denial" appears to have been responsible. The therapist simply ignored the sexual concerns. We have found this to be a rather common phenomenon among marital therapists, and we attribute it to a combination of discomfort on the part of the therapist in dealing with sexual problems, and an absence of techniques which have proven to be effective in dealing with generalized sexual concerns. This selective inattention, when it is acknowledged, is usually rationalized by the assumption that focus on other aspects of the relationship will lead to improvement in the sexual sphere. From our data, this rationalization appears to be more fantasy than reality. Happily, sexual concerns do seem to be amenable to behavioral interventions, when they are actually addressed.

As for couples complaining of a specific sexual dysfunction (n = 11), nine received attention with standard BMT interventions. Generally, specific changes in behaviors directly or indirectly related to sex were negotiated, and recorded in writing. The results were dismal. Only two of those nine couples improved substantially. To put it simply, BMT in the absence of sex therapy has little impact on sexual dysfunctions. This failure is not particularly surprising, except for the fact that most of these couples showed substantial improvement in other areas of the marriage. Thus, even if a sexual dysfunction is caused by deficits or problems in other areas of the relationship, the dysfunction often becomes functionally autonomous from its original source. Moreover, sex therapy appears to be necessary for the alleviation of sexual dysfunctions whatever their causal or temporal relationship to other marital problems.

It is of interest to note that the two couples who did reverse their sexual dysfunction were the only two in the sample who were treated outside the methodological constraints of the outcome research design. These two cases, one involving low desire and the other involving secondary orgasmic dysfunction, had been preselected for clinical training purposes. While the sample size is too small for any definitive conclusions, it may be that a flexible behavioral approach is sufficient for the reversal of sexual dysfunctions which are secondary to other marital problems. However, standard BMT techniques such as communication training appear to be insufficient for dealing with sexual dysfunctions with couples who have other significant marital problems.

CASE EXAMPLE #1

Ted and Laurie are one of the two successfully treated couples who presented with both a sexual dysfunction and marital distress. Their presenting concerns included mutual dissatisfaction with their sex life and with the paucity of open and productive communication. In addition, Laurie was dissatisfied with Ted's extramarital affairs and with the many long hours he spent at work, while she was left with the major responsibility for raising their three young children. While Ted wanted to have sex on a very frequent—preferably daily—basis, Laurie reported little or no desire for sex. As a prerequisite to entering marital therapy, Ted consented to refrain from extramarital affairs during therapy. During the course of behaviorally oriented marital therapy with one of the authors (N.S.J.), this couple was initially given a ban on sexual intercourse and taught how to exchange behaviors which increased partners' satisfaction with the marriage. They then learned communication/problem-solving skills which they applied to their major concerns, with the following change agreement developed for their sexual relationship.

Sex agreement for Ted and Laurie

1) Take two weekends off.
    (a) Laurie alone—nearby, so she feels she can get home if there are problems with Heather. November 15-16 Ted to stay home all weekend, take care of kids.
    (b) Together—after Laurie's—January 10 & 11th. No children.
2) Set criteria for sex based on mood and temperament.
    (a) No sex at all when:
        1. Ted has been drinking too much. Laurie decides.
        2. Either Ted or Laurie is feeling resentful.
            a.   Honor system. Take each other's words at face value.
            b.   Can ask partner if there is suspicion of anger/resentment.
        3. Laurie is feeling pressured (Laurie decides).
    (b) Sex is possible when:
        1. Both Ted and Laurie are feeling good about each other.
        2. Either partner has made a special effort to please (e.g.: fancy meal cooked by either one; bring home flowers or gifts; doing some chore for the other partner; watching kids so partner can go out, etc.)
        3. Laurie is rested and not feeling pressured, even though she isn't particularly interested.
    (c) Ted can make sexual advances whenever conditions under a_1 are not present.
3) Laurie not to wear sexy clothes when she doesn't want sex, or to undress in front of Ted.
    (a) low-cut, see through blouses.
    (b) bra-less look.
    (c) negligee or nude going to bed.
    (d) halter tops.
    (e) start immediately.
4) Set aside a time to touch and talk without leading to sex.
    (a) Every day. After breakfast.
    (b) Minimum of 1/2 hour between this interaction and any sexual activity.
    (c) Start 11/2/80.
5) At times of her choosing, Laurie and Ted will have a glass of wine for dinner, with no guarantee this will lead to sex.
6) Ted can masturbate when sexually frustrated.

7) Include forms of soft pornography as sexual stimulants.
   (a) Buy Playboy Magazines.
       1. Ted to buy them.
       2. Purchase first one by 11/8.
8) Ted always brush teeth immediately after dinner and clean fingernails, to start immediately.
9) Ted has the option of wearing:
   (a) gray shirt with yellow trim (by 11/8.)
   (b) avoid tight-fitting knit shirts, baggy pants.
   (c) properly fitting color t-shirts.
   (d) pants that fit snugly in the seat.
   (e) leather jacket.
10) Have regular, ongoing conversations about sex.
   (a) After having sex, each partner to mention one thing or aspect of the experience that he or she particularly enjoyed.
   (b) At some later time, mention anything or aspects which were a turnoff.
   (c) Add critique of sexual experience to the behavior checklist.
   (d) Implement immediately.
   (e) Discuss sexual contract every Sunday night (Ted's responsibility).
11) Write deadlines for this and other projects on a calendar, and update every Sunday night.

This sex agreement worked very well. Both sexual frequency and sexual satisfaction increased markedly for each of them, and in general they were both satisfied with their sexual relationship by the time therapy ended (12 treatment sessions).

CASE EXAMPLE #2

Julie and Scott presented with marital distress and low sexual desire on the part of the wife. While similar therapeutic procedures were used (initial behavior exchange strategies followed by problem-solving training), their problems were more pervasive and long-standing and their outcome was far less successful. Julie had a long psychiatric history, including multiple phobias (eight years of agoraphobia), two psychiatric hospitalizations for depression and suicidal behavior. Their presenting concerns included communication problems, little socializing or companionship, her five years of unemployment, little physical affection, and lack of sexual contact. While they frequently made love during their first months of marriage, and she was frequently orgasmic, Julie had no interest in sex for the past 12 years of their 13 years of marriage. They had no sexual contact for the two years prior to entering marital therapy and two previous efforts at sex therapy within the past four years had both been unsuccessful. Scott was extremely frustrated and felt their marriage could not continue forever without sex.

While the brief behavioral approach to marital therapy instigated changes in many facets of their relationship, including sex, the change process had only just begun after 16 therapy sessions, the maximum allowed in this treatment outcome study. Perhaps with more time the change process would have realized a more satisfying end point. By the end of therapy they had taken showers together and had mutual "touching" sessions which resembled sensate focus. However, these gains were not maintained following termination and further progress toward reintroducing sexual contact into their marriage did not occur. A referral for further marital and sex therapy was made. The following is the change agreement Julie and Scott had developed as they applied their problem-solving skills to their sexual concerns.

Sex Agreement for Julie and Scott

1) Julie will get birth control information from SISTER and other sources by a week from Friday. She will also, by that date, obtain information about groups SISTER offers for women with low sexual desire.

2) Julie and Scott will gradually move in the direction of reintroducing sex into their marriage.

   (a) Sometime between now and next Monday evening Julie will initiate taking a shower with Scott. They will have a brief (2-3 minutes) conversation with their clothes on about what is permissible in the shower.

   (b) Sexual activities they have will come after an evening spent together—this will begin this week by going out on Saturday or Sunday evening.

   (c) By a week from Sunday, Julie and Scott will go to a shop like Love Seasons or a lingerie department of a store and buy something sexy for Julie to wear.

   (d) Each week they will add an additional step to their sexual activities as they gradually increase sexual encounters—these new activities will be decided upon in therapy sessions.

   (e) Julie will make an effort to be aware of any sexual feelings (arousal, interest) and nurture them (think about them, write notes, put on "back burner" and let them simmer, etc.).

3) Scott will do things that let Julie know that she is important to him (calling by 5:30, not working every Saturday, etc.).

CASE EXAMPLE #3

The other successfully treated couple who had presented with both marital discord and a sexual dysfunction was treated by one of the authors (K.N.M.). This college-educated couple, Heather and Daniel, had been married for seven-and-a-half years and had two young children. Their chief complaints included communication problems (arguments escalated and problems did not reach resolution as they both defended their own position without listening to their partner's persepctive), secondary orgasmic dysfunction, his minimal contribution to household management and child care, and decreasing amounts of companionship. While Heather used to experience orgasms in nearly all of their sexual interactions in their courtship and early years of marriage, she had experienced only one orgasm with her husband in the four years prior to seeking therapy. This orgasm occurred about six months before therapy began while she was fantasizing about a man with whom she was having a brief, extramarital affair. She was easily orgasmic with this other man, even while kissing him. With her husband, however, she often felt angry and resentful, experiencing him as uncooperative and stubborn. She also felt unattractive, interpreting Daniel's unresponsiveness to her subtle efforts at initiation (e.g., "Let's go to bed early tonight") as meaning that he did not find her sexually attractive. For Heather and Daniel, a typical sexual encounter consisted of minimal foreplay followed by intercourse before she had achieved lubrication. Daniel had no history of sexual dysfunction.

Heather and Daniel were informed that their sexual concerns were a function of their marital distress, rather than due to any skill deficit. After only one therapy sesson, Heather experienced an orgasm with Daniel during intercourse. She reported that Daniel's agreement to work on the relationship was important to her decreased resentment and increased hope. Without any therapist prompts, Heather had spontaneously communicated her preferences for lengthier foreplay and passionate kissing. Daniel had listened and enthusiastically followed through with applying his new knowledge to satisfying Heather. Throughout the remainder of therapy, the changes in their communication/conflict resolution skills and sexual concerns were addressed and consolidated. Heather continued to experience orgasms in intercourse in over half of their weekly sexual interactions.

CASE EXAMPLE #4

Louise and Glenn presented with secondary orgasmic dysfunction and marital problems. They were an attractive, younger couple with one child. During their courtship they made love on a daily basis with Louise experiencing an orgasm during intercourse in about 20% of their sexual encounters. The quality of their marital relationship and frequency of sexual contact gradually decreased during their eight years of marriage. Presenting concerns included personal unhappiness and fatalistic attitudes, Louise's exhaustion and dissatisfaction with working and having the major responsibility for child care and household tasks, sharing few enjoyable or exciting activities, low frequency of sexual contact, and secondary orgasmic dysfunction. When they had frequent sexual encounters, having an orgasm once a week was not problematic for Louise; but now that their frequency of sex had decreased to twice a month, she was experiencing orgasms far less frequently.

While marital therapy, which focused only on communication/problem solving training, was very effective at producing significant and positive changes in their relationship and increasing the frequency of their sexual contacts from twice a month to twice a week, marital therapy had no impact on the frequency with which Louise experienced orgasms during their sexual interactions. In fact, even at the end of therapy Louise did not seem to know what contributed to her relaxation and arousal during sex. She had never masturbated and may have benefited from some sex therapy exercises to learn what she found stimulating so that she could communicate this to her partner.

SUMMARY

With some exceptions, BMT without specific sex therapy procedures was unsuccessful in reversing sexual dysfunctions, although it was successful in modifying generalized sexual concerns such as low frequency, lack of experimentation and variety, and patterns of initiation. For couples with sexual dysfunctions, the failures did not seem to interfere with the efficacy of therapy in altering nonsexual relationship disturbances. Although these findings are informal and must be considered tentative, there do appear to be some lessons in them for behavioral marital therapists, and, we suspect, for marital therapists in general. Sexual concerns need to be directly addressed in marital therapy; they do not typically disappear automatically, even when the overall outcome of therapy is favorable. For most specific sexual dysfunctions, even those that appear to be secondary to problems in nonsexual areas of the relationship, reversal of the dysfunction will not occur in most cases without interventions involving the technology of sex therapy.

In an era of clinical specialization, there is a need for "Renaissance therapists," at least where distressed couples are the clients. Since most couples who seek therapy have both sexual and nonsexual problems, therapists should be skilled in dealing with both types. The interests of our clients are notoptimally served by specialized disciplines which necessitate dual referrals. Such practices are neither clinically defensible, economically feasible, nor efficient from the standpoint of service delivery. Many couples will fail to follow through on one of the referrals, both for economic reasons and due to the psychological costs of having to establish a relationship with a second therapist. There is a compelling need for research on integrating marital and sex therapy within the same program of treatment.

REFERENCES

1. Berg. P., and Snyder D.K. Differential diagnosis of marital and sexual distress: A multidimensional approach. *J. Sex and Mar. Ther.,* 7: 290-295, 1981.
2. Crowe, M.J., Gillan, P., and Golombok, S. Form and content in the conjoint treatment of sexual dysfunction: A controlled study. *Beh. Res. and Ther.,* 19: 47-54, 1981.
3. Everaerd, W., and Dekker, J. A comparison of sex therapy and communication therapy: Couples complaining of orgasmic dysfunction. *J. Sex and Mar. Ther.,* 7: 278-289, 1981.
4. Frank E., Anderson, C. and Kupfer, D.J. Profiles of couples seeking sex therapy and marital therapy. *Amer. J. Psychiat.,* 133: 559-562, 1976.
5. Heiman, J.R., LoPiccolo, L., and LoPiccolo, J. The treatment of sexual dysfunction. *In:* A.S. Gurman and D.P. Kniskern (Eds.), *Handbook of Family Therapy.* New York: Brunner/Mazel, 1981.
6. Heiman, J.R. Personal communication, 1982.
7. Jacobson, N.S., and Margolin, G. *Marital Therapy: Strategies Based on Social Learning and Behavior Exchange Principles.* New York: Brunner/Mazel, 1979.
8. Kilmann, P.R The treatment of primary and secondary orgasmic dysfunction: A methodological review of the literature since 1970. *J. Sex and Mar. Ther.,* 4: 155-176, 1978.
9. Lansky, M.R., and Davenport, A.E. Difficulties in brief conjoint treatment of sexual dysfunction. *Amer. J. Psychiat.,* 132: 177-179, 1975.
10. Leiblum, S.R., and Pervin, L.A. *Principles and Practice of Sex Therapy.* New York: Guilford Press, 1980.
11. Libman, E., Takefman, J., and Brender, W. A comparison of sexually dysfunctional, maritally disturbed and well-adjusted couples. *Pers. and Ind. Diff.,* 1: 219-227, 1980.
12. Liberman, R.P., Wheeler, E.G., deVisser, L.A., et al. *Handbook of Marital Therapy.* New York: Plenum Press, 1980.
13. McGovern, K.B., Stewart, R.C., and LoPiccolo, J. Secondary orgasmic dysfunction. I. Analysis and strategies for treatment. *Arch. Sex. Beh.,* 4: 265-275, 1975.
14. Masters, W., and Johnson, V. *Human Sexual Inadequacy.* Boston: Little, Brown, 1970.
15. Powell, L.C., Blakeney, P., Croft, H., and Pulliam, G.P. Rapid treatment approach to human sexual inadequacy. *Amer. J. Obst. and Gyn.,* 119: 89-97, 1974.
16. Roffe, M.W., and Britt, B.C. A typology of marital interaction for sexually dysfunctional couples. *J. Sex and Mar. Ther.,* 7: 207-222, 1981.
17. Sager, C.J. The role of sex therapy in marital therapy. *Amer. J. Psychiat.,* 133: 555-558, 1976.
18. Stuart, F.M., and Hammond, D.C. Sex therapy. *In:* R. Stuart (Ed.), *Helping Couples Change: A Social Learning Approach to Marital Therapy.* New York: Guilford Press, 1980.
19. Snyder, A., LoPiccolo, L., and LoPiccolo, J. Secondary orgasmic dysfunction. II. Case study. *Arch. Sex Beh.,* 4: 277-283, 1975.
20. Zilbergeld, B., and Evans, M. The inadequacy of Masters and Johnson. *Psychology Today,* 29-43, 1980.

Chapter XXIII

A SYSTEMIC VIEW OF FAMILY
HISTORY AND LOSS

Monica McGoldrick, M.S.W.,
and Froma Walsh, Ph.D.

Editors' Summary. This paper presents a systemic view of history that takes into account the impact of the past on family functioning and asserts its utility for systems-based assessment and intervention. The systemic implications of loss, a prime issue in family histories, is discussed to illustrate how family systems approach and respond to nodal events, how patterns are transmitted over time, how they may become rigidified and replicated, and how a therapist's recognition of such patterns can be used to facilitate systemic change. In discussing the subject of history from a systemic perspective, the authors believe that it is essential to take an evolutionary view of family process over time.

The Moving Finger writes and having writ
Moves on; nor all your Piety nor Wit
Shall lure it back to cancel half a line
Nor all your Tears wash out a Word of it.
Yesterday this Day's Madness did Prepare
Tomorrow's Silence, Triumph or Despair.

—The Rubiyat of Omar Kyam

Family systems theory and family therapy have made important contributions to the understanding and treatment of dysfunction by attending to the context of symptoms. However, in emphasizing the significance of the immediate social context many family therapists, notably the structural and strategic groups (Mental Research Institute, Haley, Philadelphia Child Guidance Clinic) have not appreciated the relevance of the temporal context for system change. The purpose of this paper is to present a systemic view of history that takes into account the impact of the past on family functioning and asserts its utility for systems-based assessment and intervention. The systemic implications of loss, a prime issue in family histories, will be discussed to illustrate how families approach and respond to nodal events, how patterns are transmitted over time, how they may become rigidified and replicated, and how a therapist's recognition of such patterns can be used to facilitate systemic change.

HISTORY IN SYSTEMIC PERSPECTIVE

In discussing history from a systemic perspective it is essential to take an evolutionary view of family process over time. This perspective enables one to seek out a system's patterns, replications, redundancies, and discontinuities rather than to posit linear cause-effect relationships between "objects" or "elements," or to view the present as the "result" of the past. We stress this because recent developments in the family therapy field have contributed to confusion and polarization of so-called "historical" and "ahistorical" approaches. Family therapy approaches termed "historical," including psychodynamic approaches and the transgenerational approaches of Paul (46, 47), Boszormenyi-Nagy and Spark (7), and Bowen (9), have emphasized the uncovering and working-through of past influences on present relationships. "Ahistorical" approaches, including the structural and strategic models, focus on current patterns of interaction and tend to regard family history as either irrelevant or unhelpful for change. The work of the Milan and Ackerman groups in some ways cuts across both of these models, as will be discussed later in this paper.

Interest in historical information has been associated with psychoanalytic traditions. Sluzki (56) contrasts the psychodynamic and systems approaches as the two main orientations in the field of family therapy. He considers the former to be concerned with the genesis of symptoms, historical reconstruction, the "why" of behavior, orienting the therapist to develop a hypothesis about the interpersonal genesis of the symptom through reconstruction of the context of origin and then deducing what functions have been accomplished by the symptom. Sluzki contrasts this model with what he calls "systems approaches," which seek instead to explain the "how," to understand the collective pattern of maintenance of symptoms through here-and-now observation of interactions which support symptomatic behavior. An interesting response to Sluzki on this subject has recently been published (26), along with a rejoinder by Sluzki (57).

Fisch, Weakland, and Segal (19) also connect an interest in history with the psychodynamic approach, which emphasizes "hidden origins instead of what is presently observable, necessarily leading to extensive inquiry about the past and heavy use of inference" (p. 8).

Similarly, Madanes and Haley (32) identify one of the major dimensions on which family therapists differ as whether the emphasis should be on the past or the present. Unfortunately, they too pose this issue dichotomously, as past versus present, depending on whether one sees the "cause (sic) of a problem in the past or present situation" (p. 167).

The rejection of historical information by many systems therapists is, perhaps, an understandable reaction to the stultifying reification of history in the psychoanalytic model. Freud introduced the important observation that human beings are influenced profoundly by their consciousness, their history, and their memories, but the belief that one's fate was determined by one's history came to be taken too literally, in a linear, causal fashion by followers of the psychoanalytic movement. Many therapists came to be limited by the fixity of their view of history or to confirm their belief about historical determinism, which became a self-fulfilling prophecy. Ahistorical therapists have feared that focus on recollections and historical content distracts clinicians from observing behavior and dealing with present interactions. It was also assumed that the use of history in therapy necessitates a lengthy insight-oriented process of "working-through" the past.

Family systems, their structural patterns, communication processes, and dynamics develop, are maintained, and are altered over time. Moreover, a distinguishing feature of family systems is the shared history of their members, upon which relationship rules and mutually reinforcing transactional patterns are established and maintained. In no system can behavior in the present be comprehended apart from its motion in time, which is its history. No system is ever static. Only by some understanding of where it is coming from can one understand the direction in which a system is heading.

Limiting one's perspective to observations of a cross-section of present family patterns may be efficient if this can yield sufficient information to bring about the elimination of a problem. But in our view, observable behavior rarely provides such adequate data, apart from the history of the system, that is, the temporal context of the behavior. Like the social context, the temporal context provides a matrix of meanings in which all behavior is embedded. One needs the flexibility to expand the context as necessary to provide sufficient information to produce change. Since human beings rarely operate only in relation to immediate circumstances, it is not surprising when their behavior is not comprehensible solely from observations of the present.

In fact, since living occurs in a temporal context, it is impossible to operate apart from this dimension. Even so called ahistorical therapists necessarily use time comparisons in making sense of the behaviors they observe. They just limit the frame of history in their purview. The definition of any pattern depends on its relationship to its surrounding context, which means also the temporal context. One is always comparing a behavior at one moment with the behaviors that have preceded it. There is no other way to make sense of behavior except to look for similarities and differences from past behaviors. One could say that ahistorical therapists make an arbitrary definition of how far back in time to look, since it is impossible not to use the past for comparisons.

Of interest in this connection is the difference between healthier and more dysfunctional families on this dimension. Healthier families are better able to make accurate comparisons of the present with the past and to differentiate them from each other. More dysfunctional families seem to confound past and present and to have trouble distinguishing them (29)). Thus, in our view it is imperative for clinicians to take the family's past into account in order to understand the comparisons the family is making, and to help them gain perspective.

History is more than what Sluzki calls "mythology woven onto the tapestry of a family's reality" (58), although, of course, it includes that. History may be considered as a combination of the following aspects.

1) History is the flow of time past, present, and future. The events of history—the facts—force systemic change. There is ample research evidence that life change events are associated with a wide range of emotional and physical disorders (21).

2) History is shaped by what Reiss calls a family's "paradigm," an enduring structure of shared beliefs, convictions, and assumptions about the social world that evolves from that family's past experience, and that shapes their response to new experiences (54). The meanings ascribed to relationships and events involve a circular process of family members' perceptions of their experience, influenced by previous experiences and the meanings attributed to them, and influencing retrospectively their memory and interpretation of the past.

3) History involves the system's necessary response to change events. Families cannot *not* change in response to life change events. This involves second order adaptations to changes such as the loss or addition of a family member. The pattern of structural reorganization that will emerge depends on a variety of properties of the system, including previous multigenerational patterns of adaptation, the meanings ascribed to the present change, and the available resources. It is the fact of the evolutionary patterns to which we wish to draw attention.

4) Lastly there is the function of recalling history in the present. As Sluzki says, family histories

> . . . fix or establish or remind or fit interpersonal agreements. . . . The family history is a collective unifying principle that portrays and reminds members about agreements involving values and explanatory principles and rules of behavior. The family history thus constitutes a private (collective) code that . . . provides them with a sense of collective identity with continuity over time. (57, p. 400)

Families operate on the basis of attribution of meaning associated with their shared history. And naturally, any reconstruction of a family's historical patterns is limited. As Feinstein (17) has stated:

> Of necessity, historical reconstruction is partial, a fracturing of reality rather than the complete recovery of experience, because the past that meets an historian (that

he "discovers") depends upon the questions he asks and the tools he selects for
his research (p. 98).

Cohler, for example, has shown that people recall history differently at different
points in the family life cycle, depending on which issues in their present phase
are most salient (13).

Recognition of historical influence does not necessarily imply a linear-causal
assumption: that a particular past experience resulted in current behavior or
dysfunction (A caused B), or even that a set of past experiences combined to
produce current patterns (A + B caused C). It is an error to regard origin as
determining outcome. Rather, there is a circularity of influence over time, involving a family's organization, its approach and response to events, and its
ongoing interactional patterns. As Bateson (3) observed, humans adapt to their
experience and become emotionally committed to these adaptations. These commitments can be seen as relationship rules, which are maintained through cybernetic calibration and feedback mechanisms, upholding family "norms" and
regulating permissible deviations (66). Historical inquiry, then, is useful not to
"discover the origin" of a problem, but instead to track nodal events and transitions in order to gain information about a family's organizational shifts and
adaptive strategies in response to past stress that may be associated with current
patterns and with the present function of symptoms.
    To recognize that the past influences the present is not to assume a linear
influence any more than awareness of the influence of social context implies
linearity. There is a circularity or reciprocity of influence in both social and
temporal contexts. Current and future experience alter conceptions of the past
and relationships to it. A systemic approach to human experience should attend
to the interactional relationship between past, present, and future, rather than
assuming any single temporal context to be the cause of a problem or ignoring
the contribution of any other time dimension. Although a family cannot change
its past, change in the present and future occurs in relation to the past. Systemic
change involves a transformation of that relationship.
    Indeed, as Hoffman (22) comments,

> A problem may remain frozen until patterns connected with the original laying
> down of the problem are changed. But let it be understood that one is still dealing
> with an addiction in the present. Bowen's use of history suggests strongly that it
> is not the revisiting of the past, but the redoing of the present that counts (p. 249).

Just as Bowen (9) maintains that it is impossible to change others but only one's
relationship to others, so one can only change one's relationship to the past, not
the past itself. It may be useful to think of this as a form of detriangling from
one's relationship to the past. We propose that families need to be in balance

or harmony with their past, not in a struggle with it, whether to recapture it or to forget it.

It is an error to confuse the unidirectionality of time passage with a linear causal assumption of temporal influences. Time does, in fact, move forward despite human efforts to slow, stop, or even reverse its passage, particularly in the aging process. Nevertheless, each family's and each culture's concept of time is relative and subjective. Well-functioning families are able to accept and adapt to the inevitability of time passage, most often by maintaining a cyclical view of events and life processes (29). They orient themselves to time passage not in terms of antecedent causes and effects nor in terms of discrete beginnings or endings, but rather in terms of life cycle stages, with each transition both an end and a beginning and with each succeeding stage built on the foundation of previous stages. Likewise, they tend to view each successive generation as continuing the life cycle of past generations.

Families in trouble characteristically lack time perspective. Overwhelmed and immobilized by their immediate feelings, they tend to magnify the present moment; or they become fixed on a moment in the past that they cannot recapture or cannot escape. Others focus on a moment in the future that they dread or long for. They lose the awareness that life means continual motion and transformation of relationships. As a family's sense of motion becomes lost or distorted in periods of dysfunction, therapy involves their regaining a sense of life as motion through time from the past and into the future.

The complex process that involves three or four generations moving along together through time, in the context of their culture, has rarely been taken adequately into account. Carter (11) has represented the family's passage through time as having a developmental and a transgenerational axis. The developmental flow in the system includes the predictable stresses on the three- or four-generational family as it moves forward through time, coping with the transitions over the course of the family life cycle (12, 35). It includes both the predictable developmental stresses and those unpredictable events, the "slings and arrows of outrageous fortune" that may disrupt the life cycle process such as untimely death, birth of a defective child, chronic illness, and migration.

The transgenerational flow in the system comprises patterns of relating and functioning based on past family experience and transmitted down the generations in a family. It includes all the family myths, attitudes, taboos, catastrophic expectations, and charged issues with which people grow up. Given enough stress on the developmental axis, any family may appear extremely dysfunctional. Even a small developmental pressure on a family in which the transgenerational axis is full of intense stress may greatly disrupt the system. In our view the degree of disturbance engendered by the stress on the developmental and transgenerational axes at the points where they converge is the key determinant of how well the family will manage its transitions through life (11). It becomes imperative, therefore, to assess not only current life cycle stresses, but also their connections to past family themes, myths, and patterns around nodal transitions, which have been transmitted down the generations over time. Although all developmental change is to some extent stressful, when the developmental stress intersects with transgenerational stress, there appears to be a quantum leap in the likelihood of dysfunction in the system. The intersection of current transitions with memories of charged past family transitions or experiences complicates a family's efforts to master the current challenge.

Over time, a well-functioning system must maintain a balance between integration, stability, and continuity (morphostasis) on the one hand, and change (morphogenesis) to adapt to developmental challenges and environmental demands on the other (59). The maintenance of stability without flexibility for change leads to static rigidity; change without maintaining integration can result in chaos or disintegration of the family (60, 67).

In our view, dysfunctional families have become stopped in time and the therapist helps them get moving again. Families who are blocked in their current developmental passage are often caught in a dilemma involving the maintenance of continuity with their past and resistance to change associated with an inability to transcend it. The rigidity found in dysfunctional systems is a redundant, vicious cycle, often replaying past dramas or guarding against changes that threaten a repetition of past catastrophic consequences. At transitional points in the life cycle, when adaptational challenges resonate with painful issues from the past, the pressures against change are most likely to impede evolutionary change.

Likewise, Hoffman (22) notes that families in distress seem to be having difficulty in their evolution; they are stuck in an outmoded stage, placing too much emphasis on maintaining their equilibrium. For this reason, she sees the therapeutic task as making available to "a group that is becoming more and more like a (static) homeostatically controlled piece of machinery, the power inherent in all living systems; to transcend the stuckness and move to a different stage" (pp. 54-55). We agree with Hoffman's stance that "putting an evolutionary framework around our cybernetic analogy is in itself an evolutionary step forward in family theory and theory of change" (p. 55). Such an evolutionary framework must take into consideration family history and transgenerational patterns in order to more fully understand and treat a family's current dysfunction.

DEATH AND LOSS IN SYSTEMIC PERSPECTIVE

As a family member said of another who had committed suicide, "I don't know who suffers more, the fallen victim, who survives only in the memory of the survivors, or the survivors, who die daily in the remembering.'' In view of the profound connections among members of a family system, relationships which are not ended merely by physical separation or even death, it is not surprising that families have more difficulty adjusting to loss by death than to any other life transition (24). Most clinical and research attention to the impact of loss on the family has limited its focus to the direct dyadic relationship between the individual bearing symptoms and the dead person,* with nonsymptomatic family members presumed to be adjusting normally. Studies based on linear causal hypotheses testing whether symptomatic individuals have suffered more losses than other individuals have yielded inconsistent findings, failing to take into account the systemic impact of loss.

The family, operating as a system, both approaches and reacts to loss through a circular interactional process in which all members participate in mutually reinforcing ways. In its impact on the system, loss has implications for other family adaptational processes (27) and for members not directly related to the deceased. Symptom onset has been found to be correlated with family developmental crises of loss of members (21). Confirming the importance of transgenerational processes, Walsh (63) found symptom onset in psychiatrically hospitalized young adult patients associated with both 1) concurrent grandparent loss and 2) the patients being the same age as their parents were when a grandparent had died. Thus, loss may have an immediate and continuing impact on family development over time.

Bowen (8) has described the disruptive impact of death or threatened death on a family's functional equilibrium. He views the intensity of the emotional reaction as governed by the level of emotional integration in the family at the time of loss and by the functional importance of the member lost. A well-integrated family may show more overt reactiveness at the moment, but adapt quickly. A less integrated family may show little reaction at the time, but respond later with physical or emotional problems. Bowen defines this family process as an emotional shock wave:

> . . . a network of underground ''aftershocks'' of serious life events that can occur anywhere in the extended family system in the months or years following serious emotional events in a family. It occurs most often after the death or threatened death of a significant family member, but it can occur following losses of other types. It is not related to the usual grief or mourning reactions of people close to the one who died. It operates on an underground network of emotional dependence

---

*Important contributions to our understanding of individual intrapsychic reactions to loss can be found in the psychoanalytic literature, e.g., Pollock's work on mourning and adaptation (50, 51, 52, 53), Engel's work on grief and anniversary reactions (15, 16), as well as the work of Mintz (39), Birtchnell (5), Lindemann (30, 31), and Parkes (44) among others.

of family members on each other. The emotional dependence is denied, the serious events seem to be unrelated, the family attempts to camouflage any connectedness between the events, and there is a vigorous emotional denial reaction, when anyone attempts to relate the events to each other. (p. 339).

Bowen contends that knowledge of the shock wave provides vital information for therapy, without which the sequence of events is treated as separate and unrelated. Accordingly, he considers it essential to assess the total family configuration, the functioning position in the family of the dying or deceased member, and the overall level of life adaptation, in order to help a family before, during, and after a death.

Paul regards unresolved emotional responses to loss by death as critical factors contributing to severe dysfunction and to marital disharmony (47, 49). Paul bases his practice of transgenerational analysis on the interplay of history, experience, and a systems perspective (46). Our view expands Paul's focus on the bereaved individual and his or her "object relations," emphasizing the impact of loss on multigenerational relationship patterns. We emphasize a number of the factors involved in a family's ability to adapt to the death of a member and the modes and strategies it employs for dealing with loss:

1) *The timing of the loss in the family life cycle.* Losses that are "untimely," in terms of normative expectations, such as early widowhood or the death of a child, tend to be most difficult (43).

2) *Concurrent stress in the three-generational system:* for example, several losses that occur together or a death that occurs at the same time as a marriage or birth. Multiple change events have a cumulative stressful impact on a family. Furthermore, concurrent events may become associated and the tasks of mourning and other adaptations are likely to be confounded (64).

3) *The manner of death.* Sudden, traumatic death or lingering, painful chronic deterioration are especially stressful and require different coping mechanisms. The behavior (or unavailability) of other family members surrounding the death can generate longstanding feelings of guilt or blame for the death. Suicide is the most difficult of deaths to come to terms with.

4) *The role and function of the deceased member in the family system.* The death of a burdensome member can bring relief, and possibly accompanying guilt, while the loss of a central family support may generate great disruption. The size of the family and the length of time they have lived together, as well as the imbalance of the sexes left by the loss, will all influence the impact of the loss on the system (62).

5) *The general flexibility and openness of the system and the level of differentiation and functioning of family members.* These will, of course, affect their reactions to loss.

6) *Sociocultural supports.* Ethnic groups vary in their customs for dealing with death, so that group norms must be taken into account. The importance of culturally prescribed rituals and social supports at the time of death is well documented, particularly the value of a shared burial ceremony (20, 36).*

7) *Past losses and anniversaries.* Families with previous traumatic loss or difficulty dealing with past losses are likely to be more vulnerable to subsequent losses.

Past losses can intersect with the current life cycle passage in many ways. A couple is likely to be disrupted by the death of one spouse's parent, if it reactivates the partner's earlier unresolved parent loss, impeding support, closeness and open communication. A family may develop a protective pattern of interaction around a father as he approaches the age at which his own father died, or at which his wife's father died, or as the wife reaches the age when her mother was widowed. In a transgenerational anniversary reaction a child may become symptomatic upon reaching the same age or developmental transition at which a parent had been bereaved in childhood. It is important to understand the contributions of losses in either extended family to a current impasse. In one case a 15-year-old boy, in a dissociated episode, stabbed an old man in the street. His mother was a nurse for the elderly, who talked readily of having lost her parents early and spent her childhood in an orphanage. But it was only upon detailed inquiry that it was learned that the father, at the age of 15, saw his own father stabbed to death in the street. This terrifying scene, never discussed openly in the family, was nevertheless replicated a generation later. In our experience, such replications of earlier patterns although often hidden are especially common in families who have experienced previous traumatic and disruptive losses. An interesting example of tracking down such multigenerational patterns is Feinstein's (17) study of William James' family.

From their research on family functioning, Lewis, Beavers and their associates (29) regard the ability to accept separation and loss as at the heart of all the skills of healthy family systems. Competent families adapt to the stark realities that relationships are not unchanging, that children grow up and leave the nest, that parents grow old, and with failing functions, die. Well-functioning families show the ability to accept the future, and to acknowledge and adapt to changes brought about by growth and development, aging and death. In healthy families, a strong parental coalition, meaningful contacts outside the family, and

---

*Unlike most traditional cultures, modern society provides virtually no cultural supports to assist families in integrating the fact of death with ongoing life; the technologizing of death has removed it from everyday life and in allowing us to escape death's realities has only increased our difficulty in dealing with these dilemmas (1, 4, 41).

a functional transcendent value system are thought to be the key variables in effective adaptation to separation and loss. Less well-functioning families were found to be caught up in conflict-ridden relationships or ineffectually grieving for a long dead, idealized parent. Rather than mourning losses and seeking new relationships, they tend to keep the memory of their parents "burning bright," recreating them in other relationships. Severely disturbed families were found to be least individuated and least confident of their ability to survive change. They show the most maladaptive patterns in dealing with inevitable losses, clinging together in fantasy and denial to blur reality and to insist on timelessness and the perpetuation of never-broken bonds.

A family's difficulty in dealing with loss may be manifested in a variety of dysfunctional patterns. One family may avoid confrontation with the reality of death and the mourning process by restricting communication, distancing from one another, or by not participating in funeral rites or later visits to the grave. Another family may show an inability to stop mourning and move on with life. In maintaining a state of perpetual mourning, it is as if time stops. In some families one member may be expressing the intensity of the grief for the entire family through emotional or physical symptoms, while other members minimize or deny the impact. In other families each member may express a different component of the grief response, such as denial or sadness or anger, each fragment an integral part in maintaining the family balance (25).

Family myth and mystification processes may be employed by families unable to integrate death as a part of their life experience (18). Distorting and obscuring communication processes, more than the death per se, are the prime pathogenic elements in the loss of a family member (45). In our view it is the cutoff and emotional isolation, which follow from such disturbed communication, that have the most devastating effects on the future evolution of the system.

Patterns set in motion around the death of a family member have immediate and long-term ramifications, particularly surrounding issues of separation. Attempts to allay seemingly unbearable grief may, through patterns of interaction across generations, have consequences for members not directly related to the deceased member or event. Some families may maintain a closed, enmeshed system, unable to tolerate separation or exits from the family or to let go of their children at appropriate stages of development. Another family member may become triangulated, assuming a replacement function for the system by taking the place of the lost member.

Mueller and McGoldrick Orfanidis (42) hypothesized that the identified patient in schizophrenic families had a replacement function for a lost grandparent and enabled the family to avoid changing a family pattern over two generations. The rigid pattern would be disrupted at the point where developmentally the schizophrenic was in the transition of leaving home. Independent studies by

Mueller and McGoldrick Orfanidis (42) and Walsh (64) found that about 40% of schizophrenics had been born within two years of a grandparent's death. The incidence of death/birth concurrence was significantly greater than for siblings or for non-schizophrenic patients and normal control groups. The findings suggest that the child born around the time of loss serves a stabilizing replacement function for the family, such that the family avoids the pain and anxiety of mourning and adaptation to a new family structure. The schizophrenic breakdown typically occurs around attempts at separation in young adulthood, which threaten the family equilibrium. Others have also noted patterns of earlier experiences of loss in schozophrenic families (6, 68).

Without attention to past loss and the family's adaptation and reorganization in response to it, the protective function of the patient's symptoms and the family impasse at the normal developmental transition of launching is likely not to be recognized or understood by the therapist. It is not uncommon for parents to conceive a "replacement child" within months of learning that another child is terminally ill. While functioning to stabilize the system and to avoid the pain of loss, the process may become dysfunctional to the extent that differentiation and separation are interfered with (28).

A tenuous equilibrium may be maintained as long as the replacement member serves his or her function in the system. It is when there is a threatened separation or loss of this person, thereby destabilizing the family system, that symptoms are likely to develop. The impact of death on siblings is profound and prolonged (2, 10, 16, 53, 62).

Another process found in many families unable to deal with loss is delegation, whereby one or more members are expected to fulfill a mission for the family related to the loss. Several researchers have noted an association between the self-destructive behavior of addicts and an unresolved family mourning process. Coleman & Stanton (14) observed that addicts' families vicariously reenact through the addict's suicidal behavior the premature or unresolved traumatic deaths of other family members, most often grandparents, with the addict substituted for the deceased member, and initial drug use frequently occurring at the time of a signifcant death. Stanton (60) suggests that the addict assumes the role of savior and martyr, his death seen as a noble, cleansing sacrifice in which he willingly participates. Most addict families become stuck at the developmental transition of launching when, as for schizophrenics, the integrity of the triadic relationship is threatened. Similarly, onset or intensification of addictive symptoms at this time serves an important protective function in maintaining the homeostatic balance in the family system (61).

A pattern of disengagement may be found in other families unable to deal with loss, manifested by emotional and physical distancing and cutoffs in other parts of the system. Longstanding hostility and cutoffs between siblings may have commenced over the deathbed or the will left by a parent. Marital distancing, separation, and divorce commonly appear following the loss of a child or of the parent of a spouse. Paul and Paul (49) have been impressed by the association of parent loss with sexual dysfunction and extramarital affairs and, in some cases, incest between a parent and child. The sexualized triangulation functions as a distraction from the loss, which stabilizes the marriage while maintaining distance.

Certain losses, particularly suicide, create such an impact that families may not recover for generations. Following suicide, families typically live in an atmosphere of shame, cut off from each other and from outsiders, feeling that the suicide marks them all as pathological. Often there is no funeral and the nature of the death is denied altogether. The need to assign blame leads often to cutoffs between different segments of the family. Suicide typically leads family members to reevaluate their entire relationship with the person who has died as well as with the rest of the family and to block out or distort the painful memories, including the events surrounding the death. It also commonly leads survivors to fear that if one person could leave them in that way, others could also, or that suicide could become an option for themselves. Families who have experienced a suicide may establish particularly rigid interactional rules and prohibitions based on the fear of recurrence of catastrophic patterns they have already known.

CLINICAL UTILITY OF FAMILY HISTORY

Ideas of death (the ultimate loss) do not exist independently from ideas of time. Death, at the moment of its occurrence, seems to be a unique event that terminates the individual's life-line and thus implies a unidirectional flow of time. But only through a cyclical or evolutionary view of time that recognizes beginnings and ends, but not one absolute beginning or one unique and final end, can human beings come to terms with death. All life is motion from and toward. The therapeutic question of how much of the past motion of the system to include in one's purview is crucial.

Therapists such as Bowen and Paul emphasize the resolution of past losses in their approach to therapy, yet do so in quite different ways. Paul, with the use of video playback and photographs of deceased members, encourages an emotional confrontation and "working-through" that involves the empathic support by the spouse of a bereaved individual. Bowen's approach centers more on information-gathering to fill out a client's knowledge and perspective of a deceased member and the processes of detriangulation to change a client's relationships to other significant family members in the present through new connections with the past. Rituals such as visits to the grave are encouraged by various therapists to help families symbolically bury the dead and move on with life (42, 48, 69).

Sluzki (56) discusses the usefulness of history as metaphor. He suggests that historical information can be organized in interventions as a language that is "familiar and emotionally loaded for the members and opens the door to the proposal of a reality that is alternative to the one that locks the family into its present predicament" (p. 279).

He suggests that therapeutic interventions can tap on the family history as a code and "as a permanent reminder of rules and norms and principles governing family life and members' perceptions of reality" (p. 279). The therapist can reorganize the family's description of events in order to generate a change of their reality so that the symptoms will no longer be necessary in the present relationships. While Sluzki suggests this as a possible technique, we regard family history as a critical component of the family's current world view and approach to problem-solving, and therefore as a key element in therapeutic interventions.

Cecchin and Boscolo of the Milan Center track family systems in relation to several time dimensions: present time, historical time (particularly in relation to the time of symptom onset), future time, and hypothetical time. Through a process of circular questioning they try, as Hoffman (23) described it, to discover the systemic logic of the symptom within its family context. They track the system to decipher the meaning of symptoms in their connectedness to the context from which they derive their meaning. Present patterns make sense in relation to the evolutionary patterns of the system. The Milan goal is to free the system to get its "dance" going again. The symptom is understood as an adaptation to a dilemma created by a realignment of family relationships at a certain moment in the family's evolution. It is meant to solve the relationship dilemma, but it also stops the system's evolution. The therapist's task is to identify the points at which the system appears stuck and to introduce new connections or a reframing of time so that the system may be freed up to continue to change on its own. By reframing the family's conceptions of time, Cecchin and Boscolo's questioning frees the family from the situation in which time has stopped. By careful questioning about the differences between family relationships at the time of symptom onset and earlier periods in the family's history, they underline the continuing process of change in a family stopped in time. They do not see history as objective, but as having meaning through the interpretation families give to it. Reframing past relationships and offering new time connections provide the family with new options for their future (37).

In our own work we routinely gather family information* about the timing of diagnosis of life-threatening illness, incapacitation, and death of family members in relation to the onset of symptoms. When significant losses have occurred at the same time as symptom onset, on anniversaries, or at a similar life cycle phase, we pay particular attention to the family response patterns which may have become rigidified in the process (16).

At the start of therapy family members can be requested to prepare:

1) A family tree or genogram listing birth, marriage, separation, divorce, and death dates as well as other significant dates in the lives of family members (going back at least two generations).
2) A family chronology or time line listing in sequence family events considered significant: moves, job changes, onset of symptoms, treatment, hospitalizations, entries and exits of family members from the household, etc.

We pay particular attention to temporal patterns: concurrence of death and birth, loss and symptom onset, family anniversaries, and transgenerational anniversaries (symptom onset when a person reaches the same age or life transition as a member of the previous generation).

We also note the linkages the family makes to various events and in particular the events they cannot remember clearly. We hypothesize that those previous losses about which family members show the most discrepancy of memory are often the most problematic and likely to have rigidified family response patterns.

The following questions are useful in determining how the family has handled previous losses:

1) Did family members talk to each other about the death?
2) Did they show much reaction to the death and who was there at the moment of death?
3) Who was not present at the death who thinks s/he should have been or wanted to be?
4) Did family members feel there were unresolved issues with the person who died?
5) Who arranged the funeral and who attended?
6) Was the body cremated or buried?
7) Did conflicts or cutoffs occur at the time of death?

---

*We are currently developing standardized genogram forms and a format for an updatable computerized genogram, which will make it much easier for therapists and researchers to gather and analyse information about family patterns of loss and the impact on the system (38).

8) Was there a will (an indication that the dead person had prepared for death)?
9) Were there cutoffs or rifts over the will?
10) Who goes to the grave and how often?
11) What are family members' perceptions of each other's responses to the death?

Since families often fail to make the linkages between events which may underlie the patterns they are repeating, careful questioning is often required to elicit their beliefs about the past, and a clear picture of the family patterns. Detailed questioning about the circumstances of a death—who was there, what they did, how others responded—may be necessary to clarify the meaning of the events for family members. The aim of such inquiry is both to link and to differentiate beliefs about the past, catastrophic fears for the future, and the present realities in order to assist the family with current tasks of adaptation in a way that will not replicate their past experience.

For example, the Burns' relationship began with an affair and resulting pregnancy, while each was still married to another spouse and had other children. The couple left their spouses and married each other shortly before a baby son was born. The baby lived only four days. After the death the husband had him cremated and the ashes disposed of to ''spare'' his wife the pain of mourning the loss. Both parents became caught up in a conspiracy of silence, feeling that their illicit relationship had led to ''God's punishment.'' The older children went along with the silence. The couple proceeded to have two other children together, a son and a daughter. The family came for therapy when these two children began experimenting heavily with drugs at ages 14 and 15, the same ages as the mother's children by her first marriage at the time of her affair and divorce. Questioning about the patterns in the family indicated clearly that the family had reached a point where they would shortly outlive the previous family systems, which both parents felt very guilty about destroying by their relationship with each other. Understanding these patterns helped the therapist in the formulation of interventions, including a death ritual for the dead son and the father's reconnection with his own two sons from his first marriage, which helped them begin to set limits on their new children and moved the family toward a more adaptive pattern for both the parents and the adolescents.

CONCLUSION

In our view assessment of past events, especially losses, and family responses to those events are often crucial to therapy, not for discovering the ''cause'' or etiology of a problem, but because a family's past and the relationship they have to it provide important clues about family rules, expectations, and patterns of organization. This information helps the therapist to make more fitting interventions, which take into account the adaptive functions of a symptom and the family's stance toward change. The therapist may choose to help families achieve a new understanding of their past (a new relationship to it in the present) or may make an "interpretation" of the past for strategic purposes. Or the therapist may choose not to use the past actively at all, if the problem can be solved more directly. In either case the information is useful in understanding how the system operates and in designing the most appropriate systemic intervention, even when the intervention is limited to present action. In our view the most effective systemic interventions link past, present, and future in new ways, allowing the family more flexibility in their solutions, just as effective interventions link the members of the system in new ways. Systemic change involves a transformation that preserves stability and continuity with the past, while allowing for newness in adapting to current and future life challenges.

REFERENCES

1. Aries, P. *Western Attitudes Toward Death From the Middle Ages to the Present*. Baltimore: The Johns Hopkins University Press, 1974.
2. Bank, S., and Kahn, M. *The Sibling Bond*. New York: Basic Books, 1982.
3. Bateson, G. *Mind and Nature*. New York: Dutton, 1978.
4. Becker, E. *The Denial of Death*. New York: The Free Press, 1973.
5. Birtchnell, J. The possible consequences of early parent death. *British Journal of Medical Psychology*, 42 (1): 1-12, 1969.
6. Boszormenyi-Nagy, I. Concept of schizophrenia from the persepctive of family treatment. *Family Process*, 1: 103-113, 1962.
7. Boszormenyi-Nagy, I., and Spark, G. *Invisible Loyalties*. New York: Harper & Row, 1973.
8. Bowen, M. Family reaction to death. *In*: P. Guerin (Ed.), *Family Therapy*. New York: Gardner Press, 1976.
9. Bowen, M. *Family Therapy in Clinical Practice*. New York: Jason Aronson, 1978.
10. Cain, A., Fast, I., and Erickson, M. Children's disturbed reactions to the death of a sibling. *American Journal of Orthopsychiatry*, 34 (4): 741-752, 1964.
11. Carter, E.A. Transgenerational scripts and nuclear family stress. *In*: R.R. Sager (Ed.), *Georgetown Family Symposium, Vol. 3, 1975-76*. Washington D.C.: Georgetown University Press, 1978.
12. Carter, E.A., and McGoldrick, M. (Eds.) *The Family Life Cycle: A Framework for Family Therapy*. New York: Gardner Press, 1980.
13. Cohler, B. Adult developmental psychology and reconstruction in psychoanalysis. *In*: S. Greenspan and G. Pollack (Eds.), *The Course of Life, Vol. III*. Washington, D.C.: U.S. Government Printing Office, 1981.
14. Coleman, S., and Stanton, D.M. The role of death in the addict family. *Journal of Marriage and Family Counseling*, 4: 79-91, 1978.
15. Engel, G. Is grief a disease? *Psychosomatic Medicine*, 23 (1): 18-22, 1961.
16. Engel, G. The death of a twin: Mourning and anniversary reactions. Fragments of 10 years of self-analysis. *International Journal of Psychoanalysis*, 56 (1): 23-40, 1975.
17. Feinstein, H.M. Family therapy for the historian?—The case of William James. *Family Process*, 20: 97-107, 1981.

18. Ferreira, A. Family myth and homeostasis. *Archives of General Psychiatry,* 9: 457-463, 1963.
19. Fisch, R., Weakland, J.H., and Segal, L. *The Tactics of Change,* San Francisco: Jossey-Bass, 1982.
20. Friedman, E.H. Systems and ceremonies. *In*: E.A. Carter and M. McGoldrick (Eds.), *The Family Life Cycle: A Framework for Family Therapy.* New York: Gardner Press, 1980.
21. Hadley, T., Jacob, T., Miliones, J., Caplan, J., and Spitz, D. The relationship between family developmental crises and the appearance of symptoms in a family member. *Family Process,* 13: 207-214, 1974.
22. Hoffman, L. *Foundations of Family Therapy.* New York: Basic Books, 1981.
23. Hoffman, L. A co-evolutionary framework for systemic family therapy. *In*: B. Keeney (Ed.), *Diagnosis and Assessment,* Rockville, MD: Aspen Systems Corp., 1983.
24. Holmes, T., and Rahe, R.H. The social adjustment rating scale. *Journal of Psychosomatic Research,* 11: 213-218, 1967.
25. Howe, B.J., and S. Robinson, The "family tombstone" syndrome: An interpersonal suicide process. *Family Therapy,* 2: 17-21, 1975.
26. Jordan, J.R. The use of history in family therapy: A brief rejoinder to Sluzki. *Journal of Marital and Family Therapy,* 8 (4): 393-398, 1982.
27. Kuhn, J. Realignment of emotional forces following loss. *The Family,* 5 (1): 19-24, 1981.
28. Legg, C., and Sherick, I. The replacement child: A developmental tragedy: Some preliminary comments. *Child Psychiatry and Human Development,* 7: 113-126, 1976.
29. Lewis, J., Beavers, W.R., Gossett, J., and Philips, V. *No Single Thread: Psychological Health in Family Systems.* New York: Brunner/Mazel, 1976.
30. Lindemann, E. Symptomatology and management of acute grief. *American Journal of Psychiatry,* 101: 141-148, 1944.
31. Lindemann, E., and Greer, I.M. A study of grief: Emotional responses to suicide. *In*: A. Cain (Ed.), *Survivors of Suicide.* Springfield, IL: Charles C Thomas, 1972.
32. Madanes, C., and Haley, J. Dimensions of family therapy. *Journal of Nervous and Mental Disease,* 165: 88-98, 1977.
33. McGoldrick Orfanidis, M. Some data on death and cancer in schizophrenic families. Paper presented at Pre-Symposium Meeting of Georgetown Symposium, Washington, D.C., 1977.
34. McGoldrick, M. Ethnicity and family therapy: An overview. *In*: M. McGoldrick, J.K. Pearce, and J. Giordano (Eds.), *Ethnicity and Family Therapy.* New York: Guilford Press, 1982.
35. McGoldrick, M. and Carter, E.A. The family life cycle. *In*: F. Walsh (Ed.), *Normal Family Processes.* New York: Guilford Press, 1982.
36. McGoldrick, M., Pearce, J.K., and Giordano, J. (Eds.) *Ethnicity and Family Therapy.* New York: Guilford Press, 1982.
37. McGoldrick, M., and Garcia Preto, N. Tracking time in the therapy of Gianfranco Cecchin and Luigi Boscolo: An analysis. Videotape. Rutgers Medical School, 1983.
38. McGoldrick, M., and Rohrbaugh, M. Genograms: Developing a format for their standardization and use. Manuscript in preparation.
39. Mintz, I. The anniversary reaction: A response to the unconscious sense of time. *Journal of the American Psychoanalytic Association,* 19: 720-735, 1971.
40. Minuchin, S., and Fishman, C. *Family Therapy Techniques.* Cambridge: Harvard University Press, 1981.
41. Mitford, J. *The American Way of Death.* New York: Touchstone Books, 1978.
42. Mueller, P.S., and McGoldrick Orfanidis, M. A method of co-therapy for schizophrenic families. *Family Process,* 15: 179-192, 1976.
43. Neugarten, B. Dynamics of transition of middle age to old age: Adaptation and the life cycle. *Journal of Geriatric Psychiatry,* 4: 71-87, 1970.
44. Parkes, C.M. *Bereavement: Studies of Grief in Adult Life.* New York: International Universities Press, 1972.
45. Pattison, E.M. The fatal myth of death in the family. *American Journal of Psychiatry,* 133: 674-678, 1976.
46. Paul N. Now and the past: Transgenerational analysis. *International Journal of Family Psychiatry,* 1: 235-248, 1980.

47. Paul, N., and Grosser, G. Operational mourning and its role in conjoint family therapy. *Community Mental Health Journal,* 1: 339-345, 1965.
48. Paul, N., and Paul B.B. *A Marital Puzzle.* New York: Norton, 1974.
49. Paul, N., and Paul, B.B. Death and changes in sexual behavior. *In:* F. Walsh (Ed.), *Normal Family Processes.* New York: Guilford Press, 1982.
50. Pollock, G. Mourning and adaptation. *International Journal of Psychoanalysis,* 42: 341-361, 1961.
51. Pollock, G. Anniversary reactions, trauma and mourning. *Psychoanalytic Quarterly,* 39: 347-371, 1970.
52. Pollock, G. On time death and immortality. *Psychoanalytic Quarterly,* 40: 435-446, 1971.
53. Pollock, G. On siblings, childhood sibling loss and creativity. *Annual of Psychoanalysis,* 6: 443-481, 1978.
54. Reiss, D., and Oliveri, M. Family paradigm and family coping: A proposal for linking the family's intrinsic adaptive capacities to its responses to stress. *Family Relations,* 29: 431-444, 1980.
55. Scott, R.D., and Ashworth, P.L. The shadow of the ancestor: A historical factor in the transmission of schizophrenia. *British Journal of Medical Psychology,* 42: 13-32, 1969.
56. Sluzki, C.E. Process of symptom production and patterns of symptom maintenance. *Journal of Marital and Family Therapy,* 7 (3): 273-280, 1981.
57. Sluzki, C.E. A brief rejoinder to a brief rejoinder to Sluzki. *Journal of Marital and Family Therapy,* 8 (4): 399-401, 1982.
58. Sluzki, C.E. Systemic family therapy: An integrated model. Paper presented at *Symposium 1983: Focus on the Family,* Toronto, Canada, January 1983.
59. Speer, D. Family systems: Morphostasis and morphogensis, or is homeostasis enough? *Family Process,* 9: 259-278, 1970.
60. Stanton, M.D. The addict as savior: Heroin, death and the family. *Family Process,* 16: 191-197, 1977.
61. Stanton, M.D., and Todd, T. *The Family Therapy of Drug Abuse and Addiction.* New York: Guilford Press, 1982.
62. Toman, W. *Family Constellation,* 3rd Ed. New York: Springer, 1976.
63. Walsh, F. Living for the dead? Schizophrenia and three-generational family relations. Paper presented to the American Psychological Association, 38th Annual Meeting, 1975.
64. Walsh, F. Concurrent grandparent death and birth of schizophrenic offspring: An intriguing finding. *Family Process,* 17: 457-463, 1978.
65. Walsh, F. The family in later life. *In:* E.A. Carter and M. McGoldrick (Eds.), *The Family Life Cycle: A Framework for Family Therapy.* New York: Gardner Press, 1980.
66. Walsh, F. Conceptualization of normal family functioning. *In:* F. Walsh (Ed.), *Normal Family Processes.* New York: Guilford Press, 1982.
67. Walsh, F. Social change, disequilibrium and adaptation in developing countries. *In:* J. Schwartzman (Ed.), *Macrosystemic Approaches to Family Therapy.* New York: Guilford Press, in press.
68. Welldon, R. The "shadow of death" and its implications in four families, each with a hospitalized schizophrenic member. *Family Process,* 10 (3): 281-302, 1971.
69. Williamson, D.S. New life at the graveyard: A method of therapy for individuation from a dead former parent. *Journal of Marriage and Family Counseling,* 4: 93-101, 1978.

*Technical Interventions
in Family Therapy*

Chapter XXIV

ON ODD DAYS AND ON EVEN DAYS: RITUALS USED IN STRATEGIC THERAPY

Joel S. Bergman, Ph.D.

Editors' Summary. This paper describes the use of rituals in a brief therapy model of doing psychotherapy. Six brief case studies are given as examples of how rituals are used to change symptoms and systems in individual, couple, and family therapy.
   The effectiveness of the odd-even day rituals described in this paper is explained on the basis of the following four components: (a) *prescribing a ritual* which changes the rules and structure of the ongoing therapy, couple, or family game; (b) *prescribing the system, symptom, or resistance* in the system which produces change when there is resistance to change; (c) *differentiating into two issues an emotionally fused issue which was formerly seen as one;* and (d) *prescribing alternate behaviors on different days,* which reduces resistance to change and increases risk-taking.

In my clinical work with individuals, couples, and families, I often give prescriptions or homework assignments to do between therapy sessions. The assignments are designed (a) to help people break dysfunctional patterns of behavior which keep them "stuck" in systems; and (b) to give people practice learning new patterns of behavior which are more functional for them. Assigning homework also provides me with additional information about resistance to change, particularly when an assigned prescription is not performed by a patient or family.

One of the rituals I often use which seems effective could be called "on odd days and on even days." The idea for this ritual comes, in part, from a format for rituals developed by the Milan Associates (7). The essential context of the Milan ritual is as follows:

> On even days of the week—Tuesdays, Thursdays, and Saturdays—beginning to-morrow onwards until the date of the next session, whenever Z does (name of patient, followed by a list of his symptomatic behavior) father will decide alone, at his absolute discretion, what to do with Z. Mother will have to behave as if she were not there. On odd days of the week—Mondays, Wednesdays and Fridays—whatever Z may do, mother will have full power to decide what course of action to follow regarding Z. Father will have to behave as if he were not there. On Sundays everyone must behave spontaneously. Each parent, on the days as-

signed to him or her, must record in a diary any infringement by the partner of the prescription according to which he is expected to behave as if he were not there. (In some cases the job of recording the possible mistakes of one of the parents has been entrusted to a child acting as a recorder or to the identified patient (IP) himself, if he is fit for the task.) (p. 5.)

The ritual serves at least two functions. First, it changes the rules of the game and the structure of interaction of the family around the IP by reducing cross-parental interference with the IP. Second, it creates a competitive situation between the parents for the therapist's approval by refocusing a covert marital struggle to an overt parental struggle.

The rituals in this paper and the Milan ritual are similar in that (a) the ritual changes the rules of interaction and therefore the family structure of interacting; and (b) the ritual prescribes different behaviors on alternate days. The rituals described in this paper are different from the Milan ritual in that the presenting problem is prescribed on one day, and an alternative to the presenting problem is prescibed on the other day. The Milan ritual is an alternative to pointing out to the parents how they interfere with each other (a tactic that rarely works), while the rituals presented in this paper have some educational or informative function which probably can be used with less resistant patients or symptoms.

The rationale for and reframing of rituals in general are usually based upon an understanding of the function that a symptom serves in a system (5, 8); appreciating the resistance of a particular system to change (4, 5, 8); and presenting the ritual in a language which will be heard and acted upon by a family (4, 8, 9). The rituals presented in this paper probably work for many reasons. Prescribing a symptom, system, or the resistance in a powerful way usually mobilizes a patient or family to reject the prescription and reorganize in a different way; prescribing "old" (dysfunctional) behaviors on odd days, and new behaviors on even days reduces some of the resistance to change, since people know that the new behaviors will only last one day, which is then always followed by the old behavior.*

The following case studies illustrate the use of the odd-even day ritual with people's different symptoms and systems. Sometimes, when available, a patient's or couple's explanation will be given for why the ritual was thought to be helpful.

When prescribing a ritual, in order to help me remember which behaviors are assigned to odd versus even days, and also to give the patient a subtle message, I usually assign the ongoing behavior to be changed to *odd* days (e.g., July 11, 13, 15, etc.), and the new behaviors to even days.

---

*Incidentally, I was extremely impressed with my own personal experience of trying to stop smoking in which a technique was used to delay smoking for progressively longer intervals of time, when I knew that at the end of this nonsmoking interval I could smoke as much as I wished.

CASE STUDIES

Case #1

A fashion photographer, Jim, and his wife, Linda, a model, came in for marital counseling over a conflict which was precipitated by the husband having an affair with another model on a shooting location. Both Jim and Linda lost their mothers at early ages, Jim at age 2, and Linda at age 15. Although married for two years, both were terrified of intimacy, because of the anticipatory fear of loss if they got too close or attached.

After the affair became known, Linda was hurt, untrusting, and unsure about whether the marriage would work. Jim was guilt-laden and didn't know why he had the affair. Linda was always jealous because Jim worked out of town with beautiful women. This jealousy gave her the distance in the marriage she needed. Jim would feel guilty and uneasy on locations whenever he was attracted to a model, or when a model found him attractive, since in his mind this attractiveness meant adultery and therefore the end of his marriage, which he feared.

The following ritual was prescribed: On odd days, Jim was to practice flirting with the models and enjoy the models flirting with him. This would give him practice learning that being sexy, attractive, and flirting were normal, and not adulterous or antithetical to being happily married. Once his anxiety and obsessiveness about flirting (which he found exhausting) were reduced, he could spend his excess energy on acting more like a husband on even days.

The husband found the ritual extremely useful because, for the first time, he could make a distinction between flirting and being sexy without fearing adultery and the loss of his wife. The assignment also dealt with Linda's fear of closeness, since the closeness issue was modulated on odd days by the jealousy (distance) and on even days by having more of a husband, which would give her more practice in acting like a wife (closeness).

Besides the ritual changing the rules of the game and therefore the structure of closeness in this marital dance, it also prescribed the feared behavior on odd days and an alternative behavior on even days. In addition, it provided the husband with a chance to make an emotional distinction (discrimination) between his own sexuality and the fear of losing his wife.

Case #2

A young 23-year-old woman was having great difficulty separating from her mother. Joan was the oldest in a family of 13, living at home, and was not only the second mother in this family, but also the good mother whom Joan's mother never had. Whenever Joan opposed what her mother wanted her to do (visit grandmother, attend church, go to extended family functions), Joan would get angry, or refuse mother's requests and then be overwhelmed with guilt. Often, Joan would also be confused over whether she was acting on her own wishes or opposing her mother's wishes.

The following ritual was prescribed each day for two weeks: On odd days, Joan was to act like her mother wanted her to, and on even days she was to do whatever she pleased.

Two weeks later Joan reported that she did the ritual each day. To her surprise, she had no difficulty doing what her mother wanted her to do, which pleased her mother and brought the two women closer. On even days, Joan felt free to do whatever she wanted to do, and realized that she was not choosing what she wanted but merely opposing what her mother wanted. Joan began practicing on even days what she wanted to do, since on odd days she already paid the price of doing what mother wanted. More important, according to her self-report, Joan learned from the ritual that she was in charge of doing whatever she pleased either on odd or even days. As a consequence, she felt less helpless, less emotionally reactive to mother, more in charge of her life, and more able to begin separating emotionally from her mother.

Case #3

A similar ritual was used with a 28-year-old female patient I was seeing individually after she separated from her husband. Mary was confused and upset over whether much of her behavior was out of conformity to her mother's expectations of her, or stemmed from her own choices. The woman was in a paradoxical situation. Since the age of 12, her mother pushed Mary to maximize all social contacts, attend all parties, and meet as many people as possible. In an attempt to rebel and begin to separate, Mary did the opposite by avoiding making social contacts and parties. As a consequence, Mary remained isolated and lonely. Her choices were to conform to mother's expectations and remain an obedient child, or rebel and remain mother's child by staying isolated and alone—clearly, a no-win situation.

The prescribed ritual consisted of telling Mary that on odd days she was to think and act as her mother would want her to, and on even days, she was to act like herself.

One week later, Mary reported that she tried to do the ritual for the first few days, but became so confused that after the third day she said, "To hell with the homework—I'll act the way I want." Not only did she begin separating her mother's expectations of her behavior from her own, but she was also able to begin opposing some of the dependency in the therapeutic relationship and yet remain connected in a different way.

What is interesting, of course, is how the same ritual was used in both the present and the previous case, for what appear to be similar if not identical problems, and yet produced such different reactions, both, however, with therapeutic consequences. Joan was living at home and was able to practice the ritual in an emotional field with her mother. The ritual reduced Joan-mother tension, and Joan was able to practice discriminative choices in that emotional field which was helpful to Joan.

Mary was living alone, and her confusion was mostly cognitive, not like Joan's where there was opportunity to work differently with mother in an emotional field. Instead, Mary solved her problem by becoming so confused by the ritual that she disregarded the ritual *and* the problem, saying in effect, ''To hell with my problem.'' She also metaphorically separated from her mother by opposing both the therapist's ritual and her dependency on the therapist, and still remained connected to the therapist in a less dependent way.

Case #4

An unmarried couple in their early thirties came in for counseling because of an enormous amount of fighting and tension in their relationship. The couple were living together for the past three years and were conflictual over and focused on their inability to make joint decisions. The woman was preoccupied with her fear of his criticism if she made the ''wrong'' decision or suggestion, and therefore she always deferred to him. However, she also quietly resented that the couple always did what he decided to do. The boyfriend, on the other hand, resented always having to make the decisions, with the tacit pressure of feeling responsible if something did not work out.

The following ritual was prescribed. The couple were told that they needed practice leading and following, and that on odd days he was in charge of making all decisions for the couple, and she must graciously follow, provided the decisions were not dangerous or too kinky. On even days, she was to make all decisions for the couple and he was to follow graciously.

The couple responded well and enthusiastically to the assignment. He loved following, and she began becoming confident about making decisions. The ritual reduced one of the control issues in the relationship. Six months later, the couple continue to alternate days in decision-making. The ritual also resolved the issue of who was in charge of making the rule about the rules, since this decision was made by the therapist with the ritual.

Case #5

A couple in their early thirties came in for treatment because of the threat of their eight-year marriage breaking up. The wife was a successful pediatrician and her husband was still trying to break into show business without much success. They were college sweethearts, and the crisis was precipitated when the wife met another physician at a conference and started having fantasies about having an affair or leaving her husband. Ever since the wife met this man, the husband had become panic-stricken and began pursuing his wife with flowers, gifts, etc. The more he pursued her, the more she distanced. There was little opportunity in the first session to get crucial information about how the marriage worked because the husband was in too much of a one-down position.

The following ritual was prescribed to produce more balance in their relationship. The husband was told that on odd days he was to continue pursuing and "courting" his wife, and on even days he was to prepare himself to leave his wife. One week later, the couple system was rebalanced and "cooled down." The husband reported that he felt much more in charge of his life, since on even days he didn't fall apart as he feared he would. In a subsequent session, the husband reported that he always feared that his mother would fall apart if she left his father, which in the husband's mind was the reason mother never left his father.

The wife enjoyed the distance even days gave her, and felt more respect and attraction towards the husband because he no longer showed the dependency and anxiety he displayed on odd days. Most important, however, was that now the couple-system was more balanced, which permitted the therapist to get the necessary information for doing marital counseling.

Case #6

A remarried, middle-class, Hispanic-American family was seen by myself and co-therapist, Gillian Walker. The patient was a 17-year-old female who was just released from a hospital for her third psychotic break. The family consisted of mother, Marilyn, age 40, her two daughters, Suzanne (the identified patient), and another daughter Ann, age 16, and the stepfather, Ben, age 42. The two daughters came from Marilyn's first marriage. This was Ben's second marriage, and he had little contact with his ex-wife or children from the first marriage.

After a few sessions, it became clear that one of the family's conflicts centered around the issue of parenting. When Suzanne was becoming psychotic or was psychotic, the newly married couple were close—Marilyn would worry about Suzanne, and Ben would comfort and give support to Marilyn. When

Suzanne was not psychotic, she would have huge fights with Ben over discipline, which would lead Marilyn to become overprotective of her two daughters. Suzanne, of course, was acting out mother's differences with father, a conflict which could never be overtly expressed. So, in part, the closeness issue within the couple was modulated by Suzanne's psychosis (the couple were close when Suzanne was psychotic, and distant when not).

Also contributing to the family dysfunction were the opposing myths which each of the parents carried into this new marriage from their respective families of origin. In Marilyn's family, she was taught by her divorced mother, who lived alone, that all men are barbarians and women must be aware of this and also protect their children (particularly daughters) from them. From Ben's family came the message that all women are basically whores and you must watch them and protect them from their own impulses and keep a close eye on young girls until they marry.

Most of the overt differences between the couple centered around Marilyn's complaints that Ben was too strict, didn't let the girls out at night, and was scrutinizing the daughter's friends too closely. Marilyn thought that she was much more flexible and that the girls should come and go as they pleased.

The ritual we gave the couple consisted of the following. On odd days, both parents were to remain loyal to their parents' teachings, which for Ben was "all women are whores and should be watched," and for Marilyn was "all men are beasts and daughters should be protected from them." Therefore, on odd days, Ben should fight to stop the girls from going out and Marilyn should fight to protect the girls and their rights from this beast. On even days, the parents should use their own thoughts on parenting and find some agreement on boundaries for their daughters that they both could live with.

The ritual was devised in a way to provide a contest between the parents' loyalty to their respective parents' teachings on child-rearing, and their own thoughts on parenting. We knew that prescribing their loyalty to their parents' teachings would keep them from acting in their old way. We also hoped that pitting their loyalty to their parents in deference to their own thinking would mobilize the parents to think for themselves for the first time and find some common ground on parenting.

What we did not realize at the time was the danger of the parents finding a common, middle ground to parent. For if the parents got together on parenting, the following sequence was probable: Suzanne would begin to behave, become more independent and eventually leave, which in Marilyn's mind was too threatening, because Marilyn would then be more married to Ben, which in turn would be disloyal to Marilyn's mother's belief that you cannot be happily married to men.

The prescribed ritual unwittingly became a no-win situation for the family, which was confirmed when Suzanne became psychotic again. After this fourth break, the family dropped out of treatment. In retrospect, I would have changed the ritual to the following: On odd days, both parents should remain loyal to their parents' teachings; on even days, both parents should use their own thoughts on parenting; and Suzanne should keep a close watch over the family, particularly grandmother (Marilyn's mother), and "show psychosis" whenever she feels grandmother will be endangered. Prescribing the psychosis would be an attempt to block the psychosis and place more pressure on the couple to succeed in finding a common ground in parenting, and in their marriage—the original source of their struggle.

DISCUSSION

The odd-even day rituals could be analyzed in four components. Each of these components, taken individually, has known therapeutic value and, when combined, appears to make the ritual a more powerful possibility for therapeutic change.

One feature of the ritual known to produce change is that prescribing a ritual changes the rules and structure of a game that's being played. Here, the term *game* comes from the Milan work (8) and could address the game between a patient and therapist, or a couple game, or a family game. The game is the overt way in which a patient, couple, or family presents the presenting problem to a therapist or even to themselves. The game differs from the covert struggle, feelings, and thoughts, which are not presented. Since acting upon an effectively prescribed ritual changes the structure of family interaction around a symptom, the ritual challenges the game and often eliminates it, since the covert struggle and issues become overt when the family engages in the ritual. This is also true when the prescribed ritual is not acted upon or is defied by the family (6). Often, when a patient or family is expected to defy a ritual or assignment because of resistance, it is then prescribed precisely with the expectation that this act will change the game, make the overt covert, or eliminate the symptom (1, 2).

Another component of the odd-even day ritual involves prescribing the system, symptom, or the resistance inherent in the system. The therapeutic effectiveness of prescribing symptoms and systems when there is resistance to change is well-known and amply documented in the brief therapy literature (1, 2, 4-9).

A third component of the odd-even day ritual involves the discrimination of two issues which are emotionally fused and experienced as one issue for an individual. Here, the term *fusion* is used in a Bowenian sense (3), and the ritual might be called a counter-fusion (differentiation) task. For example, in Case

#1, it was important that Jim was able to make a distinction (both emotional and intellectual) between being attractive, sexy, etc., and being an adulterer. Equally important were the distinctions in Cases #2 and #3 which both women were able to make between their own wishes and their mothers' expectations of them.

The final component of the ritual thought to have therapeutic effect is the daily alternation of "symptomatic" behavior with an alternative behavior. Many patients feel that the alternating-days ritual helps them with the discrimination between two issues which are emotionally experienced as one. The alternation of days also seems to reduce resistance and increase risk-taking, since change appears to be facilitated for many patients more in half- rather than in full-steps.

REFERENCES

1. Bergman, J.S. The use of paradox in a community home for the chronically disturbed and retarded. *Fam. Proc.,* 19: 65-71, 1980.
2. Bergman, J.S. Paradoxical interventions with people who insist on acting crazy. *Am. J. Psychother.,* 36: 214-222, 1982.
3. Bowen, M. Toward the differentiation of self in one's family of origin. *In:* F. Andres and J. Lorio (Eds.), *Georgetown Family Symposium Papers.* Washington, D.C.: Georgetown University Press, 1974.
4. Haley, J. *Strategies of Psychotherapy.* New York: Grune & Stratton, 1963.
5. Haley, J. *Advanced Techniques of Hypnosis and Therapy: Selected Papers of Milton Erickson, M.D.* New York: Grune & Stratton, 1967.
6. Papp, P. The Greek chorus and other techniques of family therapy. *Fam. Proc.,* 19: 45-58, 1980.
7. Selvini Palazzoli, M., Boscolo, L., Cecchin, G., and Prata, G. A ritualized prescription in family therapy: Odd days and even days. *J. Mar. Fam. Coun.,* 4: 3-9, 1978.
8. Selvini Palazzoli, M., Boscolo, L., Cecchin, G., and Prata, G. *Paradox and Counterparadox: A New Model in the Therapy of the Family in Schizophrenic Transaction.* New York: Jason Aronson, 1978.
9. Watzlawick, P., Weakland, J., and Fisch, R. *Change: Principles of Problem Formation and Problem Resolution.* New York: W. W. Norton, 1974.

Chapter XXV

SEVEN OPPORTUNITIES FOR BRIEF THERAPY: A RECIPE FOR RAPID CHANGE

Douglas C. Breunlin, M.S.S.A., and Rocco A. Cimmarusti, A.C.S.W.

Editors' Summary. The authors identify seven aspects of therapy which they maintain constitute opportunities to achieve brevity in working with families. These are: 1) engaging the family; 2) conducting an assessment; 3) setting goals; 4) working in a session; 5) working between sessions; 6) linking sessions; and 7) ending the therapeutic process. Following a discussion of the therapeutic opportunities for brevity, a case example is presented to illustrate their application.

INTRODUCTION

In the last decade the literature on brief therapy has grown to the point where this body of writing is now recognized as a distinct approach to therapy, albeit one which embraces several models. The emphasis on brevity can be attributed in part to a shift in focus from the individual as client to his/her context, with a change in that context often swiftly eliminating the presenting problems and altering both the people and the relationships in which they are involved (3, 12). But interest in brevity is also related to the consumer mentality of clients, the accountability consciousness of administrators, and the simple fact that in most outpatient clinics 50% of the client population has abandoned therapy by the eighth session (2, 11).

Some models of therapy may be defined exclusively as brief therapy (3, 13, 14, 15) while others are commonly recognized as such because the length of therapy associated with them is generally less than ten sessions (4-10, 13). If one examines the literature associated with these models, a number of therapeutic principles may be identified which facilitate brevity. Unfortunately, the reader of this literature could easily conclude that therapy can always be brief if these principles are followed. However, therapy is generally brief only insofar as the therapist approaches each aspect of the total process of therapy in a highly economical and effective manner. In this paper we will identify seven key aspects of therapy which constitute opportunities to achieve brevity. We believe that when these opportunities are combined with the principles of brief therapy and executed economically and effectively, a successful outcome to therapy is usually reached in a short period of time. Following a discussion of the opportunities, we will illustrate their application with a case example.

PRINCIPLES OF BRIEF THERAPY

Although styles and emphases vary, most brief therapists ascribe to the following principles. First, the therapist takes responsibility for therapy and acts in an active and directive way (3-10, 13-15). Although the presenting problem is usually accepted as the goal of therapy (1, 4, 6, 7, 14), it is operationalized as solvable and presented as such to the family. Once the goals are established, they constitute a consistent focus for the therapy and are used to gain leverage in the therapeutic system (5, 6, 7). The therapist adopts a positive stance toward the family, avoids power struggles (3, 4, 7, 14) and uses the strengths and resources inherent in the system (3, 4, 7, 9). The therapist also gains access to the family by understanding and using its language (3, 4, 5, 14). The way the family presents its views about the problem is seen as its preferred punctuation of repeating sequences; these sequences take on new meaning when they are given a different punctuation by the therapist (14). In this way the therapist presents new realities to the family (8, 9). Interventions are carefully prepared and designed to impact as many levels of the system as possible (10, 13). Finally, built into the therapy is a clear definition of when therapy is to end, either because it is to last a specified number of sessions or because the agreed-upon goals have been reached (10, 15, 16).

THE THERAPEUTIC OPPORTUNITIES

In addition to the principles defined above, we believe the process of therapy viewed as a whole offers the following seven opportunities to achieve brevity: 1) engaging; 2) assessing; 3) setting goals; 4) working in each session; 5) working between sessions; 6) linking sessions together; and 7) ending. When each opportunity is executed in an economical and effective manner, therapy is shortened; conversely, if any of the opportunities are mishandled, ignored, or taken lightly, therapy will be lengthened. Even greater economy can be achieved through a careful combination of the opportunities such that they enhance rather than limit their respective therapeutic potential. We believe that the structural (1, 8, 9) and strategic (4-7, 10, 14, 15) models of family therapy approach these opportunities in a complementary way and hence the following discussion is based on the operating principles of these models.

Therapy can be brief if, like the sprinter, the therapist gets a fast start. This not only assures a productive beginning, but also sets the pace for the entire therapy. Starting quickly is not easy, however, because of the complexity involved in beginning therapy. For in the first session, the therapist must accomplish four tasks: *engage* the family, conduct an *assessment,* define *goals* and initiate the process of *change in the session.* Time is wasted if the therapist approaches these tasks sequentially, or spends more time than necessary on any one of them. Time is saved if the therapist can weave the tasks together with one dominant thread. We believe this thread is the concept of a *workable reality* (9) which is constructed by shifting the world view of the family from one in which it cannot solve the presenting problem to one in which it can (7, 9, 14). Although we will describe them separately, engaging, assessing, and setting goals become different emphases of the same process: creating a workable reality. We believe that skilled therapists execute this process with precision and economy, and frequently complete it within the first half of the initial session.

Engaging

In the beginning, the family presents its view of the problem as well as a view of itself as unable to solve that problem (10). To engage the family, the therapist must use the family's language to hear and understand their view but must quickly translate it into one involving a solution which includes the family. This process need not be time-consuming and is accomplished by searching for strengths and highlighting competence in and among family members. These constitute a basis for a workable reality by defining the resources in the family to be used to solve the problem. This process begins immediately with the therapist's first contact with each family member, and continues until the therapist has located the family resources needed to solve the problem. It is our experience that most families engage in therapy once they accept a reality which defines them as able to solve their problems.

Assessing

The length of therapy can often be correlated with the emphasis placed upon assessment. Not only is an elaborate assessment time-consuming, but also the information it generates can confuse and demoralize both therapist and family, thus paralyzing the capacity of the therapeutic system to act. Therapy is shortened when only that information is gathered which is essential to construct a workable reality. Of course, this stance toward information requires a therapist who accepts the relativity of reality (14, 15).

We prefer to base our initial assessment upon the information available from the family-therapist interactions. This information inevitably contains isomorphs indicative of family structure (8, 9). These isomorphs, which appear regardless of content, tell the therapist how the family maintains the problem and what new behaviors are needed to solve it. They contain all of the information needed to construct a workable reality, and hence initiate the process of change in the session. Of course, more information may be needed to develop strategies for between session change, but much of this information will emerge spontaneously in the session. Time is thus spent gathering information only when and if it is needed.

Setting Goals

Our experience is that setting goals is far more difficult than is depicted in the literature. If a single client presents a single symptom, setting goals is relatively easy; however, families more often present multiple and diffuse problems, and often no consensus exists among members concerning either the seriousness or priority of the problem. A therapist can easily get lost in this maze, spending sessions trying to set goals only to see them shift again. We believe the goals should be modest and fit the needs of successful therapy. They are pragmatic in so far as they create a focus for work, motivate the family to cooperate, and act as a measuring stick of change.

In our view, setting goals is simply a matter of reaching agreement with the family on a workable reality which includes a problem to be solved and a change in family functioning that will bring about a solution. The problem must be solvable by the family, hence psychiatric problems are reframed in behavioral terms (e.g., depression as laziness) (6, 9) and problems beyond conscious control (e.g., enuresis) may be shifted to collateral behaviors which are metaphorically equivalent (e.g., talking baby talk is acting childishly as is wetting oneself) (5, 7, 9).

Likewise, the change in family functioning required to solve the problem must be both understandable and acceptable to the family. Operating within the frameworks of structural (8, 9) and strategic (5, 6, 7) family therapy, the areas of family functioning most often targeted for change are hierarchy and subsystem boundaries. Most parents accept a correction in the family hierarchy when the therapist communicates clearly that parents, not children, should run the family. Likewise, most parents want their family to function effectively and hence respond favorably to a change in subsystem composition or the degree of proximity or distance between subsystems if that change solves the problem (8, 9).

In addition to the goals derived from the workable reality, a therapist should also establish operational goals for each session, which define the work to be accomplished. Without such subgoals, the workable reality is easily lost, and so are the opportunities of working in a session and linking sessions.

In summary, the workable reality the therapist strives to create in the beginning fits the following formula: You, the family, using such-and-such strengths can function (organize) in such-and-such a way, and in doing so the problem you have presented, framed in such-and-such a way, will be solved. When the family accepts the therapist's workable reality, the beginning is complete: the family is engaged, the assessment is sufficient, and the goals have been set.

Working in and Between Sessions

The therapist has two opportunities in which to produce change: the time spent in the session, and the time between sessions. Although most brief therapies emphasize one or the other, and the literature abounds with examples of successful outcomes in which only one was used, we believe progress in therapy is often dramatic when both opportunities are used. To do so, however, requires not only a grasp of the mechanisms by which change occurs both in and between sessions, but also a plan by which to combine the two. Otherwise each opportunity may be diluted and ineffective, or one may cancel the other. In either instance therapy is lengthened.

We believe the major strength of the structural model is its clear grasp of the mechanisms by which change occurs in a session (8, 9), whereas the major strength of the strategic model is a clear grasp of the mechanisms by which change occurs between sessions (5, 7, 10, 14); hence we attempt to maximize the opportunities for brevity afforded by working in and between sessions by applying these models where they are most effective.

During the session the therapist, in effect, asks the family to experience the workable reality. Through the use of carefully constructed enactments, the family is pushed to develop new ways of functioning which solve the problem. Such enactments often involve many repetitions as the family successively approximates the behaviors needed to solve the problem.

The opportunity afforded by "in session" work can be wasted and therapy lengthened, if the therapist terminates the enactment before it produces a successful outcome. Unfortunately, this often happens because the intensity created when people interact in new ways is threatening. On the other hand, the therapist must also be skilled at recognizing new behaviors when they appear and be able to punctuate the enactment in such a way as to indicate success, otherwise the session can end with the family abandoning hope in its ability to solve the problem.

Change is produced between sessions through directives which sustain the new ways of functioning needed to solve the problem. The selection of a directive takes into account the forces for and against change as well as the nature of the therapist's relationship with the family. Directives may directly organize the family to live the workable reality between sessions, or they may anticipate disruptive forces by indirectly and/or paradoxically encouraging the family to slow down the rate of change, postpone it, or abandon it altogether. Such directives cannot be conceived and delivered as an afterthought at the completion of a session; therefore, the therapist must either work with a team or colleague, or leave sufficient time to do this work him/herself (10). Otherwise, the directive will contain loopholes which the family will discover, and the directive will fail. The time will then be wasted, and therapy will be lengthened.

Working both in and between sessions poses a timing problem for the therapist. A directive given at the end of one session must be followed up in the next; hence sufficient time must be allotted to obtain feedback about the impact of the directive. We believe that the way this feedback is elicited is crucial because too much feedback can consume much of the session and jeopardize the opportunity to work in the session. We believe the therapist should elicit feedback which preserves a focus upon the workable reality. Such feedback can be evoked quickly and then used as a point of entry for the work to be done in the session.

Linking Sessions

Although the concept of making the sessions of a therapy relate to one another is simplistic, therapists often fail to apply this concept in practice. The longer the therapy, the more information emerges, and the more the therapist is tempted to add new goals and hence prolong the therapy. When sessions are linked together, therapy is more economical and impactful and hence shorter. It is economical because time is not wasted on extraneous matters, and impactful because the sessions accumulate (like compound interest). In this way, when change does occur the linking of subsequent sessions sustains and reinforces that change. Or if change is slow to come, the linking of sessions builds pressure to the point where a threshold in the family is exceeded and change is triggered.

The focus around which linking takes place is the workable reality. This is not to say that the therapist adheres rigidly to this reality. On the contrary, it evolves as therapy progresses and the family changes, but the evolution is along the lines of expansion or reframing to take into account new information or other family members. The therapist should abandon the reality with reluctance and only when it becomes clear that it was selected incorrectly. From session to session, the problem to be solved acts as the point of leverage with the therapist requesting the family, in complementary ways, to use its resources to solve it.

Another way to link sessions is to vary the length of time between them. In the beginning, sessions may be held weekly and a major emphasis placed on the work in the sessions. As the problem is solved, sessions may be spaced at longer intervals and emphasize the process of change between sessions. This spacing can also facilitate the final opportunity: ending.

Ending

Therapy can be brief if the therapist achieves the goals and then terminates. Ending therapy, however, is not easy because it involves reaching a consensus between therapist and family on three agendas: that the problem has been solved; that the family is functioning as it should; and that family and therapist agree to separate. Failure with any of these agendas prolongs therapy.

The workable reality is the vehicle for achieving consensus on the agendas of the problem and family functioning. If the problem was operationalized properly, in most cases it will be clear whether it has been solved. In some cases, however, the therapist believes the problem is solved but the family does not. They may express doubt that the problem is completely gone, that others have taken its place, or that it will return in the future. These concerns often indicate that some family members have been harboring a belief that the problem behavior is a sign of "madness" or "badness." This impasse can be circumvented if, in the course of therapy, this same behavior is placed on a continuum wherein it is seen as normal so long as it occurs only intermittently. If the therapist has preserved a focus on the workable reality, then family functioning is also readily evaluated. Unfortunately it is all too easy to include other dimensions of functioning which are not actually needed to solve the problem. Each additional dimension complicates the process of reaching consensus on family functioning. We recommend that, whenever possible, the therapist maintain a tight focus on only those dimensions of family functioning involved in the workable reality, and when other dimensions arise these are either incorporated into the workable reality or ignored.

The final agenda, ending the relationship between therapist and family, is perhaps the most difficult. If the therapeutic experience has been positive, there will exist a natural pull to prolong it. Also the family will, at least partially, attribute change to the therapist. We recommend that the therapist work with a team or at least have colleagues who know the case and can help the therapist recognize when therapy is no longer needed. By becoming a peer to the family, the therapist can also step out of the role of expert and thus mitigate against the family's need to cling to therapy for the sake of holding onto the therapist.

In the last session, we also recommend that the therapist communicate primarily in metaphor (5, 7, 10, 14). At this level, a quantifying of behavior is avoided so it is easier to reach a consensus regarding outcome. Metaphors also allow the therapist to comment on family relationships in a nonthreatening way, and to subtly achieve a peer relationship with the family.

In the above discussion, we have operationalized seven opportunities to achieve brevity using the models of structural and strategic family therapy. The therapist begins quickly by using a workable reality to engage, assess and set goals. The process of change involves working in and between sessions and linking all sessions together, again with the workable reality. The pattern of therapy involves intense work in each session followed by carefully designed directives which sustain and augment this work between sessions. Finally, the therapy has a clear way to end. Unfortunately, the necessity to define and operationalize each opportunity has made it difficult to capture an equally important concept: how the opportunities combine to define the whole process of therapy. At some level, skilled therapists always have in mind all of the relevant opportunities. Hence, in the beginning, as the therapist searches for a workable reality, he/she is also aware of engaging, assessing and setting goals. In setting goals, the therapist is also aware that these same goals must enable therapy to end. Although in any session the therapist may find him/herself immersed in an intense enactment, he/she remains aware that time must be allotted to plan a directive to produce change between sessions. The therapist tries to anticipate how each session links with those which have preceded and will follow it.

CASE EXAMPLE: THE B FAMILY

To illustrate this use of opportunities to achieve brevity, we now present an example of therapy which lasted four sessions. Even such a brief therapy is difficult to describe succinctly; consequently in the discussion to follow, the major emphasis is placed upon the ways the opportunities operate to achieve a successful outcome in four sessions.

The clinical context for the therapy was an externship program in family therapy conducted by the Family Systems Program of the Institute for Juvenile Research in Chicago, Illinois. The therapist, who at the time was a trainee in the program, worked with a team consisting of two supervisors and two other trainees. A contract for four sessions was made with the family at the beginning of therapy and the family was seen every two weeks.

The B's were an Italian family consisting of the mother, Ann, her seven-year-old son, Jim, and the maternal grandparents, who occupied a separate residence but saw Ann and Jim daily.* The parents had been divorced three years earlier after episodes of wife and child abuse, and the father was reported to have no contact with the family. The identified patient was Jim whose behavior at home and at school was described as out of control.

Session One

The therapist's task in the beginning was to *engage, assess,* and *set goals.* The family presented several isomorphs at the outset which facilitated assessment. First, Jim and grandmother sat together while mother sat by herself. When asked about the problem, the mother excused Jim's misbehavior stating it was a reaction to her own hysterical ways of dealing with him. When the grandmother was asked, she mumbled that Jim did sometimes misbehave, to which Jim responded by punching her in the arm. Grandmother stated that the punching was nasty, but did nothing to stop it. At this point mother reasserted that Jim's behavior was her fault, and taking this cue, Jim left his chair and wandered to the blackboard in the room. Although the session was only minutes old, these isomorphs provided enough information to construct an initial assessment: Jim's misbehavior was maintained by an incongruous mother-son hierarchy (how could the mother control that which she believed she had created?) and a crossgenerational coalition of Jim and grandmother.

To have accepted mother as the cause of Jim's misbehavior would have led to goals which defined her, rather than her son, as the problem. Such goals would have further lowered mother in the hierarchy and justified the grandmother-son coalition as protection against an irrational mother. A different and more *workable reality* was needed which would elevate the mother in the hierarchy, enabling her to parent her son and to break the grandmother-son coalition, and hence solve the problem of her son's misbehavior. This was accomplished by eliciting from the grandmother a firm commitment of support that Ann was competent to do something about Jim's misbehavior without any interference. The workable reality which emerged included both a workable problem (Jim is disrespectful), and a functional family capable of solving that problem (grand-

---

*In order to protect the confidentiality of the family we have changed the names of mother and son, and refer to the grandparents as grandmother and grandfather.

mother had taught Ann how to be respectful, therefore mother was competent to teach Jim how to be respectful without grandmother's interference).

The acceptance of the workable reality by both women signaled successful engagement. The therapist could next capitalize upon the opportunity to work in the session. Although the mother still expressed concern about her handling of Jim, she stopped blaming herself and indicated readiness to try something different. An enactment was initiated in which the mother assumed the superior position in the hierarchy by demanding respect from her son by holding Jim in a manner that would safely show him that she was in control, while at the same time grandmother was excluded by sending her behind the mirror to watch and discuss the proceedings with the team. The enactment, which lasted 30 minutes, required many repetitions of transactions in which Jim showed subtle but clear evidence of disrespect followed by a demand from mother that he act respectfully.

Meanwhile, behind the mirror, the team highlighted to grandmother the positives of the mother-son interaction and made a pact with her that in the next two weeks she would not interfere or spoil Jim by buying him toys, thus providing a directive which blocked her interference between sessions. She was then instructed to practice by reentering the therapy room and ignoring Jim and mother. She was able to do so successfully and by the end of the session Jim was complying with mother's requests and acting in a respectful fashion.

The fast start coupled with the work in the session resulted in an economical and effective first session in which the family had actually demonstrated a solution to the problem of Jim's disrespect. If these changes could be maintained between sessions, therapy could indeed be brief.

Session Two

At the outset of the session Jim was relaxed and compliant. Mother reported that on several occasions Jim had misbehaved and she had held him as she had in the first session, but overall he was behaving more respectfully. Grandmother had not interfered, but Jim had only visited once in the two weeks since the previous session. Again, grandfather did not attend. With this feedback, the therapist established the following sub-goals for the session, taking into account the opportunities afforded by *in-session work* and *linking sessions*: 1) to consolidate mother's efforts to solve the problem; 2) to continue to block grandmother's interference; and 3) to intervene to assure the grandfather's presence in the third session.

The therapist's first in-session intervention was an expression of concern over the swiftness of the changes in Jim's behavior. The mother agreed, stating that she too feared it might fall apart, but insisted she wanted to solve the problem. Encouraged by this commitment, the therapist pointed out that like all children Jim would still misbehave occasionally and require limits and consequences. While mother and son negotiated these rules and consequences, grandmother was given the task to silently consider how both she and her husband would keep from interfering. This in-session work, though less spectacular than the first session, was vital to insuring that between sessions the mother would have effective ways to handle Jim. Not surprisingly, from her new position in the hierarchy mother competently defined issues of behavioral control and established reasonable consequences, and grandmother did not interfere.

Since it was vital that grandfather attend the third session, two directives were devised to assure his presence. Both directives were based on the language of the family's Italian heritage shared in common with the therapist. The first intervention appealed to the grandmother's pride as the "behind the scenes" ruler of an Italian family. The therapist assured her that from this position she would surely get her husband to attend the next session. Second, the team requested a meal, tapping one of the family's strengths—its culinary expertise. The grandfather would surely have some interest in a therapist who wanted to eat Italian food, and besides, if he missed the session, he also missed his dinner.

Session Three

The directive for grandmother had worked, and not only had she convinced her husband to attend the session, but she also presented another dimension of expertise by providing a delicious Italian meal. The therapist used the meal to praise grandmother and engage the grandfather. This positive atmosphere was broken, however, by mother, who appeared demoralized when she reported that, despite following through with the rules made in the previous session, Jim had been disrespectful. To maintain the workable reality was crucial if the third session was to be linked to the first and second; however, to do so successfully, it was necessary for this feedback and grandfather's presence to be incorporated into the reality.

The first opportunity to do so occurred when mother stated that Jim had been disrespectful while visiting the grandparents. The therapist asked the grandfather if he, too, had noticed this disrespect. He not only had noticed it, but he also readily accepted the therapist's view of the problem: Jim was disrespectful and mother could teach him how to be respectful. In addition, he implied how the reality could be maintained and how he could be incorporated into it in such a way as to help solve the problem: grandfather could be defined as a resource in the family because, like mother, he tried to make Jim be respectful. Hence, the only change in family functioning which still needed to be addressed was grandmother's intrusiveness, and this had been included as part of the original workable reality.

To complete the expanded reality and prepare for the work in the third session, all that remained was to find a way to frame grandmother's intrusiveness in a way that would help her save face. The team phoned in a message saying that it was clear that grandmother had tried not to interfere, but she had had a relapse because, like many grandmothers, she had a soft heart. With this reality, an enactment was initiated in which the grandfather was asked to talk to his wife and help her overcome her softness. As the grandfather pushed his wife not to interfere, the mother also became more insistent. Through the repetition of many transactions concerning grandmother's softness, a strong affiliation between grandfather and mother was developed, excluding the grandmother as one of the executives in the family. This enactment placed pressure on the grandmother until finally she interrupted and scolded Jim, showing that she too could be firm with him.

The therapist quickly highlighted this show of firmness as evidence that the enactment was successful: All of the adults were acting together to help Jim be respectful. To complement this work and provide a link to the fourth session, the team devised a directive which took into account the daily routine of the family. The directive was as follows: On Monday Jim was to go to the grand-parents' home where, as usual, grandmother would look after him; however, grandfather was to watch carefully, and if grandmother became soft and allowed Jim to be disrespectful, grandfather would report this to mother, and the following day Jim would not be allowed to visit. On the next day after that, the procedure was to be repeated. The task preserved the affiliation between mother and grand-father and encouraged grandmother to remain firm or be deprived of her grandson for a day.

Session Four

The primary concern of the therapist for the final session was to orchestrate a successful *ending*. Therefore, the subgoals for the session were to reach con-sensus that the problem had been solved, that the family was functioning as it should, and that the family no longer required the therapist. Throughout the session, the therapist introduced and discussed metaphors to achieve these goals.

On her own initiative, the mother had prepared a lasagne dinner for the family and team. Jim helped organize the room for the meal and politely received his food. The therapist commented on his helpfulness (a metaphor for respect) and all of the adults nodded. He then listened to grandmother relate a story, with disdain in her voice, in which a family allowed a child to misbehave in a restaurant. Again, the story became a metaphor for the grandmother's conviction that such behavior was disrespectful, and were she involved, it would have been controlled. This story allowed the grandmother to admit that she had changed while still saving face, and nods of approval from grandfather and mother indicated that the matter of her softness could be closed.

It was also recognized that the meal was a metaphorical statement of the mother's competence: Like the grandmother, she too was a competent Italian mother. The meal, and more generally, variations in Italian recipes became a metaphor for commenting on relationships in the family, in particular, the capacity of the family to tolerate some differences as they jointly worked together to raise Jim. Each member of the family had a recipe for dealing with Jim and though there were variations in the recipes, the outcome was the same, a respectful young boy.

The therapist punctuated the family's ability to continue functioning without him by discussing Jim's future plans as well as mother's plans for herself. The feedback received indicated that mother and son were handling these issues appropriately. Noticing that this discussion triggered a smile from grandfather, the therapist normalized the relationship of the grandparents as a resource to Ann and Jim, and closed the session. A six month follow-up showed the gains of therapy were being maintained.

CONCLUSIONS

Underpinning the above discussion of opportunities for brevity should be a recognition that considerable skill is required to operate in this manner. Beginning therapists should not expect nor should they be expected to operate as economically as their more experienced colleagues.

Finally, lest we imply that the correct application of these opportunities constitutes an infallible recipe for brief therapy, we should add that in some cases conditions will mitigate against brevity. The therapist cannot always control the time frame of therapy, and circumstances such as death, illness, or divorce may control the length of therapy. In other cases, the inability to generate or hold onto the necessary treatment unit can prolong therapy. In still other cases it may just take longer to solve the problem, and when this happens, the therapist's patience may, in fact, be the most important opportunity for success.

REFERENCES

 1. Aponte, H. Organizing treatment around the family's problems and their structural bases. *Psychiatr. Q.*, 48: 209-222, 1974.

2. Baekeland, F., and Lundwall, L. Dropping out of treatment: A critical review. *Psychol. Bull.,* 82: 738-783, 1975.
3. DeShazer, S. Brief therapy. *Family Process,* 14: 79-93, 1975.
4. Haley, J. *Uncommon Therapy.* New York: Ballantine Books, 1973.
5. Haley J. *Problem-Solving Therapy.* New York: Harper and Row, 1976.
6. Haley, J. *Leaving Home.* New York: McGraw-Hill, 1979.
7. Madanes, C. *Strategic Family Therapy.* San Francisco: Jossey-Bass, 1981.
8. Minuchin, S. *Families and Family Therapy.* Cambridge: Harvard University Press, 1974.
9. Minuchin, S., and Fishman, H.C. *Family Therapy Techniques.* Cambridge: Harvard University Press, 1981.
10. Papp, P. The Greek chorus and other techniques of paradoxical therapy. *Family Process,* 19: 45-57, 1980.
11. Rogers, L. Drop-out rates and results of psychotherapy in government aided mental hygiene clinics. *J. Clin. Psychol.,* 16: 68-92, 1960.
12. Selinger, D., and Barcai, A. Brief family therapy may lead to deep personality change. *Am. J. of Psychother.,* 31: 302-390, 1977.
13. Selvini Palazzoli, M., Boscolo, L., Cecchin, G., and Prata, G. The treatment of children through brief therapy of their parents. *Family Process,* 13: 428-442, 1974.
14. Watzlawick, P., Weakland, J., and Fisch, R. *Change: Principles of Problem Formation and Problem Resolution.* New York: W.W. Norton, 1974.
15. Weakland, J., Fisch, R., Watzlawick, P., and Bodin, A. Brief therapy: Focused problem resolution. *Family Process,* 13: 141-168, 1974.

Chapter XXVI

A METHODOLOGY FOR CONSULTING
WITH FAMILIES

Robert Garfield, M.D.,
and Linda Schwoeri, M.A., M.F.T.

Editors' Summary. Live consultation interviews have become popular formats for teaching family therapy. This paper presents a methodology for consulting families in therapy. Guidelines for preparing the family and therapist beforehand, conducting the interview, and follow-up procedures are introduced. An in-depth case is presented to illustrate these aspects of the process.

Live family consultation interviews have become extremely popular devices for teaching family therapy practitioners. The opportunity to observe an experienced therapist directly intervene when an impasse arises in treatment can be exciting and instructive. The benefits of increased visibility and direct access to the work of the therapist with the family have been described at length in the family literature on supervision and training (1, 5, 6).

Risks accompany these benefits, however. The family movement has been criticized for promoting an attitude of "spontaneity without reserve," or unnecessary, extremist actions with regard to treatment of families. While we obviously do not agree with this criticism as a representative statement, certain events seem to occur with annoying frequency in family consultation interviews that lend credibility to the critics' views. Families, unprepared and overly anxious, may fail to show up for the consultation. The consultant may demonstrate dazzling therapeutic pyrotechnics, but offend the family in the process, undermine the therapy, or fail to make any impact at all. The lack of follow-up plans by the consultant and therapist often puts the consultation's effectiveness in doubt.

This paper attempts to present a methodology for conducting effective con-

---

The masculine pronoun is used in this paper with no intent for sexual discrimination.

sultations with families. It was inspired by our appreciation and respect for the potential helpfulness of live consultation, as well as the problems that can arise as a result. We have witnessed, and participated in, both these aspects, and believe much can be learned from both. A clinical example of the consultation process is included to illustrate the procedures used.

BACKGROUND

In a previous paper (2) we described a conceptual framework for understanding the consultation process. This model was originally developed in a family training seminar at Hahnemann Medical College and Hospital (4). Students were invited to bring in their treatment families for one-shot consultations. The interviews were videotaped in front of other student trainees. Repeated problems in arranging and conducting these interviews forced us to carefully analyze our efforts and gradually refine our procedures. Over the years these consultations have been carried out in other settings as well, including private and community mental health centers, psychiatric inpatient services, and day treatment centers. A teaching videotape (3) demonstrating these procedures has recently been released.

Our original paper introduced several principles applicable to family consultation. These are briefly summarized, before presenting the methodology:

1) Consultation is a procedure that is applied to the therapeutic system. The therapeutic system consists of the network of relationships that includes therapist, family, as well as extended family members, important friends, neighbors, and helping professionals.

2) Consultation's purpose is to improve the system's functioning and the level of trust between members and subsystems.

3) Family members and the therapist reciprocally influence each other. The consultant is not immune to the emotional forces generated between them. He must be able to alternately join and disengage with members, modeling dual capacities for intimacy and individuation, to be successful.

4) The therapeutic system has its own evolving structure and history. It demonstrates generative and healing properties; its members experience developmental crises and can grow from these. The consultant must respect these processes and intervene to facilitate them.

5) The consultant's role is both leader and collaborator. He borrows power and authority from members to redirect the system's efforts to grow. He operates as a temporary, but critical, agent of change.

CONSULTATION METHODOLOGY

Consultation can best be conducted when the participants have a clear set of guidelines for participating. The procedures we have developed include: 1) preparing the family and therapist for the consultation; 2) conducting the interview and; 3) planning follow-up measures. These three aspects of the consultation process must be judiciously observed in order to insure the consultation's effectiveness.

Preparing the Family and Therapist

Consultation seems to fare best when the family members are well prepared and know what to expect in advance. The therapist can help alleviate their anxiety this way. Two to four weeks' advance notice is usually optimal, as well as explaining why the consultation is being asked for, when it will occur, and who must be there. It must be assumed that the family will naturally be anxious about an "outsider" entering their private world and need reassurance that this can be helpful and not dangerous. If an audience will be present and/or videotaping done, they must consent and sign a release of information form.

The therapist, likewise, should be prepared. Writing up the case in advance and focusing on what areas of the therapy are progressing and which need further resolution can be helpful. The therapist should also have some contact with the consultant prior to meeting the family. This is for the purpose of briefing him (or her) on the case and clarifying the expectations and structure of the consultation. While in-depth discussion of the family might be avoided at this point, in order to preserve the spontaneity of the eventual interview, this "touching base" can help ease the sense of strain that the therapist may feel in presenting his work, especially for the first time.

Case Example

The T. family consisted of father, Herb, 39, mother, Barbara, 37, and three children, Rebecca, Charles and Joan, ages 10, eight, and five respectively. The therapist had been seeing them for six months, initially because of mother's problem of "wanting to run away from my children."

Mother and father were both overweight—she having dieted down to 150 pounds in the last year, and he having ballooned up to 450. Both had been obese as children and adolescents. After they married, mother began to lose gradually and, during the past year, she began to withdraw more and more from the house, leaving cooking responsibilities and chores to her husband. The husband spent most of his time running his business out of their basement. He had installed an intercom system throughout the house, so there was little direct communication between anyone in the family.

Since mother had returned to work as a clerk, her daughters had become symptomatic with "screaming fits" or tantrums. These were the same behaviors mother had previously employed when she felt desperate for her husband's attention. Now that she was away more often, the daughters proceeded to irritate their father with these tantrums.

When the therapist first met the family she witnessed one of these fits in her office. Colleagues from down the hall inquired, either annoyed or concerned, as to what were those bone-chilling shrieks emanating from her office.

The therapist was gradually able to set limits on the children's behavior in the sessions. Mother's further withdrawal from the house was forestalled by getting the couple to begin to examine their marital problems and the breakdown of their parenting relationship. The therapist recognized that both parents were immature and still deeply enmeshed with their own families of origin. Each was an "overstuffed" child, whose parents used food to manipulate and infantilize their children. Each was still actively involved with their parents. The therapist was able to form an alliance with mother, whose struggle for independence she was able to appreciate in the symptomatic behavior. Father was more difficult to reach. He insisted on his incompetence and remained in the basement. Crisis intervention around the children's tantrums and his visits to his parents' house were the only incentives to get him out. He pouted about his wife's inattention to him, but refused to confront her. The daughters' screaming fits would return when the parents' withdrawal increased dangerously.

After six months, consultation was requested. The therapist described the previous case and listed the following questions: a) What is the best intervention in this rigid system? b) What resources are there for the parents to better raise the children? c) How can we better understand and redefine constructively "screaming fits" for this family? The parents wanted to deal with the "fits" by yelling, threatening and arbitrarily punishing the children.

The family agreed to the consultation and videotaping. Mother was more reluctant, asking that only Rebecca be seen. Father was more agreeable, however, and persuaded her that the family should all come. An appointment was arranged.

Conducting the Interview

The interview process should allow enough time for introductions, an initial exchange with the therapist, the family interview, and finally a summary and recommendations by the consultant. The entire process usually requires between one and one and a half hours. This time can be modified on the basis of the family's size, the number of outside helping persons or extended family members attending, and the nature and extent of the problem. In one family, for example, the mother discovered that she had multiple sclerosis immediately prior to the consultation. Relatives who were attending could not be notified of this in advance. Therefore, the consultant and therapist planned as an option to have a second session if this seemed necessary.

When the interview begins the consultant first addresses the therapist. He asks the therapist to introduce the family and to describe his experience with them. Here the consultant pays special attention to "clues" about the therapist's relationship with the family—which aspects of it seem to be progressing and which seem blocked. He listens to the facts, but also to subtle messages: What is the level of the therapist's involvement? Does the therapist seem to care about this family? Are they a burden, a struggle, or merely "a job to do"? Is the therapist working harder than the family? All these things the consultant notices—and keeps to himself—in order to formulate hypotheses about the therapeutic relationship that can be helpful in the subsequent interview with the family. No a priori discussion or planning can substitute for the information gained at this point.

If the consultant feels that the therapist is too abstract or clinically distant, the therapist may be invited to share personal feelings about the family. For example, is the therapist optimistic about the case? Does he enjoy working with the family? Does he think the central issues have really been addressed?

This initial dialogue also helps the consultant gain entry to the family's emotional system. One way to view the therapist is as a "professional parent" of the therapeutic system. Therefore, in speaking with the consultant the therapist may grant temporary authority to intervene in the family system. Conversely, the consultant's acknowledging the therapist's leadership position can reassure the family members and secure their cooperation in the interview. This ritual entry process may also help to prevent covert power struggles and competition between the therapist and consultant. The key here is the consultant's demonstrated respect for the nature and depth of the relationships in the therapeutic system.

Addressing the family, the consultant may introduce himself by stating, "I'm glad to meet with you and hope that I can add something to the work that you are already doing with Dr. Jones," or a similar statement. This kind of remark brings him in as a collaborator, rather than someone who might usurp the therapist's role. The consultant is then free to use his full powers to intervene with the family.

During the interview, the therapist usually observes silently. We do not view the therapist as a co-therapist or a co-interviewer. Rather, the therapist utilizes the emotional distance provided to gain a more objective view of the family and learn new techniques for working with them. The therapist's benign presence also supports the consultant's effort to explore and help the family.

Case Example (Continued)

The T. family arrived for the consultation interview with all members present. The therapist was also present. The session was videotaped. The consultant began by addressing the therapist.

Dialogue	Commentary
C: Can you catch me up on what's been happening with the family?	
T: The other night we started to work on roles in the family. Herb and Barbara decided they wanted to change their roles. It seems that Herb has more to offer than just being a sergeant to come up and yell at the kids . . . that maybe he could discover some new way to relate to his family.	The therapist is generally positive about the family. She asks for help in getting the parents to work with each other, and to get father more involved. The consultant probes about the interactional role of other family members in father's withdrawal.
C: Do other members of the family want him more involved too?	
T: Yes, I think the kids also want him involved. Not just as a sergeant but for support and affection. Barbara says she would really like him to come out of the basement. And that she wants a daddy for the children. (The consultant then addresses the father)	
C: (to the father) I'm confused. While you seem to be very present in your house, your therapist and family seem to think of you as absent. Can you explain this?	
F: I am tired of just being around to discipline. The only one who pays	

any attention to me is Charles. There is constant fighting between everyone, and I am really annoyed at the way they ask me to help. For example, I was sleeping the other day. I try to sleep as long as I can. They wake me up with yelling and screaming and I know I am in trouble already.

C: Do you have any sense that they have to come up with some sort of tornado or explosion in order to get your attention?

F: The explosions don't necessarily get me.

C: That's what I meant. They are desperate for a way to get you involved. (to mother) How much do you weigh? I would like to know how much all of you weigh, Mom and the kids, in the family.
(The mother and the children all reveal their weight and the consultant adds these figures up.)

C: If I add up the score, all together they don't add up to as much as your husband. You all are really struggling to build up some concentrated force to get him involved. (to the mother) How much of an explosion do you think it will take to get him to move toward you?

M: One the size of an atom bomb. I just lose complete control. I start screaming and can't get a hold of myself.

C: This is a problem for you. You used to weigh much more, was it almost a 125 pounds more? Now you don't have as much weight to throw around and maybe you need more

The consultant immediately challenges the father's impotence in his family. He redefines the children's and mother's screaming fits as helpful methods to get the father involved. He identifies weight or obesity both as resistance to, as well as resources for, achieving intimacy. He finally underscores the family's

help. 150 pounds doesn't have
enough impact to get him moving.
Have the kids been trying to help
you with their fits in order to build a
cumulative bomb big enough to bring
him into the family?

R: I try to get Daddy to come upstairs
to help take care of things but then
when I start yelling I just get
punished for this.

C: So you don't have enough power all
by yourself? How about with Joan?
(Joan nods negatively). So all the
screaming fits haven't succeeded.
Have you been able to figure out any
other ways to get dad involved?
(The consultant continues to dialogue
with the father)

C: Have you had any sense of your
absence in the eyes of your family?

F: The other night I was with the kids
in the basement, watching the
Wizard of Oz. Susie was scared so I
gave her a magic pencil. It helped to
scare off the witch. Susie is very
moody. But I enjoy being with her
and all the rest of them.

C: I just had a strange thought! For
some reason, when you were talking
about witches, I thought of your
mother. Have you been scared and
hiding from her?

F: I have never gotten along very well
with my mother.

C: Does she haunt you?

F: She doesn't know when to stop.
She's always on the telephone,
telling me what to do. She just won't
relinquish the phone call once I get
on. Always telling me this or
that—nag, nag, nag.

failure to resolve this
problem, and raises for the
first time the question of
exploring alternative ways to
proceed.

C: Did you hope to be free of her when you got married? Or were you afraid you would be nagged the same way by your wife?

F: I do more for myself now. I buy my own clothes and shop for myself. Mother used to buy all these things for me.

C: (to father, later) Do you have a sense of yourself as "cut off" behind your fat? *Is* there a self behind all that weight, do you think?

F: There is a self there that wants to get out. And that's a big problem for me. I can't participate in boy scouts with Charles, like I want to. I've been on so many diets. None of them work.

C: You must be very disappointed not to participate with your son. I can tell you want to be close to him. And your wife and your daughters haven't been able to help you out with their screaming fits.

F: I have to lose weight, I know it. But it's too difficult. You want to know what? I have this crazy fear that if I get down to normal size I'll get killed by a car at Broad and Vine Street. I guess I feel safe behind my fat. If I lose it I'm losing my safety. (slightly later)

C: Do you worry that other family members would feel endangered if you lost weight? For example, do you feel your wife would become more vulnerable?

F: No. (hesitatingly) I can't really see how that would happen.

C: Do you think others in the family would feel better or worse if you lost

The consultant accepts the father's invitation to participate in primary process thinking. In sharing, the two men moved closer, and the discussion becomes more personal—about father's family of origin and his wishes to be close to his son.

weight? You don't seem to be sure.
Can you find out about this from
each person?
(Consultant directs the father to find
out his family's reaction to his losing
weight)

M: Well yes, of course I'd feel better.

F: It's just that I am not a person to
make my own breakfast! I'm not
motivated to cook for myself. And I
just can't do these things for myself.
(silence) I guess I'm just making
excuses here.

C: You really don't seem to trust your
wife. I don't think you are really
willing to confront her to find out for
sure if she supports your losing
weight.

M: You do have my support. But
eventually you always give up and I
feel foolish cooking all your meals,
being careful measuring things, and
then finding cookie wrappers and
McDonald papers in the back seat of
the car!

C: (to mother) Do you think he thinks
you are his mother in disguise?

M: I tell him I'm not his mother.

C: (to father) Until you are really clear
in your own head about what you
want to do with your weight, you'll
be less likely to change. You seem
still more apt to hide from your wife
rather than find this out. You are
going to have to work very hard to
find this out. (turns to younger
daughter) What do you think? Would
it be better if Daddy lost weight?

J: Yes. It would be very nice. Then he
could wear pajamas again.
(everybody laughs)

The consultant attempts
to enlist other family
members in supporting
father's weight loss. He
challenges mother's role
indirectly here and redefines
Herb's problem as not
trusting her. Just as quickly
however, he returns the
responsibility for change to
the husband. The younger
daughter's humorous remark
suggests the wish for the
return of appropriate
interpersonal boundaries in
the family.

At the close of the interview the consultant should present a simple summary of his findings, an evaluation of the state of progress of the therapy, and concrete suggestions for immediate and long-range steps to be taken. This aspect should be judiciously carried out in every consultation. The pressure of time should not truncate it. Here the consultant passes the "mantle of authority" back to the therapist. He directs his remarks to the entire group and indicates that their future work be conducted by the therapist. The consultant "low keys" himself and defers to the family's and therapist's future relationships without him. He points out what might be useful to add to an "already productive relationship," and may even introduce some discussion about his plans to return to a setting. As the consultant has carefully worked to enter the therapeutic system, now he moves with the same deliberateness to exit from it.

Dialogue

C: (to the family) I see you all trying very hard to be close to each other. To lose weight, or control yourselves, or really communicate you may feel might be dangerous. It would be good if there would be a way to break down these barriers. (to the father) I think it would be very sad if you want to participate in activities with your son, and you feel there is no support in the family. You seem to not trust people, and you need to know if there is really support for you to lose weight and be a member of this family. All of you have to decide if you feel it would be really better for the family to drop these barriers.

M: I for one want this. Then I could have a husband.

C: (to the therapist) I think the women are doing a beautiful job already at having fits if they need an explosion to bring father into the family. They already know how to do this well. Maybe they can learn better ways to get him involved. Father has to

The consultant leaves the family with a challenge to decide whether to keep their defenses or strive for intimacy. He introduces his suggestions to the therapist, compliments her work, and tells her she is free to do whatever she wants with his explore if he wants to stay in his basement, or whether he feels it's safe enough to come out of hiding and be a father and husband. These are refinements that I might add, but I am impressed with how calmly they seem to be communicating to each other today. Please use these suggestions however you feel they can be useful. I think you and the family already seem to be on the right track.

recommendations. This way he attempts to enlarge the possibility that they will incorporate his suggestions.

Follow-up

Consultation is viewed as vitally linked to the ongoing therapeutic process. Prior to the consultation interview, we recommend that a follow-up session between the therapist and family be scheduled soon after the consultation interview. The purpose of this is to review the consultant's recommendations, to process these suggestions, and to inventory the family's reactions to the session. This can help the family and therapist better integrate what was brought up in the session. The consultant should have made clear that the family is absolutely free to use or disregard whatever he suggests. The overall benefits of consultation are much greater when the family and therapist are free to choose what to use. There is no expectation that the therapist begin to treat the family in the same way as the consultant. Such expectations are discouraged and generally counterproductive.

It is useful for the consultant to include some communication with members of the therapeutic system in his follow-up planning. Depending on the geographical location and proximity to the consultant's place of work, this follow-up might be an interview in three or six months or a phone call or letter to the therapist. Future consultation efforts are best served by informed comments and impressions gained through this practice. Here the consultant can gauge the effectiveness of his work, as well as determine the relative merits of different techniques and models of consultation. It is this concern, built into the structure of consultation, that best seems to reinforce the positive direction of the therapy, and insures its continuity.

Case Example (Conclusion)

The therapist met with the T. family a few days after the consultation. The family was somewhat confused by the consultation and wanted to know why the consultant had spent so much time focusing on "weight" in the family. The therapist had gained an understanding of the symbolic meaning of the screaming fits as attention-getting devices. She reviewed this with the family, and began to push them in this and subsequent sessions to assume more control themselves over the children's fits. She was also impressed by the consultant's confrontation of the father, but at that point did not push him too hard. Now recognizing the importance of mother's expectations, the therapist began to challenge her, first, about how much she really wanted her husband to lose weight. Mother became more assertive herself toward her husband, spent fewer evenings running away from the house, and demanded more participation from him. The therapist joined her by gradually but consistently provoking the father. She told him that if he didn't want to participate in the therapy that had to be his choice, and that she had serious doubts about how long he was going to continue to survive without taking care of his obesity problem. During the month following the consultation session, the children's tantrums dramatically diminished.

Eight months after the consultation the therapist reported to the consultant that the father had decided to enter an obesity clinic. At that point the marriage began to improve dramatically. As father's weight reduced, he had more insights about how he had scheduled his whole life around meals, and had reduced a whole complex set of needs to food and eating. One year later the marriage remained intact and the children's screaming fits virtually disappeared. Both parents continue in therapy. The father was still involved with the obesity clinic, and each of the parents was working on problems related to their families of origin.

SUMMARY

Family consultation is best done with a clear set of guidelines to structure the experience for the family, therapist, and consultant. These procedures include administrative preparation for the consultation, careful consideration of the therapist's role at the beginning and end of consultation interview, and follow-up procedures built into the consultation process. These guidelines insure that the consultation will protect the integrity and confidentiality of family members, as well as support the previous efforts of the therapeutic system to grow and develop in a positive direction. With these in mind, the consultant is free to join with the family and intervene in a spontaneous and direct fashion, assured that his efforts would be utilized in the most beneficial manner. As the family field continues to grow, we anticipate that other models will develop and provide the opportunity to refine consultation methods and provide data for follow-up research in this area.

REFERENCES

1. Andolfi, M. *Family Therapy: An Interactional Approach*. New York: Plenum Press, 1979.
2. Garfield, R., and Schwoeri, L. Consulting With the Therapeutic System: When An Impasse Arises In Family Therapy. *International Journal of Family Psychiatry*, 2: 251-267, 1981.
3. Garfield, R. (Producer) *The Family Consultation Interview: When An Impasse Arises In Therapy*. New York: IEA Corporation, 1982 (Videotape).
4. Garfield, R. Family therapy training at Hahnemann Medical College and Hospital. *In*: M. Andolfi and I. Zwerling (Eds.), *Dimensions of Family Therapy*. New York: Guilford Press, 1980.
5. Montalvo, B. Aspects of live supervision. *Family Process*, 12: 343-359, 1973.
6. Selvini Palazzoli, M., Boscolo, L., Cecchin, G., and Prata, G. *Paradox and Counterparadox*, New York: Jason Aronson, 1978.

Chapter XXVII

PARADOXES OF ALWAYS-NEVER LAND

Stephen E. Levick, M.D.

Editors' Summary. An extension of the concept of paradox is offered by pointing out what is referred to as the "always-never" form of certain pragmatic paradoxes. An interdisciplinary perspective is used to evaluate different manifestations and levels of the "always-never" form. Family rituals, stereotyping, and certain psychological defenses receive special focus. Family rituals are viewed as having the always-never form implicit in their structure, and corresponding family myths may take on the form explicitly. Stereotyping is viewed as a process conforming to the always-never form. Social-cognitive data consistent with this view are cited. The always-never form is also shown to be usefully correlated with important negatory, universalizing, and temporal aspects of a variety of defense mechanisms.

INTRODUCTION

Some families, groups, and individuals are rigidly fixed in patterns of behavior, ideation, and interaction that are pragmatically if not logically paradoxical. What are the varieties of paradoxes in operation, and how would one recognize them? A growing body of literature addresses these questions and goes on to describe how paradoxical interventions may be selectively employed for therapeutic purposes.

A particular linguistic form reflecting and generating pragmatic paradoxes is what I call the "always-never" form. "Always" and "never" are logically antithetical terms. They are the ultimate generalizing descriptors. They not only respectively affirm or deny the statements they precede, but do so for all past and future times. When applied in the realm of pure abstraction, they are useful concepts. Systems of mathematics are of this form by definition: In the decimal system, $1 + 1$ always equals 2 and never equals anything else. "Always" and "never" are the implicit or explicit event quantifiers of formal rules of any sort.

Meta-rules are formal rules within which lower order formal rules and pragmatic behavioral rules are generated. We all know that formal rules for human beings need not follow the form of Aristotelian logic. Formal rules of

---

I am grateful for the helpful comments of Nathaniel Laor, M.D., Ph.D., Leonard Hill, M.S.W., and Behnaz Jalali, M.D., all of Yale University, who read earlier drafts of this article, and to Diana Daimwood who assisted in manuscript preparation.

the unconscious have been described by Freud as falling within what he called the "primary process." Arieti has described aspects of this process, naming it "paleologic." (2).

If there is one group of people who ideally operate with the knowledge that overarching formal rules are tentative assumptions, it is the practitioners of science. However, the sociology of science reveals that the tentative nature of scientific generalization is too often forgotten. There is a tendency toward allowing such generalizations to assume the status of always holding and never admitting of exception or revision. This is especially true of the most basic accepted generalizations—or meta-rules. Thomas Kuhn refers to these as "paradigms" (12). He argues that it takes a "revolution" in thought to change them.

What Searles (20) has called the "non-human environment" tends to be more easily described in always-never form than the environment of interpersonal interaction. As we develop from infancy onwards, through our interactions with our environment, we make and refine generalizations about it until they are generally functional. Piaget describes this process as schemata formation. (18). On a propositional level, we strive to understand our environment sufficiently to be able to make always-never predictions about it.

The child strives to name objects, people, and events. The name serves as a condensation of descriptions, predictions, and interactions. Naming reifies always-never assumptions into a word. If an individual is functioning at a concrete level, he does not progress beyond reified literal meaning. Arieti describes this phenomena in schizophrenics (2). Always-never rules for the non-human environment come to be generated with a high level of confidence. However, the use of the always-never form with the human environment inevitably leads not only to frustration for the individual holding those views as his cognitive schemata fail him, but also to a dehumanization of the person he is describing or with whom he is interacting.

Much in the clinical examples that follow can be understood from a developmental-object relations and ego-psychological perspective in the tradition of Mahler (15), Kernberg (10, 11) and Jacobson (9). The prototype of the always-never form is to be found in the psychological mechanism of splitting. Splitting is said to have its developmental roots in the cognition and affective life of the pre-ambivalent infant, whose object representations do not initially permit positive and negative feelings to be affixed to the same person (6). Instead, separate good and bad internal objects come to represent what is in fact the real object. (9).

Calling special attention to the linguistic and logical aspects of the structure of the always-never form and demonstrating the various ways it is used allow for a level of formulation that enriches more traditional models of clinical behavior. Because it is linguistically and logically based, it is a level of formulation with easier objective validity. The always-never form is often explicitly employed. Then it is an easily detectable manifest signal to the clinician in the midst of clinical interaction. It could be noted in transcripts of therapy for research purposes. Implicit demonstrations of the always-never form reveal it in more latent fashion.

The always-never form is a level of formulation regarding action, interaction, cognition, and affect that may be applied to human systems varying from one member to many. This type of conceptualization can be more readily and consistently applied to the realms of group and social psychology than can a developmental-object relations approach alone, with its own special theoretical base being that of the individual organism.

CLINICAL ILLUSTRATIONS

Polarizing and consciously unintended results of employing the always-never form in interactions occur not infrequently in couples. The following case illustrates the explicit use of the form. A couple in their early forties presented with the wife, Angela, depressed and agitated, and histrionic in her personality style, and the husband, Florio, withdrawn and depressed. His personality style was obsessive and mildly paranoid. Like the classical hysterical-obsessive marriage described by Barnett (3), the more she pursued him for affection, the more he backed away.

One aspect of the pursuit for this couple was that every time Angela felt that Florio was not meeting her needs she would assail him with always-never statements: "You never want to have sex. You're always too tired." From what could be gathered, Florio initially responded by trying harder to please. These overtures were too often met by statements like "You're just doing that to prove me wrong. You really don't want to. Don't deceive me." These statements indicated Angela's inability to allow Florio to change and her unwillingness to modify her always-never views.* Having already decided how he always has been and never will be, counter-examples did not alter her view. She saw them as attempts at pacification and deception. These sorts of interactions led Florio into tremendous financial debt which he kept secret from Angela, as he tried to "give her what she deserved" by buying a house they could not afford. Bankruptcy ensued and Angela pursued him with why he "never" talked with her about their monetary status and "always" handled those matters himself. One might ask why she never-always did the obverse.

Florio required hospitalization for depression and alcohol abuse, and their youngest daughter needed hospitalization several times for suicidal behavior.

---

*What has been called a "be spontaneous" paradox by Watzlawick et al. (21) helps this always-never paradox to survive.

She had been triangulated into a position in which the parents attacked each other for how the other "always" and "never" treated her. Eventually, the couple was helped to separate, and after a time this had beneficial effects for all concerned.

Pathologic family rituals are implicitly always-never in form, being relatable to myths which, if stated clearly, would take explicit always-never form. Levick et al. (14) recently described a case of the family of a schizophrenic young man in which a laughing ritual occurred within the context of what would usually be sadness-evoking circumstances or events in any family. The laughing ritual was conceived of as the behavioral manifestation of the pragmatic paradox: "We laugh even though we are sad." This was felt to be consistent with and perhaps a derivative of an unstated but implied family myth: "We are always happy and never sad." It is important to note that the identified patient did not laugh, but rather displayed a flat affect manifested by a weak, uncomfortable, and inane-looking smile. The rest of the family could behave, think, and feel according to the "always-never" rule of their family myth. The schizophrenic young man could not. His silly half-hearted smile was a permanent and paradoxical compromise between his deeper feelings and the family's myth that "We are always happy and never sad."

Many pieces of literature could serve to illustrate the use of the always-never form by unfortunate characters trapped in tragic situations of their own unconscious making. The writer, Milan Kundera, warns us that

> . . .every love relationship is based on unwritten conventions rashly agreed upon by lovers in the first weeks of their love. . . . O lovers! Be wary during those perilous first days! If you serve the other party breakfast in bed you will be obliged to continue same in perpetuity or face charges of animosity and treason! (13)

The conventions of which Kundera speaks are implicitly always-never in form, and are usually unconscious until they are violated. Abrogations of such conventions can bring out charges and counter-charges often explicitly phrased in always-never form.

STEREOTYPING

Let's look at some clinical data of a family with a hospitalized 17-year-old daughter, Debby. Her drug-abusing, sexually promiscuous, and generally oppositional behavior had brought her a large share of emnity from her father. Father used Debby as a stereotype when relating to their other daughter, Sally. When Sally began to become increasingly troublesome to the couple, her father told her that he did not want her to "become another Debby." Bateson (4) explains how the substitution of names for complex interactional descriptions can impede understanding and scientific progress, but it is particularly dangerous when the noun that the interactions are collapsed into is a person's or group's name. Through the process of being stereotyped, Debby had the misfortune of this being done to her name as she came to be viewed in always-never form.

Since stereotypes are the material for scapegoating, it should not be surprising to learn that projective and delegative processes were prominent features in the dynamics of Debby's family. Projection is a dangerous and interactionally destructive defense which the always-never form serves well. Zinner (22) shows how projective identification leads to polarities in the descriptions that members of a marital couple have for each other. These polarities fit into our always-never form.

When anti-Semites say, "He's such a Jew," a similar mechanism is at work. The implication is that Jews and Debby are "always" one way and "never" another. What these ways are is left vague. The result is an always-never form with a content open to the projections of the person making such statements and those listening to him. Sartre (19) sketched out this process from his own unique perspective. Sartre described the anti-Semite as wishing to "exist all at once and right away," as not wanting "any acquired opinions," seeking "only what he has already found," and he "becomes only what he already was. . . . He tries to project his intuitive certainty to a plane of discourse." For both the anti-Semite and for Debby's father a tenuous sense of self and a fear of self-awareness breed projective tendencies which enhance not only shaky self-esteem but provide a sense of secure existence and certitude serving to fend off fears of personal dissolution. Clearly, this is a process that may transcend individuals and families. It found virulent expression in the Nazi-perpetrated holocaust. It continues as a destructive force not only for Jews, but for other groups and nations whose faces are inhumanely painted by some as "the enemy."

Some work in specifying cognitive processes in stereotyping behavior utilizes the concept of "illusory correlation." Hamilton (7) summarizes data on this concept, showing that people recall distinctive events more frequently than they actually occurred, and that descriptions incongruent to expectations are recalled with a lower than actual frequency. These findings demonstrate a cognitive basis for polarization in perceived probabilities, based on event and description distinctiveness and incongruence to expectation, and are, therefore, evidence for a cognitive basis for the always-never form.

DEFENSIVE MECHANISM

In the pragmatic sphere of human existence, verbal use of the always-never form or interacting by unstated always-never rules constitute manifestations of the defensive process of denial, and often projection as an elaboration of that defense mechanism.

In Freud's paper "Negation" (5), he begins to look at negation as a linguistic form used in the service of psychological defense. His dictum that there is no "not" in the unconscious is well-known in this regard.

Opposite action, thought, or feeling statements are often linked together by the always-never form. Simple negation of statement "A" blocks out "A" but gives no direction to attention. I would speculate that "Never A" provides a reciprocal attentional vector to an opposite response, "Z." The reverse would also hold, where "Always Z" points to "Never A." "Always" and "never" are thus tied to opposite terms in the semantic space of an individual or group. Osgood (17) has shown us how semantic space may be mapped.

One may capitalize on the principles regarding the always-never form to use it therapeutically. For example, a family member may be moved from a simple negatory statement to the always-never form, thus dialectically polarizing the defended-against opposite. This may lead the subject to look beyond his negation. If the patient is operating by means of reaction formation, introducing the always-never form may be experienced as an absurdity by him, as reaction formation is a developmentally more advanced mechanism than splitting. Nonetheless, the experienced absurdity may point to a paradox he had not confronted.

In the context of couples therapy in which splitting and projective identification loom large, offering a "never the opposite" counterpart to an "always" statement or vice versa generates a therapeutic counterparadox. For example:

Wife: He is always preoccupied.
Therapist: Harry, Edith feels you *never* pay attention to her.
Wife: I guess that's not what I mean.
Husband: What do you mean?
Wife: I wish we spent more time together.

The "always" statement of the wife is here countered with the therapist making a "never" statement regarding something perceived by him to be a bipolar opposite in the wife's organization of reality. If this special restatement is accurately chosen by the therapist, it can have powerful effects. If the wife negates it, she is either obliged to modify the initial statement or change her tendency to view both statements in bipolar fashion. This will necessarily destabilize aspects of the husband's "always-never" perceptions of her.

By adding an infinite temporal dimension with the words "always" or "never" to what is denied or projected, an extra dimension is added to the defense. Rather than repeatedly having to deny or project in the present moment, adding temporal infinity to it attempts to extend the defense mechanism infinitely into the past and future. To the extent it can extend into the future, the psychic energy of constantly having to recreate denial and projection is partially spared by their cognitive manipulation into the infinite future. ''Never'' thus symbolizes the retrograde and anterograde spreading of denial, and often of projection, when ''never'' is paired with its opposite ''always.'' In that sense, the use of the always-never form constitutes a defensive mechanism that can be layered over the classic defenses of denial and projection, and which may be the cognitive mechanism for repression. When asked about repressed experiences, people may explicitly use the always-never form. People diagnosed histrionic are likely to use it in the service of denial and repression, but they are not the only people to use it.

As stated earlier, splitting is the prototype for always-never form usage. The psychotic or borderline individual is unable to maintain unitary internal object representations for an object with both good and bad attributes. This process is manifested implicitly and explicitly in interactions and verbalizations in the always-never form.

Compulsive rituals may be always-never phenomena in the service of myths meant to deny a person's aggression. The obsessive's decision-making difficulty may be in part understood from his rigid disinclination to explicitly use the always-never form. His manifest form of thought is best described by ''either-or,'' although his oscillating repulsion between opposite alternatives indicates the operation of the always-never form at a deeper level. To the obsessive, decisions take on an always-never character. What is about to be decided becomes experienced as what will be always. This perceived threat to his autonomy paralyzes action and sends him oscillating between alternatives until uncertainty-induced anxiety forces an impulsive decision. The paranoid's prejudices and frank delusions are examples of the always-never form applied to the content of his projections.

TIME AND DIMENSIONALITY

The always-never form effectively obliterates time by dedifferentiating it. It may also be a manifestation of a more primary dedifferentiation of temporal experience. Apprehension of the future may lead some people to want to make the present the past and the past the future—to make it all one moment, and so do away with uncertainty. The undifferentiated timelessness of the always-never form and the timelessness that Freud said applied to the unconscious point to the fact that the predominant mode of thought in each is that of primary process. The sense of undifferentiated timelessness is, in my experience, a dominant feature of therapy groups with marginally compensated psychotic patients.

The clinical situation for the couple, family, or group is reminiscent of the adventures of A. Square in Abbott's *Flatland* (1). Living in a two-dimensional world, he had generated certain always-never schemata for experiencing reality, which he only came to understand by being forced to travel into three dimensions. There, he also had the opportunity to witness the behavior and listen to the ideas of beings living in one and zero dimensions. Therapy groups and family therapy provide individuals living in Always-Never Land with analogous opportunities for increasing the dimensionality of their lived-in world of behavior, ideas, and feelings.

"Never" or "always" can be violated by a single counter-example, but the forces at work to maintain well-established schemata fight back with a variety of often rigidly employed defense mechanisms. Extreme measures to retain an always-never form by an individual, group, or family result in a variety of individual, family, and larger system pathologies.

Marcuse (16) writes of the society which produces a "pattern of *one-dimensional thought and behavior* in which ideas, operations and objectives that, by their content, transcend the universe of discourse and action are either repelled or reduced to forms of this universe" (p. 12). Larger human systems are not only trapped within their own meta-rule framework, but the subsystems within are likewise constrained by not only their own meta-rules but those of higher system levels. The struggle of the individual within the family and the minority group within the society is the struggle for self-definition within larger systems—systems that have already defined themselves and so have implicitly or explicitly defined their members.

Hoffer's "true believer" (8) is a representative of many individuals existing in societies in which the always-never form is paramount for values and beliefs, regardless of what those values and beliefs are. The "true believer" may exchange one set of beliefs for another in a sudden conversion but he does not give up the inflexible always-never form into which his belief systems are molded.

This limited dimensionality of perception, cognition, and action is by no means limited to our patients. Other than having our own personal always-never rules for ourselves and others, the theoretical orientations to which therapists subscribe have their own higher level meta-rules which are of the always-never form. Striving to explicitly specify these implicit assumptions is essential to seeing the limits of our various theories.

The always-never form works for the "n" dimensions over which it rules. The therapist strives to introduce the previously unseen or poorly understood "n + 1" dimensional view to his patients. Therapists may unwittingly share more limited dimensional views with patients as they join a family, group, or dyadic system. Joining with a clear and explicit awareness of the always-never forms at work requires that the therapist maintain himself in several dimensions simultaneously.

Solution of always-never paradoxes involves the skillful explicit and implicit introduction of "sometimes" and other modifiers. This process may proceed by a variety of therapeutic strategies and techniques, and by therapists of differing orientations. The variegations introduced by "sometimes" build another dimension onto the limited dimensional world of what I call "Always-Never Land." Not unlike Peter Pan's Never-Never Land, Always-Never Land is passionately believed by those living in or, hopefully, passing through it.

The homogeneous, timeless uniformity of infinity is eliminated by introducing and by inviting the patient to introduce modifiers. Time, then, becomes discrete and capable of containing events that may be perceived, imagined, and remembered—events which may contradict always-never statements. Flexibility in perception and attribution of meaning can build out of this, and hence greater flexibility and efficacy in action.

It must be emphasized that rather than reflexively identifying a surface structure containing "never" as constituting a component of an always-never form, one should listen not only to the form but also to the content to arrive at the deeper structure. Content related to permanent separation or death may quite rightly be presented in a "never . . . again" format. This "never . . . again" of actual separation from or death of a previously existing person or family points to the true implications of "never" in the pragmatic sphere of human existence. The overwhelming sense of loss that may accompany such circumstances may lead the surviving person or family into the paradoxical always-never form in their remembrances of the lost object(s). Idealization, devaluation, or a confused mixture of both may result.

CONCLUSION

It is hoped that by underlining the always-never cognitive and linguistic aspects of a variety of clinical phenomena some help has been provided in conceptualizing their paradoxical nature. The always-never form has been demonstrated to apply to family rituals and stereotyping. It is an aid to better understanding certain psychological defenses, because it highlights their temporal and dimensional qualities. The always-never nature of the meta-rules for any individual or system of people is emphasized. This points to the need for the therapist to learn both his own and his patients' meta-rules to avoid unconsciously using the always-never form. Its thoughtful therapeutic use is then permitted.

REFERENCES

1. Abbott, E.A. (1884) *Flatland.* New York: Dover, 1952.
2. Arieti, S. *The Intrapsychic Self.* New York: Basic Books, 1967.
3. Barnett, R. Narcissism and dependency in the obsessive hysteric marriage. *Fam. Proc.,* 8: 75-83, 1971.
4. Bateson, G. *Mind and Nature: A Necessary Unity.* New York: E.P. Dutton, 1979.
5. Freud, S. (1925) Negation. *In*: J. Strachey (Ed.), *The Standard Edition of the Complete Psychological Works of Sigmund Freud, Vol. 19.* London: Hogarth Press, 1961, pp. 235-239.
6. Greenspan, S.I. Intelligence and adaptation. *Psychological Issues,* 12 (47-48): 297-379, 1979.
7. Hamilton, D.L. Illusory correlation as a basis for stereotyping. *In*: D.L. Hamilton (Ed.), *Cognitive Processes in Stereotyping and Intergroup Behavior.* Hillsdale, N.J.: Lawrence Erlbaum Associates, 1981, pp. 115-144.
8. Hoffer, E. *The True Believer.* New York: Harper and Row, 1951.
9. Jacobson, E. *The Self and the Object World.* New York: International Universities Press, 1964.
10. Kernberg, O. *Internal World and External Reality.* New York: Jason Aronson, 1980.
11. Kernberg, O. *Object Relations Theory and Clinical Psychoanalysis.* New York: Jason Aronson, 1977.
12. Kuhn, T. *The Structure of Scientific Revolutions* (Second Edition). Chicago: University of Chicago Press, 1970.
13. Kundera, M. *The Book of Laughter and Forgetting.* New York: Penguin Books, 1980, pp. 36-37.
14. Levick, S.E., Jalali, B., and Strauss, J.S. With onions and tears: A multi-dimensional analysis of a counter-ritual. *Fam. Proc.,* 20: 77-85, 1981.
15. Mahler, M. Symbiosis and individuation: The psychological birth of the infant. *Psychoanalytic Study of the Child,* 29: 89-106, 1974.
16. Marcuse, H. *One-Dimensional Man.* Boston: Beacon Press, 1964.
17. Osgood, C.S., Suci, G.J., and Tannenbaum, P.H. *The Measurement of Meaning.* Urbana, IL: University of Illinois Press, 1957.
18. Piaget, J. *The Origins of Intelligence in Children.* New York: W.W. Norton, 1966.
19. Sartre, J.P. (1946) *Anti-Semite and Jew.* New York: Schocken Books, 1965.
20. Searles, H. *The Non-Human Environment.* New York: International Universities Press, 1960.
21. Watzlawick, P., Beavin, J.H., and Jackson, D.D. *Pragmatics of Human Communication.* New York: W.W. Norton, 1967.
22. Zinner, J. The implications of projective identification. *In*: H. Grunebaum and J. Christ (Eds.), *Contemporary Marriage: Structure, Dynamics and Therapy.* Boston: Little, Brown and Co., 1976, pp. 293-307.

Chapter XXVIII

FAMILY THERAPY WITH CANCER PATIENTS: A MODEL

David K. Wellisch, Ph.D.

Editors' Summary. The first section of this article deals with the family problems of the cancer patient which often center around a ''conspiracy of silence'' and drastic difficulties with finances. The second deals with family risk factors in ability to adapt to cancer. These include isolation, problems in role flexibility, and historical problems in interaction personified by interpersonal hostility or abandonment. The third section attempts to take all of these factors into account to suggest a model for family treatment. This model presents some fundamental departures regarding who is included, when the family is seen, and for how long and where. The model also focuses on issues of intervention as well as the therapist's countertransference problems.

INTRODUCTION

''Cancer is like the main member of our family now. It moved in, took over and shoved me out.''

—67-year-old wife of man with colon cancer

The above remark was a particularly apt observation of the potential effect of cancer on a family's experience. The woman's observation presents important implications for the therapist attempting to help a family live with the reality of a cancer. Perhaps the primary issue in working with such a family is enabling the family to maintian a semblance of normality in the face of this frightening and chronic stressor. The incidence of this problem is very large. One of three Americans can expect a diagnosis of cancer in their lifetime, while three out of four American families will have to confront and learn to live with a diagnosis of cancer in a family member. However, three of every eight people with a cancer diagnosis, at present, will live at least five years beyond diagnosis (1).

The implications of these statistics for the family of the cancer patient and for the family therapist are profound. Medical science and technology have now enabled cancer patients to live longer and for some cancer sites the notion of cure has become a realistic notion. Psychologically, however, longer-term cancer survivors cannot be guaranteed quality of life parallel to longevity of life. Living with the rigors of cancer treatment, in the form of surgery, radiation, chemotherapy, or combinations of these, can exert a powerful and sometimes negative impact on the family milieu. More time, then becomes not only a precious commodity to be enjoyed by the family, but also a burden for the patient and family now joined together in a period of fearful waiting. Family members have likened this to living in prison with an indeterminate sentence.

One writer (24) who has had extensive experience in the psychological treatment of cancer patients delineated four factors which he felt reflect behavior ranging from adaptive to maladaptive in the cancer patient requiring intervention. These include:

1) When the emotional reaction of a patient prevents him from cooperating with treatment or interferes with treatment.
2) When the patient's behavior causes more pain and distress than the disease itself or increases that which is present. This may be manifested by various physical complaints, or in difficult and uncooperative behavior with others around him.
3) When the emotional responses interfere with everyday functions (such as work and interpersonal relations) or cause the individual to entirely give up his usual sources of gratification.
4) When the emotional responses appear as conventional psychiatric symptoms. The patient may misinterpret his (interpersonal) environment, including the people in it, in terms of his feelings and he may also suffer a considerable loss of self-esteem.

It is noteworthy that at least three of these four conditions (2, 3, 4) directly interface with the patient's family environment. The cancer patient and family form a system, which ultimately incorporates the health care delivery team in an intimate psycholgocial fashion. Any of these parts can influence the other and it cannot be concluded that the only direction of negativity is from the cancer patient toward the family. The family can influence the patient; the patient can influence the health care team; the health care team can influence the family, and so on through all the permutations and combinations of this system. This chapter proposes that the cancer patient be evaluated and treated psychologically in a systems context which includes family and health care deliverers. To do less is to lose a critical focus in the etiology of dysfunctional coping of the cancer patient.

Three areas will be addressed:

1) What are the issues which confront the family of the cancer patient? In this overview of the family problems, a brief review of the literature will be carried out which will emphasize breadth rather than depth.
2) What are the risk factors of family-based dysfunction in coping with cancer? What does the family bring to cancer? This section will meld review of the literature with clinical observations.
3) What are the elements of a viable model for the family therapy of the cancer patient based on these problems and risk factors? How this model contrasts with non-cancer-oriented family intervention will be an important focus of this subsection.

A most important theme of this chapter is what the cancer situation can teach us about families and family therapy. The introduction of cancer into a family brings the resources and shortcomings of the family into bold relief. It can also force the family therapist to modify technique in ways which are potentially useful for family therapy in general.

WHAT ARE THE ISSUES FACED BY FAMILIES WITH A CANCER PATIENT?

In a large scale review of the literature of the interpersonal processes of the cancer patient, two major issues were found to be relatively widespread in regard to family behavior toward cancer patients. These involved avoidance of communication about the illness, and physical avoidance of the patient (32).

In regard to avoidance of communication, several studies have shown that high percentages of cancer patients feel they do not have emotional access to a significant other with whom to share their feelings about their disease (9, 15). There are several reasons why this may be true. Cancer may be unique among other diseases in its ability to present spouses or family members with feelings of fear and vulnerability (12). Several studies have shown that open communication often will be avoided by family members toward cancer patients. This may be because open communication is regarded by many people as being deleterious for the cancer patient's emotional well-being (7, 10, 11). In addition to not communicating with cancer patients in the family, studies have shown that family members can actively discourage cancer patients from expression of feelings (5, 20). Family members may do this because listening to such feelings is unpleasant, makes them feel helpless, and intensifies their own feelings of anger, guilt, and grief (3, 11, 18). As cancer patients become more ill, family members must spend more time caring for them, which often produces very normal feelings of resentment and a sense of being overburdened (5, 28). Family members become guilty about such feelings of resentment, trying to obscure them by becoming over-solicitous and patronizing toward the patient (33). This can be understood as a reaction-formation to the feelings of resentment.

In terms of physical avoidance of the cancer patient, this is not limited to family members but also includes physicians and nurses (2, 22). With this as a model, families can respond similarly. Studies of patients with colon or gastrointestinal malignancies reflect decreased sexual activity and decreased levels of assistance by spouses, persisting many years after surgery (5, 28). Decreased levels of post mastectomy sexual activity and intimacy have also been found with breast cancer patients and their partners (30). Thus, avoidance of physical contact can span across different cancer sites and is not limited to those cancers where potentially obvious stressful issues such as colostomy management are developed.

The patient can also engage in behaviors that limit and bind family interactions. One study evaluated major concerns of adult cancer patients. It was found that worries about the adverse effects of their illness upon the families' financial and emotional resources were prime concerns for cancer patients (25). In more than one study, the notion of patients not communicating distress and protecting the family members' feelings due to perceiving them as overburdened by their illness has been presented (23, 29).

The literature points to two net outcomes in regard to the importance of family interaction for the cancer patient. First, the cancer patient with a supportive family where open communication is possible is likely to cope with cancer in a more functional manner than patients lacking such a resource (9, 29). Second, the patient with a supportive family unit has been shown to be more willing and able to cooperate with treatment regimes (4, 26). Thus, the issue of resolution of family conflict and organization of family support may not only have implications for patient coping with and adjustment to cancer, but may also impact on patient compliance and subsequently on survival and longevity of life itself.

RISK-FACTORS—WHAT DOES THE FAMILY BRING TO THE CANCER SITUATION?

In this section, more specific clinical variables and illustrative clinical examples of these will be described. The point of this is to orient family therapists toward earlier intervention with these families, which may ensure coping and treatment compliance by the patient.

A study of 273 families extracted four factors which correlated with effective interaction with a sick member in the family and also in effective bonding and interaction between the family and the health care deliverers (19). The factors involved are presented below.

1) *Varied contacts with other groups and organizations in the community in an active attempt to cope and master their lives.* As a case example, a couple in their late seventies were presented to this writer by a visiting nurse agency for consultation. The man had metastatic colon cancer and was homebound. The couple had so limited their contacts in the community that the patient's wife was resisting leaving their apartment for food shopping. Although they knew they needed the visiting nurse, they resisted her suggestions and interventions in passive-aggressive ways. The couple were persuaded to have a volunteer visitor from the agency. This allowed the wife to feel a bit more comfort in leaving the home to do errands and shop. The reduction in her isolation and depression seemed to help the patient slightly.

2) *Fluid internal organization, including flexible role relationships* (i.e., sharing tasks such as housecleaning or sick care). As a case example, a couple in their fifties was seen by this writer for family therapy. The woman had an esophageal malignancy which was metastatic. She obviously had been the maternal figure to not only their three children but also him. As she became more ill, he drank and became erratic in his dependability, which forced their 18-year-old daughter to become more responsible and maternal toward him. The husband-wife relationship had neither the emotional nor situational (task-related) flexibility to tolerate the changes presented by the woman's illness-related deterioration. Family therapy, which included the treating oncologist, was directed toward getting the husband to accept a live-in nurse who would help him learn to organize the household and let his daughter "off the hook" from a role which she could perform only with great difficulty. This intervention led to stabilization of the situation.

3) *Shared power, with each family member participating in decisions that affect him or her.* As a case example, a family was seen in the in-patient oncology service by this writer with a 16-year-old son with metastatic osteo-sarcoma. The mother was making unilateral decisions, many of which reinforced and protected her over involvement with her son. Both the boy's father and her second husband (the boy's stepfather) were being excluded from decisions. The mother's needs in this area overrode her ability to hear that she needed to include these family members in the decisions. The boy's father became increasingly alienated from the son and the stepfather separated from the mother shortly after the boy's death.

4) *Maintaining a high degree of autonomy with the family and relationships among members that support personal growth.* As a case example, a family was

seen for family therapy by this writer where the woman had metastatic breast cancer and should not have necessarily been homebound, but presented as a total invalid. She remained bedridden at home and refused to be alone for one moment of the day. If she was left alone in her room, she began having anxiety attacks which became somatic, with her becoming short of breath. This, in turn, panicked the family. Family interviews revealed this woman to have always been a dependent person and fearful of being left even prior to the illness. In short, the woman's suffocation was symptomatic of the family emotional suffocation in the situation. Intensive marital work was done with the couple when it became evident that there had been significant pre-illness ambivalence on the part of the husband, combined with some acting-out on his part which fueled her fears. The husband was supported in saying to his wife that he absolutely would not leave her, but also that her behavior was intolerable and made any quality time between them impossible. A compromise was struck: The patient's mother would be brought into the family home if the patient would agree to embark on a program of anxiety management that included some time spent alone with less hysteria-tinged demands on the family. In addition, a religious person was contacted and began visiting the patient. The patient did settle down and grew to accept her terminality. She did not die in a state of hysteria.

Problems with these general family factors do appear, therefore, to indicate family level dysfunction in coping with cancer. In a more strictly clinical sense, five additional family history variables require attention in the initial assessment of a family's ability to functionally cope with cancer. They are as follows:

1) Upon being confronted with a stressor (such as diagnosis of a cancer in a family member) does the family historically react with a pattern of hostility and aggression? As an example, a family was presented with the diagnosis of (terminal) pancreatic cancer in their 83-year-old mother. The sisters and brother fought among themselves and were not able to openly express grief. One family member had a combative episode with a nurse on the floor of the cancer center. It was felt subsequently by the staff that family intervention might have eliminated this unfortunate episode that seemed to represent displaced hosility about the diagnosis itself.

2) Does the family contain a member (who is *not* the patient) with a history of a major psychiatric disorder which the family unit has organized around in such a way as to protect this family member? As an example, a couple in their fifties was seen by this writer in multiple family therapy. The cancer patient was the wife who had breast cancer and had recently undergone mastectomy. She was also undergoing adjuvant chemotherapy. The husband had always been an unstable, emotional, reclusive figure who stayed at home doing menial tasks,

while the wife earned the family living in a responsible job. She now was turning to him for support where previously she had emotionally supported him. He presented in the group with frank clinical mania and described concurrent mood alterations involving suicidal depression. The couple was referred to a private psychiatrist for a combination of lithium treatment for him and marital therapy.

3) Does the family contain a member (who is *not* the patient) with a history of a major alcohol or drug problem which the family unit has organized around in such a way as to protect that family member? As an example, a family was seen by this writer in consultation on the inpatient cancer center unit. They had a 15-year-old son who had osteo-sarcoma and was to immediately undergo amputation of his leg. The father, a recovered alcoholic with several years' sobriety, began presenting on the ward "falling down drunk," as described by the staff. He was seen with his wife and strongly encouraged to return to active A.A. meetings. Prior to this, no one knew or had inquired into his past history of difficulties with alcohol.

4) Does the family flee in the face of stress and abandon the member in crisis? As an example, a 50-year-old man with malignant melanoma was seen on the inpatient cancer center unit threatening to jump out of the window. He indicated that his wife was basically abandoning him. She in fact was refusing to come to the hospital or to offer him emotional support. Upon interviewing her, it became clear that this was a long-term, reciprocal style for this couple. This marital relationship has been termed "façade marriage" by Sutherland in his classic article on the impact of cancer and its therapy (26). The wife was not pushed to support her husband, but outside support in the form of a psycho-therapist was arranged for the patient. He ultimately came to accept the reality of his marital situation. The couple divorced. He did not suicide, but rather died from his disease one year after the divorce.

5) How old is the family in question? In our research project on homebound cancer patients, age of the couple appeared to be a major risk factor in family-based coping problems with very ill homebound cancer patients (31). As can be observed (see Figure 1), the rate of spouses verbalizing feelings of being over-whelmed in this circumstance is about 14% for couples aged 50 or less. For couples in their seventies this rate doubles, and for couples aged 80 or more better than one-third of the caretaking spouses verbalized feeling overwhelmed.

Currently no viable model exists of which we are aware that attempts to predict family-based dysfunction with cancer patients. To date, we have a large project in progress assessing family management of homebound cancer patients. This project has thus far developed an instrument entitled "Psychosocial Problem Categories for Homebound Cancer Patients" which is designed to assess patient records of homebound patients which are generated by visiting health care de-liverers (30).

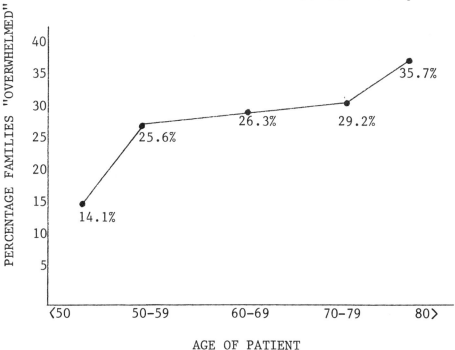

Figure 1
DIFFICULTY IN FAMILY ABILITY TO COPE WITH HOMEBOUND PATIENT

A currently viable model for prediction which has not been utilized to date with cancer patients but which we plan to use is the "Circumplex Model" designed by Olson, Sprenkle, and Russell (17). This model, which locates families on a grid, utilizes the Family Adaptability and Cohesion Evaluation Scales (FACES) test to achieve this location. The model is based on the utilization of two basic dimensions: Cohesion and adaptability.

Cohesion is subdivided into a range of four styles. They range from disengaged, to separated, to connected, to enmeshed. Cohesion is of importance to families with cancer patients in many ways. The family that is chronically disengaged reflects exactly the family style just described of family flight in face of stress. On the other end of this continuum is the enmeshed family previously very well described in the writings of Minuchin (14). This type of family, also described previously, tends to overprotect the patient which is usually a function of the family members' needs rather than the needs of the patient. This type of family brings problems with separation into the cancer situation which then become very severe with the result of neither the patient nor family being able to achieve any resolution of feelings if and when terminality is an issue. As Lansky (13) masterfully observes:

> Such marriages are organized around the containment and expression of massive rage, by the collusive exchange of projective defenses warding off the experience of inadequacy and the humiliating realization that abandonment (or even the threat) results in debilitating anxiety and fragmenting experiences (pp. 169).

Abandonment, carried forth in the form of terminal illness, can be a central theme with cancer and is ultra-conflict-inducing with these types of marriages. Adaptability, the second dimension of the Circumplex Model, is sub-divided into a range of four styles. They range from chaotic, to flexible, to structured, to rigid. This dimension is potentially more central to the task organization necessary for a family to manage the care of a cancer patient, especially when that patient is homebound and deteriorating. Cancer calls for much role flexibility and task flexibility, especially if the ill patient was a pivotal family member such as a breadwinner or home-maker, regardless of sex. The family that is chaotic has no structure to rework; the family that is rigid provides no room to restructure an inflexible interactional/organizational pattern.

Thus, the model focuses in on two crucial dimensions of family experience with cancer patients, one more emotional-interactional, and the other more task-interactional.

A MODEL FOR FAMILY INTERVENTION
WITH THE CANCER PATIENT

In the first section some of the situational dilemmas in the cancer patient's interpersonal environment were reviewed. In the second section, some clinical risk factors for problematic coping at a family level were described. In this third section, all of the foregoing are considered, with an attempt made at developing a preliminary model for cancer-based family therapy, with five areas of consideration. These are:

1) What is the setting for the family based intervention?
2) Who are the participants in the family therapy?
3) What is the course of the family therapy?

4) What are the special features in intervention and how might they be handled?
5) What are the therapist's vulnerabilities in this type of family therapy?

1. Setting for Family Therapy

In conventional family therapy (not involving the issue of cancer) the most frequent and usual setting is the therapist's office. With the cancer patient and family, the family therapist is almost mandated to see the family in a variety of settings. Besides the therapist's office, the family can be seen in the patient's hospital room, the treating oncologist's office or clinic during outpatient visits, and especially in the family home. These additional settings can become necessary given the effects of the illness. For example, if the patient is very ill, it can be all a patient and family can do to come to the oncologist's office. An additional trip from that office to the family therapist's office may overtax the patient completely. Thus, it should not be viewed as resistance when the therapist sees the family at the oncologist's office. In fact, such a move by the family therapist can be viewed by the family and oncologist as an important joining move into the "treatment team." The value of family therapy home visits has been previously discussed in the literature (6). Such visits take on a special significance for the family with a homebound cancer patient. Besides the naturalistic observation advantage, home visits can allow the family therapist to form liaisons with nurses who may be working in the family home. This further facilitates the coordination of the health care delivery team. In addition, home visits counteract for these families the fearful sense of isolation they can experience when the illness is worst and medical intervention and involvement are often the least.

2) Participants in the Family Therapy

In conventional family therapy there is almost never a health care team involved with the family. In dealing with cancer patients and their families there is always a primary medical physician and very often hospital, clinic, or office nurses, as well as visiting or home care nursing personnel. All of these health care providers impact on the family in crucial ways and must be considered in making successful family-based interventions. Inclusion of home care personnel in family sessions is this writer's usual practice, and inclusion when needed, of physician and nurses who are hospital-based, can have significant advantages. As a case example, a 42-year-old woman with breast cancer including nodal involvement was undergoing the usual three-drug adjuvant chemotherapy pro-

tocol. She was having a very difficult time and felt like quitting her chemotherapy. She was very frightened that if she told this to the chemotherapy nurse
she would be viewed as an "ungrateful patient" by the staff. The chemotherapy
nurse was brought in for two family sessions. Two important things happened.
The patient found the chemotherapy nurse to be empathic, supportive, and accepting of her feelings. In addition, the nurse's inclusion allowed us to begin
a systematic desensitization/relaxation intervention with the nurse present. This
has been shown to be effective for anticipatory nausea and vomiting from chemotherapy (16). The nurse and patient were then able to take this behavioral
intervention back into the actual clinical setting, and the patient was able to
finish her course of chemotherapy. Often, strategic inclusion of the treating
oncologist into a family session can facilitate the family therapist's leverage
around necessary points of intervention. A good and frequent example is getting
the family to deescalate their efforts in pushing the patient to eat, which has
built to a high level of anxiety for patient and family alike. The oncologist has
the authority and transference with the family to reduce the anxiety loop around
the eating.

3) Course of the Family Therapy

In conventional family therapy the family presents with a symptom or
problem and meets with the therapist for a series of sessions until change has
occurred or a stalemate is reached. This is usually not the case when cancer is
the impetus for family therapy. The course of cancer-related family therapy often
runs parallel to the crisis periods of the disease course, with the need and wish
for family sessions being absent between these crises. For example, the family
members are often catastrophically upset by the diagnosis and urgently request
to meet in reference to how they can talk with their family member about his/her
cancer. As treatment is started, they usually do not continue in family therapy
during the early treatment phase. If treatment is particularly stressful in an
ongoing way, as exemplified by chemotherapy, the frustration tolerance of all
family members often grows short and they may once again ask to meet. If not,
the family might not return until a recurrence of disease is noted. This may take
months or even years to occur. This is a very stressful crisis, because the potential
threat of terminality becomes very real at this time and often requires a longer
series of sessions than previously. If death occurs, the family members in mourning may return for another series of sessions. The picture emerges, therefore,
of a series of blocks of sessions, often separated by long periods of time, which
are crisis-oriented in nature. For families who were maladaptive prior to the

cancer, family therapy may extend in an uninterrupted fashion throughout the illness and thereafter, but this is not usually the case.

4) Special Features of Intervention

The issue of family resistance is perhaps the greatest area of difference between cancer-oriented family therapy and conventional family therapy. While the handling of resistance is usually a major problem in family therapy, the reverse is true with families living with cancer. The essence of family resistance centers around fear of change manifested by clinging to outmoded, nonfunctional patterns of interaction. The family facing cancer and potential loss is often so distressed by the obvious changes that are occurring that the theme becomes, "How do we adapt to these overwhelming changes that are so upsetting to us?" The focus, therefore, is learning to accept and cope with chronic and catastrophic change. Given this reality, the task of the family therapist is not to gain access to the family (as is the primary problem in conventional family work) but how to avoid engulfment by the family. The problem of maintaining functional therapeutic distance with these families is often a major area of supervision with our trainees.

In conventional family therapy a major fundamental problem is getting the family to shift their focus from the symptoms of the identified patient to the wider context of the family relationship. With cancer families, the difficulty, at least initially, is in the opposite direction. As was evident in the first section the family members have a very difficult time focusing directly on the patient, their feelings about his or her illness, and verbalizing these feelings in the presence of the patient. This, then, becomes an initial task in the family therapy of the cancer patient.

Another major difference between conventional and cancer-oriented family therapy can be in the area of direction of frustrated or angry feelings. In conventional family therapy the family often directs enormous displaced anger onto the identified patient who reinforces this cycle by acting-out and protecting the family from other more problematic foci of anger. The task is to get the family members to direct both their attention and anger more appropriately. In the cancer area, the family usually would not dream of becoming angry at the cancer patient, which can often be a reaction formation to underlying feelings of anger about the changes brought by the patient's illness. The patient may act in obnoxious, presumptive, and disturbing ways while being artificially insulated from feedback. An important task of the family intervention here is to remove this artificiality and make the cancer patient, once again, a normal family member who receives reality-based feedback. This intervention can sometimes be very difficult for such families to accept but can deescalate tension very dramatically.

5) Therapist-induced Problems

The feelings that the family therapist introduces to the conventional family therapy situation can be radically different from those of the therapist working with the cancer patient and his or her family. The feelings of the family therapist in facing the cancer situation can be translated into behaviors that are often puzzling to the therapist. For example, in a recent supervision session a trainee indicated she felt like taking the family of a cancer patient with whom she is working grocery shopping. She indicated she never had a thought like this before, even though she had previously worked with many families. This impulse toward radical modification of technique is quite reminiscent of the process described by Renneker more than two decades ago in his classic paper, "Countertransference Reactions To Cancer" (21). Renneker, at that time, observed his analytic colleagues to impulsively break from technique with cancer patients based on underlying feelings of impotence in response to fantasized attempts to use the therapy to control the course of the cancer. He viewed this process as a response to an undermining of omnipotence and a type of narcissistic injury to the therapist. Thus, the trainees' fantasy of grocery shopping with the family begins to make sense in a paradoxical fashion. It was almost as if she was saying to herself, "If my interventions cannot change the basic physical reality of this family, which so controls their psychic pain, maybe I can feed them in a different way which will reduce their painful feelings of emptiness."

The most frequent problem in supervision of psychiatric residents and psychology interns treating families on the oncology services is the maintenance of optimal clinical distance. This is certainly not unique to the family therapy of the cancer patient but is a universal issue in all family therapy work. What is unique with cancer families is the almost irresistible pull to become over-involved and lose all clinical objectivity. With the absence of usual forms of resistance and the presence of extreme family desperation, powerful omnipotent rescue fantasies (as described by Renneker) are induced in the therapist. We have very commonly seen trainees do two things with these feelings. First, they will see the family too often, up to daily in the hospital setting. Second, they will see the family for too long per session, sometimes spending several hours with the family at one time. The trainees verbalize the notion that their other cases or responsibilities are less grave, less important, or have no real meaning in comparison to the cancer-burdened families. This is a tip-off to us to watch for countertransference problems with loss of effective boundary-keeping being high on the list.

Another critical, therapist-induced countertransference problem can be over-identification with the family such that the family therapist attempts to rework past losses with the family in treatment. An example from supervision involved a trainee who had lost his mother to cancer and who now was seeing a family with the patient being a 50-year-old woman with lung cancer who was the mother of three sons. What became apparent in the supervision was that the trainee was competing with the sons in subtle ways for the approval of the mother. He was attempting to be "her best boy" by being the smartest. This was at the expense of the three sons who needed support from the therapist, not competition. The therapist was able to identify his sense of loss with his mother mainly in regard to the absence of support and praise from her which he was trying to rework with this living mother who was his patient.

The faculty members who treat cancer patients and their families in psychotherapy on our consultation-liaison service have met in group supervision for themselves for several years. We recognize the power of the family context of the cancer patient. We have learned that in spite of our experience with families, these cancer-oriented situations have a special force to induce very problematic countertransference feelings.

REFERENCES

1. American Cancer Society. *1983 Cancer Facts and Figures*. New York: American Cancer Society, 1983.
2. Artiss, K.L., and Levine, A.S. Doctor-patient relation in severe illness. *N. Eng. J. Med.*, 288: 1210-1214, 1973.
3. Buehler, J.A. What contributes to hope in the cancer patient? *Am. J. Nursing*, 75 (8): 1353-1356, 1975.
4. Cobb, S. Social support as a moderator of life stress. *Psychosom. Med.*, 38: 300-314, 1976.
5. Dyk, R.B., and Sutherland, A.M. Adaptation of the spouse and other family members to the colostomy patient. *Cancer*, 9: 123-138, 1956.
6. Fisch, R. Home visits in a private psychiatric practice. *Family Process*, 3: 114-126, 1964.
7. Garfield, C. Impact of death on the health care professional. *In*: H. Feifel (Ed.), *New Meanings of Death*. New York: McGraw Hill, 1977.
8. Harker, B.L. Cancer and communciation problems: A personal experience. *Psychiat. in Med.*, 3: 163-171, 1972.
9. Jamison, K.R., Wellisch, D.K., and Pasnau, R.O. Psychosocial aspects of mastectomy: I. The woman's perspective. *Am. J. Psychiat.*, 134 (4): 432-436, 1978.
10. Kalish, R.A. Dying and preparing for death: A view of families. *In*: H. Feifel (Ed.), *New Meanings of Death*. New York: McGraw Hill, 1977.
11. Kastenbaum, R., and Aisenberg, R. *The Psychology of Death*. New York: Springer, 1972.
12. Knopf, A. Changes in women's opinions about cancer. *Soc. Sci. and Medicine*, 10: 191-195, 1976.

13. Lansky, M. Treating the narcissistically vulnerable marriage. *In*: M. Lansky (Ed.), *Family Therapy and Major Psychopathology*. New York: Grune & Stratton, 1981.

14. Minuchin, S. *Families and Family Therapy*. Cambridge: Harvard University Press, 1974.

15. Mitchell, G.W., and Glicksman, A.S. Cancer patients: Knowledge and attitudes. *Cancer*, 40: 61-66, 1977.

16. Morrow, G.R. Behavioral treatment of anticipatory nausea and vomiting during treatment. *Pro. Am. Soc. Clin. Oncol.*, 22: 396, 1981, abstract.

17. Olson, D., Sprenkle, D., and Russell, C. Circumplex model of marital and family systems I: Cohesion and adaptability dimensions. *Family Process*, 14: 1-35, 1979.

18. Parkes, C.M. The emotional impact of cancer on patients and their families. *J. Laryngology and Otology*, 89: 1271-1279, 1972.

19. Pratt, L. *Family Structure and Effective Health Behavior: The Energized Family*. Boston: Houghton-Mifflin, 1976.

20. Quint, J.C. Institutionalized practice of information control. *Psychiatry*, 28: 119-132, 1965.

21. Renneker, R. Countertransference reactions to cancer. *Psychosomatic Med.*, 19: 409-418, 1957.

22. Schulz, R. *The Psychology of Death, Dying and Bereavement*. Reading, MA: Addison-Wesley, 1978.

23. Schwartz, M.D. An information and discussion program for women after surgery. *Arch. Surg.*, 12 (3): 276-281, 1977.

24. Senescu, R. The development of emotional complications in the patient with cancer. *J. Chron. Dis.*, 16: 813-832, 1963.

25. Sheldon, A., Ryser, C.P., and Krant, M. An integrated family oriented cancer care program: The report of a pilot project in the socio-emotional management of chronic disease. *J. Chron. Dis.*, 22: 743-755, 1970.

26. Silver, R., and Wortman, C.B. Coping with undesirable life events. *In*: M.P. Seligman and J. Garber (Eds.), *Human Helplessness: Theory and Applications*. New York: Academic Press (in press).

27. Sutherland, A.M. Psychological impact of cancer and its therapy. *Med. Clin. North Am.*, 40: 705-720, 1956.

28. Sutherland, A.M., Orback, C.E., Dyk, R.B., and Bard, M. The psychological impact of cancer surgery. I. Adaptation to the dry colostomy: Preliminary report and summary of findings. *Cancer*, 5: 857-872, 1952.

29. Weisman, A.D. *Coping with Cancer*. New York: McGraw-Hill, 1978.

30. Wellisch, D.K., Jamison, K.R., and Pasnau, R.O. Psychosocial aspects of mastectomy: II. The man's perspective. *Am. J. Psychiat.*, 135 (5): 539-546, 1978.

31. Wellisch, D.K., Landsverk, J., Guidera, C., et al. Evaluation of psychosocial problems of the homebound cancer patient: I. Methodology and problem frequencies. *Psychosom. Med.*, 45 (1): 11-21, 1983.

32. Wellisch, D.K., Landsverk, J., Fawzy, F., Pasnau, R.O., and Wolcott, D. Evaluation of psychosocial problems of the homebound cancer patient: II. The relationship of disease and patient sociodemographic variables to family problems. *J. Psychosocial Onc.*, 1 (3) in press, 1983.

33. Wortman, C.B., and Dunkel-Schetter, C. Interpersonal relationships and cancer: A theoretical analysis. *J. Soc. Issues*, 35 (1):120-155, 1979.

SUBJECT INDEX

Achievement-oriented family, 230
Acting-out behavior, 16
  of oedipal age experiences, 112
  rejection and, 122
  sexual, 63, 201
  transference in the group and, 25-26
Activity Group Therapy, 3, 11-12
Adjustment disorder, 221
Adolescents, 115-116, 136, 153-154, 213,
  231
  see also Children
Advisement, 13
Affect see Emotional expression
Affiliation, 83
Aggressor, identification with the, 113, 117
Aim attachment, 18
Alcoholism, 326
Always/never paradoxes, 310-318
American Group Psychotherapy Association,
  3, 9, 11, 19
Anger:
  death and, 262
  families of cancer patients and, 331
  illness and, 130-131, 136
Anxiety, 115, 118, 192-193
Assessment, 213-215
  brief therapy and, 284-285, 290
  of families with cancer patients, 325-326
Associated thinking, 15
Atmosphere in supervision, 144-146
Attachment and loss see Loss; Separation
Authority, 92, 95
  childhood conflicts with, 117
  definition, 189-190
  the family and, 190
  in leaderless groups, 162
  parental relationships and perception of,
    175-185
  therapist's role and, 190-192
Autonomy, 191, 324-325
Avoidance, 322-323

Bad self-object, 98
Behavioral approach, 214-218
Behavioral marital therapy see Marital ther-
  apy
Blind window, 98
Brain damaged, 61

Brief therapy, 46-55, 282-294
Bulimia, 213

Cancer, 320-333
Casualties of therapy, 59-62
Catharsis, 17, 131, 135
Character disorders, 14
Child abuse, 110, 200
Children:
  acting-out behavior and, 16
  mother-child reciprocities, 103-105
  oedipal development and, 104-107
  patterns of behavior passed on to, 37-38
  role in the family, 213
  scapegoating in group therapy and, 115-
    124
  see also Adolescents; Families; Fathers;
    Mothers; Parents
Circumplex model, 327-328
Clarification, illness and, 130, 135
Coalitions, 290
Cognitive constructs, 207-218
Cognitive therapy, 18
Communication, 132, 322-323
Compromise, 212-213
Coney Island Hospital Rap Group, 197-198
Confidentiality, 93, 96-97, 109
Conflct-oriented family, 230, 240
Conflict resolution within groups, 80-82, 85
Confrontation, 133-134
Congenial-affectionate relationship, 240
Consultation, 296-308
Contracts:
  initial contract to become a group, 70
  quid-pro-quo, 216
  sex agreement, 246-248
Control-mastery theory, 48
Co-therapy, 51, 154-156, 159
  use of consultants and, 301
Counseling, definition, 13-14
Countertransference:
  aim attachment and, 18
  demise of a group and, 62, 65
  hostility expression in groups and, 5-6
  leader of single mother's group and, 112-
    114
  reactions to cancer and, 332-333
  response to attachment and loss, 158

335

NAME INDEX